Bakery:
Flour Confectionery

Books by
L. J. HANNEMAN

Modern Cake Decoration
Cake Design and Decoration
  (with G. Marshall)
Patisserie
Bakery: Bread & Fermented Goods

Bakery:
Flour Confectionery

L. J. HANNEMAN
F.Inst.B.B., F.H.C.I.M.A., F.C.F.A.(C.G.), A.M.R.S.H.

*Head of Department of
Service Industries (formerly Food and Catering)
Lancaster and Morecambe College
of Further Education*

HEINEMANN:LONDON

William Heinemann Ltd
10 Upper Grosvenor Street, London W1X 9PA
LONDON   MELBOURNE   TORONTO
JOHANNESBURG   AUCKLAND

© L. J. Hanneman 1981
First published 1981
Reprinted 1984

434 90710 3

Filmset by Willmer Brothers Limited, Birkenhead, Merseyside
Printed in Great Britain by REDWOOD BURN LIMITED, Trowbridge.

Preface

This book is written especially for the Baking Industry and contains a wide variety of recipes of varying quality, using methods generally in common use in most small bakeries with specialized bakery materials and equipment.

Some of the products described have the same name as those which appear in the sister publication *Patisserie*, but being made from recipes very restricted in both variety and size and using traditional catering materials and equipment, *Patisserie* is more suited to the practising patissier employed by the catering industry than to the baker and confectioner.

Flour Confectionery is not only written for the craftsman baker and confectioner, but also for the ambitious cooks who may wish to bake in their own homes. Teachers of home economics will find this volume as useful as students who, it is hoped, will find within its pages most of the subject matter covered by the syllabus of the City and Guilds of London Institute 120 parts I, II and III.

Readers of this publication are recommended to read the first volume *Bakery: Bread and Fermented Goods* which has an extensive glossary and contains chapters relating to flour confectionery, raw materials and legislation.

Every effort has been made to ensure that this book contains the latest information about regulations and legislation relating to the various baked products described.

QUANTITIES USED IN THIS BOOK

	Metric (grams)	Imperial (oz)	% based upon flour weight (%)
Flour	1000	1000	100.0
Fat	500	500	50.0
Sugar	125	125	12.5
Water	125	125	12.5
Baking Powder	10	10	1.0
Totals	1760	1760	176.0%

Suppose we require a recipe in Imperial units which will give us 5 lb of pastry = 80 ounces, we would require:

			Actual weight in ounces	Weight used in practice	
Flour	$= \dfrac{80}{176} \times \dfrac{100}{1}$	$=$	45.4545	2 lb	$13\frac{1}{2}$ oz
Fat	$= \dfrac{80}{176} \times \dfrac{50}{1}$	$=$	22.7272	1 lb	$6\frac{3}{4}$ oz
Sugar	$= \dfrac{80}{176} \times \dfrac{12.5}{1}$	$=$	5.6818	–	$5\frac{5}{8}$ oz
Water	$= \dfrac{80}{176} \times \dfrac{12.5}{1}$	$=$	5.6818	–	$5\frac{5}{8}$ oz
Baking Powder	$= \dfrac{80}{176} \times \dfrac{1.0}{1}$	$=$	.4545	–	$\frac{1}{2}$ oz
Totals			79.9998 oz	5 lb	0 oz

So a recipe which will give us exactly 5 lb of finished pastry will now read:

Flour	2 lb	$13\frac{1}{2}$ oz
Fat	1 lb	$6\frac{3}{4}$ oz
Sugar		$5\frac{5}{8}$ oz
Water		$5\frac{5}{8}$ oz
Baking Powder		$\frac{1}{2}$ oz
	5 lb	0 oz

A recipe for any given quantity in metric units can be calculated in the same way. For exact equivalents refer to the tables in the Appendices.

Acknowledgements

My grateful thanks are given to all who have helped me in the preparation of this book. In particular I wish to record my appreciation to the following:

The Principal and Governors of the Lancaster & Morecambe College of Further Education who permitted me to use facilities of the College for making many of the examples of the work illustrated; my colleagues, Mr Arthur Green and Mr Ray Ward, for their assistance and helpful advice, Mr Donald Bland for allowing the use of his bakery to produce some of the examples shown and Mr Andrew Davidson for some of his ideas on Bridal Cakes used in the chapter on Celebration Cakes.

Throughout the preparation of this book I have been encouraged, advised and sustained by my wife to whom I give my gratitude.

Finally I wish to dedicate this publication and acknowledge the debt I owe to those many craftsmen and women, past and present, who gave so freely of their knowledge, and without whom this book could not have been written.

L. J. H.

Contents

Aeration – Mechanical by lamination – Mechanical by beating – Beating action – Stabilizers – Chemical aeration – Recipe balance – Basic rules for a normal balanced recipe – Recipe balance of high-ratio cakes – Cake quality – Batter flow – Quantity of baking powder used – Effects of materials on recipe balance – Overbeating – Underbaking – Judging correct baking – Baking temperatures – Protection of cakes – Sugar boiling – Hand tests for sugar boiling – Sugar boiling, methods and precautions – Sugar syrups – Use of saccharometer – Making of confiture fruit – Use of crumbs and scraps

Choice of method – Choice of ingredients – Egg custard tarts – Fruit pies – Fruit tarts – Fruit meringue tarts – Large tarts and pies – Mince pies – Flans – Fruit flans – Apple meringue flan – Lemon meringue flan – Frangipane – Frangipane slices – Apple and sultana slices – Date and fig slices – Frangipane tarts – Maids of honour – Cheese curd – Sweet pastry cut-out shapes – Strudel – Faults

Choice of ingredients – Consistency – Turning – Resting and cutting-out – Washing – Oven temperature – Use of scrap – Storage – Method of making dough – Methods of turning: English, French, Scotch – Vol-au-vent – Bouchees – Pineapple haloes – Cream puffs – Royal puffs – Apricot or pineapple purses – Cushions – Bows – Victorias – Windmills – Slices – Sausage rolls – Turnovers – Eccles – Banburys – Mince pies – Coventries – Cream horns – Cream rolls – Frangipane slices – Apple strudel – Fruit slices – Bakewells – Palmiers – Fantails – Petals – Fans – Accordians – Butterflies – Eventails – Currant slices – Tarts – Faults

1. Flour Confectionery Technology

An understanding of the way ingredients interact either on their own or with each other, under the influence of such things as temperature, acidity or alkalinity (pH), mechanical agitation or work input, etc., is very important if first class goods are to be produced and faults to be corrected.

Aeration

Most bakery goods are aerated in one way or another. We can divide the number of different methods used into *three* broad categories as follows:

Biological

Produced by carbon dioxide gas through the action of yeast (explained in greater detail in the first volume of *Bakery: Bread & Fermented Goods* chapter 3). *Examples –* Bread, buns, etc.

Mechanical

(a) Produced by steam through the technique of lamination (explained in greater detail in chapter 3, page 38. *Examples –* Puff pastry and Danish pastry. (The latter is also aerated by yeast.)
   (b) Produced by air being incorporated by beating or whisking
      (i) Eggs and egg white.
      (ii) Fat and sugar.
      (iii) Fat and flour.
      (iv) Cream.
Special mixing machines are in use which can control the amount of air admitted, to be incorporated into a batter, i.e. the continuous mixer for cakes and sponges. Air admitted under pressure, therefore, is another technique used for aeration purposes and this greatly speeds up the process. *Example –* Air pressure whisk.

Chemical

Produced by carbon dioxide liberated from
(a) Sodium bicarbonate by the action of
      (i) Heat only, e.g. some ginger goods.
      (ii) Acid and heat, e.g. baking powder.
(b) Ammonium bicarbonate (VOL) by the action of heat.

Mechanical by beating or whisking

If any liquid or semi-solid is beaten in air, some of the latter will become incorporated. Even water when whisked will become aerated. The important fact as far as bakery goods are concerned, is to trap the air in the mixing until the goods go into the oven. Although the mixing is already aerated before heat is applied, baking expands the trapped air and causes more aeration to occur resulting in the batter or mixing expanding in the oven. Therefore the less air incorporated at the mixing stage, the less the expansion which can occur in the oven. Over-beating causes too much air to be incorporated and this in turn causes too great an expansion in the oven which can result in a collapsed texture – *see* Faults, page 152. Factors affecting the degree of aeration achieved in this method are as follows:

Beating action

Type of beater This is usually shaped like a grid, the size and pattern depending upon the machine and the shape of the bowl used. However, the beater should only just clear the bowl when revolved so that the whole mixture gets agitated in one revolution. For liquid mixes, e.g. egg whites, a wire whisk is used. This is very much more efficient than a beater for aerating purposes, because it has more cutting surfaces. However, by the very nature of its manufacture, it is not of sufficient strength to be used for semi-solid mixtures like fat. Aeration can be just as easily achieved by beating with the hand, and because this is sensitive to the consistency of the batter, it can be used to advantage to mix cake batters.

Speed The speed of beating or whisking has an important effect. Aeration is achieved at a much faster pace if the speed of beating or whisking is accelerated, but this will affect the texture. Rapid beating entangles larger air cells which show up as a more open and coarse texture of the goods being made. For exhibition work, fast beating is avoided for this reason.

Temperature The warmer the temperature, the quicker will aeration be achieved, but again at some sacrifice of good texture. Beating a warm mixture will also result in larger air cells being incorporated.

To achieve a good texture, all other things being equal, we need to keep the batter or mixture cool and beat at a moderate speed over a longer period of time.

Consistency Very little aeration can be produced by beating a solid. Materials such as fat have to be brought to a plastic semi-solid condition by applying heat prior to being subjected to beating. It should *not*, however, be over-heated, e.g. fat to an oil, which in this state cannot trap the air incorporated.

Type of ingredients used We have shown that it is important to use materials which are capable of forming a batter of a consistency which can be beaten. Fats with high melting points such as puff pastry margarine, whilst being ideally suited to lamination techniques, are unsuitable for cakes because their high melting points will not allow them to be sufficiently aerated by beating.

For fat to be successfully aerated, it must have a fine crystalline structure, and manufacturers of fats market such products especially recommended for creaming purposes. Lard, and to a lesser extent, butter, do not have good creaming and aerating properties because of their crystalline structure.

Butter is often used in cakes, primarily for flavour, but when employed it is recommended that a proportion should be replaced with a high grade shortening, which has very good creaming properties, so that this deficiency in butter is partially compensated. Extra beating is also another method we can use to achieve adequate aeration when using butter.

Stabilizers

When we make a cake batter we are delving into the realms of emulsion chemistry. Once we start to incorporate egg into a mix of fat and sugar, we form an oil-in-water emulsion in which air cells encased in fat are dispersed in the liquid phase of the egg. The more perfect this emulsion, the finer these aerated cells of fat will be, the greater the number which will be present and therefore the greater will be the amount of air incorporated.

To help us obtain a perfect emulsion we can use agents called stabilizers, some of which have the ability to increase fat dispersion by reducing the size of the fat particles present, besides making the emulsion more stable (i.e. reduces the risk of separation of the fat from the liquid phase).

Ethyl Methyl Cellulose (EDIFAS) is marketed in either flakes or a powder and is used as a 5% solution with water.

Lecithin is a naturally occurring stabilizer which is found in eggs, and this is one of the functions of egg in a cake mixture.

Glycerol monostearate and other agents of a similar type may also be used for this purpose.

High-ratio fats which have been specially compounded for use in high-liquid cakes contain such stabilizers and may also be used.

The more thorough dispersal of fat by the use of stabilizers will not only increase volume, but will result in a much finer texture. Keeping properties will also be improved. Stabilizers may also be used in fat-less mixes like egg sponges. Here their function is similar, enabling smaller cells of air to be trapped by the egg which are more difficult to break down when the flour is stirred in. This results in a finer texture and more volume. They are also used to prevent the breakdown of unstable mixtures such as egg sponges and japanese when flour and/or fat is incorporated.

Special Note Certain substances owe their usefulness to the fact that they lower the surface tension and therefore act in exactly the opposite way to stabilizers which increase surface tension. Therefore if traces of this are present it can have disastrous effects upon aeration. Silicone is such an agent and there have been cases reported of sponges failing to whip because the sugar was weighed on silicone paper.

Chemical Aeration

When we heat bicarbonate of soda, we liberate some carbon dioxide gas but there is a chemical change which takes place and after the gas has been expelled we are left with sodium carbonate, which is washing soda. Although harmless to eat, the flavour of this product is unacceptable if left in baked goods, besides which there is a yellowing of the crumb due to interaction between it and the protein present. However, it is still used on its own in some ginger goods where the yellowing of the crumb and the carbonate flavour left, is masked by the ginger used. A certain amount of the bicarbonate also reacts with the natural acid in the syrup which is present in these goods.

To liberate all the available gas from sodium bicarbonate we need to mix it with an acid. This chemical reaction can be expressed as follows:

Sodium bicarbonate + acid   ⟶ Carbon dioxide gas + Residual salt
   (baking powder)   (heat & moisture)   (aerates the goods)   (left in goods)

Tartaric

This acid used on its own reacts immediately with the sodium bicarbonate in the cold and is therefore unsuitable for use as the acid ingredient of a baking powder.

Cream of Tartar

This white crystalline powder is the derivative potassium salt of tartaric acid. It meets most of the criteria for a perfect acid as follows:

(1) As an acid ingredient naturally present in many fruits, it is not only harmless, but beneficial to eat.
(2) As a fine crystalline powder it mixes very well.
(3) The residual salt formed is called Rochelle salt which as an aperient present in some medicines, can be regarded as beneficial. It has a slightly saline taste undetectable in the baked goods.
(4) Over half of the gas of the reaction is produced in the cold before the goods are baked. Although this is a disadvantage especially if goods are left for a considerable time prior to baking (*see* scones page 73), not all the gas is lost. Research carried out by the author some years ago revealed that a considerable

amount was retained by the mixing, i.e. scones prior to baking, provided a medium to strong flour was used.

(5) Costs are relative and whilst it may be true that this product costs more than its phosphate counterpart, the advantage gained in (3) above might well be regarded as a compensating factor.

Phosphoric Acid

There are three different types of phosphoric acid and these can produce a very large number of different acid salts from the metals of sodium, potassium and calcium. Since these were originally used to replace cream of tartar in baking powders, they were known and sold as "Cream Powders". The usual chemicals used are – monocalcium phosphate and sodium acid pyrophosphate. They may all be used with sodium bicarbonate in a baking powder, and in fact most, if not all of the commercially prepared baking powders, contain one or a mixture of these acid derivatives. Like cream of tartar, it meets most of the criteria for a perfect acid, only falling short of (3):

(1) All the acid derivatives used are harmless.
(2) As a white powder it mixes well.
(3) The residual salt is easily detected in goods in which a lot of baking powder has been used. Although harmless, it leaves a burning sensation on the palate that some people would find objectionable (*see* note at end).
(4) It reacts very slowly with the sodium bicarbonate in the cold, most of the gas being produced in the oven once heat is applied. This factor gives this type of acid a superior advantage because goods may be left for a considerable time before baking off without loss of aeration.
(5) It is relatively inexpensive – cheaper than cream of tartar.

Recently a new generation of phosphate acid powders have been developed for use in baking powder. These are the sodium aluminium phosphates. It is claimed that because it is only soluble in cold water the gas production is much more delayed and it leaves an insoluble residue which betrays no flavour of its own.

Another acid ingredient which has found acceptance as an ideal acid to mix with bicarbonate of soda in baking powder formulations is G.D.L. (Glucono Delta Lactone). This substance does not react until it comes into contact with water. Then it changes to gluconic acid and at this stage is available to react with the bicarbonate of soda. Because of the delayed action of the chemical reaction, very little gas is given off initially in the cold.

Note The residual salt leaves a slightly sweet aftertaste which is quite acceptable to leave in the baked goods. In fact it is an ideal product, its only disadvantage being its cost which is higher than other baking acids.

Proportions Used

When cream of tartar and sodium bicarbonate were extensively used, they were mixed as follows:

2 parts cream of tartar
1 part sodium bicarbonate.

This ratio had been initially arrived at by trial and error, but when examined by chemists who became interested in bakery problems, it was found that there was a good scientific reason for such a ratio. When two chemicals are made to react with each other we can calculate how much of each is required for the reaction to become complete by adding up the atomic weights of the elements they contain, to find their molecular weight and applying these to the equation.

It was found theoretically that we actually needed $2\frac{1}{4}$ parts of cream of tartar to 1 part of sodium bicarbonate to effect a complete reaction.

However, one has to consider that most cake mixes are acid and this can account for some of the extra acid required by this theoretical balance. The exception is in such goods as meringues and angel cake. Because they carry such a high percentage of egg whites, making them strongly alkaline, they require extra acid for this to be neutralized.

Research carried out by the author some years ago showed that more gas was evolved from a baking powder compounded from a 2:1 mix than a $2\frac{1}{4}$:1 mix.

This ratio of 2 acid : 1 bicarbonate has been retained as the recommended mix for all the baking acids now available. Although each acid will have a different molecular weight and therefore different proportions of the acid would normally have to be used, by adding an appropriate quantity of *filler* the ratio of 2 : 1 can be maintained. The filler referred to is usually finely ground rice flour which, besides helping to adjust the ratio, also helps in keeping the acid mixture free from lumps. This is due to the hygroscopic nature of rice which absorbs any moisture present.

Vol

This is a mixture of ammonium bicarbonate and ammonium carbonate. When heated it disintegrates into carbon dioxide gas, ammonia gas and water, the product leaving no residual salt. Although it may seem the ideal aerating agent, its use has one serious drawback. The ammonia gas is very soluble in water, and in a normal cake containing a high moisture content, it is impossible to get rid of the strong objectionable ammonia flavour. Its use is therefore confined to biscuits which have a low moisture content. Because these are thin, and are baked at a high temperature, it is possible to drive all the ammonia gas away.

Effect of Steam

When goods containing a considerable amount of moisture are baked, some of this moisture is transformed to steam and whilst some of this escapes to cause loss of weight in the baked goods, it also contributes to the aeration of the goods. As with puff pastry, the aeration produced by steam generation will depend upon the strength of the batter and the temperature at which it is baked. The stronger the structure and the higher the baking temperature, the greater the volume of steam which can be trapped, and therefore the greater the aeration which can be achieved (*see* Choux paste page 62).

RECIPE BALANCE

An understanding of the basic rules of recipe balance is of immense importance to a craftsman. Not only will this knowledge enable him to alter and perfect existing recipes according to the materials used, but he will be able to create new recipes with confidence. Furthermore, he will be able to correct faults caused by an imbalance of materials.

A convenient starting point is to consider the main commodities used in cake making, and classify their functions under four group headings.

Group 1
Materials which provide the strength and structure of a cake: Flour, egg.
Group 2
Materials which have to be carried by the ingredients of Group 1: Sugar, fat, egg.
Group 3
Materials which have a lifting or opening effect: Sugar, fat.
Group 4
Materials which have the effect of closing the texture, i.e. opposite to Group 3: Milk.

BASIC RULES FOR A NORMAL BALANCED RECIPE

(1) The quantity of egg used in any cake recipe should be equal to or greater than the fat. The latter not only helps to achieve the aeration but also contributes to the eating quality of a cake. However, since it can give no strength to the crumb, we must use sufficient egg to provide the structure for it to be carried.

(2) 1 kilo (2¼ lb) flour, requires an equal quantity of egg for it to be moistened, but only 875 g (31½ oz) of milk. If using egg for the moistening function, replacement with milk is possible on this basis.

(3) The opening function of sugar can be balanced by adding 510 g (1 lb 2 oz) milk to each kilo (2¼ lb) sugar. The sugar content of a cake should be between 20–25% of total weight.

(4) The closing effect of milk can be offset by the use of 50 g (1.8 oz) of baking powder to each litre (1¾ pints) milk.

RECIPE BALANCE OF HIGH RATIO CAKES

In the previous rules we note that (3) and (4) indicate that we can increase the sugar content and still retain a balanced recipe by also increasing the milk and baking powder. There are limits to the extent by which these ingredients, in a normal cake, can be increased, but to help absorb the extra liquid, the use of two specially prepared raw materials are necessary:

1 (a) High-Ratio Flour

This is a top-patent cake flour usually milled from English wheats to a very fine particular size. Since a considerable portion of moisture is held in a cake by surface adsorption*, it follows that the finer the particle size of the flour, the more water it can hold. To demonstrate this fact let us take a cube of 2 cm. The surface that is exposed on this cube is the area of one side multiplied by the number of sides – $2 \times 2 \times 6 = 24$ cubic centimetres.

If we now break up this cube into 8 smaller cubes of 1 cm we have the area of a cubic cm $\times$ 6 for each cube = 6 cubic cm, but now we have 8 cubes the total exposed area is $6 \times 8 = 48$ cubic centimetres.

Therefore by splitting the 2 cm cube into the 8 smaller 1 cm cubes, we have doubled the surface to which the liquid will be absorbed.

The specially milled high ratio flour is also heavily chlorinated which not only bleaches it but raises its acidity and denatures some of the gluten.

1 (b) High-Protein Cake Flour

This is manufactured in the same way as the normal cake flour but from a stronger blend of wheats. Its use is recommended for high-ratio fruit cakes where the extra strength is required to support the fruit.

2 High-Ratio Fat

These are hydrogenated 100% shortenings† which are made to contain an emulsifying agent such as a monoglyceride or lecithin. Such fats are capable of excellent emulsifying properties so that a greater proportion of liquid can be incorporated into the batter – emulsion.

---

*ADSORPTION = the attraction of molecules of a gas or liquid to a surface, thereby weakening it. Adsorption also lowers the temperature at which starch gelatinizes.
†Hard solid fats produced by combining hydrogen gas with vegetable oils.

The term *high ratio* refers to the ratio of sugar and liquid to flour. Based on a flour weight of 100 it is possible to devise recipes in which the sugar content is 124 and the liquid as high as 148. This latter balance is often to be found in angel layer cake recipes in which up to ⅔ of the liquor may be egg whites (*see* recipes on page 136).

Merits of High Ratio Cakes

These cakes have a number of advantages not enjoyed by normal cakes.
(1) The high sugar content gives the cakes a longer shelf-life. Since sugar is hygroscopic, it attracts moisture to the crumb thereby preserving a soft texture.
(2) Angel cakes made with egg whites are white and are ideally suited to cake colour. Layer cakes and battenburgs look very attractive when made with appropriately coloured angel cake.

Not all British palates are suited to the extra sweetness of these cakes, and hence there is not such a market for them as in the U.S.A. where this type of recipe originated.

Cake Quality

The quality of a cake is dictated by the fat content. The higher the fat content the richer the cake and vice versa. However, the fat quantity should never exceed that of the flour. A good quality cake fat should be able to form a stable emulsion with $1\frac{1}{4}$ times its weight of egg, but this should never be exceeded.

Batter Flow

Both sugar and baking powder have the effect of causing the batter to flow so that we can cause a flat top of a cake to be created by increasing either of these and adding more milk to effect the correct balance.

Quantity of Baking Powder Used

The amount of baking powder used is also to some extent governed by the size of the cake to be made. Small cakes may require up to 6% of the weight of flour in excess of egg whilst for large cakes only 2% may be required.

EFFECTS OF MATERIALS ON RECIPE BALANCE

Milk or Liquid

This used in excess produces a classical fault known as the X *fault*, as this represents the shape of the resultant cake. Whilst the excess liquid is present in the cake in the hot oven, no noticeable fault can be seen, since the excess liquid is in the form of steam and actually contributes to the aeration causing well volumed cakes to be apparent.

On cooling, however, the steam from the excess liquid condenses back to the liquid phase and settles as a seam at the base of the cake. At the same time the structure collapses and the cake shrinks. The effect is caved-in sides with loose bands and a shrunken appearance.

A deficiency of liquid results in a cake of poor volume with a bound appearance. The crumb will be dry with a poor, harsh texture.

When we refer to liquor in a cake recipe it can apply to any liquid, but it would be wrong to assume that for this purpose water can be used to replace egg or milk. Since egg only contains 75% and milk 88% approx. water, it is obvious that less water is required to replace them. Thus in moistening power 1 kilo ($2\frac{1}{4}$ lb approx.) egg can be replaced by 750 g (1 lb $10\frac{1}{2}$ oz approx.) water and 1 kilo ($2\frac{1}{4}$ lb approx.) milk can be replaced by 880 g (1 lb 15 oz approx.) water.

Sugar and Baking Powder

Used in excess both of these will cause the structure of the cake to be weak, and this will result in a collapse of the top – another classic fault known as the M *fault* since it is a representation of the shape of the cake so formed. Outwardly it is sometimes difficult to detect which of these materials has been responsible for this fault. Excess baking powder will cause a darkening of the crumb at the base of the cake. Excess sugar may be detected by its extra sweetness which may result in a slightly sticky crumb and crust. This fault could be caused by a slight excess of both materials, in which case diagnosis can sometimes be difficult.

Deficiency of these aerating agents will cause a cake to be of small volume with a bound appearance and a cracked, peaked top.

Fat

An excess of fat results in a weakening of the structure which manifests itself in a sunken top. Further examination will reveal a greasy crumb and crust.

A deficiency will result in a reduction of volume with a bound appearance and a cracked peaked top.

Cocoa Powder

Cocoa is added to many recipes to make a chocolate variety of the same product.

However, to conform with the Code of Practice, before we can describe and sell a cake as a *chocolate cake*, we must have a minimum of 3% of dry non-fat cocoa solids in the moist crumb. (The latter is defined as the crumb of the baked product as sold excluding additions such as fruit, nuts, fillings, etc.)

All cocoa powders contain cocoa butter, and an average would be 25%. Therefore if we add 4% of cocoa to our recipe we would comply with the Code of Practice.

Cocoa powder usually replaces flour in such recipes and therefore the balance of the recipe is affected. Assuming that we have a recipe with 1000 g of flour, after substitution we have 960 g flour and 40 g of cocoa powder. Since cocoa powder has a greater water-absorbing power than flour, we would now have to increase the milk content by an amount equal to the cocoa powder used. Also since we have now increased the milk content we need to increase the baking powder to achieve the same degree of aeration.

Thus our recipe of 1000 g now has to be adjusted as follows to make it into a chocolate cake:

Flour 860 g
add Cocoa powder 40 g
add Milk 40 g
add Baking powder 2 g

Ground Almonds

With the exception of goods which are termed almond goods, e.g. macaroons, japanese, frangipane, etc., ground almonds are usually added to a recipe for flavour purposes only. However, it is not always realized that because it absorbs liquid and it contains about 50% of fat, its use can affect the balance of the recipe. It is usual to calculate that 50% of ground almonds in a recipe can replace flour if used in small amounts, say up to $12\frac{1}{2}$%. The fat content is not so critical except for higher quantities involved.

Cornflour

Weight for weight cornflour can replace flour in cake recipes, but because it contains no gluten, both the texture and the stability of the crumb is modified. Whilst the use of some cornflour would be an advantage if a strong or medium flour were used, say for Madeira cakes, it might be disastrous for fruit cakes where we require a certain amount of strength in order to keep the fruit from sinking.

Colour of Chocolate Cakes

The natural colour of chocolate is influenced by the acidity or alkalinity of the batter, the former giving a greyish colour, whilst an alkaline one enhances the attractive rich chocolate colour. It is usual therefore to add a slight excess of bicarbonate of soda to achieve this purpose.

Most chocolate cakes have added colour and this can usually be improved by the addition of some red colour with the chocolate.

Fruit

One of the main faults with fruit cakes is sinking fruit and there are three main causes.
(1) Fruit has been washed and left wet before being incorporated into the mix.
(2) The cake structure is too weak to support either the weight of fruit added or the size of the fruit, e.g. cherries.
(3) Too cool an oven temperature.

The remedy for (1) is self evident. It is a good idea to wash fruit and let it drain overnight before incorporating it into the batter.

The remedy for (2) is not so easily corrected if we want to preserve a good and moist texture. There are three ways by which we can strengthen the texture sufficiently to support fruit:
(*a*) Addition of acid. The addition of tartaric acid strengthens the flour and hence the batter.
(*b*) Use of a stronger flour.
(*c*) Toughening the batter slightly by beating.

With (3), when the temperature is too low the fruit slides to the bottom before the other ingredients have set, and so arrests their movement. This applies particularly to cherry cakes which should be put initially into a hot oven to set the structure, thereafter baking at a cooler temperature.

Besides the faults due to a wrong balance of materials there are two others which should be mentioned here, because they produce cakes very similar to the appearance of cakes made with an excess of sugar, baking powder and fat.

Overbeating

This will produce excessive aeration which will weaken the structure of the cake resulting in the fault of a sunken top and weakened texture. The crumb is not darkened as in a cake with excess baking powder and this is a clue in its diagnosis. In any case this fault usually occurs with good class recipes in which aeration has to be achieved by beating, there being little or no baking powder present. The use of machines for beating the cake batter encourages this fault.

Underbaking

This is a common fault, especially with rich fruit cakes where the correct degree of baking is sometimes difficult to judge accurately. The last part of the cake to set and bake is just below the centre of the top crust. If cakes are withdrawn from the oven before this part has baked, it collapses and the top sinks after it has been withdrawn from the oven and cooled. However, once the cake is cut open, this fault is easily detected by a wet patch about 6–12 mm ($\frac{1}{4}$–1 in) below the top crust. In extreme cases this patch is almost unbaked batter but more usually it manifests itself as a damp seam or a patch of close texture.

Disturbing a cake in the oven by moving it, or knocking it, or by even allowing a draught of cold air to strike it, will also form a seam of close texture just below the top crust as the un-set portion of cake partially collapses.

Often underbaking is the result of baking a cake in too hot an oven, the operative withdrawing the cake before time in order that the crust should not be burnt. In such circumstances the crust formed may be so rigid that it fails to sink but on cutting open the cake, not only will there be a damp seam but possibly a hole as well.

Judging Correct Baking

Judging that a cake has been perfectly baked can only be done by applying slight pressure with the finger tips on the top centre of the cake. This sensitive part of the hand should be able to detect the resistance to pressure which a perfectly baked cake will exert. The top crust of an underbaked cake will collapse under the pressure applied. Another method advised in most domestic cookery books, is to insert a fine skewer into the cake. On withdrawal, if the skewer is free of any adhering cake batter, it is properly cooked.

BAKING TEMPERATURES

As a general rule, baked goods require to be baked at the highest possible temperature for the shortest time compatable with the crust colour, and sometimes crumb colour, required.

The correct baking temperature depends upon several factors as follows:

Richness

Goods containing a high content of enriching agents, i.e. fat, sugar, eggs and fruit require to be baked at a lower temperature than goods which are lean in such agents.

Size and Thickness

Goods are mainly baked by the transfer of heat from the top and the bottom rather than through the sides. Therefore, although the size of the individual product will slightly affect the baking temperature required, it is influenced more by its thickness. Small and thin ones require a hotter oven temperature than large or thick.

Steam

The presence of steam in the oven will allow goods to be baked at a higher temperature because the steam will delay crust formation. This will in turn reduce the crust colour which would normally dictate a lower baking temperature if steam were not present. When an oven is fully loaded, there is enough steam generated from the goods themselves to enable them to be baked at a higher temperature. With small batches however, we can overcome steam deficiency by baking in large lidded tins such as cream bun tins.

Besides enabling goods to be baked at a higher temperature, the presence of steam keeps the crust from forming in the initial stages, and so allows full volume to be reached unrestricted by crust formation.

Top Dressings

If goods are dressed with materials which colour readily in the oven, then the temperature has to be reduced to prevent these materials taking on too much colour or becoming burnt. Such materials are nuts and sugar. Here the use of steam can help. Another way this problem can be solved is to cover the cakes with paper after the top has set.

Protection of Cakes

Besides protecting the top of cakes against the oven heat by a sheet of paper, we often need to protect the sides and bottom.

This is especially important for large heavily fruited cakes. For the protection of bottom heat it is useful to use corrugated brown paper since this gives a useful layer of air as well as paper.

For the sides of cakes, a fairly thick piece of paper or thin card cut so that it projects above the cake by 5–7½ cm (2–3 in) is useful for subsequently laying on a sheet of paper for protection without it touching the top of the cake.

Sometimes ovens have more bottom heat than top, or vice versa. Some goods benefit from this imbalance whilst with others protection has to be employed. Excessive bottom heat is often a problem and can be easily overcome by use of a double tray. If too much bottom heat is used it can manifest itself either by giving too much colour to the bottom crust, or discolouring the crumb. This latter occurs especially in cakes containing honey which caramelizes at a lower temperature than ordinary sugar.

Tins should always have a dulled surface before being used for baking. One way heat is transferred is by radiation which is in the form of waves behaving like light. If, therefore, we use bright tins, the radiant heat waves will be reflected away from the product it contains instead of being used to bake it. New shiny tins should be dulled by placing them in a hot oven for a few hours, before putting them to use.

Rich fruit slab cakes are best baked in wooden frames since these are poor conductors of heat and will therefore allow the slab cake to bake slowly with less risk of the sides scorching.

SUGAR BOILING

There are many products used by the flour confectioner which are made from boiled sugar, these include fondant, fudges, marshmallow, boiled meringue etc. Therefore an understanding of the underlying theory of sugar boiling is important to the craftsman.

When we add cane sugar to water it dissolves to form a syrup. At normal room temperature it is possible to form a syrup from twice as much sugar as water. Such a solution is termed saturated. To get a clear syrup it is recommended that cube or preserving sugar is used since this is more likely to be free from dust which would form scum in the syrup and possibly make it cloudy.

If we increase the temperature of this syrup, we find it is possible to add more sugar until a clear syrup is formed in which the sugar content is just over three times that of the water. If we now allow this syrup to gently cool without any disturbance we form what is called a super-saturated solution, and this has particular properties.

When we boil a sugar solution made from cane sugar (sucrose) we bring about a chemical change in which one molecule of water is added to the sucrose molecule. This then forms invert sugar which is made from one molecule of glucose and one of fructose. This chemical reaction is called "inversion" and is speeded up by the presence of an acid which acts as a catalyst.

If we agitate a supersaturated solution we find it will crystallize to give a mass of coarse grained crystals. We can control the size of these crystals in two ways:
(1) Adding a crystal of a definite size, in which case the whole mass of syrup will crystallize out into crystals of the same size. (This process is called *seeding*).
(2) Carefully controlling the rate of inversion. Since invert sugar does not readily crystallize, it follows that the more sugar that can be inverted, the less sugar there remains to be crystallized. In fact crystallization can be completely inhibited by inversion, particularly in the presence of an acid.
Examples of how we use these theories in practice may be given as follows:

(*a*) Fondant is made by agitating a super-saturated sugar solution which has been boiled to 115°C (240°F). This creates millions of minute sugar crystals which thicken the syrup to form an icing which is a brilliant white due to the light-reflecting properties of the crystals.

(*b*) Fudge is made by adding fondant to a mixture of sugar and fat to bring about the production of fine crystals.

Another substance used to inhibit or modify crystallization is confectioners' glucose. This is often used instead of acid in recipes because the use of the latter can often carry out the inversion too far.

Besides the chemical changes which take place, there is a very obvious physical change which occurs. As boiling of the sugar proceeds, some of the water evaporates and the resulting syrup becomes more viscous resulting in the syrup setting firm when cold. As the syrup becomes thicker so its boiling temperature progressively increases, so we can determine its temperature by its physical state as follows:

Hand Tests for Sugar Boiling

Temperature °C	°F	Name of Degree	How to Test
104.5	220	Boiling	Effervescence.
107	225	Thread	Touch the surface of the boiling sugar with a dry finger. Join the thumb and this finger together and separate them. An elastic thread of sugar will be formed.
110	230	Pearl	Repeat the foregoing. The sugar will form a pearl-like bead at the ends of the thread as it breaks.
113	235	Blow	When a loop of wire is inserted into the syrup and removed, a thin film will be produced which can be gently blown.
115	240	Feather	At this stage the film of sugar syrup can be blown into feather-like pieces.

Note Up to this stage, the syrup is still fairly thin although it is becoming noticeably thicker. To test the next few stages, it is necessary to take out some of the syrup and shock-cool it by plunging it into cold water to test its characteristics. This is done with the fingers by first immersing them in cold water then plunging them into the syrup for just as long as it takes to collect a little of the syrup, then quickly putting them back into cold water again. The syrup will set and can be worked with the fingers.

Temperature °C	°F	Name of Degree	How to Test
118	245	Soft Ball	The syrup at this stage sets into a very plastic ball when manipulated with the fingers.
121	250	Hard Ball	A very much firmer ball is now formed. At this stage the syrup is becoming really thick and the temperature rises rapidly.
132–138	270–280	Soft Crack	The ball of sugar which is formed at this temperature forms a thin skin which will crack slightly.
138–154	280–310	Hard Crack	The ball of sugar now sets with a very thick skin which requires considerable pressure before it is shattered. (Many confectioners crunch this ball of sugar with their teeth to ascertain the correct degree.)

Beyond this stage, the syrup begins to turn to a pale and then a dark amber colour emitting acrid fumes, until eventually a very dark, almost black mass is formed.

| 154 | 310 | Caramel | Very dark amber colour. |
| 177 | 350 | | |

Notes 1. If glucose or acid is used, this should be added at 104.5°C (220°F).

2. The above sugar boiling degrees are only approximate and there are of course differences which can be detected between the extremes of 121°–132°C (250°–270°F) and 154°–177°C (310°–350°F). Only a sugar-boiling thermometer can obtain an accurate indication of the correct degree for any particular purpose and its use is to be strongly recommended. In the final stages, the temperatures at which the sugar syrup finally boils or colours is also modified by the percentage of inversion which has taken place and the percentage of confectioners' glucose or invert sugar (e.g. honey) used in the initial syrup. This is because invert sugar and dextrose colour at a much lower temperature than sucrose.

Sugar Boiling Method and Precautions

(1) Place sugar and water in a clean pan (preferably copper) and dissolve by stirring gently on low heat.
(2) Once dissolved, raise the temperature to boiling. If glucose or acid is used, add it at this point (moisten the acid with a little water first).
(3) Whilst boiling *do not stir*. Keep the sides of the pan and the thermometer continuously washed down with a little water to re-dissolve any sugar crystals which might form. Boil as rapidly as possible to the required temperature.
(4) If any scum appears on the surface remove it with a spoon.
(5) When the required temperature has been reached, remove the pan quickly from the heat and plunge it into a pan of cold water for a few seconds to prevent the temperature rising further due to heat absorbed by the pan.

Sugar Syrups

For many types of goods, e.g. confiture fruits, etc., a sugar syrup of a definite density is required. This is ascertained by the use of an instrument called a saccharometer. This is a hydrometer which may be calibrated in either *brix* or *beaumé* degrees. The instrument is a hollow glass tube sealed at each end. At one end it is weighted with lead shot so that when it is placed into a solution it floats upright. The scale marked in either *brix* or *beaumé* indicates the depth at which the tube floats. This is influenced by the density of the sugar which in turn is controlled by the ratio of sugar to water used for the solution. This instrument can thus measure the amount of sugar in solution.

Use of Saccharometer

(1) Make sure that the solution to be tested is at 68°F (20°C). As the density changes with temperature, the *brix* or *beaumé* tables have been standardised at this temperature.
(2) Pour the solution to be tested into a tall cylinder (a 500 ml glass cylinder is ideal).
(3) Insert the hydrometer and take the reading with the eye looking horizontally.
(4) To adjust the density of the sugar solution, add a syrup with a high concentration of sugar but at the same temperature of 68°F (20°C).

Making of Confiture Fruit

This process is only suitable for hard or semi-hard fruits such as pears, apples, peaches, apricots, plums, cherries or pineapple.
Method
(1) Select perfect, almost ripe fruit. Remove skins and if large, cut into suitably sized pieces.

(2) Make sufficient sugar syrup with a density of 18°B to cover the fruit.

(3) Place the fruit into this syrup and bring to the boil.

(4) Remove from the heat and leave for 24 hours.

(5) On the second day carefully remove the fruit. Add sugar or heavy syrup to bring the syrup to a density of 20°B.

(6) Replace the fruit, bring to the boil, remove from the heat and leave for 24 hours.

(7) On each successive day, repeat 5 and 6 above, increasing the density of sugar by 2°B each day, until the 6th day, when the density should be 28°B.

(8) At this stage of 28°B, add confectioners' glucose to bring the density up to 30°B.

(9) Repeat the process for the successive 3 days, adding glucose until on the 9th day the syrup is 34°B.

(10) On the tenth day remove the fruit and store in a clean airtight tin until required.

Note   If the fruit is required to be candied, add sugar at (8) instead of glucose. The fruit will then crystallize out when stored.

An alternative method of making confiture pineapple from tinned fruit is given on page 231.

Mould

Notes on mould and anti-mould agents will be found in the first volume of *Bakery: Bread & Fermented Goods* – chapter 3, page 59.

THE USE OF CRUMBS AND SCRAPS

In any bakery, cuttings from cakes and pastries are inevitable, but provided they are carefully collected and stored, they form a valuable material from which many types of cakes and pastries can be made. Some of these appear under the various chapter headings and reference to these recipes will be made at the end of this chapter.

Firstly, any crumbs or cuttings which are collected must be kept scrupulously clean. Usually one has to wait for a few days until sufficient has been collected before it is economic to use them for a particular recipe. Ideally, they should be placed immediately into a polythene bag and placed into a deep-freezer. If they are left for any length of time in a polythene bag at normal room temperature or even in a refrigerator, mould will soon make its appearance and the crumbs would become unfit for use.

If a deep-freezer is not available, it is best to leave the cuttings exposed to the air, for example, in a wooden tray in a cupboard free of dust so that they stale and become dry. Alternatively, if the cuttings are of cake, it may be crumbed immediately and these left thinly spread out on trays in a cupboard to dry. However, such crumbs should be used as quickly as possible, preferably in a recipe which has to be baked.

Always remember that good quality products demand high quality crumbs or cuttings.

Besides cake, cuttings from pastries like vanilla slices may be used, the various components of pastry, cream or custard and icing being smashed to a paste for inclusion into the recipe. Such cuttings are best used in recipes which have to be baked.

Bread crumbs are also a valuable material which can be recycled. One master baker makes a very acceptable loaf replacing up to 6% of dry-flour weight with bread crumbs. He also uses these to dress the bread after washing it with water prior to baking. The result is a loaf with a pleasantly flavoured crust having an attractive appearance.

Up to 15% of the flour in chemically aerated bread or *farls* may be replaced with bread crumbs without very much noticeable difference.

Other uses for bread crumbs include the replacement of up to 50% of rusk in pies and 25% in sausage meat.

Recipes which include cake crumbs and pastry cuttings are shown as follows:

page 28 Frangipane
page 103 Biscuit Base
page 151 Farmhouse Cake
page 252 Truffles
page 253 Rum Truffle Slice

2. Short and Sweet Pastry

Traditionally the difference between short pastry and sweet pastry is that the former should contain no sugar whilst the latter can contain as much sugar as 50% the weight of flour. Besides sweetening, sugar in pastry imparts some shortening property, colour and bloom and prolongs its shelf life. It is not surprising, therefore, that most bakers and confectioners employ sugar in all their short pastry recipes. The exception is of course with savoury goods in which the sugar is replaced with salt.

When making this item of confectionery it is important *not* to overmix as this will make it tougher, causing difficulties when handling and producing shrinkage in baking. There are four methods of mixing as follows:

Method 1
(1) The fat, margarine (or butter) is rubbed by hand or machine into the flour, until no lumps are left and the mixture has the consistency of ground almonds.
(2) The rest of the liquid in which sugar or salt is dissolved, is now added either into a bay made in the dry mixture, or poured in slowly whilst the machine mixes on slow speed.
(3) Mix ingredients to a smooth paste.
Note   If mixing by a machine use the hook or pastry knife for each stage.

Method 2
(1) Beat the fat and sugar to a light cream.
(2) Continue beating, adding the egg or liquid.
(3) Slowly stir in the flour and ground almonds and mix ingredients to a smooth paste.
Note   For machine mixing use the beater for (1) and (2) and change to the hook for (3).

Method 3
(1) Cream the fat with an equal quantity of flour.
(2) Slowly add the liquid in which has been dissolved the sugar or salt.
(3) Carefully blend in the flour and mix to a smooth paste.
Note   For machine mixing use the beater for (1) and (2) and change to the hook for (3). This method is more suited to the production of paste suitable for blocking purposes.

Method 4
   Place all the materials into a high speed mixer and mix for 20–25 seconds. On no account must this be exceeded otherwise the paste will be sticky and difficult to handle.
Note   In the above methods it is assumed that if any baking powder is used it is previously well sieved into the flour prior to mixing.

Choice of Method
   The choice of the method used is largely dictated by the recipe employed and whether made by hand or machine. Method 1 is more suitable for lean recipes containing little sugar and egg and made by hand, whilst method 2 is more suited to rich sweet paste recipes. For large-scale recipes methods 3 and 4 are recommended. The latter method entails the use of a specialized high-speed mixing machine.
   Sweetpastry recipe No. 3 is best made using Method No. 2 making sure that the pastry fat is softened before blending with margarine. Because of the nature of pastry fat, little aeration will be achieved at the creaming stage.

Short and Sweet Pastry

	Short Pastry				Flan Pastry				Sweetpastry 1				Sweetpastry 2				Sweetpastry 3			
	kg	g	lb	oz	kg	g	lb	oz	kg	g	lb	oz	kg	g	lb	oz	kg	g	lb	oz
Soft flour	1	000	2	4	1	000	2	4	1	000	2	4	1	000	2	4	1	500	2	4
Strong flour	—	—	—	—	—	—	—	—	—	—	—	—	—	—	—	—	—	500	1	2
Baking powder	—	10	—	⅓	—	10	—	⅓	—	—	—	—	—	—	—	—	—	—	—	—
Shortening	—	250	—	9	—	—	—	—	—	—	—	—	—	—	—	—	—	—	—	—
Margarine/butter	—	250	—	9	—	625	1	6½	—	555	1	4	—	600	1	5½	—	335	—	12
Puff pastry fat	—	—	—	—	—	—	—	—	—	—	—	—	—	—	—	—	—	335	—	12
Fine castor sugar	—	125	—	4½	—	250	—	9	—	390	—	14	—	—	—	—	—	335	—	12
Icing sugar	—	—	—	—	—	—	—	—	—	140	—	5	—	390	—	14	—	110	—	4
Egg	—	—	—	—	—	195	—	7	—	—	—	—	—	—	—	—	—	—	—	—
Water	—	125	—	4½	—	—	—	—	—	—	—	—	—	—	—	—	—	—	—	—
Ground almonds	—	—	—	—	—	—	—	—	—	—	—	—	—	290	—	10½	—	—	—	—
Lemon juice (optional)	—	—	—	—	—	55	—	2	—	—	—	—	—	55	—	2	—	—	—	—
Totals	1	760	3	15⅓	2	135	4	12⅚	2	085	4	11	2	335	5	4	2	115	4	12

CHOICE OF INGREDIENTS

Flour
With the exception of savoury pastes and recipe No. 3 in which a proportion of strong flour is used, pastry is best made from soft or cake flour so that the gluten formation is kept to the minimum to prevent a toughened paste.

Fats Any special compounded shortening is ideal for use in pastry making. Margarine and butter can also be employed, but are best used in combination with a shortening. For savoury pastes a good quality lard is recommended. The use of puff pastry fat is reserved for the special sweet pastry recipe No. 3.

Sugar If the percentage of sugar is high, there will be some difficulty in getting it dissolved into the paste. In methods 1 and 2 where the sugar is first dissolved into the liquid, the cheaper granulated sugar may be used, but for methods 3 and 4 the use of a fine grained castor sugar is recommended.

Liquid Water, milk or egg, or a mixture of these, can be used depending upon the richness of the pastry being made.

Baking Powder Except for rich pastes in which a higher proportion of eggs is used, a small amount of baking powder helps to lighten the paste and make it friable. This should be well sieved together with the flour.

VARIETIES

Short pastry is used to produce a large number of varieties in combination with various fruits, jams and other fillings.

Jam and Curd Tarts (Using short pastry recipe)

Preparation of the filling

Before jam or curd can be used as a filling for tarts, it should be brought to a soft consistency to facilitate easy depositing into the pastry case and also to flow during baking and fill the case. This is simply done by mixing it with sufficient water to obtain the consistency desired.

Method
(1) Line the pastry pans with short pastry in either of the following ways:

By Machine Roll out a rope of pastry approx. 4 cm (1½ in) diameter and with a knife cut into slices about 12 mm (½ in) thick. Place these into the patty pans, give them a light dusting of flour and block out the shape on the machine. The size of the pastry slice will depend upon the patty tin size and may have to be adjusted. The aim should be to collect only the minimum amount of trimming. Ensure that the patty tins, tray and base plate of the machine are clean so that the trimmings are not contaminated and can be used again.

By Hand Pin out the pastry to the required thickness – approx. 3 mm (⅛ in), dusting the bench and the pastry with sufficient flour to prevent sticking. Brush off surface flour and using an appropriately sized cutter, either fluted or plain, cut out the required number of pieces.

Pick these up and stack about six at a time into the hand. Invert and place the pieces into the patty tins so that the surface, free from flour, is in contact with the tin, whilst the floured underside is now on top. This will facilitate the shaping of the pastry to the tin.

Hand Notching Commercially this is no longer a viable proposition, but for exhibition work it is still retained for demonstrating traditional skills. It is done by first building up a plain wall of pastry at the edge of the patty tin. Then, using a sharp knife, the notching is produced by cutting the wall towards the centre against the thumb or finger at intervals around the edge.

(2) Jam or curd is now deposited into the lined pastry case by one of the following methods:

    (*a*) An automatic depositor.

    (*b*) The use of a funnel.

    (*c*) The use of a savoy or greaseproof paper bag.

    (*d*) By hand.

The quantity of filling will depend on a number of factors and has to be determined after experimentation. Too much jam will result in it boiling over the edge to give unsightly tarts and burnt debris on the tray. Insufficient will give tarts of poor appearance which taste dry.

It is important to ensure that an equal amount of filling is placed into each tin so that every tart is uniformly baked.

(3) Bake in an oven at approx. 215°C (420°F). If the jam begins to boil before the pastry is coloured the temperature should be lowered. Conversely, if the pastry starts to colour before the jam has boiled – increase the temperature.

Syrup or Treacle Tarts

Syrup or treacle may be baked in tarts in the same way as jam, but breadcrumbs are required to be added first of all at the rate of approx. 195 g (7 oz) per kilo (2¼ lb) of golden syrup. To facilitate the filling of the tarts, the syrup should be warmed. A lower baking temperature is required for these tarts, i.e. 193°C (380°F).

Use of Foil Containers

Many bakers are now using aluminium foil cases instead of patty pans and tins. They have the following advantages:

    (*a*) They are more hygienic.

    (*b*) They are labour-saving because the tins do not need cleaning.

    (*c*) They facilitate packing and cause less risk of breakage (particularly with custard tarts).

Packing Small Tarts

Once cold, the tarts can be packed in pairs, one being inverted over the other. This not only reduces packing space but the filling is protected from the dust in the air, which can spoil its appearance. The filling will obviously have to be set firm otherwise it will run out of the tart when placed upside down.

Egg Custard

Yield – 36 tarts

	k	g	lb	oz
Fresh milk	1	000	2	4
Fresh eggs (6)	—	280	—	10
Sugar	—	140	—	5
Nutmeg		Pinch		Pinch
Totals	1	420	3	3

Method

(1) Beat milk, eggs and sugar.

(2) Transfer to a jug with a good pouring lip.

Note   The best quality custard is made with fresh eggs, but frozen or reconstituted A.F.D. egg may also be used.

EGG CUSTARD TARTS

(1) Line deep patty tins or cases with short pastry similar to the technique described for jam and curd tarts. If done by hand, use a plain cutter and thumb pastry to form a good wall above level of tin. Ensure that the pastry is thick enough to prevent collapse after baking and air from being trapped between the pastry and the case. This will expand on heating and force the custard to overflow. Also ensure that the pastry is not punctured as this will cause the custard to leak into the tin and prevent its release. The use of machine-blocked aluminium foil cases will prevent these faults occurring. Alternatively, the use of paper cups inserted into the patty pan is recommended.

(2) Carefully pour the liquid custard to $\frac{3}{4}$ fill the pastry case.

(3) Sprinkle some grated nutmeg in the centre of each tart to improve the appearance and to give it flavour.

(4) Bake in an oven at approx. 205°C (400°F) until the pastry has slightly coloured and the custard has set. On no account must the custard boil, as this will completely ruin its consistency causing separation of the liquid it contains. Great care must be exercised to ensure that the temperature is correct for the size and that it is not left to bake for too long. Larger tarts require an oven at least 20°C (36°F) cooler.

Figure 1. Custard tarts—machine stamped in foil cases

FRUIT PIES

(1) Line deep patty tins or cases with short pastry in the same way as for custard tarts.
(2) Pin out some pastry approx. 1½ mm (⅛ in) thick and from this cut circles to fit inside the top of the case. Stack these for use later. These can be cut from pastry trimmings.
(3) Deposit an appropriate quantity of fruit filling into each case.
(4) Cover with the pastry circles.
(5) Pierce top with a knife. The enclosed filling may be thus identified by the number of cuts, e.g. 1 for apple, 2 for blackcurrant etc. if more than one variety is being made at the same time.
(6) Bake in an oven at approx. 205°C (400°F) for about 15–20 minutes or until the pastry case is coloured.
(7) Give each tart a dusting of castor sugar.
(8) Remove from the tins once the tarts are cold.

Preparation of Fruit Fillings

Most fruits require partial or complete cooking prior to their use in this way. In addition the juice is thickened by the addition of starches such as cornflour or arrowroot. Most bakers purchase fruit fillings already prepared for use in tarts, but the use of fresh fruits purchased during their seasons can be advantageous.

Fruits commonly used are – apple, plum, blackberry, bilberry, gooseberry, blackcurrant and cherry.

If stewed fruit is used solely for the fillings, the juice content should not exceed 125 gm per kilo (2 oz per lb).

Usually a fruit filling is made as follows:

Fruit Filling
Yield – 36 tarts

	kg	g	lb	oz
Solid Fruit	1	000	2	4
Juice	—	500	1	2
*Cornflour or arrowroot approx.	—	50	—	1¾
Totals	1	550	3	7¾

(1) Make a thin paste from the cornflour and cold juice.
(2) Bring the remaining juice to the boil.
(3) Stir the boiling juice into the paste.
(4) Return the mixture to the heat and boil for a few minutes.
(5) Allow to cool and then incorporate the fruit.

Quantity of Jellying Agent (*cornflour or arrowroot)

This will depend upon the natural pectin content of the fruit chosen and whether the fruit is under-ripe. The actual consistency required can only be determined by experience, just sufficient thickening agent being used to set the juice when cold.

Quantity of Sugar

The amount of sugar which needs to be added depends upon the natural sweetness of the fruit used. Ideally the sugar should be added with the fruit at the initial stage of boiling, but often only a proportion is added at this stage and the rest later to bring the filling to the desired sweetness.

Preparation of Fruit

If fresh fruit is used, there must obviously be some pre-preparation such as peeling, removal of cores, stalks and stones etc. Also the fruit must be ripe, sound and clean prior to cooking. The removal of skins and stones may be more easily accomplished after cooking. Fruits such as apples and pears brown very easily if left exposed to the air. As these are peeled they should be placed into salted water and then rinsed free of the salt immediately prior to cooking. Lemon juice may also be used to preserve colour and impart flavour. For flavouring apple tarts, a clove bud should be placed into each case after filling. Ground cloves can be used as an alternative.

INDIVIDUAL FRUIT TARTS

These are baked cases made from either short or sweet pastry into which is placed either fresh soft fruit such as raspberries, strawberries or bananas, or more usually tinned fruit. This is covered in a glaze or jelly to enhance appearance. Alternatively the baked case may be filled with a custard (*see* page 180), wine cream (*see* page 179) or fresh cream and fruit placed on top in a decorative way and glazed (*see* figure 2).

(1) Line patty tins or cases with short pastry and prick base.
(2) Bake in an oven at approx. 205°C (400°F) until the pastry case is golden brown in colour.

This is known as baking blind. Some confectioners used to fill the pastry case with dried beans or peas to keep the centre from rising. If the patty tin or case has been properly lined with pastry, this is not necessary.

(3) When the case is cold, drain the fruit well. Arrange it in the case in a pattern.
(4) Cover with a glaze whilst still hot, (*see* opposite).

Figure 2. Individual fruit tarts: (1) Banana (2) Mandarin Orange (3) Cherries (4) Pineapple (5) Grapes (6) Apricot

	kg	g	lb	oz
Fruit Juice	1	000	2	4
Arrowroot	—	50	—	$1\frac{3}{4}$
Totals	1	050	2	$5\frac{3}{4}$

(1) Make a thin paste from the arrowroot and cold juice.
(2) Bring the remaining juice to the boil.
(3) Stir the boiling juice into the paste.
(4) Return the mixture to the heat and boil for a few minutes.
(5) Sweeten with sugar if necessary.
(6) Pass through a strainer.

Note Arrowroot is used in preference to cornflour, because it gives a more transparent jelly allowing the fruit to be more easily seen.

Use of Quick Set Jelly

This is a preparation made from a fruit-flavoured pectin syrup which, when citric acid is added, will set to a firm jelly. The directions for using these preparations are clearly explained by each manufacturer for his own particular product.

FRUIT MERINGUE TARTS

Instead of covering the fruit with a pastry case, it may be covered with a boiled meringue as follows:
(1) Prepare individual fruit pies in one of the following ways:
  (a) As explained for fruit pies on page 21 but without pastry lids. After baking allow to cool.
  (b) Bake the pastry case blind and when cold fill with the appropriate fruit, e.g. pineapple, raspberries, either tinned or fresh as explained on page 22.
(2) Make a boiled meringue (*see* page 110) and pipe a rosette on top of each pie with a star tube to cover the fruit completely.
(3) Flash off by putting them back into an oven at 260°C (500°F) to slightly colour the meringue.
(4) One method of identifying the fruit filling is to pipe on the top with meringue using a 6 mm ($\frac{1}{4}$ in) tube, the initial letter of the fruit used.
  For example: A – Apple, B – Blackcurrant, P – Pineapple, R – Raspberry.

Where two types of fruit are used having the same initial, e.g. blackberry and blackcurrant an alternative method of identification needs to be made such as either leaving off the piped initial altogether or baking the pie in a different shaped patty tin.

These fruit tarts may be decorated with a rosette of fresh cream immediately before sale.

LARGE TARTS AND PIES

These can be made on plates of metal, paper or foil and also in flan rings.

It is difficult to be dogmatic about the difference between a *TART* and a *PIE*. The accepted definition is that in a pie the filling is enclosed, whilst in a tart the filling is open to view. However, we can partially enclose the filling with a lattice of pastry which allows only part of the filling to be seen.

As in the small tarts, large ones can also be blocked out by machine onto foil plates. *By hand* the method is as follows:

Tarts
(1) Pin out the pastry to the required thickness [approx. 3 mm ($\frac{1}{8}$ in)].
(2) Brush off surface flour and cut circles with a large cutter.
(3) Invert the pieces over the plate and press flat with the fingers or a piece of pastry.
(4) Trim edge with a sharp knife and notch if desired.
(5) Deposit the filling and spread level.

Pies
(1) At stage 3 above, deposit the filling and spread level. Brush the sides with water.
(2) Cover with a circle of pastry pinned out to 3 mm ($\frac{1}{8}$ in) thick, large enough to overlap.
(3) Trim the edges with a sharp knife and notch if desired.
(4) Prick the centre with fork, or spear with a pointed knife, and identify the type of filling by the number of incisions made.

Baking
Large tarts and pies require an oven approx. 20°C (36°F) cooler than their smaller counterparts.

The surface may be washed with egg or milk or water and/or dusted with sugar either before or after baking.

Mince Pies
(Yield – 56)

	kg	g	lb	oz
Shortpastry	1	000	2	4
Mincemeat	—	830	1	10
Totals	1	830	3	14

(1) Line or block the patty tins or cases with short pastry as with jam tarts.
(2) Roll the pastry to about 1$\frac{1}{2}$ mm ($\frac{1}{8}$ in) thick and cut out circles sufficiently large to cover the tin or case.

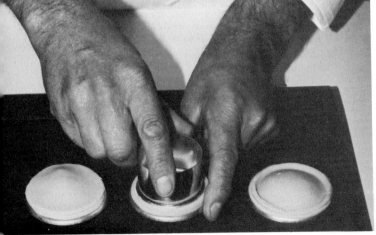

Figure 3. Mince pies: pressing in the tops using a round cutter

(3) Deposit mincemeat either by machine or in one of the following ways:
    (*a*) Using a savoy bag with a large nozzle.
(With this method it will be necessary to pinch off the required quantity of mincemeat with a clean finger)
    (*b*) Using a spoon and a clean finger.
(4) Splash with water or cover with a fine spray to seal the top lid.
(5) Place the circles of pastry over each case.
(6) Press down with the rolled edge of a smaller cutter so that the top is secured to the bottom (*see* Figure 3).
(7) Prick with a fork or spear with a pointed knife.
(8) Bake in an oven at 215°C (420°F) until golden brown.
(9) Liberally dust with icing sugar on removal from the oven.

SWEET PASTRY

This is sometimes referred to as sugar pastry or flan pastry especially by patissiers. As the name implies, it is much richer than short pastry, containing a higher proportion of sugar and fat, and is usually bound with egg instead of water. It is used for flans and cases for various types of fancies.

Flans   (Use Flanpastry Recipe on page 17).
The method of lining flans is as follows:
(1) Place the clean flan ring onto a thin circular metal plate or a cardboard disc.
(2) Divide the pastry into appropriately sized pieces and hand up into balls. 250 g (9 oz) pieces should suffice to produce a 20 cm (8 in) flan. This obviously requires to be scaled down for smaller flans.
(3) Using a rolling pin, extend the ball of pastry to a diameter of approx. 26 cm (10 in) for a flan of this size – enough to cover the base and extend up the sides of the flan ring.
(4) Carefully pick up the pastry by wrapping it around the rolling pin and laying it over the flan ring.
(5) Press the pastry firmly into the base and work it up the sides of the ring, ensuring that no air pockets are formed.
(6) Trim off the surplus pastry from the edge of the flan with a sharp knife.
(7) Prick the base thoroughly with a fork or docker and bake in an oven at 215°C (420°F) until light golden brown colour.
Some confectioners recommend that before baking, the flan should be filled with dried beans or peas to prevent the base from buckling. Such a precaution is unnecessary if the flan has been properly prepared before baking.

Fruit Flans

These are finished off in the same way as the small fruit tarts, covering the baked cases with fruit and then afterwards with a glaze.
The larger surface area of a flan gives greater scope for the imaginative confectioner to devise attractive patterns using a variety of tinned and other fruits which not only provide colour but texture and shape to any design.
Allow about 250 g (9 oz) of fruit for each 20 cm (8 in) flan. The following shows how much tinned fruit is approx. equal to 60 g (2 oz):

1 Pineapple ring (small)	4 Apricots
16 Mandarin oranges	20 Cherries
1 Peach	1 Pear

Glaze with one of the preparations shown on page 23.

Figure 4. Fruit flan prior to glazing: (1) Centre of mandarin orange segments with a cherry, surrounded with half apricots and cherries (2) Sliced peaches with a small peach in the centre (3) Half cherries (4) Pineapple rings and segments (5) Centre of a pineapple ring and cherry surrounded with sliced peaches (6) Sliced pears with a centre of apricot

Apple Meringue Flan (or Pie)

Yield – 1 at 20 cm (8 in)

	kg	g	lb	oz
Flan pastry (*see* page 17)	—	250	—	9
Apples	—	780	1	12
Italian meringue (*see* page 110)	—	165	—	6
Totals	1	195	2	11

(1) Line a flan ring with pastry and bake blind.
(2) Peel, core and cut the apples into small slices into salt water to prevent browning. Rinse and cook with a very small amount of water to a purée.
(3) When cold, place the purée into the flan and spread level.
(4) Using a savoy bag with a star tube, cover the apple with meringue in a decorative pattern.
(5) Place the finished flan into a hot oven at approx. 232°C (450°F) for a few minutes to colour the highlight of the meringue pattern a golden brown.

Filling for Lemon Meringue Flan

	kg	g	lb	oz
Sugar	1	000	2	4
Water	1	250	2	13
Cornflour	—	195	—	7
Butter or margarine	—	250	—	9
Egg yolks	—	250	—	9
Lemon juice	—	500	1	2
Totals	3	445	7	12

(1) Dissolve sugar in half the water and bring to the boil.
(2) Add the cornflour mixed with the remaining half of the water and cook until it thickens, stir well.
(3) Add the zest and juice of the lemon and the melted butter.
(4) Lastly whisk in the egg yolks.

Lemon Meringue Flan

Yield – 1 at 20 cm (8 in)
(1) Use the same amount of sweet pastry and meringue as with the apple meringue pie but with 400g (14 oz) of the lemon filling.
(2) Line a flan ring with pastry and bake blind.
(3) Pour 400 g (14 oz) of the lemon filling into the cold baked case.
(4) Cover with meringue piped in a decorative fashion.
(5) Place into a hot oven at 232°C (450°F) for a few minutes to colour.

FRANGIPANE

(Recipes page 28)
Method for mixing filling   Normal sugar batter method in which the ground almonds replace the flour – *see* page 128.
Yield from recipe – 320 small tarts.
Yield from recipe – 16 large tarts (18 cm) (7 in) diameter.
Yield from recipe – $1\frac{1}{2}$–2 full size (36 in × 18 in) baking tins (depending upon thickness).

(*See* page 30 for yields for slices).

Flavoured frangipane

Hazelnut   Replace ground almonds with ground hazelnuts.
Coconut   Best quality recipe – replace $\frac{3}{4}$ ground almonds with coconut flour. Medium quality recipe – replace all the ground almonds with coconut flour.
Coffee   Add 140 g (5 oz) coffee extract.
Chocolate   Add 200 g (7 oz) melted unsweetened chocolate, vanilla flavour and chocolate colour.
Pineapple   Add 400 g (14 oz) drained chopped glacé pineapple and yellow colour.
Orange or Lemon   Add orange or lemon paste with the juice or an orange or lemon. Add the appropriate colour.

Besides flavouring the frangipane filling, various fruits etc. can first be placed into the pastry case and the filling put on top before baking. Fruits and fillings suitable for this treatment are:
(*a*) Various preserves.
(*b*) Pineapple crush.
(*c*) Ginger crush.
(*d*) Chopped glacé cherries.
(*e*) Apple.
(*f*) Dates.
(*g*) Sultanas.
(*h*) Apricots.

Method for Large Tart (*see* page 23)

(1) Line the flan ring with pastry.
(2) Prick the base well with a docker or fork.
(3) Spread jam over the base.
(4) Deposit 220 g (8 oz) of the frangipane filling and spread level.

Fillings for Tarts 1

	Frangipane 1				Frangipane 2				Frangipane 3				Maid of Honour				Cheese curd 1				Cheese curd 2			
	kg	g	lb	oz	kg	g	lb	oz	kg	g	lb	oz	kg	g	lb	oz	kg	g	lb	oz	kg	g	lb	oz
Castor sugar	1	000	2	4	1	000	2	4	1	000	2	4	1	000	2	4	1	000	2	4	1	000	2	4
Butter/margarine	1	000	2	4	1	000	2	4	1	000	2	4	—	—	—	—	1	000	2	4	1	000	2	4
Eggs	1	000	2	4	1	000	2	4	1	000	2	4	1	000	2	4	1	835	1	14	1	110	2	8
Ground almonds	1	000	2	4	—	500	1	2	—	375	—	13½	1	000	2	4	—	—	—	—	—	—	—	—
Sponge crumbs	—	—	—	—	1	000	2	4	—	375	—	13½	—	—	—	—	—	—	—	—	—	—	—	—
Flour	—	60	—	2¼	—	60	—	2¼	—	250	—	9	—	—	—	—	—	—	—	—	—	—	—	—
Melted butter	—	—	—	—	—	—	—	—	—	—	—	—	1	000	2	4	—	—	—	—	—	—	—	—
Milk curds	—	—	—	—	—	—	—	—	—	—	—	—	—	—	—	—	—	—	—	—	2	660	6	—
Currants	—	—	—	—	—	—	—	—	—	—	—	—	—	—	—	—	—	—	—	—	—	415	1	14
Nutmeg	—	—	—	—	—	—	—	—	—	—	—	—	—	—	—	—	—	10	—	3/8	—	15	—	½
Milk	—	—	—	—	—	—	—	—	—	—	—	—	—	—	—	—	5	000	11	00	—	—	—	—
Rennet	—	—	—	—	—	—	—	—	—	—	—	—	—	—	—	—	—	85	—	3	—	—	—	—
Lemon paste or zest	—	—	—	—	—	—	—	—	—	—	—	—	—	—	—	—	—	10	—	3/8	—	—	—	—
Totals	4	060	9	2¼	4	560	10	4¼	4	000	9	0	4	000	9	0	7	940	17	9¾	6	200	14	14½

Fillings for Tarts 2

	English				Swiss				Rice				Lemon				Bakewell				Coconut			
	kg	*g*	*lb*	*oz*	*kg*	*g*	*lb*	*oz*	*kg*	*g*	*lb*	*oz*	*kg*	*g*	*lb*	*oz*	*kg*	*g*	*lb*	*oz*	*kg*	*g*	*lb*	*oz*
Castor sugar	1	000	2	4	1	000	2	4	1	000	2	4	1	000	2	4	1	000	2	4	1	000	2	4
Butter/margarine	—	500	1	2	—	500	1	2	—	750	1	11	1	000	2	4	1	000	2	4	—	500	1	2
Shortening	—	165	—	6	—	165	—	6	—	250	—	9	—	—	—	—	—	—	—	—	—	—	—	—
Eggs	1	000	2	4	—	—	—	—	—	750	1	11	1	110	2	8	—	500	1	2	—	—	—	—
Ground almonds	—	335	—	12	—	—	—	—	—	—	—	—	—	—	—	—	—	500	1	2	—	—	—	—
Sponge crumbs	1	000	2	4	—	665	1	8	—	—	—	—	—	—	—	—	—	180	—	6½	—	—	—	—
Soft flour	—	335	—	12	—	—	—	—	1	000	2	4	—	415	—	15	—	—	—	—	—	190	—	6¾
Milk	—	625	1	6½	—	—	—	—	—	625	1	6½	—	55	—	2	—	—	—	—	—	625	1	6½
Currants	—	500	1	2	—	—	—	—	—	—	—	—	—	220	—	8	—	—	—	—	—	—	—	—
Mashed potato	—	—	—	—	1	335	3	0	—	—	—	—	—	—	—	—	—	—	—	—	—	—	—	—
Salt	—	—	—	—	—	20	—	¾	—	—	—	—	—	—	—	—	—	—	—	—	—	—	—	—
Ground rice	—	—	—	—	—	—	—	—	—	500	1	2	—	—	—	—	—	180	—	6½	—	—	—	—
Baking powder	—	—	—	—	—	—	—	—	—	30	—	1⅛	—	10	—	⅓	—	—	—	—	—	10	—	⅓
Med. desiccated coconut	—	—	—	—	—	—	—	—	—	—	—	—	—	—	—	—	—	—	—	—	—	375	—	13½
Golden syrup	—	—	—	—	—	—	—	—	—	—	—	—	—	—	—	—	—	—	—	—	—	500	1	2
Cornflour	—	—	—	—	—	—	—	—	—	—	—	—	—	250	—	9	—	—	—	—	—	—	—	—
Lemon peel (finely chopped)	—	—	—	—	—	—	—	—	—	—	—	—	—	55	—	2	—	—	—	—	—	—	—	—
Lemon peel (paste)	—	—	—	—	—	—	—	—	—	—	—	—	—	10	—	⅓	—	—	—	—	—	—	—	—
Totals	5	460	12	4½	3	685	8	4¾	4	905	11	0⅝	4	125	9	4⅔	3	360	7	9	3	200	8	3 1/12

Figure 5. Frangipane flans, *left*: lattice of piped jam, *right*: lattice of softened sweet pastry

(5) The tart may now be finished off in several different ways:
  (a) Pin out pastry approx. 3 mm ($\frac{1}{8}$ in) thick, cut into strips approx. 1 cm ($\frac{3}{4}$ in) wide and lay these on top in a lattice pattern.
  (b) Proceed as (a) above but instead of cutting into strips use the lattice cutter on a strip of pastry approx. 10 cm (4 in) wide. After cutting, expand this strip and lay it onto the filling. Trim the edges.
  (c) Soften the pastry with egg to make it a mixture which can be piped. Transfer to a savoy bag with a 3 mm ($\frac{1}{8}$ in) tube and pipe the lattice pattern onto the filling. [*see* Figure 5 (right)]
  (d) Instead of a lattice, cut out suitable figures, such as rabbits, and lay these carefully in the centre.
  (e) Instead of pastry, pipe the lattice pattern onto the filling with raspberry jam [*see* Figure 5 (left)].
(6) Bake in an oven at 182°C (360°F).

Slices

A large number of slices may be made with either a pastry base covered with a suitable filling such as frangipane, or a filling sandwiched between two layers of pastry. Allow approx. 1 kilo ($2\frac{1}{4}$ lb) pastry for each layer to cover a 76 cm × 46 cm (30 in × 18 in) baking sheet. Puff pastry may also be used for the top layer of some slices.

Frangipane Slices

(1) Line a baking sheet with pastry and dock well.
(2) Spread with raspberry jam.
(3) Deposit the filling and spread level.
(4) Lay on strips of pastry or alternatively pipe on a lattice using softened pastry in a savoy bag.
(5) Place into an oven at 204°C (400°F) and bake until golden brown in colour.
(6) Brush over with water-icing whilst still hot.
(7) When cold, cut into an appropriate number of slices.

Two aids which will speed the cutting of slices and ensure that each slice is uniform in size is a tray cutter for cutting the tray into strips and the use of a cutting bar.

Yields

The number of slices obtained from a baking sheet will obviously be dictated by the type of business and the price charged. A useful approx. size is 50 mm × 25 mm (2 in × 1 in). This would entail cutting the tray widthwise into 15 strips and cutting each strip into 18 slices making a total of 15 × 18 = 270. Because allowance has to be made to trim the edges the actual size needs to be slightly smaller than indicated. The yields for slightly larger slices are as follows:

$15 \times 17 = 255$
$15 \times 16 = 240$

14 strips cut into 18 = 252
14 strips cut into 17 = 238
14 strips cut into 16 = 224
13 strips cut into 18 = 234
13 strips cut into 17 = 221
13 strips cut into 16 = 208
12 strips cut into 18 = 216
12 strips cut into 17 = 204
12 strips cut into 16 = 192

If one carefully peruses these numbers it becomes immediately apparent that there are several options with only marginal differences in yields.

Other Slices and Squares

Many other types of slices may be made using different fillings.
The basic method is the same:
(1) Roll out the shortpastry approx. 3 mm ($\frac{1}{8}$ in) thick and cover the baking sheet.

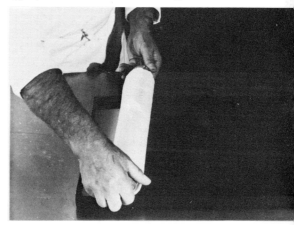

Figure 6. Method of covering a tray with paste by first wrapping it around the rolling pin and unwrapping it to fall onto the tray

(2) Place in an appropriate quantity of filling and spread level.
(3) Cover with a thin layer of pastry pinned out to 3 mm ($\frac{1}{8}$ in) thick.
(4) Pass the rolling pin over the top to press the pastry level, dock and cover with egg wash.

Figure 7. Using a roller docker

(5) A tracy cutter can be used to mark the surface of the pastry prior to baking to facilitate its cutting afterwards into either slices or squares.

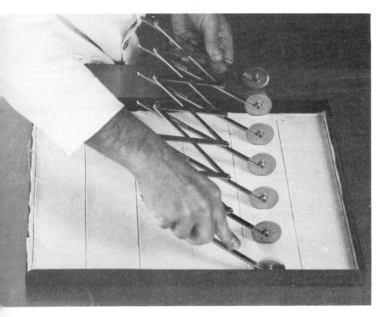

Figure 8. Using a tracy cutter to cut the paste into squares or rectangles. This cutter can be adjusted to any width.

(6) Bake in an oven at approx. 204°C (400°F).

If a sheet has to be cut into squares we have far fewer options open to us as the following figures show. Whichever unit we choose to divide, the width must also be used to divide the length:

Division of length (30 in)	Division of width (18 in)	Yield
20	12	240
18	11	198
16	10	160
15	9	135
14	8	112

Filling for Apple and Apple-and-Sultana Slices and Squares.

These can be made from either fresh or tinned apple.

Fresh Apple

(1) Peel, core and dice or firmly chop the fresh apple.
(2) Sweeten with sugar and add a few cloves. If required, add sultanas or chopped dates.
(3) Use this filling raw as cooking is achieved in the oven.
(4) A few minutes before baking is complete, remove from the oven, dust with castor sugar and replace to finish.

Solid-Pack Tinned Apple

Finely chop, or place in a machine with a whisk, sweeten and use in the same way as for fresh apples.

Note If dates are used less sugar will be required for sweetening.

Date and Fig Fillings

	Date Filling				Fig Filling			
	kg	*g*	*lb*	*oz*	*kg*	*g*	*lb*	*oz*
Dried dates	1	000	2	4	—	—	—	—
Dried figs	—	—	—	—	1	000	2	4
Sugar	—	335	—	12	—	335	—	12
Water	—	250	—	9	—	555	1	4
Totals	1	585	3	9	1	890	4	4

(1) Mince the dried figs or dates.
(2) Add the sugar and water and bring to the boil.
(3) Allow to cool before spreading over the pastry.

Yields

This will depend upon the thickness required of the filling. A normal 76 cm × 46 cm (30 in × 18 in) baking tray will take about 3 kg (6 lb 12 oz) of filling.

Frangipane Tarts for Individual Fancies

The type of patty tin usually reserved for this type of goods has a raw edge and this makes their lining with pastry easy if the method shown in Figure 9 (A) and (B) is adopted. Furthermore, shapes other than circular can be lined just as easily.

These small cases are filled in the same way as with the larger tarts, jam or fruit being put in before the filling.

Baking temperature: 185°C (365°F).

The decoration of these tarts is shown in chapter 17 page 233.

Figure 9 (A & B). Method of lining small patty pans with pastry.

A. After covering the tins with a thin layer of pastry, press into the tin with a piece of scrap pastry.

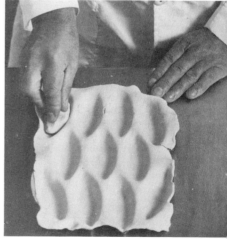

B. Using the rolling pin, pass it over the tins to cut off excess pastry

OTHER SMALL TARTS

See pages 28–9 for recipes for fillings.

General Method for Mixed Fillings

(1) Mix the sugar, fat and egg by the sugar-batter method (*see* page 128).
(2) Stir in the dry ingredients, i.e. flour, ground almonds, rice, etc. If baking powder or spice is used, this should first be sieved with the flour.
(3) Lastly, blend in the other ingredients.
    Baking temperature range: 185°C (365°F) to 199°C (390°F).

Method for Maid-of-Honour Filling

No beating is required in this recipe. Mix all the ingredients except the butter until homogeneous. Lastly add the melted butter and stir until thoroughly blended.

Method for Making the Curd for Cheese Curd Filling

Add the essence of rennet to the warm milk and leave to set in a warm place. Separate the whey from the curds by passing them through a muslin bag or a fine hair or nylon sieve.

Alternatively, curds may be obtained from heavily soured milk.

Note   Only the curds are used in the recipe.

Besides the many types of fillings shown on page   other fillings may be used as follows:

Almond and other nut fillings–Chapter 16 page 228.
Chemically aerated goods   –Chapter 6 page 72.
Meringue goods   –Chapter 8 page 104.

A variety of finishes may be applied to the tarts after they are baked and the following are examples:

Water icing or fondant	– suitably coloured and flavoured and decorated with a cherry.
Chocolate	– for chocolate-flavoured fillings.
Coconut	– coconut tarts can be iced and then dipped into desiccated or thread coconut.

Notes   Many of these fillings may be used with puff pastry bases, especially for the curd recipes.

Yields for Small Tarts

It is difficult to give exact yields because small patty pans not only vary in size but also in shape and particularly in depth. The following list must therefore be regarded as a guide only and is based on the approx. weight of the filling for each individual tart so that quantities can be easily calculated.

Jam and Curd	–35 g (1¼ oz).	
Fruit and Mincemeat	–40 g (1½ oz).	
Frangipane with filling	–10 g (⅜ oz)	–filling 3·5 g (⅛ oz).
Frangipane without filling	–15 g (½ oz).	
All other fillings	–15 g (½ oz).	

Sweet Pastry Cut Out Shapes

Sweet pastry may be used for various shapes cut out with various special cutters. After baking they may be finished off with marzipan (*see* page 87).

Baking temperature: approx. 199°C (390°F).

Strudel Dough

STRUDEL

	kg	g	lb	oz
Strong flour	1	000	2	4
Water	—	500	1	2
Egg	—	100	—	4
Lard	—	100	—	4
Salt	—	20	—	$\frac{3}{4}$
Totals	1	720	3	14$\frac{3}{4}$

Oil – 55 g (2 oz)

(1) Make a smooth dough from the above ingredients and leave to rest for at least half an hour.

(2) Use the oil to grease the hands, stretch the dough to wafer thickness, without breaking the skin. This is a difficult operation and only achieved after much practice. It is done by laying the dough over the hands which are made to circulate in a horizontal position in a flapping motion.

The above dough should cover an area of 1.5 × 1.8 m (5 ft × 6 ft), but for practical reasons the amount of dough used for each rolling should be half or even a quarter of the recipe given. The stretching is facilitated if a table of the appropriate dimensions is available, so that the dough can be extended over the ends. The dough should be so thin that it should be possible to read newsprint when placed underneath the pastry.

(3) Cover the dough with filling up to within approx. 5 cm (2 in) from the long edge. This is left to seal after rolling.

(4) Roll up Swiss roll fashion and place onto a baking sheet.

(5) Brush with a mixture of butter and egg and bake in an oven at 204°C (400°F).

(6) After baking it is dusted with icing sugar and cut into convenient lengths.

Filling

	kg	g	lb	oz
Apples	1	000	2	4
Breadcrumbs	—	100	—	3$\frac{1}{2}$
Butter	—	100	—	3$\frac{1}{2}$
Sugar	—	100	—	3$\frac{1}{2}$
Cinnamon	—	7	—	$\frac{1}{4}$
Raisins	—	100	—	3$\frac{1}{2}$
Totals	1	407	3	2$\frac{1}{4}$

Note The sugar quantity depends upon the sourness of the apples used.

(1) Heat the butter and fry the breadcrumbs to a delicate brown shade. Sprinkle them over the dough at stage 3.

(2) Finely slice the apples, mix with the sugar and cover the breadcrumbs.

(3) Sprinkle with the raisins and cinnamon. Some rum spirit can also be splashed on at this stage.

(4) Proceed with stages 4 and 5.

Cherry Strudel

Instead of apple, use stoned cherries.

FAULTS IN SHORT and SWEET PASTRY

FAULTS	Insufficient fat/egg/sugar used.	Use of too strong a flour.	Poor rolling out technique.	Insufficient moistening agent used.	Excessive moistening agent used.	Insufficient rest prior to baking.	Insufficient aeration.
PASTRY FAULTS:							
Tough pastry.	√	√		√	√		
Shrinkage.	√	√			√	√	
Distorted shape.	√	√	√		√	√	√
Poor texture.	√	√		√			√
Too much oven colour.							
Insufficient oven colour.							
Pastry too short.							
Brown spots on crust.							
FAULTS IN GOODS MADE:							
Jam in tarts boiling over.							
Jam in tarts spilling over.							
Custard boiling.							
Custard spilling over.							
Custard breaking through pastry.							
Lids of tarts becoming detached.							

CAUSES

Oven temperature too low.	Insufficient fat/egg used.	Excessive fat/egg used.	Insufficient sugar used.	Excessive sugar.	Seal insufficiently dampened.	Under mixing.	Over mixing.	Undissolved sugar.	Jam too thin.	Too much filling.	Excessive shrinkage of pastry.	Poor blocking or thumbing.	Pastry too thin.
							√						
							√						
							√						
	√						√						
				√									
√			√										
		√		√		√							
								√					
									√				
										√	√		
										√	√		
										√			
												√	√
					√					√			

3. Puff Pastry

This is a pastry made by forming layers of dough interleaved with layers of fat by the process known as *turning*. There are three basic methods of manufacture, but the purpose of each is to achieve about 700–1000 layers of dough and fat. When these very thin layers of dough are subjected to heat, steam is generated, the pressure of which forces the layers apart and so causes the *puff* in the pastry. Besides being the agent used to keep the dough layers separate, the fat melts and is absorbed into them thereby imparting a shortening effect.

CHOICE OF INGREDIENTS

Flour

Since it is the gluten which is responsible for trapping the steam in the dough layers, we must use a flour rich in this respect. A medium-strength flour with gluten of good elasticity is to be desired for most commercial practices. Very strong flour should be avoided, since this will make a very tough pastry with a risk of the layers fracturing during the manufacture and shrinkage of the finished pastry afterwards. The author has seen first-class exhibition puff pastry made with butter and English flour; however, the care and time involved in hand-rolling such pastry makes it an uneconomic commercial proposition. Power-rolling of puff pastry requires the use of a medium-strong flour as well as the specially manufactured fats which are available.

Fat

As previously mentioned, top quality puff pastry is made with butter, but the temperature of the paste needs to be kept cooler to maintain the right consistency. The use of a softer flour and a dough of softer consistency is also essential for the best results. The flavour of such pastry, however, is supreme and may well justify the trouble taken for high quality goods.

Fats and margarine made especially for puff pastry are manufactured from oils and fats with a high melting point and have good spreading characteristics (i.e. they are plastic). The high melting point delays the fat melting and being absorbed into the dough layers until they have begun to set. Whilst the use of such fats helps the manufacturer to produce pastries of attractive appearance, and good volume with power-rolling methods, there is often a waxy taste left in the cooked pastry afterwards (*palate cling*).

The fat manufacturers have made available a number of different products for puff pastry manufacture. Some of these are margarines whilst others are 100% fats and emulsions containing up to 20% water.

The quantity of fat used is not critical and provided there is enough present to insulate the dough layers, the pastry will *puff*. It can vary between 50% to 100% of the flour weight. For the best results with the lower quantities, less turns must be given and this will result in a slightly reduced and more irregular lift. We usually define the type of pastry made by the amount of fat used:

Half pastry	–	50% of fat based upon flour weight
Three quarter pastry	–	75% of fat based upon flour weight
Full pastry	–	100% of fat based upon flour weight

It is usual to add about 10% to 12½% of shortening to the dough to increase its tenderness.

Acid

The use of cream of tartar or lemon juice is often recommended to make the gluten more extensible and this might be true if a very strong flour is used. However, this is difficult to prove, and it is the author's experience that perfectly good puff pastry can be made without the aid of acid in the dough.

Proteinase

The use of the enzyme proteinase is advocated by some to reduce the resting time necessary prior to goods being baked off. The use of very small quantities is stated to have a mellowing effect on the gluten thereby preventing shrinkage.

Salt

If a butter, margarine or fat is used which is already salted, it renders a further addition unnecessary.

Yellow Colour

This is widely used in industry and a little certainly helps to make goods look more attractive. However, it should be used with discretion and the pastries should never appear to be bright in colour.

NOTES ON PUFF PASTRY MANUFACTURE

Consistency

Ideally the consistency of both the dough and the fat must be the same in order to get perfectly interleaved layers. If the dough is stiffer than the fat, the latter will be squeezed out and conversely if the fat is stiffer, the dough will be extruded. Care to see that the fat is of the correct consistency is very important in winter when it may have to be kneaded in a warm environment. The use of soft fats such as butter demands a very much softer dough for the correct result.

Turning (Rolling)

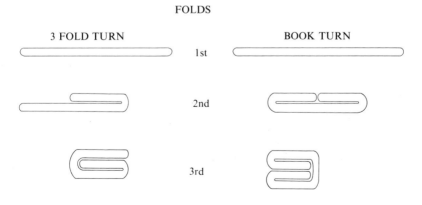

Figure 10. Sectional diagrams of the stages of the 3 fold and book turns

There are two different methods by which we can achieve the number of layers necessary to produce good pastry.

(1) Rolling out and folding into three.

(2) Rolling out, folding the ends in first and then again like a book (Book Turn).

A combination of both methods may also be used.

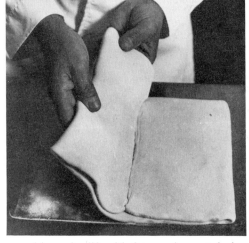

Too few turns will result in a poor and irregular lift with fat running out during baking.

Too many turns will result in the merging of the layers with the fat to form a kind of shortpastry. This too will result in poor lift.

To ensure that the layers are kept separate during manufacture, the pastry must not be rolled too thinly and given sufficient rest between turns. (A special exception is made to dough made on a high-speed mixer – *see* later).

If a pastry brake is used, the reduction of thickness of the pastry must be done gradually otherwise rupturing of the layers will occur, resulting in poor lift.

Resting and Cutting Out

Besides giving pastry resting periods between turns to overcome this toughening action, it is desirable to allow the individual cut-out pieces of pastry to rest prior to being baked. It is also an advantage to thoroughly relax the rolled out pastry before cutting and ensure that stresses caused by the rolling pin are equalized. Circles of pastry cut out of a piece of pastry in which stresses have been set up by rolling it in one direction only, will result in ovals once they are baked. There is no special merit in resting the pastry for too long before it is baked, in fact whilst it might aid perfection in shape, it will lose some of its lift. Puff pastry should not be more than 3 mm (⅛ in) in thickness prior to cutting. Thick pastry will not result in a greater volume but will result in unbaked thick layers in the finished goods.

If puff pastry is made and left overnight it is advisable to leave the last turn to be done on the following day prior to finishing off. Ensure it is covered either with a polythene sheet or damp cloth to minimize the risk of skinning.

Washing

For washing the goods prior to baking, egg whites beaten with a little water undoubtedly gives the best results for sugar-dipped items. For a glaze and good colour without sugar, whole egg should be used. This should be done just prior to baking to minimize the risk of surface drying and cracking giving unsightly marks on the surface after baking.

Oven Temperature

A hot oven is essential for good puff pastry in order to quickly generate sufficient steam to effect the lift. Plain and egg washed varieties should be baked up to 232°C (450°F). Varieties coated with sugar, or almond nibs, must of course be baked at lower temperatures otherwise the surface will take on too much colour and could burn.

Figure 13. Showing the effect of temperature on puff pastry. The pieces illustrated were all cut from the same piece of pastry rolled out to the same thickness, given the same period of rest, but baked at the following temperatures: (1) 260°C (500°F); (2) 232°C (450°C); (3) 204°C (400°F); (4) 177°C (350°F)

Use of Scrap

Some varieties are required to be cut out of fresh virgin pastry whilst others like palmiers can be made entirely from scraps. Most varieties however are made from pastry in which a proportion of scrap is incorporated. The usual method is to fold back the top layer, assemble the scrap in an even layer and replace the top flap, before rolling out.

For lift such as is required for vol-au-vents, virgin pastry is essential but where flakiness only is required, a mixture of virgin and scrap is quite acceptable. The production of puff pastry goods should be planned in such a way that all the scrap can be used.

Storage of Puff Pastry

Puff pastry should always be covered to prevent skinning due to exposure to the air. The best material for this is plastic film which besides being impervious can be washed repeatedly and so is more hygienic than other types.

It can be kept indefinitely in a deep freeze from where it may be defrosted by either leaving it in the bakery for six hours or placing it in a refrigerator overnight or up to two days. Once brought to room temperature, however, it should be used up and baked off. Keeping raw pastry at above refrigeration temperature will result in the production of acids formed by bacteria which will cause sourness to develop and make the pastry unusable.

Puff Pastry

	1st quality full				2nd quality full				2nd quality $\frac{3}{4}$			
	kg	g	lb	oz	kg	g	lb	oz	kg	g	lb	oz
Medium flour	1	000	2	4	—	—	—	—	—	—	—	—
Strong flour	—	—	—	—	1	000	2	4	1	000	2	4
Cream of tartar	—	—	—	—	—	3	—	$\frac{1}{8}$	—	3	—	$\frac{1}{8}$
Lemon juice	—	15	—	$\frac{1}{2}$	—	—	—	—	—	—	—	—
Butter (salted)	—	110	—	4	—	—	—	—	—	—	—	—
Cake margarine or shortening	—	—	—	—	—	110	—	4	—	110	—	4
Tough butter (salted)	—	890	2	0	—	—	—	—	—	—	—	—
Pastry margarine or fat	—	—	—	—	—	890	2	0	—	640	1	7
Cold water	—	530	1	3	—	530	1	3	—	530	1	3
Salt	—	—	—	—	—	30	—	$\frac{1}{2}$	—	30	—	$\frac{1}{2}$
Totals	2	545	5	$11\frac{1}{2}$	2	563	5	$11\frac{5}{8}$	2	313	5	$2\frac{5}{8}$

METHOD FOR MAKING DOUGH (ENGLISH AND FRENCH METHODS)

(A) (1) Rub the 120 g (4 oz) of butter, margarine or shortening into the flour.
     (2) Add the water and mix into a well blended and developed dough.
(B) (1) Place the flour, 120 g (4 oz) of butter, margarine or shortening, and water into the high speed mixer and mix to a dough in 15–20 seconds.

METHODS OF TURNING

There are four methods for making puff pastry, but only the first three explained are commercial.

1. English Method (*see* Figures 14 and 15)

(1) Roll out the dough to a rectangle approx. $\frac{1}{2}$ cm ($\frac{1}{4}$ in) in thickness.
(2) Plasticise the butter, margarine or fat, and spread it over $\frac{2}{3}$ of the dough.
(3) Fold the remaining $\frac{1}{3}$ of the dough over the portion spread with the fat and fold over again so that there are two layers of fat and three layers of dough.
(4) Roll out this piece to about the same size as previously and fold into three. This constitutes a normal *turn* sometimes referred to as a *half turn*.

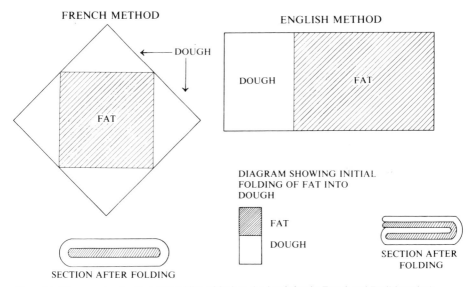

FRENCH METHOD

DOUGH

FAT

SECTION AFTER FOLDING

ENGLISH METHOD

DOUGH

FAT

DIAGRAM SHOWING INITIAL
FOLDING OF FAT INTO
DOUGH

FAT

DOUGH

SECTION AFTER
FOLDING

Figure 14. Diagrams showing the initial folding of fat into the dough for the French and English methods

Figure 15. The initial folding for the English method.

(5) Repeat (4) another five times so that six turns have been given with resting periods between. If two turns are given in succession it is advisable then to leave the dough to rest for at least 30 minutes. Alternatively four book turns may be given.

2. French Method (*see* Figures 14 and 15)

(1) Mould the dough into a ball, make a knife cut at right angles and with the rolling pin form a square with the corners rolled extra thinly.

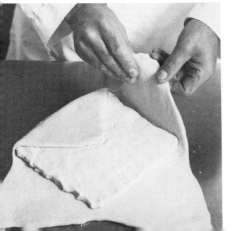

(2) Plasticise the butter, margarine or fat and form it into a square.

(3) Place this diagonally in the centre of the dough and fold over each corner of the dough to meet in the centre, so completely enveloping the fat.

(4) Proceed to give the required turns as in (4) and (5) above.

Figure 16.

3. Scotch or Rough Puff

(1) In this method the 120 g (4 oz) of butter, margarine or fat is first rubbed into the flour.
(2) Dice the remaining fat into 2½ cm (1 in) cubes and mix into the flour.
(3) Proceed to give turns in any of the conventional ways.

This pastry is suitable for varieties in which scrap would normally be used – especially for pies.

Scotch Method Using High Speed Machine

The high speed machine may be used for mixing the dough and the fat.

The mixing time is critical. If it is too long the fat lumps will not remain intact, resulting in a type of shortpaste being made. The time should not exceed 9 seconds and on some of the latest machines even this is reduced to 7 seconds.

4. Swiss Method

One other method used in Switzerland reverses the roles of the fat and the dough, the latter being rolled into the fat to which some of the flour has been added. The first two turns are difficult without plenty of flour to prevent sticking, but after this initial stage the rolling feels the same as in the traditional method. One great advantage of this method is that as the fat layer is always on the outside, it never skins and does not require covering. Having tried this method the author is of the opinion that some of the lift associated with the traditional method is sacrificed.

VARIETIES USING VIRGIN PASTRY

Vol-au-Vents or Open Puff Tarts

This is an open-baked puff pastry case which may be either filled with a savoury filling, jam, curd, fruit or cream. They can be made either large, approx. 16 cm (6 in) or individual 6 cm (2½ in). There are two methods for the *individual vol-au-vent*.

Figure 17.
A vol-au-vent

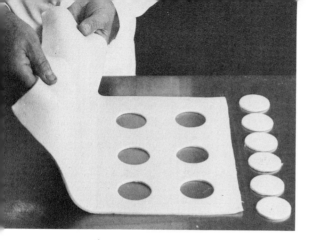

Figure 18. Stages in the making of vol-au-vents

Figure 19.

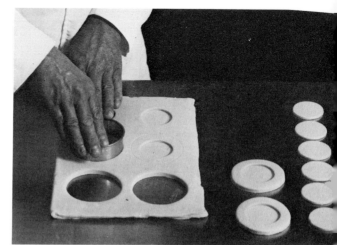

Method 1 This method produces the best-shaped pastry and is well worth the trouble involved.
(1) Roll out well rested virgin pastry to approx. 3 mm ($\frac{1}{8}$ in) thick.
(2) Divide roughly in half and on this piece mark out with a 6–8 cm ($2\frac{1}{2}$–3 in) cutter.
(3) In the centre of these marked circles, cut out a piece using a cutter $2\frac{1}{2}$ cm (1 in) smaller.
(4) Lightly wash the piece containing the cut out holes, with water.
(5) Cover this with the other sheet of pastry and then reverse both pieces so that the holes can be seen (*see* Figure 18).
(6) Using the larger cutter, cut through both layers of pastry with the hole exactly in the centre (*see* Figure 19).
(7) Lay the cut out pieces onto a clean tray and prick the centres with a fork.
(8) Brush the top outside edge with egg wash.
(9) Allow a resting period of 30 minutes to one hour, and egg wash a second time if desired.
(10) Bake in a hot oven at 227°C (440°F) until crisp and light brown in colour.
(11) If lids are required, the pieces cut out with the 4 cm ($1\frac{1}{2}$ in) cutter must also be egg washed and baked off separately. (*Not on same tray, as these will take less time to bake.*)

Method 2
(1) Roll out the pastry to 3 mm ($\frac{1}{8}$ in) in thickness and cut out discs, using a 6–8 cm ($2\frac{1}{2}$–3 in) round cutter.
(2) Using a cutter $2\frac{1}{2}$ cm (1 in) smaller, cut out the centre from half of the discs.
(3) Lay the remaining ones onto a clean baking tray and damp tops with water.
(4) Place on the discs cut out in 5 cm (2 in).
(5) Egg wash, allow to rest and bake as in Method 1.
(6) If tops are required, egg wash and bake off the centres also.

Method 3
(1) Roll the pastry to approx. 6 mm ($\frac{1}{4}$ in) in thickness.
(2) Cut out discs with a 6–8 cm ($2\frac{1}{2}$–3 in) cutter.
(3) Using a cutter $2\frac{1}{2}$ cm (1 in) smaller, cut three-quarters through the pastry in the centre of the disc.
(4) After resting and egg washing, bake in the usual way.
(5) When cold, the centres can either be removed by hand or pressed in to form the cavity for the filling.

Note Commercially Method 3 is the most economical in terms of labour, but it does not produce such a well volumed case. Special vol-au-vent cutters are available which may be used to cut out the pieces with the hole impression in one operation. These are widely used in industry.

Bouchées

Same method as for vol-au-vent, but using smaller cutters, i.e. $2\frac{1}{2}$ cm and $4\frac{1}{2}$ cm (1 in and $1\frac{3}{4}$ in).

Large Vol-au-Vents

For this the pastry needs to be slightly thicker, approx. $\frac{1}{2}$ cm ($\frac{3}{16}$ in) and cut out with a 15–20 cm) (6–8 in) cutter. Use a cutter approx. 4 cm ($1\frac{1}{2}$ in) smaller for the hole. Bake in a cooler oven at approx. 204°C (400°F).

Pineapple Haloes

(1) Before baking, pipe some vanilla custard (*see* page 180) into the centre hole, place on a small ring of tinned pineapple, and finish by putting a cherry in the centre.
(2) Bake for approx. 20–25 minutes at an oven temp. of 220°C (430°F).
(3) When baked, brush over the pineapple with well boiled apricot purée.

Figure 20. Puff pastry varieties as follows:

(1) Banburys	(2) Eccles	(3) Victorias	(4) Vol-au-vent variety
(5) Turnover	(6) Windmill	(7) Cream puff	(8) Apricot puff
(9) Coventry	(10) Bow	(11) Cream horn	(12) Apricot purse

Other Shapes

Square, rectangular and oval open cases may also be made using appropriately shaped cutters. An indication of the sizes of these is as follows:

Square – 60 cm (2½ in).
Oval – 5 × 7½ cm (2 × 3 in).
Rectangular – 4½ × 9 cm (1¾ × 3½ in).
Cut circles out with a 3 cm (1¼ in) cutter.

Using two differently coloured and flavoured fillings such as jam and curd, a very attractive variety is made (*see* Figure 20(4)).

Cream Puffs [*see* Figure 20(7)]
Yield – round 48, square 54.
  1 kg virgin puff pastry.
  7–8 dl (1¼ pts) fresh cream.
  200 g jam (7 oz).
(1) Roll out the puff pastry to 3 mm (⅛ in) in thickness and approx. 40 × 60 cm (16 × 24 in) in size.
(2) Dock well and cut into various shapes equivalent to an 8 cm (3 in) circle. The shapes may be squares, rectangles, ovals, hearts, diamonds or half-moons cut with either plain or fluted cutters. Commercially the best shapes are either square or rectangular since these can be cut with the minimum of scraps, with tracy cutters to speed up production.
(3) Before baking, the top surface may be dressed in one of the following ways:

A. Royal Puffs

Before cutting, evenly spread royal icing on. Further varieties may be made by piping on jam, either diagonally from corner to corner (called *cream coronets*) or in a lattice pattern. If left plain, these are usually called *batons glacé*.

B. Dressed in sugar or almond nibs Brush tops with either water or egg whites and dip into castor sugar or nibbed almonds.

C. Egg washed If the top is egg washed, leave the finished piece plain.

D. Dusted If the top is to be dusted with icing sugar, it should be left plain.
(4) Allow the pieces to rest for a minimum of half an hour.
(5) Bake off at the following temperatures:

  A 200°C (390°F);   B 215°C (420°F);   C and D 226°C (440°F)

(6) When baked and cold, split into two and remove the top piece.
(7) Pipe a small bulb of cream on the bottom piece and then pipe on a bulb of sweetened whipped fresh cream.
(8) Replace top.
(9) With variety D, dust top with icing sugar.

Apricot Puffs
(1) Proceed as for cream puffs, cutting the pastry into squares and washing with egg.
(2) Lay half an apricot on top.
(3) Cover with a strip of pastry for decoration.
(4) After recovery, bake at 226°C (440°F).

Note Besides jam and cream, tinned or fresh fruits in season such as strawberries may be added.

Figure 21. Cutting the apricot purse with the special cutter as shown

Apricot/Pineapple Squares/Purses
Yield 36.

	kg	g	lb	oz
Virgin pastry	1	000	2	4
Apricot/Pineapple	—	500	1	2
Icing sugar	—	250	—	9
Apricot purée	—	250	—	9
Totals	2	000	4	8

(1) Roll out the pastry to 2 mm ($\frac{1}{10}$ in) in thickness and approx. $40\frac{1}{2} \times 62$ cm ($17\frac{1}{2} \times 24\frac{1}{2}$ in).
(2) Cut this into squares of 90 mm ($3\frac{1}{2}$ in).
(3) Make an impression in the centre, of approx. $2\frac{1}{2}$ cm (1 in).
(4) Pipe vanilla custard (*see* page 180) into the centre and onto this place a well drained apricot half.
(5) Place a narrow strip of pastry diagonally across the square for decoration.
(6) Rest for a minimum of half an hour before baking in an oven at 220°C (430°F) for approx. 20–25 mins.
(7) On leaving the oven, brush over with a well boiled apricot purée and thin water icing.

Apricot or Pineapple Purses (*see* Figure 20)

(1) Roll out the pastry to 3 mm ($\frac{1}{8}$ in) in thickness and cut out with the special cutter indicated.
(2) Moisten the cut edge with water and fold over to the opposite end of the shape. Press down to seal.
(3) Bake for approx. 20 minutes at a temperature of 200°C (430°F).
(4) When cold, pipe into the cavity formed, a whirl of whipped sweetened fresh cream.
(5) Decorate with a segment of glacé pineapple and a cherry.
    Alternatively, an apricot half may be used.

Cushions, Bows, Victorias and Windmills

Roll out virgin puff pastry to 2 mm ($\frac{1}{10}$ in) in thickness and cut it into 10 cm (4 in) squares.
    From this the following four varieties may be made:

Cushions

(1) Damp the centre of each square and fold in the corners to meet in the centre.

Figure 22. *Right to left* Row 1–Stages in the making of Bows

Right to left Row 2–Stages in the making of Victorias

Right to left Row 3–Stages in the making of Windmills

(2) Press down firmly and wash with egg white.
(3) Pin out a piece of pastry 1½ mm ($\frac{1}{16}$ in) in thickness and cut a circle 4 cm (1½ in) diameter.
(4) Place this in the centre and wash also with egg white.
(5) Dip into castor sugar and place them on baking trays.
(6) Allow to rest for a minimum of half an hour and bake in an oven at 215°C (420°F).
(7) When baked they may be finished off with jam or curd piped into the corners. A good decorative effect can be made by using two differently coloured jams or curds piped in at opposite corners.

Bows [*see* Figure 20(10) and 22 (row 1)]

Follow the same method as for cushions but only fold over the two opposite ends to the centre.

Victorias [*see* Figure 20(3) and 22 (row 2)]
(1) Fold the square into a triangle.
(2) Make a knife cut at the places indicated approx. 1 cm ($\frac{3}{8}$ in) from the edge and unfold.
(3) Damp the square and then fold the point A to meet B, and the point C to meet D. Press these down firmly.
(4) Allow a minimum of half an hour's rest.
(5) Egg wash the edges and bake in an oven at 226°C (440°F).
(6) When cold fill the centre with jam or curd.

Windmills [*see* Figure 20(6) and 22 (row 3)]
(1) Cut the square at the places indicated.
(2) Damp with a brush and fold the corners into the centre. Press these down firmly.
(3) Place in the centre a circle of pastry cut from 1½ mm ($\frac{1}{16}$ in) thick pastry and 2½ cm (1 in) in diameter.
(4) Allow a minimum of half an hour's rest.
(5) Egg wash and bake in an oven at 226°C (440°F).
(6) When cold fill the cavities with jam or curd.

Slices

Yield – 36 slices

	kg	g	lb	oz
Virgin puff pastry	1	000	2	4
Fresh whipped cream or custard	—	550	1	4
Jam	—	195	—	7
Totals	1	745	3	15

Figure 23. Cream Slices: the slices illustrated consist of two layers of puff pastry sandwiched with cream. The top layer is iced in fondant and has a dressing of browned desiccated coconut at the edges.

Method
(1) Roll out a piece of well rested virgin puff pastry to 3 mm ($\frac{1}{8}$ in) in thickness and approx. 30 × 35½ cm (12 × 14 in).
(2) Cut into 3 strips of 10 cm (4 in) width and lay these pieces of pastry onto a clean baking tray.
(3) Well dock.
(4) Allow to rest for at least 30 minutes and bake in an oven at 227°C (440°F) until crisp and light golden brown in colour.
(5) When baked turn over and split the pieces in two lengthwise.
(6) Remove the top (which was the base) and on the remaining piece spread on a layer of jam followed by a layer of either whipped fresh cream or vanilla custard.
(7) Spread the top piece first with boiling apricot purée and then suitably flavoured and coloured warm fondant.
(8) Allow the fondant to set and then cut the piece into slices approx. 4 cm (1½ in) wide.
(9) Replace the cut slice on top of the creamed base and finish by cutting through.
Notes
 (a) The top or edge could be suitably decorated with coralettes, browned desiccated coconut, etc.
 (b) The cream sides could also be spread evenly and masked with a suitable dressing, e.g. browned nibbed almonds.
 (c) Instead of one piece of virgin pastry, the slice could be made from two strips of thinly rolled pastry 1½ mm ($\frac{1}{16}$ in) in thickness. In this event some scrap pastry could be worked in.

VARIETIES USING A PROPORTION OF SCRAP PASTRY

Sausage Rolls
Yield – 48 rolls

	kg	g	lb	oz
Puff pastry	1	000	2	4
Sausage meat	—	665	1	8
Totals	1	665	3	12

(1) Roll out the pastry to about $2\frac{1}{2}$ mm ($\frac{1}{10}$ in) in thickness and into a rectangle approx. 30 cm × 35 cm (12 in × 21 in).
(2) Cut pastry into four strips 8 cm (3 in) wide.
(3) Mould the sausage meat into 2 long ropes approx. 2 cm ($\frac{1}{2}$ in) in diameter and lay these in the centre of each strip.
(4) Wash with egg or water between each roll of sausage meat so that the edge of each strip is dampened.
(5) Fold over and press edges together firmly.
(6) Cut lengths of roll into suitable lengths of approx. 6 cm ($2\frac{1}{2}$ in).
(7) Mark the surface with the back of a knife.
(8) Wash over with a mixture of egg and water.
(9) Place the individual rolls onto a clean baking sheet.
(10) Allow a resting period of at least 30 minutes.
(11) Bake in an oven at approx. 232°C (450°F) until crisp and light golden brown in colour.

Note The sausage rolls described are dainty enough for a cocktail buffet. If larger rolls are required, the quantities of pastry and sausage meat would have to be increased proportionally.

Turnovers [*see* Figure 20(5) and 24 (top row)]
Yield 36 turnovers

	kg	g	lb	oz
Puff pastry	1	000	2	4
Sugar (for dredging)	—	85	—	3
Jam (filling)	—	335	—	12
Almond/frangipane/ apple (fillings)	—	500	1	2
Totals for jam filling	1	420	3	3
Totals for other fillings	1	585	3	9

For frangipane recipe see page 28

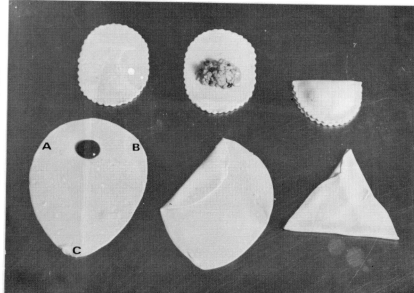

Figure 24.
Right to left Top row – Stages in the making of Turnovers.

Right to left Bottom row – Stages in the making of Coventries.

(1) Roll out pastry to 2½ mm ($\frac{1}{10}$ in) thick.
(2) Cut out with a 10 cm (4 in) fluted cutter.
(3) With a rolling pin, elongate these discs, keeping the centre thin and the edges thick.
(4) Place in a quantity of the filling, except for the fruit or cream varieties.
(5) Damp the edges with egg or water and fold over so that the two meet.
(6) Wash with egg whites or water and dip into castor sugar.
(7) Place onto a clean baking tray and leave to rest for at least 30 minutes.
(8) Bake in an oven at 215°C (420°F) until crisp and golden brown in colour.

Almond Turnovers

Almond Filling

Recipe 1   Soften marzipan with egg whites until it can be piped easily by using a savoy bag.

Recipe 2   Mix ground almonds and castor sugar in equal proportions and make into a soft paste with egg whites.
(1) Roll out the pastry to 2 mm ($\frac{1}{10}$ in) in thickness and cut into squares approx. 9 cm (3½ in) square.
(2) Pipe approx. 15 g (½ oz) of one of the fillings above into each square. If rectangles are required, pipe a rope of the filling, and if triangles are to be made, pipe a bulb into the centre of the pastry square.
(3) Damp the edges with water, fold over and press to seal.
(4) Wash with egg whites and dip into nibbed almonds.
(5) Bake at 204°C (400°F) until almonds are coloured.

Other Varieties   Other varieties may be made by varying the shape. For example from squares we can get either rectangle shapes by folding in half, or diamond shapes by folding diagonally.

Eccles [*see* Figure 20(2)]

Yield 36

	kg	g	lb	oz
Puff pastry	1	000	2	4
Eccles or Banbury filling	—	500	1	2
Totals	1	500	3	6

Mix all ingredients together thoroughly.
(1) Roll out the pastry to 1½ mm ($\frac{1}{16}$ in) in thickness.
(2) Cut out discs using a 10 cm (4 in) cutter.
(3) Place a tablespoonful of the filling in the centre of each piece.
(4) Fold the edges into the centre, sealing in the filling and then turn over.
(5) Either flatten with the palm of the hand or roll out with a rolling pin to approx. 8 cm (3 in) diameter.
(6) Wash the tops with egg white or water and dip into castor sugar.
(7) Place the pieces onto a clean baking sheet.
(8) Make two or three slits in the top with a knife so that the filling shows through.
(9) Allow a minimum of 30 minutes resting period.
(10) Bake in an oven at 215°C (420°F) until crisp and golden brown in colour.

Eccles and Banbury Fillings

	1				2				3			
	kg	g	lb	oz	kg	g	lb	oz	kg	g	lb	oz
Currants	—	250	—	9	—	—	—	—	—	330	—	12
Brown sugar	—	85	—	3	—	—	—	—	—	85	—	3
Golden syrup	—	40	—	1½	—	—	—	—	—	—	—	—
Cake crumbs	—	125	—	4½	—	165	—	6	—	—	—	—
Mixed spice		pinch			—	—	—	—		pinch		
Mincemeat	—	—	—	—	—	335	—	12	—	—	—	—
Butter	—	—	—	—	—	—	—	—	—	85	—	3
Totals	—	500	1	2	—	500	1	2	—	500	1	2

Banburys [*see* Figure 20(1)]

Yield – 36

(1) Repeat 1, 2 and 3 as for Eccles.
(4) Fold over the top and bottom edges to meet in the centre but mould it into a boat shape, keeping the filling sealed in.
(5) Flatten with the palm of the hand or rolling pin to approx. 5 cm × 10 cm (2 in × 4 in).
(6) Finish off as for Eccles.

Mince Pies
Yield – 24

	kg	g	lb	oz
Puff pastry	1	000	2	4
Mincemeat	—	390	—	14
Icing sugar	—	40	—	1½
Totals	1	430	3	3½

(1) Roll out the pastry to 2½ cm ($\frac{1}{10}$ in) thick.
(2) Cut out half the pastry with a 7 cm (2¾ in) cutter (either fluted or plain).
(3) Place the pieces onto a clean baking sheet.
(4) Damp the edges with water or, alternatively, splash the whole tray with water.
(5) Place about a teaspoonful of mincemeat in the centre of each cut out piece.
(6) Cover the pieces with discs cut from the remaining half of the pastry with an 8 cm (3 in) cutter (rolling the pastry slightly thinner to enable the same number of tops to be cut out).
(7) Using the back rolled rim of a 5 cm (2 in) cutter, press down the edges to seal in the mincemeat.
(8) Brush over with egg wash and pierce the top with a fork or knife.
(9) Allow to rest for half an hour.
(10) Bake in an oven at 232°C (450°F) until golden brown in colour.
(11) Sprinkle with icing sugar when baked.

Coventries [*see* Figure 20(9) and 24 (bottom row)]

(1) Roll out the puff pastry to 3 mm ($\frac{1}{8}$ in) in thickness and cut out circles using an 8 cm (3 in) cutter.

(2) Using a rolling pin, extend this circle into a pear shape as shown in figure 24.

(3) Damp the edges with egg whites.

(4) Place a spoonful of filling into the centre where indicated. This filling could be jam, curd, mincemeat, pineapple crush, etc. Allow 15 g ($\frac{1}{2}$ oz) of jam or curd to fill each pastry.

(5) Fold over first (A) and (B) and cover the join with (C) so that a perfect triangle has been formed sealing the filling into the centre.

(6) Place the triangles on the bench so that they rest into each other.

(7) Wash with water or egg whites.

(8) Dip into castor sugar and place closely together on the tray.

(9) After half an hour's rest, bake in an oven at 215°C (420°F) until golden brown in colour.

Note It is important to ensure that the filling is sealed inside the folds to prevent it running out during baking leaving an empty shell.

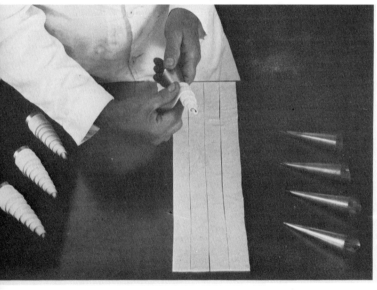

Figure 25. Making cream horns

Cream Horns [*see* Figure 20(11) and 25]

Yield – 36

	kg	g	lb	oz
Puff pastry	1	000	2	4
Jam	—	120	—	4$\frac{1}{2}$
Castor sugar	—	120	—	4$\frac{1}{2}$
Sweetened fresh cream	—	500	1	2
Totals	1	740	3	15

(1) Roll out the puff pastry to $1\frac{1}{2}$ mm ($\frac{1}{16}$ in) in thickness and 60 cm (24 in) long.
(2) Cut into strips $2\frac{1}{2}$ cm (1 in) wide.
(3) Dampen with water.
(4) Wrap the strip carefully round a clean cream horn mould so that each strip overlaps half the other. Start at the point and work towards the open end.
(5) Wash top with egg white or water and dip into castor sugar.
(6) Place onto a clean baking tray and allow at least a $\frac{1}{2}$ hour resting period.
(7) Bake in an oven at 215°C (420°F) to a golden brown colour.
(8) Remove the moulds whilst the horns are still warm by first giving them a slight twist.
(9) Pipe in a small bulb of jam.
(10) Using a savoy bag with a star tube, fill the horn with suitably flavoured and sweetened whipped fresh cream. Finish neatly with a little rosette and decorate with a cherry.

Cream Rolls

(1) Instead of cream horn moulds, wrap the strips of pastry around small cylinders of metal approx. $2\frac{1}{2}$ cm (1 in) in diameter.
(2) Remove when baked and fill the cavity with a bulb of jam and sweetened fresh dairy cream from both open ends.
(3) Decorate using a glacé cherry.

Frangipane Slices

Yield – 48 slices

	kg	g	lb	oz
Puff pastry	1	000	2	4
Frangipane (*see* page 28)	1	000	2	4
Jam	—	180	—	$6\frac{1}{2}$
Totals	2	180	4	$14\frac{1}{2}$

The jam is spread on the strips before the frangipane filling is added.

These goods are *not* finished with apricot purée and water icing, but are usually either left plain or dusted with icing sugar and returned to the oven for glazing.

Apple Strudel (German)

Yield – 48 slices

	kg	g	lb	oz
Puff pastry	1	000	2	4
Fresh apples (unpeeled)	2	000	4	8
Sultanas	—	220	—	8
Sugar	—	180	—	$6\frac{1}{2}$
Strip of sponge	—	335	—	12
Apricot purée	—	250	—	9
Water icing	—	250	—	9
Totals	4	235	9	$8\frac{1}{2}$

(1) Roll well-rested puff pastry to a thickness of $1\frac{1}{2}$ mm ($\frac{1}{8}$ in).
(2) From this cut strips 10 cm (4 in) wide and place onto a clean baking sheet.
(3) Place a 5 cm (2 in) wide strip of sponge along the centre of this strip.
(4) Wash, peel and core the apples. Chop very finely.
(5) Mix in the sultanas and sugar.
(6) Place this mixture on top of the sponge. It should form a mound about 5 cm (2 in) in height. Brush the edges of the puff pastry with egg.
(7) Using another strip of pastry, fold in half lengthwise and cut slits from the folded edge at 6 mm ($\frac{1}{4}$ in) intervals. This is best done on a flat strip of metal or wood so that operation (8) can be more easily accomplished.
(8) Keeping this strip folded, carefully lay it over one half of the filling and unfold it over the other half.
(9) Press each side to make a perfect seal.
(10) Egg wash and bake in an oven at 171°C (380°F).
(11) When baked and whilst still hot, brush over with hot apricot purée and then water icing.
(12) When cold, cut into slices approx. 4 cm ($1\frac{1}{2}$ in) in width.

Notes
(1) Instead of fresh apples, stewed or tinned apples may be used. In the latter case only $\frac{3}{4}$ of the stated quantity will be required.
(2) The purpose of the sponge strip in the base of these slices is to soak up the juice which will be formed from the mixture. Alternatively, bread or cake crumbs could be added to the filling and the sponge strip omitted.
(3) These goods may also be made from scrap puff pastry.

Fruit Slice

Yield – 36 slices

	kg	g	lb	oz
Puff pastry	1	000	2	4
Sugar	—	110	—	4
Apricot purée	—	110	—	4
Fruit	1	000	2	4
Totals	2	220	5	0

(1) Roll out the puff pastry $1\frac{1}{2}$ mm ($\frac{1}{16}$ in) thick and about 35 cm (14 in) in length.
(2) Cut a strip approx. 12 cm ($4\frac{1}{2}$ in) wide.
(3) Dampen each edge with water and lay on a strip of similar thickness 2 cm ($\frac{3}{4}$ in) wide.
(4) Press these strips down firmly and decorate with the back of a knife.
(5) Well dock and let it rest for at least half an hour.
(6) According to the type of fruit used either:
    (*a*) Put the fruit (i.e. apple) onto the slice and bake together in an oven at 215°C (420°F).
    (*b*) Bake the slice without the fruit in an oven at 227°C (440°F). Afterwards, finish off with custard or cream and fruit or just the fruit itself.
(7) Cover with well boiled apricot purée, pectin jelly or glaze.
(8) Cut into slices.

Other Varieties

Other fruits, such as cherries, apricots, pears, etc. could be used instead of apples.

Varieties Using All Scrap Pastry

	kg	g	lb	oz
Puff pastry	1	000	2	4
Fresh cream	—	610	1	6
Castor sugar	—	195	—	7
Jam	—	120	—	$4\frac{1}{2}$
Totals	1	925	4	$5\frac{1}{2}$

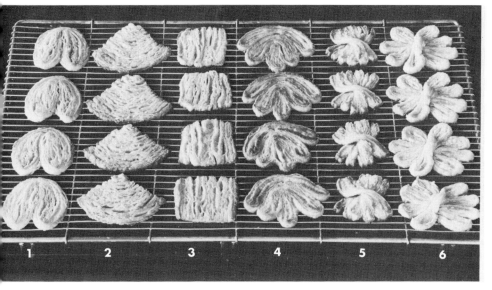

Figure 26. Row 1 – Palmiers: Row 2 – Fans: Row 3 – Accordions: Row 4 – Eventails: Row 5 – Butterflies: Row 6 – Petals

Palmiers

Yield 36 (sandwiched in pairs)

(1) Roll out the pastry to 3 mm ($\frac{5}{8}$ in) in thickness and to at least 45 cm (18 in) in length.
(2) Brush the surface with water and sprinkle liberally with castor sugar.
(3) Starting at each end and folding in three results in six folds altogether, giving a strip approx. 12 mm ($\frac{1}{2}$ in) thick and 6 cm ($2\frac{1}{2}$ in) wide.
(4) Cut this strip into slices 1 cm ($\frac{3}{8}$ in) thick and lay, with the folds showing, onto a well greased baking tray. Space about 8 cm (3 in) apart.
(5) Allow to rest for at least $\frac{1}{2}$ an hour, and then bake in an oven at 215°C (420°F) until just tinged with colour.
(6) Turn over with a palette knife and finish off by baking to a golden brown colour with a glaze of caramelized sugar.
(7) When cold, sandwich two palmiers with a little jam and a bulb of sweetened whipped fresh cream.

Fantails
(1) Roll out the pastry to 3 mm ($\frac{1}{8}$ in) in thickness and to at least 45 cm (18 in) in length.
(2) Brush the surface with water and sprinkle liberally with castor sugar.
(3) Starting at each end and folding in three results in six folds altogether, giving a strip approx. 12 mm ($\frac{1}{2}$ in) thick and 6 cm ($2\frac{1}{2}$ in) wide.
(4) Cut off the open end as indicated.
(5) Cut the strip into slices 1 cm ($\frac{3}{8}$ in) thick.
(6) Give the piece a twist and lay with the folds showing, onto a well greased baking tray. Space about 8 cm (3 in) apart.
(7) Allow to rest for at least half an hour and then bake in an oven at 215°C (420°F) for 12–15 minutes.
(8) When cold finish with a whirl of cream and a cherry.

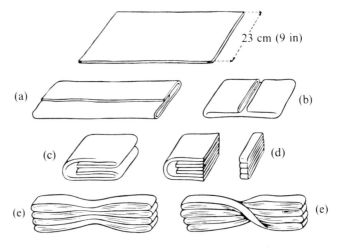

Figure 27. Stages in the making of Petals

Petals [*see* Figure 26(6) and 27]
(1) Roll out the pastry to 3 mm ($\frac{1}{8}$ in) in thickness and cut strips 23 cm (9 in) wide and 30 cm (12 in) in length.
(2) Brush the surface with water and dredge with castor sugar.
(3) Bring one edge to the centre and then the other to slightly overlap. Press to seal. The strip is now approx. 11 cm ($4\frac{1}{2}$ in) wide.
(4) Repeat (2) and then fold the two ends into the centre again but leaving a slight gap.
(5) Wash with water and dredge again with sugar.
(6) Fold the pastry in half to form a piece 11 cm ($4\frac{1}{2}$ in) wide but now a quarter of its original length (*see* Figure 27(c)).
(7) Cut off the folded edge and then cut into slices approx. $\frac{1}{2}$ cm ($\frac{3}{16}$ in) in width [*see* Figure 27(d)].
(8) Press down the centre of each piece, give it a twist and place with the fold showing onto a well greased baking sheet spaced at least 8 cm (3 in) apart [*see* Figure 27(e)].
(9) Bake in an oven at 215°C (420°F) until tinged with colour.
(10) Turn over with a palette knife and finish off, baking to a golden brown colour with a glaze of caramelized sugar.

Fans [*see* Figure 26(2)]

(1) Roll pastry to $1\frac{1}{2}$ mm ($\frac{1}{16}$ in) in thickness and from this cut strips 40 cm (16 in) in width.
(2) Brush with water and liberally dredge with castor sugar.
(3) Roll as for Swiss roll and seal the edge.
(4) Cut into slices approx. 8 mm ($\frac{1}{4}$ in) thick and place onto a well greased baking sheet approx. 4 cm ($1\frac{1}{2}$ in) apart.
(5) Cut through each slice from the centre to the outside edge at the point of sealing.
(6) Proceed as for Palmiers (5, 6, 7).

Accordions [*see* Figure 26(3)]

(1) Prepare the pastry in the same way as for Palmiers.
(2) Cut off both folded ends.
(3) Proceed as for Palmiers 4–6.
(4) When cold they are sandwiched with cream or a conserve and the ends may be dipped into chocolate.

Butterflies [*see* Figure 26(5)]

(1) Prepare the pastry as for Accordions 1 and 2.
(2) Twist the pieces in the centre before laying them onto a well greased baking sheet.
(3) Proceed as for Palmiers 4–6.
(4) If this variety is required to be sandwiched, only twist half. Use these for the top of the sandwich and a plain accordian slice for the bottom.

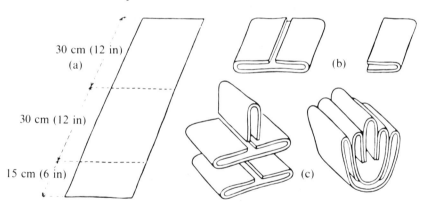

Figure 28. Stages in the making of Eventails

Eventails [*see* Figures 26(4) and 28]

(1) Roll the pastry to a thickness of 3 mm ($\frac{1}{8}$ in) and from this cut two pieces 30 cm (12 in) in length and one piece 15 cm (6 in) in length [*see* Figure 28 (a and b)].
(2) Wash, liberally dredge with sugar and fold as indicated in the diagram [*see* Figure 28(c)].
(3) Cut into slices of 1 cm ($\frac{3}{8}$ in) and lay onto a well greased baking sheet at least 4 cm ($1\frac{1}{2}$ in) apart.
(4) Proceed as for Palmiers.

Note Although these crisps are commercially satisfactory when made from scrap puff pastry, they are superior when made from virgin pastry and for exhibition purposes this ought to be considered.

PUFF PASTRY FAULTS

FAULTS	Incorrect rolling technique.	Fat unevenly distributed.	Insufficient rest before baking.	Uneven heat distribution in oven.	Too many turns given.	Pastry rolled out too thinly.	Flour used was too weak.
Uneven lift.	√	√	√	√			
Poor volume.	√				√	√	√
Distorted shape.	√		√	√			
Shrinkage.			√				
Loss of fat during baking.		√					
Tough eating.					√		
Cores.							
Filling spilling out.			√				
Skinning.							

Currant Slices

These are made with a short pastry base and a puff pastry top in the following manner.
(1) Use 1½–2 kg (3 lb 6 oz–4 lb 8 oz) short pastry to line a full size baking sheet and dock it well.
(2) Wash 1 kg (2¼ lb) of currants by first soaking in very hot water for half an hour.
(3) Drain and sprinkle evenly over the short pastry.
(4) Follow this with a sprinkling of sugar and if desired cinnamon spice.
(5) Pin out 1 kg (2¼ lb) puff pastry to 3 mm (⅛ in) in thickness and cover the currants.
(6) Using a small rolling pin, roll the puff pastry firmly down on the currants.
(7) Brush over with either egg or water and dress with sugar.
(8) Using a tracy cutter, mark the surface into squares or rectangles for ease of cutting after baking (*see* pages 30–32 for sizes).
(9) Bake in an oven at 215°C (420°F).
(10) Cut into the squares or rectangles already marked.

Tarts

Yield – 60 small tarts

Scrap puff pastry may be used for tarts in the same way as short pastry, and provided the pastry is well rested for at least an hour prior to baking, it should retain a good shape, whether hand raised or blocked by machine.

Fat used is too soft for process.	Temperature of making too high.	Too much fat employed.	Insufficient fat employed.	Oven temperature too low.	Incorrect cutting out/or shaping.	Tough pastry fat was used.	Flour used was too strong.	Dough made too tight.	Dough made too slack.	Skinning.	Poor sealing.	Insufficient turns given.	Paste left uncovered.
					√					√	√	√	
√	√	√	√	√	√			√	√	√			
					√				√		√		
							√	√	√				
√		√		√								√	
					√		√	√	√	√			
										√			
					√						√		
													√

	kg	g	lb	oz
Puff pastry	1	000	2	4
Raspberry jam	—	445	1	0
Filling	2	000	4	8
Totals	3	445	7	12

(1) Roll out puff pastry to 3 mm ($\frac{1}{8}$ in) thick and from this cut circles to fit the patty pan used. The cutter may be plain or fluted.

(2) Thumb these up by hand or block on the machine. If the latter method is adopted, the thickness of the paste and the size of the cutter used must be carefully chosen to avoid too much scrap.

(3) Pipe in a bulb of raspberry jam followed by the filling.

(4) Bake in an oven at 204°C (400°F).

Finishes

Bakewell Spread a thin layer of water icing over the filling and decorate with a glacé cherry.

Frangipane and Curd Sprinkle a few flake almonds onto the filling prior to baking.

4. Choux Pastry

Yields – Cream Buns
    – Éclairs } 120

	Cream Buns				Éclairs			
	kg	g	lb	oz	kg	g	lb	oz
Strong flour	1	000	2	4	1	000	2	4
Water	1	250	2	13	1	670	3	12
Butter, margarine or shortening	—	500	1	2	—	665	1	8
*Eggs	1	610	3	10	1	725	3	14
Vol (Ammonium bicarbonate)	—	7	—	$\frac{1}{4}$	—	—	—	—
Totals	4	367	9	13$\frac{1}{4}$	5	060	11	6

* The amount of eggs required depends upon the strength of the flour used and the amount shown may have to be adjusted to produce a paste of the correct consistency which should be just capable of holding its shape when piped. The éclair recipe should be of a softer consistency than that of the cream bun. The more eggs which can be beaten in the better the result.

An acceptable alternative to the cream bun recipe is the éclair recipe but with a little less egg to keep it stiffer. This is useful if both cream buns and éclairs have to be made. The éclair recipe can then be divided into two, one half to which Vol is added and used for cream buns, and the other into which extra egg is beaten for éclairs.

Note   Whilst the use of Vol (Ammonium bicarbonate) is recommended to give cream buns of good volume, these can be made of quite acceptable volume without its use.

General Method

(1) Place the fat and water in a saucepan and bring to the boil.
(2) Add and mix in the flour. Cook for at least a minute or until the paste leaves the sides of the pan cleanly.
(3) Allow to cool.
(4) Beat in the eggs a little at a time making sure each addition is well incorporated.
(5) For cream buns add the Vol just before the last addition of egg.

Cream Buns [Figure 29 (centre)]

	kg	g	lb	oz
Fresh cream	2	225	5	0

These are baked in steam, either in special metal cream bun tins which are fitted with lids, or alternatively baked under inverted bread tins on a baking sheet.
(1) Transfer the choux paste to a savoy bag fitted with a large star tube.

62

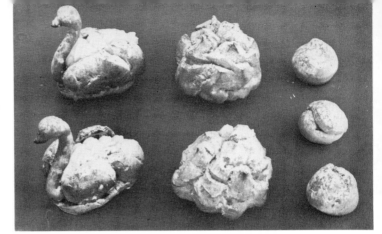

Figure 29. Choux pastry varieties:
Left – Swans
Centre – Cream buns
Right – Petits choux

(2) Pipe rosettes or bulbs onto the greased bottom of the cream bun tin or the greased baking sheet if inverted bread tins are to be used. Ensure that each bun is of the same size and leave sufficient room for each to expand during baking.
(3) Place on the cream bun tin lid (or invert the bread tins) and bake in an oven at 232°C (450°F) for approx. 25 minutes.
(4) Remove the lids (or bread tins) and allow the cream buns to get quite cold.
(5) Finish by splitting them open, filling with fresh cream and dusting the top with icing sugar.

A spot of jam could also be piped in. The jam and cream may also be inserted into the cream bun without splitting them open, by using a cream filling machine.

Notes
(1) It is very important that these goods should be thoroughly baked before withdrawing from the oven, otherwise they will collapse. To ensure that the buns baked in the cream bun tin are not removed from the oven before they are baked, it is a good idea to bake one or two under a bread tin. These can be inspected before the cream bun tin is removed and if it is premature, only one or two buns will be spoiled instead of the 24 or so piped in the tin.
(2) These goods may only legally be sold as *cream buns* if they are filled with fresh dairy cream. If filled with an alternative filling such as imitation cream, they should be differently named, e.g. *choux buns*.

Éclairs [Figure 30 (3 and 4)]

	kg	g	lb	oz
Fresh cream	2	225	5	0
Fondant	—	445	1	0
Totals	2	670	6	0

(1) Make up the choux paste and transfer to a savoy bag fitted with a 12 mm ($\frac{1}{2}$ in) or 16 mm ($\frac{5}{8}$ in) plain tube.
(2) Pipe out on a lightly greased baking sheet or onto silicone paper. An average size is approx. 10 cm (4 in) long. Avoid leaving a point at the end of the piped shape by moving the tube forwards and upwards at the same time as stopping the paste from coming out of the tube.
(3) Bake in an oven at 221°C (430°F) for approx. 20 minutes until they are crisp and dry.
(4) When cold, split open and fill with fresh cream.
(5) Ice the tops in one of the following:
   (*a*) Fondant to which chocolate flavour and colour have been added.

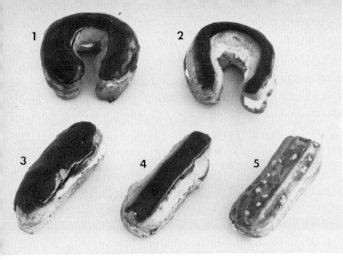

Figure 30. Choux pastry varieties:

(1) Horseshoe with top coated with chocolate icing
(2) Horseshoe with bottom coated with chocolate icing
(3) Éclair with top coated with chocolate icing
(4) Éclair with bottom coated with chocolate icing
(5) Leopold

(b) Fondant to which chocolate or block cocoa (unsweetened chocolate) has been added.

(c) Chocolate couverture.

(d) Fondant to which an alternative flavour and colour has been added, e.g. coffee.

(e) An alternative icing such as the chocolate icing on page 167. The fondant is first conditioned as described on page 165.

Usually the flat base of the éclair is iced because it offers a better surface. However, such iced éclairs need to be placed into paper cases for sale, otherwise they roll about.

Notes

(1) The baked éclair should be bold with a good cavity for the filling of cream. If small and round looking, the paste has been made too tight, whilst if the eclairs are mis-shapen or flat looking, it has been made too soft.

(2) To ice large quantities a special wide flat tube can be used to pipe a strip of fondant on top of the éclair in one simple operation. The tube can be made by flattening a metal savoy tube.

Deep Freezing

Provided chocolate couverture is used the finished éclairs and cream buns will deep freeze quite satisfactorily. They are usually first packed in transparent film.

Petits Choux [*see* Figure 29 (right)]

Yield 240

These are small buns piped from the cream bun recipe, but with no Vol.

(1) Pipe small bulbs on a lightly greased baking sheet.

(2) Bake at 221°C (430°F) without a cover.

(3) When cold, fill with a suitably flavoured cream and ice with an appropriately coloured and flavoured fondant.

Notes

(1) Small éclairs may be made in the same way.

(2) Petits choux are also used in the making of gâteaux St. Honoré (*see* page 206).

(3) Small petits choux or éclairs are very suitable to be made into savouries by filling with a savoury filling.

OTHER VARIETIES

Leopolds [*see* Figure 30(5)]

Yield 120

(1) Proceed as for éclairs but using a star tube.

(2) Sprinkle with nib sugar and carefully bake at 204°C (400°F).

(3) When cold fill with fresh cream.

Rognons

Yield 120

(1) Using the éclair choux paste, pipe out kidney shapes onto a lightly greased baking sheet or silicone paper.
(2) Bake as for éclairs.
(3) When cold split open and fill with fresh cream.
(4) Lightly ice the tops in coffee fondant and dip in roasted flaked almonds to finish.

Horseshoes [*see* Figure 30 (1 and 2)]

Yield 120

(1) Pipe out horseshoe shapes onto a lightly greased baking sheet or silicone paper using the éclair choux paste.
(2) Bake at 215°C (420°F).
(3) When cold split open and fill with fresh cream.
(4) Ice the top in coffee flavoured or an alternatively flavoured and coloured fondant.

Rings

(1) Pipe out rings onto a lightly greased baking sheet using the éclair paste.
(2) Proceed as for the horseshoe shape.

Swans [*see* Figure 29 (left)]

Yield 120

(1) Using the éclair choux paste, pipe out ovals onto a lightly greased tray or silicone paper using a savoy bag fitted with a 12 mm ($\frac{1}{2}$ in) tube.
(2) Transfer the paste to a savoy bag with a 6 mm ($\frac{1}{4}$ in) tube and pipe the neck and heads. These should resemble the Roman numeral 2. Pipe the neck at the base and finish by the head so that when the tube is pulled away, the beak is formed.
(3) Bake as for éclairs.
(4) When cold cut right through the body and cut the top section in half lengthways.
(5) Pipe fresh cream on the base, set in the neck and head and arrange the two half top sections to resemble the wings.

GOODS MADE FROM PUFF PASTE AND CHOUX

Copenhagens

(1) Roll out well rested puff pastry trimmings very thinly and dock well.
(2) Cut out with a 6$\frac{1}{2}$—8 cm (2$\frac{1}{2}$–3 in) round plain cutter, place onto a clean baking sheet, brush the edge with egg and allow to rest for at least 1 hour.
(3) Using an éclair paste in a savoy bag fitted with a 12 mm ($\frac{1}{2}$ in) tube, pipe a ring of choux paste approx. 1 cm ($\frac{3}{8}$ in) from the edge of the puff pastry disc.
(4) Bake at 221°C (430°F) for approx. 20 minutes.
(5) When cool, dip the ring of choux paste into chocolate.
(6) Fill the centre with some fruit and fresh cream.
(7) The top can be embellished with a piece of fruit according to the filling used, e.g. apricot half, wedge of pineapple, cherry, etc.

Note With imagination these rings can be made into quite attractive fancies. One example is to pipe squiggly lines of sweetened chestnut purée, chocolate buttercream or ganache all over and in the centre, place three little sugar eggs. This is made to represent a bird's nest and is very suitable for sale at Eastertide.

Gâteaux St. Honoré – see page 206.

5. Meat Pies and Pasties

LEGISLATION

In Britain there are statutory standards for certain types of meat pies as outlined by the Meat Pie and Sausage Roll Regulations 1967. These require that the following minimum meat contents in each case *raw meat equivalent* by weight of the product as sold should be as follows:

Pork, Mutton, Veal and Ham

Total meat content 25%.

Steak and Kidney

Total meat content 25%. It is suggested that 15–20% kidney, expressed on the total weight of steak plus kidney used in the recipe, would probably be acceptable as a minimum standard.

Meat and Potato Pie and Cornish Pasties

Total meat content 25%.

The regulations give an allowance for *excess fat* in the pastry used for pies but it is recommended that these are discounted in any calculation to determine the meat quantity present.

The *meat content* refers to raw meat before processing. Therefore if cooked or processed meat is used, the *raw meat equivalent* requires to be calculated.

In the recipes given, the raw meat equivalent of the filling is well over the minimum quoted and if used with an equal weight of pastry, will produce pies which should adequately meet the regulations.

SAVOURY PASTES

	Cold				Hot or Boiled			
	kg	g	lb	oz	kg	g	lb	oz
Flour (medium strength)	1	000	2	4	1	000	2	4
Lard	—	445	1	0	—	500	1	2
Salt	—	15	—	$\frac{1}{2}$	—	15	—	$\frac{1}{2}$
Water	—	265	—	$9\frac{1}{2}$	—	250	—	9
Totals	1	725	3	14	1	765	3	$15\frac{1}{2}$

Cold Paste

Make by using Method 3 of short pastry (*see* page 17).

Hot Paste

(1) Rub the lard into the flour.

(2) Add the water *boiling*.
(3) Partially mix until it is cooler.
(4) Finish off to a clear paste by mixing lightly.
Note This paste should not be used until it is *cold*.

Boiled Paste

(1) Boil water, lard and salt.
(2) Add flour to the boiling mixture.
(3) Mix to a clear smooth paste.
(4) Use immediately whilst still hot.

Seasonings

The amount of seasoning used is a matter of individual preference and may have to be adjusted to suit individual taste. In some cases, i.e. Quiche Lorraine, the amount of salt to be added will be influenced by the saltiness of the bacon and cheese used and must be adjusted accordingly.

	Recipe 1				**Recipe 2**
	kg	*g*	*lb*	*oz*	
Salt	—	500	1	2	2 parts
Pepper	—	250	—	9	1 part
Ground Nutmeg	—	—	—	$\frac{1}{4}$	—
Ground Mace	—	—	—	$\frac{1}{4}$	—
Totals		750	1	$11\frac{1}{2}$	

Use of Boiled and Hot Pastes

Hand-raising Use the boiled paste whilst still hot.
Blocking by machine Use the hot paste whilst still warm.

HAND-RAISED PIES

Yields	Weight of filling	Weight of pastry	Baking temp.	Baking time
225 g ($\frac{1}{2}$ lb)	85 g (3 oz)	115 g (4 oz)	210°C 410°F	50 mins
455 g (1 lb)	210 g ($7\frac{1}{2}$ oz)	200 g (7 oz)	204°C 400°F	1 hour
910 g (2 lb)	455 g (16 oz)	400 g (14 oz)	204°C 400°F	1 hour 40 mins

The above are minimum weights of meat filling.

Filling
(1) Finely chop the pork.
(2) Add and thoroughly mix the other ingredients.
   To shape a pork pie case successfully we need wooden blocks of approx. 10 cm (4 in) diameter. If these are not available the bottom of a large jar may be used.
   (1) Make a ball of the boiled paste whilst still hot.
   (2) Form a cup shape with the heel of the hand.
   (3) Reverse and press onto the block.

Fillings for Meat Pies

	Pork				Mutton/Lamb				Veal & Ham				Steak & Kidney				Meat & Potato				Cornish Pasties			
	kg	g	lb	oz	kg	g	lb	oz	kg	g	lb	oz	kg	g	lb	oz	kg	g	lb	oz	kg	g	lb	oz
Lean pork	—	665	1	8	—	—	—	—	—	585	1	5	—	—	—	—	—	—	—	—	—	—	—	—
Fat pork	—	335	—	12	—	—	—	—	—	—	—	—	—	—	—	—	—	—	—	—	—	—	—	—
Mutton or lamb	—	—	—	—	1	000	2	4	—	—	—	—	—	—	—	—	—	—	—	—	—	—	—	—
Veal	—	—	—	—	—	—	—	—	—	415	—	15	—	—	—	—	—	—	—	—	—	—	—	—
Lean steak	—	—	—	—	—	—	—	—	—	—	—	—	—	835	1	14	—	390	—	14	1	000	2	4
Kidney	—	—	—	—	—	—	—	—	—	—	—	—	—	165	—	6	—	—	—	—	—	—	—	—
Seasoning No 1	—	30	—	1	—	30	—	1	—	20	—	¾	—	30	—	1	—	—	—	—	—	—	—	—
Seasoning No 2	—	—	—	—	—	—	—	—	—	—	—	—	—	—	—	—	—	15	—	½	—	15	—	½
Water	—	220	—	8	—	665	1	8	—	110	—	4	—	665	1	8	—	250	—	9	—	—	—	—
Rusk or bread	—	125	—	4½	—	60	—	2¼	—	—	—	—	—	110	—	4	—	195	—	7	—	500	1	2
Onion	—	—	—	—	—	180	—	6½	—	—	—	—	—	—	—	—	1	000	2	4	1	000	2	4
Potato	—	—	—	—	—	—	—	—	—	—	—	—	—	—	)	—	—	—	—	—	—	—	—	—
Totals	1	375	3	1½	1	935	4	5¾	1	130	2	8¾	1	805	4	1	1	850	4	2½	2	515	5	10½

(4) Pressing firmly, rotate the block to raise the paste up the side. The aim should be to produce a thicker paste at the base with the sides tapering off at the top.

(5) Allow the paste to set and remove from the block.

(6) Fill with the meat filling. This should be done by first making a ball, placing into the case and then flattening with pressure to exclude any air.

(7) Roll out some paste approx. 3 mm ($\frac{1}{8}$ in) thick and from this cut out a circle to fit the top of the pie.

(8) After trimming the top edge, egg wash, lay on the top and press with fingers or nippers to seal.

(9) Make a hole in the centre to allow the steam to escape and egg wash top and sides.

(10) Place on a pattern of leaves cut from the paste and egg wash again. Make sure that the steam hole is left uncovered.

(11) Bake for at least 1 hour at 204°C (400°F).

(12) After baking and whilst still hot, fill through the hole in the top with a good stock, into which 30 g (1 oz) approx. of gelatine per 6 dl (1 pint) has been added.

Proprietary pie jellies may be used for this purpose. They are usually used at the rate of 45 g ($1\frac{1}{2}$ oz) powder to 3 litres (5 pints) of cold water brought to a vigorous boil and used immediately to fill the pie.

The use of jelly serves two purposes:

(*a*) It ensures that the pie eats and keeps moist.

(*b*) Final weight may be adjusted by the quantity added.

Note   The pink colour associated with pork pies may be obtained by either allowing the meat to be steeped for a little time in a mature brine solution or 10% of cured pork and bacon trimmings added to the recipe.

Mutton/Lamb

Filling

(1) Mince the meat.

(2) Add the other ingredients and thoroughly mix.

(1) Line pie tins with the hot or boiled paste.

(2) Place in the filling and proceed as for pork pies.

(3) Bake in an oven approx. 215°–226°C (420–440°F) depending upon the size.

(4) Finish as for pork pies.

Veal and Ham

Filling

(1) Coarsely chop the veal and pork.

(2) Add the other ingredients and thoroughly mix.

Usually these are made in rectangular tins so that they may be cut into slices. Hard-boiled eggs may be incorporated either by laying in individual eggs or the proprietary *long egg*.

(1) Line the rectangular tin with the hot paste.

(2) Half fill with the meat filling.

(3) Lay in the egg if required.

(4) Complete the filling, compacting it well.

(5) Proceed as for pork pies.

(6) Bake in an oven 215–226C (420–440°F), depending upon the size.

Steak and Kidney

Filling

(1) Finely chop the meat, shred the onion, add the water and seasoning.

(2) Cook gently until tender.
(3) Strain off the juice and thicken by boiling it with 70 g (2½ oz) flour moistened with a little water.

(1) Line or block the pie tin with the cold savoury paste.
(2) Deposit the required amount of meat and cover with gravy.
(3) Proceed in the same way as for pork pies.
(4) Bake in an oven at approx. 218°C (425°F).

	kg	g	lb	oz
Cold savoury paste	1	000	2	4
Filling	1	805	4	1
Totals	2	805	6	5

Yield depends upon size of tins used and the ratio of pastry to meat given must be considered as a guide only.

Meat and Potato
Proceed as for Steak and Kidney pie, but only part-boil the potatoes.

Quantities for Individual Pies (Steak and Kidney and Meat and Potato)
Paste   45–55 g (1½–2 oz)
Filling   100 g (4 oz)

Cornish Pasties
Yield – 30

	kg	g	lb	oz
Cold savoury paste	1	670	3	12
Filling	2	515	5	10½
Totals	4	185	9	6½

Filling   Finely chop or coarsely mince the ingredients and use *raw*.
(1) Divide the paste and roll out to a diameter of approx. 13 cm (5 in).
(2) Place the filling in the centre of the paste discs.
(3) Wash the edges of the paste with either water or egg.
(4) Draw up each side of the paste to the centre to cover the filling, pinching them firmly together.
(5) With the thumb and finger notch the seam. Finish moulding it into a boat shape with the fluted seam on top.
(6) Egg wash and bake in an oven at 204°C (400°F) for approx. 30 minutes, or until the filling is thoroughly cooked.
Note   Other pasties may be made in a similar way using different fillings such as veal, ham, potatoes and carrots.
   They may also be made into turnover shapes. A special machine is available for forming both these shapes and its use greatly speeds up production.

Further Varieties of Savoury Goods

A very large variety of savouries may be made from the following bases:

Flans and Tarts These are made from a savoury short pastry and baked either containing the filling or baked blind and the filling added afterwards. Appropriate fillings for such goods are: egg and bacon; cheese and onion; cheese; cheese, bacon and onion.

Puff Pastry Vol-au-vents and bouchees may be filled with a variety of savoury fillings including mushroom, chicken, ham, prawns, salmon, cheese etc. with a suitable sauce.

Cheese straws can be made by incorporating 50% of cheese into puff pastry.

Likewise salt can be incorporated to make salt sticks. Horns, turnovers and crescents can all be made into savouries by incorporating fillings especially cheese and ham.

Further savoury goods may be found in the sister book *Patisserie* written by the author and published by Messrs. W. Heinemann Ltd.

6. Chemically Aerated Goods

Baking Powder

Since the aeration of these goods is mainly achieved by the use of baking powder, the quality and quantity required to achieve the best result is a matter of some importance and further information on this is found on page 3.

Cream-of-tartar baking powder is superior from the taste point of view but because it reacts fairly quickly in the cold, goods containing it need to be baked off with the minimum of rest, otherwise the volume will suffer. The outside crust will also not be so smooth as when other *cream* powders are used.

The use of a baking powder containing an acid of a phosphate type (so-called *cream* powder) will allow goods to stand a considerable time, up to 1 hour before baking because less gas is generated in the cold. This means that goods can be deliberately toughened at the dough stage, a great advantage for scone rounds which can be made softer as a result and yet still retain their shape. A finer texture can also be developed as a result.

Flour

A medium flour is recommended for recipes which are low in fat, sugar and egg, such as scones. The use of too strong a flour in these goods will cause toughness to be developed with all the corresponding faults which occur with cakes. The use of too soft a flour will cause loss of volume since the gluten would not be strong enough to hold the carbon dioxide gas produced. The liquid absorption will be affected by the strength and quality of flour used. For goods in which the aeration is assisted by the fat, sugar and egg, such as raspberry buns, a soft flour can be used since this will impart the more tender crumb associated with cake.

Fats

Low melting point fat, margarine, butter or mixtures of these may be used as well as cooking oil.

Fruit

This should be pre-prepared (*see Bakery: Bread & Fermented Goods*).

Milk

Sour milk (or buttermilk) is often used in this type of goods, especially in Scotland where some advocates hold the opinion that scones with a better crumb and texture can be obtained by its use.

METHODS

There are four methods used:

Method 1 (Used for recipes low in fat and egg).
(1) Thoroughly sieve the flour, salt and baking powder.
(2) Rub in the fat by hand or on the mixer with a hook.

Basic Scone Recipes

	Rounds				Victoria 1st quality				Victoria 2nd quality				Tea			
	kg	*g*	*lb*	*oz*	*kg*	*g*	*lb*	*oz*	*kg*	*g*	*lb*	*oz*	*kg*	*g*	*lb*	*oz*
Medium flour	1	000	2	4	1	000	2	4	1	000	2	4	1	000	2	4
Baking powder	—	55	—	2	—	55	—	2	—	55	—	2	—	50	—	$1\frac{3}{4}$
Milk (approx.)	—	555	1	4	—	555	1	4	—	665	1	8	—	610	1	6
Butter/margarine/fat/oil	—	155	—	$5\frac{1}{2}$	—	165	—	6	—	125	—	$4\frac{1}{2}$	—	250	—	9
Sugar	—	155	—	$5\frac{1}{2}$	—	165	—	6	—	125	—	$4\frac{1}{2}$	—	220	—	8
Salt	—	7	—	$\frac{1}{4}$	—	7	—	$\frac{1}{4}$	—	7	—	$\frac{1}{4}$	—	7	—	$\frac{1}{4}$
Egg	—	—	—	—	—	—	—	—	—	—	—	—	—	60	—	$2\frac{1}{4}$
Egg whites	—	60	—	$2\frac{1}{4}$	—	—	—	—	—	—	—	—	—	—	—	—
Totals	1	987	4	$7\frac{1}{2}$	1	947	4	$6\frac{1}{4}$	1	977	4	$7\frac{1}{4}$	2	197	4	$15\frac{1}{4}$

(3) Dissolve the sugar into the milk and eggs (if used) and add it to the flour/fat mixture.

(4) Mix until a clear dough or paste is formed.

(5) Add any fruit, etc., last.

Method 2 (Used for recipes with high fat/egg content).

(1) Thoroughly sieve the flour, salt and baking powder.

(2) Cream the sugar and fat and add the egg or milk, beat to form a sugar batter (*see* page 128).

(3) Add the flour and proceed with (4) and (5) of Method 1 above.

Method 3 (Used for plain recipes using oil, i.e. scones).

(1) Thoroughly sieve the flour, salt and baking powder.

(2) Whisk the oil, milk and egg to form an emulsion.

(3) Add the flour and proceed with (4) and (5) of Method 1 above.

Method 4

Same as Method 4 of short pastry (*see* page 17). Mix any fruit into the dough by hand afterwards.

Note If the scone dough is made by hand, some will stick to the hands and this should be removed by first scraping with a celluloid scraper. Coating the hands with flour and rubbing them together will rub off the remainder which should then be worked back into the dough as carefully as possible. Leaving these scraps or rubbings will cause cores to develop in the crumb afterwards.

Dusting Flour

Some of these goods are very soft and cannot be handled without dusting flour. Strong flour should be used for this purpose and the amount kept to the minimum necessary.

SCONES

The amount of mixing given to a scone dough depends upon two factors:

(1) The type of baking powder used (*see baking powder* under choice of materials page 72).

(2) By toughening we can get a better shape, i.e. in scone rounds. To overcome the effects of toughening we must give a reasonable resting time prior to baking, and this dictates the use of a baking powder other than cream of tartar if we are to get good volume with appearance. Some of the baking powder may be replaced by yeast when we get a scone with different characteristics requiring a little proof prior to baking for the best results.

VARIETIES

Fruit (Selected Sultanas or Currants)

Rounds Add 155 g (5½ oz)
Tea Add 250 g (9 oz)

Yields

Rounds and Victoria 9 at 220 g (8 oz) approx.
 7 at 280 g (10 oz) approx.
Tea 44 at 50 g (2 oz) approx.

Scone Rounds [*see* Figure 31(1)]

(1) Using method 1, 3 (or 4) (*see* page 73), make the dough and scale into the appropriately sized pieces.
(2) Mould round, flatten to a thickness of approx. 2 cm (¾ in) in the centre, but tapering slightly towards the edge. Place onto greased baking sheets leaving at least 5 cm (2 in) between each for expansion. The technique of moulding very soft doughs like scones is called *chaffing*. The rounds are shaped one at a time, one hand employing the moulding action and throwing the round against the flat of the other hand which is used like a shield.
(3) The dough rounds are now cut into 4 equal segments by using a Scotch scraper.
(4) Slightly separate these segments to give a gap of approx. 6 mm (¼ in) between.
(5) Using beaten egg, wash each segment carefully so that no wash runs down between.
(6) Rest if required and bake at 232°C (450°F) for approx. 20 minutes.

Note An alternative method is to cut the flattened rounds into four whilst on the table and transfer the segments only onto the baking sheet assembling them in the form of a round or individually, depending on what is required.

Victoria Scones [*see* Figure 31(2)]

The dough is treated in the same way but flattened slightly more with a rolling pin without the edges being tapered. They may be cut into 4 or larger rounds made to be cut into 6 or 8 segments.

Both the first and second quality recipes may be made into the following varieties:

Turnover [*see* Figure 31(3)]

(1) After egg washing, place the individual segments onto a slightly greased baking sheet and bake at 232°C (450°F).
(2) Using a palette knife turn the segments over when they are half baked.
(3) Return to the oven to finish baking.

Farmhouse

Proceed as for turnover scones but instead of egg washing dust the segments with flour.

A method often adopted by bakers, especially in Scotland is as follows:

Figure 31. Scones (1) Rounds   (3) Turnover scone
          (2) Segment of a Victoria scone round   (4) Tea scone dusted with flour

(1) Lightly mix the dough.
(2) Dust well with flour and pin out to fit the bun divider tray.
(3) Divide and place the individual pieces without further handling upon the baking sheet and bake off.
The size of the recipe shown will give 36 scones.

Hotplate

Proceed as either turnover or farmhouse scones, but baked on a hotplate.

Potato

Omit the sugar.
Replace half of the flour with mashed potatoes or potato flour with added milk. These may be baked either in the oven or on the hotplate.

Fried

(1) Roll out the dough to 12 mm ($\frac{1}{2}$ in) in thickness.
(2) Cut into strips 6 cm ($2\frac{1}{2}$ in) wide and then into fingers approx. 12 mm ($\frac{1}{2}$ in) wide.
(3) Drop into boiling fat. When one side is cooked, turn over to cook the reverse side.
(4) When cooked, roll in cinnamon-flavoured sugar.
(5) These may be split open and filled with jam or cream afterwards.
Note Segments or round shapes may also be made and finished in the same way. A similar dough made slightly softer is used for American Doughnuts and Rings.

Tea Scones [*see* Figure 31(4)]

(1) Using method 2 (page 73) make the dough and roll out to approx. 12 mm ($\frac{1}{2}$ in) in thickness.

(2) Using a 5 cm (2 in) round cutter, cut out pieces and place them onto a slightly greased baking sheet.

(3) Wash the tops with well beaten egg and after an appropriate rest, bake in an oven at 226°C (440°F) for approx. 15 minutes.

(4) When baked and cool, these may be split open and served with butter, fresh cream and/or jam.

The following varieties may be made from either recipe:

Treacle

Replace the sugar with black treacle and bake at 221°C (430°F).

Wholemeal or Wheatmeal

Replace the white flour with wholemeal or wheatmeal.
Increase milk by 60 g (2 oz).

Coconut

Add 60 g (2 oz) desiccated coconut to recipe. Allow 140 g (5 oz) desiccated coconut for top dressing.

(1) Proceed as for turnover scones but cut into 6 segments.

(2) Egg wash and dip each segment into desiccated coconut.

(3) Place onto slightly greased baking sheets and bake at 221°C (430°F).

Oatmeal

Replace half the flour with oatmeal.

CHEMICALLY AERATED BUNS

Research into the published recipes of these buns reveals an astonishing variety of recipes which when they are carefully analysed can be resolved into one basic recipe with various additions to satisfy the requirements of the different varieties. Within the proportions governed by this basic recipe it is possible to slightly change the character and taste by varying the ingredients used as follows:

Fat

Butter will give a superior flavour, but goods will not eat so short and unless well creamed in the mixing, aeration may suffer.

Margarine will give good aeration, but not impart so much shortness.

Shortening will give superior shortness, but goods will lack flavour.

To overcome the shortcomings of all these used on their own, it is recommended that a blend of equal quantities of butter or margarine with shortening is used.

Egg

This may be replaced entirely by milk, although the texture and aeration will suffer.

Milk

The quantity of milk used is largely dictated by the type of flour employed and the variety of goods being made. This can only be determined after experience. Given the same type of flour, rock cakes, for example, may require *less* milk than raspberry buns which should flow slightly in the baking. The basic recipe shown gives an average milk content which may need some adjustment to suit these factors.

Flour

Since we are relying upon the aerating properties of the fat, sugar and egg, the use of a medium flour is not so essential. It is more important to obtain a soft texture and therefore a soft flour is recommended.

BASIC CHEMICALLY AERATED BUN DOUGH RECIPE

	kg	g	lb	oz
Soft flour	1	000	2	4
Baking powder	—	50	—	$1\frac{3}{4}$
Shortening	—	125	—	$4\frac{1}{2}$
Margarine or butter	—	125	—	$4\frac{1}{2}$
Castor sugar	—	250	—	9
Whole egg	—	125	—	$4\frac{1}{2}$
* Milk	—	555	1	4
Salt	—	4	—	$\frac{1}{8}$
Totals	2	234	5	$0\frac{3}{8}$

*Variable (*see* note on page 76).

The above recipe is made by Method 2 (page 73) taking care not to overmix and so toughen the dough.

Additions such as fruit, coconut etc., may be incorporated just before the dough has received its final mixing.

Rock Cakes

Yields – 60 at 40 g ($1\frac{1}{2}$ oz)
45 at 55 g (2 oz) approx.

	kg	g	lb	oz
Basic dough	2	234	5	$\frac{3}{8}$
Currants	—	125	—	$4\frac{1}{2}$
Sultanas	—	125	—	$4\frac{1}{2}$
Peel	—	55	—	2
Totals	2	539	5	$11\frac{3}{8}$

Mix prepared fruit and incorporate into dough before finishing, mixing to clear.
(1) Allow 100 g (4 oz) sugar for dressing.
(2) Deposit in rocky heaps onto a slightly greased baking sheet, approx. 4 cm ($1\frac{1}{2}$ in) apart.
(3) Sprinkle castor sugar on top in the centre of each cake.
(4) After a rest of 15 minutes, bake in an oven at 221°C (430°F) for approx. 15 minutes.

Chocolate Variety

Replace the fruit with 250 g (9 oz) of coarsely grated chocolate (free of dust).

Raspberry

Yield – 53 at 40 g (1½ oz) and 40 at 55 g (2 oz) approx.

Allow 140 g (5 oz) sugar for dressing.

Divide the dough into the appropriate number of buns and mould round using dusting flour. This dough is very soft and sticky and is best moulded lightly on a cloth rather than the table.

There are two methods of finishing as follows:

First Method

(1) Slightly flatten the pieces by hand (or canvas roller) and wash with egg.
(2) Dip into castor sugar and place upon greased baking trays approx. 4 cm (1½ in) apart.
(3) Make an indentation with a clean finger in the centre of each bun and fill with raspberry jam.
(4) After a rest of 15 minutes, bake in the oven at 226°C (440°F) for approx. 15 minutes.

Second Method

(1) After moulding, place upside down and flatten.
(2) Pipe some raspberry jam in the centre of each and fold it into the centre.
(3) Mould very lightly into a round shape, reverse and place on the table with the fold underneath.
(4) Wash with egg or milk and dip into castor sugar.
(5) Place onto greased baking sheets approx. 4 cm (1½ in) apart and with a sharp knife make 3 or 4 cuts on the top so that when baked the jam will show through.
(6) After a 15 minute rest, bake in an oven at 226°C (440°F) for approx. 15 minutes.

Lemon or Orange

Use the basic plain bun recipe.

Allow 140 g (5 oz) castor sugar for dressing.

(1) Add lemon or orange flavour and colour to the basic dough.
(2) Proceed as for raspberry buns, using either method, but employing the appropriate curd instead of jam.

Almond

Almond Filling

	kg	g	lb	oz
Ground almonds	1	000	2	4
Granulated sugar	1	000	2	4
Ground rice	—	55	—	2
Egg	—	335	—	12
Totals	2	390	5	6

165 g (6 oz) flaked or nibbed almonds for dressing.

(1) Add almond flavour to the basic dough.
(2) Proceed as for raspberry buns, but employing the filling instead of jam.
(3) Finish off by washing with egg or milk and dipping into small flaked or nibbed almonds.
(4) After a 15 minute rest bake in an oven at 221°C (430°F).

Spice

Use the basic plain bun dough.
Allow 500 g (1 lb 2 oz) for filling.
Allow 140 g (5 oz) demerara sugar for dressing.
Filling – equal quantities of treacle and cake crumbs.
(1) Add 15 g ($\frac{1}{2}$ oz) ground mixed spice to the basic recipe.
(2) Proceed as for raspberry buns using Method 2, but employing the treacle filling instead of jam.
(3) Dip into demerara sugar instead of castor.
(4) After a 15 minute rest bake in an oven at 221°C (430°F).
Note If spice buns and coffee buns are being made at the same time, to avoid confusion the latter should be made into finger shapes.

Rice

(1) After scaling, mould round, slightly flatten and place on the table.
(2) Wash with egg or milk, dip into small sugar nibs and place 4 cm ($1\frac{1}{2}$ in) apart on a greased baking sheet.
(3) After a 15 minute rest, bake in the oven at 221°C (430°F) for approx. 15 minutes.

Coconut

Make the basic bun recipe but substitute 220 g (8 oz) flour with desiccated coconut. Yield same as raspberry buns.
Allow 110 g (4 oz) desiccated coconut for dressing.
(1) Proceed as for rice buns, but dip the buns in desiccated coconut instead of sugar nibs.
(2) Place onto a greased baking sheet 4 cm ($1\frac{1}{2}$ in) apart and with a knife score a lattice pattern on top.
(3) After a 15 minute rest, bake in the oven at 221°C (430°F).

Coffee and Chocolate Buns

Yield – Same as for raspberry buns.

	Coffee				Chocolate			
	kg	*g*	*lb*	*oz*	*kg*	*g*	*lb*	*oz*
Soft flour	1	000	2	4	—	945	2	2
Baking powder	—	55	—	2	—	55	—	2
Shortening	—	125	—	$4\frac{1}{2}$	—	125	—	$4\frac{1}{2}$
Margarine/butter	—	125	—	$4\frac{1}{2}$	—	125	—	$4\frac{1}{2}$
Brown sugar	—	290	—	$10\frac{1}{2}$	—	290	—	$10\frac{1}{2}$
Milk	—	555	1	6	—	610	1	8
Salt	—	4	—	$\frac{1}{8}$	—	4	—	$\frac{1}{8}$
Coffee extract	—	50	—	$1\frac{3}{4}$	—	—	—	—
Cocoa powder	—	—	—	—	—	55	—	2
Totals	2	204	5	$1\frac{3}{8}$	2	209	5	$1\frac{5}{8}$

Allow 140 g (5 oz) demerara sugar for dressing, unless they are to be iced (*see* over).
(1) Proceed as for rice buns, but dip into demerara sugar. They may be moulded into finger or oval shapes if desired.

(2) After a 15 minute rest, bake in an oven at 221°C (430°F).
Alternative Variety   Leave plain and after baking, cover with a thin appropriately coloured and flavoured water icing or fondant.

Queen or Fairy Cakes

1st Quality – Yield 58 at 55 g (2 oz) approx.
2nd Quality – Yield 50 at 55 g (2 oz) approx.

	1st Quality				2nd Quality			
	kg	g	lb	oz	kg	g	lb	oz
Soft flour	1	000	2	4	1	000	2	4
Baking powder	—	15	—	$\frac{1}{2}$	—	40	—	$1\frac{1}{2}$
Shortening	—	165	—	6	—	110	—	4
Butter/margarine	—	500	1	2	—	335	—	12
Castor sugar	—	750	1	11	—	555	1	4
Egg	—	805	1	13	—	415	—	15
Milk	—	—	—	—	—	415	—	15
Totals	3	235	7	$4\frac{1}{2}$	2	870	6	$7\frac{1}{2}$

(1) Deposit the batter either by hand or through a savoy tube into well greased, deep, fluted tins to within 12 mm ($\frac{1}{2}$ in) from the top.
(2) Decorate with pieces of cherry, dried fruit or nuts and bake in an oven at 204°C (400°F) for approx. 20 minutes.
Notes
(1) Chopped cherries, flaked almonds and currants may be sprinkled into the tins prior to filling with batter and when baked, these goods are displayed upside down to show the decoration. This variety would demand flat tops and to achieve this the mixing must not be toughened.
(2) Superior quality queen cakes of exhibition standard can be made by using a first quality fruit cake recipe (*see* page 142) with the addition of a little baking powder and milk.
(3) If raised centres (cauliflower head) are required, the mixing must be toughened by beating, but should be rested for at least 30 minutes prior to baking.

Cup Cakes

Method for Recipe 1   Make on the traditional sugar batter method (*see* page 128).
Method for Recipe 2
(1) Mix all the dry ingredients including the margarine together to form a crumble. This can be done on a machine using a beater.
(2) Mix the egg and water and add it to the crumble mix.
(3) Beat well for 4 minutes to form a smooth batter.
Notes
(1) For the good quality Recipe No. 1 butter may be used instead of margarine.
(2) Up to 890 g (2 lb) of mixed fruit may be added to the above recipe.
Baking and finishing
(1) Prepare a tray of deep custard tart tins in which are placed greaseproof paper cases. Alternatively prepare special frames with the cases.

Yields – 96 at 35 g (1¼ oz) approx.
80 at 40 g (1½ oz) approx.

	Recipe 1				**Recipe 2**			
	kg	*g*	*lb*	*oz*	*kg*	*g*	*lb*	*oz*
Soft flour	1	000	2	4	—	—	—	—
Special cake flour	—	—	—	—	1	000	2	4
Baking powder	—	20	—	¾	—	40	—	1½
Salt	—	—	—	—	—	10	—	⅛
Cake margarine	—	665	1	8	—	520	1	2¾
Castor sugar	—	665	1	8	—	680	1	8½
Milk powder	—	—	—	—	—	80	—	3
Whole egg	1	000	2	4	—	860	1	15
Water	—	—	—	—	—	160	—	5¾
Totals	3	350	7	8¾	3	350	7	8⅝

(2) Transfer the batter to a savoy bag fitted with a 12 mm (½ in) plain tube and pipe a quantity of the mixing into each paper case to within 12 mm (½ in) from the top.
(3) Decorate with glacé cherries or currants, if required. These may be left plain for future decoration as fancies (*see* chapter 17).
(4) Bake in an oven at 204°C (400°F) for approx. 15 minutes.

Note Good cup cakes can be made with the Genoese recipes on page 140, adding a little more baking powder and milk.

Ginger Buns

	kg	*g*	*lb*	*oz*
Soft flour	1	000	2	4
Cream of tartar	—	7	—	¼
Bicarbonate of soda	—	7	—	¼
Butter	—	250	—	9
Shortening	—	250	—	9
Egg	—	555	1	4
Golden syrup	—	500	1	2
Castor sugar	—	375	—	13½
Ground spice	—	7	—	¼
Ground ginger	—	30	—	1
Milk	—	55	—	2
Totals	3	036	6	13¼

(1) Sieve the flour, spices and chemical raising agents.
(2) Cream the fat and sugar.
(3) Add the eggs a little at a time, beating in each addition.
(4) Blend in the golden syrup.
(5) Add the sieved flour, etc., and mix to a clear smooth batter with the milk.

(6) Deposit by means of a savoy bag into well greased plain or fluted pans into which a split almond or a sprinkling of flaked almonds has been placed.
(7) Place into an oven at 182°C (360°F).
(8) When baked, immediately turn out of the pan or tin and present for sale with the almond surface showing.

Scotch Pancakes
Yield – 65 approx.

    Like crumpets, these are usually eaten at afternoon tea, sometimes toasted and buttered.

	kg	g	lb	oz	
Soft flour	1	000	2	4	A
Baking powder	—	50	—	$1\frac{3}{4}$	
Castor sugar	—	305	—	11	
Salt	—	15	—	$\frac{1}{2}$	B
Eggs	—	140	—	5	
Milk	—	890	2	0	
Butter/or edible oil	—	75	—	$2\frac{3}{4}$	C
Totals	2	475	5	9	

(1) Sieve the flour and baking powder (A).
(2) Whisk the ingredients of (B). Egg colour may be added if desired.
(3) Add (A) to (B) and mix until a smooth batter is formed.
(4) Pour the ingredient (C) into the batter and mix until clear. (If butter is used this must be first melted with gentle heat.)
(5) Slightly grease the hotplate and heat to a temperature a little cooler than that required for crumpets.
(6) The batter is now deposited in blobs onto the hotplate giving each sufficient room to flow. This may be done by piping the batter through a savoy tube, using a dropping funnel, a small ladle or by hand.
(7) When one side is cooked, the pancakes are turned over using a wide chisel scraper. The pancakes should be quite flat and browned on both sides.

Figure 32. Scotch pancakes

7. Biscuits

In Britain although there are no regulations laying down the composition of biscuits, it has been agreed between the Customs & Excise authorities, and a committee representing the biscuit industry, that for the purpose of labelling, a biscuit is defined as follows:

"*A biscuit* shall be deemed to be a baked product of a mixture having *not less than 8% flour content* calculated on the weight of the finished article. The biscuit content must be readily recognizable as substantially a whole biscuit or as one or more continuous layers of cut biscuit or wafer. The finished product shall have a *moisture content of not more than 10%*.

"Processes subsequent to baking, such as sandwiching or coating with jam, fruit, etc., which may affect the total moisture content of the product, shall not be taken into account provided the biscuit falls within the scope of the foregoing paragraph. Flour shall be taken to mean any cereal product, for example: wheat, oats, maize, etc."

The term *biscuit* means literally *twice baked* but this definition no longer holds good today. Any small baked confection could be termed a biscuit and even goods like macaroons are referred to as macaroon biscuits.

Biscuits may be savoury, unsweetened or sweetened. They may be sandwiched with cream or iced after baking. Indeed it is difficult to give a general description which could cover every permutation.

In Britain a whole section of the baking industry has been developed to produce biscuits of the type which can be manufactured by automatic plants. These are wrapped and packaged and can be found on the shelves of every grocery shop in the country. Recipes for such biscuits, however, i.e. Marie, Lincoln, etc., are not given in this book.

Very few bakers now make a large variety of biscuits for their customers, but there are a few lines which can easily be made to give a handsome profit for the master baker. Many of these like shortbread and Shrewsbury biscuits are traditional lines which have always been made. Others included here are recommended as well worth while attempting to increase the range of goods offered.

The inventive baker and confectioner will be able to increase the variety of the biscuits described even further by the addition of different types of dried fruit, nuts and dressings. The flour content of many of these recipes may be replaced as follows:

Chocolate – Replace 110–165 g (4–6 oz) flour with cocoa powder.
Almond   – Replace 110–165 g (4–6 oz) flour with ground almonds.
Hazelnut   – Replace 110–165 g (4–6 oz) flour with ground hazelnuts.
Coconut   – Replace 110–165 g (4–6 oz) flour with coconut flour.

CHOICE OF MATERIALS

Flour

Most biscuits are made with a soft flour and in fact a specially milled English flour is available for this purpose. However with a few of the cheaper varieties a medium flour may be used.

Sugar

Because many of these biscuits are made with the minimum of liquid a soft-grained sugar should be used (castor or brown). Where little or no moistening agent is used, pulverized sugar is recommended.

Syrup and Treacle

Where this is used, e.g. in ginger goods, it should be brought to a consistency which will mix readily with the other materials. Therefore in cold conditions it will be necessary for heat to be applied to lower the viscosity and so allow it to flow more readily.

Weighing

Weighing of the aerating materials and spices must be done with care when the amounts used are very small as instanced in many of these recipes (*see* technique of weighing small quantities in the first volume of *Bakery: Bread & Fermented Goods*).

Baking

Since biscuits are very thin, special baking precautions must be observed. Too much bottom heat is a problem with many goods and can be easily overcome by the use of a double tray. The use of silicone or greaseproof paper upon which to bake goods also reduces bottom heat. Biscuits which are dressed with sugar must always be double trayed.

Shortbread

This should contain at least 24% fat of which at least 70% should be butterfat. (Under the Labelling of Food Regulations 1970, shortbread is classified as *flour confectionery*.)

Scotch Shortbread

	1				2				3				4			
	kg	g	lb	oz	kg	g	lb	oz	kg	g	lb	oz	kg	g	lb	oz
Soft flour	1	000	2	4	1	000	2	4	—	890	2	0	1	000	2	4
Butter	—	555	1	4	—	500	1	2	—	665	1	8	—	500	1	2
Castor/pulverised sugar	—	250	—	9	—	250	—	9	—	375	—	13½	—	500	1	2
Whole egg	—	—	—	—	—	110	—	4	—	—	—	—	—	85	—	3
Ground rice	—	—	—	—	—	—	—	—	—	110	—	4	—	—	—	—
Totals	1	805	4	1	1	860	4	3	2	040	4	9½	2	085	4	11

CHOICE OF MATERIALS

Flour

This should be a soft English or Scottish variety. Specially milled biscuit flour is ideal for use in these goods.

Fat

No self-respecting Scotsman would make shortbread from anything other than butter, and in fact it is this that imparts the traditional flavour.

Sugar

The use of a very soft fine-grained sugar is essential to ensure that it is dissolved in the mixture. Pulverized sugar is to be preferred in recipes containing no egg. This is coarser than icing but fine enough to easily dissolve in this type of mixing. The use of hard-grained sugar in these goods will result in black specks of caramelized sugar appearing on the underside surface.

Baking

The temperature at which shortbread should be baked depends mainly upon its thickness and will vary between 188°C (370°F) and 204°C (400°F) for goods between 1–2 cm ($\frac{3}{8}$–$\frac{3}{4}$ in) in thickness. Petticoat Tails, which are very thin, can be baked at temperatures higher than this approx. 215°C (420°F). The aim is to get an even thorough bake without excessive colouring either of the crust or the crumb. When baked it should be crisp and break cleanly.

Storage

Like biscuits, shortbread will rapidly lose its crispness and soften if not stored in an air-tight tin.

Methods of Mixing the Paste

Method One
(1) Beat the butter and sugar to a cream.
(2) If there are eggs in the recipe, add and beat these in too.
(3) Blend in the sieved dry ingredients.
(4) Mix to a smooth paste.

Method Two (suitable for recipes 3 and 4)
(1) Cream the butter with half the flour.
(2) Mix the egg and sugar and beat into the fat/flour cream.
(3) Blend in the sieved dry ingredients.
(4) Mix to a smooth paste.

VARIETIES

Large (Yield 13)

Variety One
(1) Scale the dough at 220 g (8 oz) and mould round.
(2) Roll out to approx. 20 cm (8 in) in diameter, ensuring that the edges are kept free from cracks.
(3) With the thumb and forefinger, crimp the edge.
(4) Dock the centre thoroughly and place the piece onto papered baking sheets (use either greaseproof or silicone paper). It is a good idea to roll out the pieces on a flat circular disc of the same dimension as the shortbread as this will facilitate an easy transfer to the baking sheet without any distortion of shape.
(5) With either a knife, Scotch scraper, or a special shortbread cutter cut into 8 sections without disturbing the shape.
(6) Bake at approx. 199°C (390°F).
(7) When baked, and whilst still hot, dredge with fine castor sugar.
(8) When cold it may be broken into individual sections.

Note If 110 g (4 oz) is used so that the shortbread is very thin, it may be baked at 215°C (420°F). This variety is called Petticoat Tails.

Variety Two Proceed as for the previous variety, but instead of cutting into segments, decorate with cherries and other crystallized fruits before baking.

Variety Three Instead of moulding by hand, shortbreads may be moulded in a carved wooden block in the following manner:

Figure 33. Scotch shortbread: *Left* – The wooden mould.
Right – The moulded shortbread.

(1) Scale the dough at a weight appropriate to the size of the block used.
(2) Mould round and roll out to the size of the block.
(3) Make sure the block is clean and dry, and dust it with rice flour.
(4) Place in the round of shortbread and use the rolling pin to force the dough into the mouldings of the block.
(5) Trim the edge clean with a knife.
(6) Turn upside down and gently tap the block to help the moulded shortbread piece to release itself and fall onto a papered baking sheet.
(7) Dock the centre thoroughly.
(8) The shortbread may now receive either of the treatments of varieties 1 or 2 or left plain, before being baked in the same way.

Special Decoration In Scotland these large round shortbreads are often decorated with special water or royal icing and inscribed with traditional Scottish sayings, such as "For Auld Lang Syne", "Should Auld Acquaintance Be Forgot", "A Guid New Year Tae Ane An A".

Individual Shortbreads (Yield 64)

Variety One
(1) Weigh 30 g (1 oz) dough for each piece.
(2). Use small carved wooden blocks and proceed in the same way as for the large moulded shortbread.
(3) They may be decorated with a cherry prior to baking if desired.
(4) Bake at 204°C (400°F) and dredge with castor sugar on withdrawing from the oven.

Variety Two
(1) Roll out the dough to approx. 12 cm ($\frac{1}{2}$ in) in thickness.
(2) Dock well and cut into fingers approx. 5$\frac{1}{2}$ cm (2$\frac{1}{4}$ in) × 2$\frac{1}{2}$ cm (1 in) (*see* note 3 below).
(3) Proceed as with 4 above.

Notes
(1) To be able to cut the dough given into 64 fingers, we need to roll out the dough to cover an area of 46 cm (18 in) × 20 cm (8 in). This may be conveniently done by making a frame of this size and after lining with paper, rolling out the dough within same.
(2) Alternatively, the dough may be cut first into strips of 5$\frac{1}{2}$ cm (2$\frac{1}{2}$ in) and cut into 8.
(3) After cutting into fingers the individual pieces may be either left attached to each other, baked and separated by breaking at the cut afterwards, or baked separated on the baking sheet.

Cut Out Shapes

Animal and other shapes can be cut out of shortbread by the use of an appropriate cutter. Animal cutters can be used and after baking, the shapes may be finished with marzipan as shown in Figure 34.

Figure 34. Animal shapes cut out of shortbread. The second row in each case shows the figures covered with marzipan with has been textured with the roller above. A bulb of royal icing and a spot of chocolate makes the impression of the eye.

Easter Biscuits

Use shortbread recipe No. 3 with the following amendments:

Increase	Egg	60 g (2 oz)
Add	Baking powder	15 g ($\frac{1}{2}$ oz)
Add	Ground mixed spice	7 g ($\frac{1}{4}$ oz)
Add	Currants	95 g ($3\frac{1}{2}$ oz)

(1) Roll out paste to 3 mm ($\frac{1}{8}$ in) in thickness.
(2) Egg wash and dredge with castor sugar.
(3) Cut out rounds using a 9 cm ($3\frac{1}{2}$ in) finely fluted cutter.
(4) Place onto papered baking sheets and bake at 199°C (390°F).

Rice Biscuits

(1) Use shortbread recipe No. 4 (page 84) with the following amendments:
    Substitute   165 g (6 oz) flour with ground rice.
    Add   70 g ($2\frac{1}{2}$ oz) whole egg.
(2) Proceed as for Easter biscuits but bake at 204°C (400°F).

Dutch Biscuits

Use shortbread recipe No. 1 with the following amendments:
Substitute flour for the ground rice   110 g (4 oz)
Add baking powder   10 g ($\frac{1}{3}$ oz).

Variety A
(1) Divide the dough into four and colour one quarter chocolate.
(2) Make a long roll. The diameter depends upon the size of the finished biscuit, but an average size is 4 cm ($1\frac{1}{2}$ in).
(3) Roll out the chocolate paste to 6 mm ($\frac{1}{4}$ in) in thickness, and cut into approx. 11 cm ($4\frac{1}{2}$ in) strips.
(4) Egg wash and wrap the chocolate strips around the roll. The paste should join butt on and not overlap.
(5) Cut this composite roll into slices 6 mm ($\frac{1}{4}$ in) thick and place onto papered baking sheets.

Variety B
(1) Roll out the two differently coloured pastes approx. 6 cm ($\frac{1}{4}$ in) in thickness.
(2) Damp the surface of one and lay the other on top.
(3) Cut into strips 23 cm (9 in) approx. and roll up Swiss roll fashion to form a roll of approx. 5 cm (2 in) diameter.
(4) Repeat (5) of previous variety.

Variety C (*see* Figure 35)
(1) Roll out the two differently coloured pastes approx. 12 mm ($\frac{1}{2}$ in) in thickness.
(2) Damp the surface of one and lay the other on top.
(3) Cut in two, dampen the surface of one and lay the other on top to give four layers of alternate colours.
(4) Cut strips 12 mm ($\frac{1}{2}$ in) wide and dampening the surface, join four of these to each other so that chocolate is against white and vice versa.
(5) Roll out some white dough 3 mm ($\frac{1}{8}$ in) in thickness and cut into strips 20 cm (8 in) wide.
(6) Damp the surface and wrap it around the composite piece.
(7) Repeat (5) of *Variety A*.
Note   This will give a checkerboard design of 16 squares. Rolling the paste to $2\frac{1}{2}$ cm (1 in) and cutting the white and chocolate layer into two $2\frac{1}{2}$ cm (1 in) strips we make a checkerboard design of 4 squares.

Figure 35. Dutch biscuits.

A 9 square checkerboard design can just as easily be made by the same technique.

Variety D
(1) Using the plain dough, roll out ropes approx. $1\frac{1}{2}$ cm ($\frac{5}{8}$ in) in diameter and cut these into 13 cm (5 in) lengths.
(2) Damp the surface with water and dip into castor sugar.
(3) Arrange on a papered baking tray in the form of a horseshoe.
(4) When cold the ends may be dipped into chocolate for decoration.

American Cookies

	kg	g	lb	oz
Medium flour	1	000	2	4
Baking powder	—	10	—	$\frac{1}{3}$
Butter or cake margarine	—	720	1	10
Fine castor sugar	—	720	1	10
Whole egg	—	195	—	7
Totals	2	645	5	$15\frac{1}{3}$

These biscuits are sold by weight.
(1) Make the paste by Method 2, detailed for short or sweetpastry, page 17.
(2) Chill the dough in a refrigerator so it can be more easily handled.
(3) Roll out into ropes of $2\frac{1}{2}$ cm (1 in) diameter and place in a refrigerator to chill.
(4) Cut into slices 12 mm ($\frac{1}{2}$ in) thick and place flat onto a baking sheet either papered with silicone paper or lightly greased.
(5) Bake at 188°C (370°F) without too much colour.

Varieties
(1) Egg wash the ropes and before cutting into slices roll in one of the following:
    (*a*) Castor sugar
    (*b*) Desiccated coconut
    (*c*) Fine nibbed almonds.
(2) Add glacé fruits, sultanas, currants or nibbed nuts to the dough prior to cutting out.
(3) Decorate with cherries or nuts.
(4) Divide paste into two or more portions and add a different colour to each. These may now be finished off in the same way as Dutch biscuits (*see* page 88) but

keeping the overall size to approx. 2½ cm (1 in) diameter. Squares may also be made up and if formed from three colours, can be most attractive.

(5) Up to one quarter of the weight of flour may be replaced by the following:
   Ground almonds, ground hazelnuts, coconut flour.
   For chocolate replace 110 g (4 oz) flour with cocoa powder.

Note If coloured paste is used it is very important to ensure that the biscuits do not take on too much colour in the oven.

These biscuits are best sold by weight in mixed varieties.

Small Wine Biscuits (These are sold by weight)

	Recipe 1				Recipe 2			
	kg	*g*	*lb*	*oz*	*kg*	*g*	*lb*	*oz*
Soft flour	1	000	2	4	1	000	2	4
Butter/cake margarine	—	500	1	2	—	500	1	2
Soft castor or pulverized sugar	—	750	1	11	—	500	1	2
Whole egg	—	155	—	5½	—	220	—	8
Totals	2	405	5	6½	2	220	5	0

(1) Make the paste in the same way as sweetpastry, *see* page 17.

(2) Roll out the paste to 3 mm (⅛ in) in thickness on a perfectly flat surface. For varieties which are not egg washed or dressed before baking, fluted rollers may be used. It is important for these biscuits to be of uniform thickness to achieve even baking. If a pastry break is not available for this purpose, it may be achieved by using two slats of the required thickness, placing one each side of the piece of paste and reducing its thickness until the ends of the rolling pin are running on the slats. In this way the paste is reduced to the same thickness as the slats (Figure 36). Use rice flour for dusting purposes.

Figure 36. Showing how the biscuit paste can be uniformly rolled out between two slats of a definite thickness. The rolling pin used in this illustration has ball bearings for easy rolling.

(3) With small cutters of different shapes, plain or fluted, cut out and place the pieces upside down onto a clean baking sheet. This technique is speeded up by the use of tapered cutters which will allow several pieces to be cut out, the pieces being removed by inverting the cutter onto the hand which can then place about ten biscuits in one operation. Not only cutters of different shapes and sizes, but also two cutters of different sizes may be used to produce rings.

(4) Ensure that the biscuits are evenly placed upon the tray which when full should be baked at 204°C (400°F) to a light golden brown colour. The colour should be the same throughout.

VARIETIES

Note All the additions shown are mixed with 1 kg (2¼ lb) of the basic wine biscuit paste. Currants need care to ensure they are not bruised and so discolour the paste. Only the variations from the method of producing the basic plain wine biscuit are given. Two recipes are given, one being very much sweeter than the other. For those varieties which are dressed in sugar the recipe containing the least sugar should be used.

Almond (*see* note above)
(1) Add 110 g (4 oz) roasted ground almonds to the high sugar recipe.
(2) Brush over with a dilute egg wash and dredge with ground almonds.

Raspberry Almond (*see* note above)
(1) Proceed as for the previous variety but using plain ground almonds instead of roasted and raspberry colour and flavour.

Currant (*see* note above)
(1) Add 110 g (4 oz) of small currants to either the plain recipe or the raspberry almond.
(2) Brush over with a dilute egg wash and dredge with castor sugar.

Currant Nib
(1) In addition to the currants, add 220 g (8 oz) nibbed almonds.
(2) Roll the dough into a rope 2½ cm (1 in) diameter, and harden by placing into the refrigerator.
(3) Cut into 3 mm (⅛ in) slices.
(4) Egg wash the slices and dip each into nib almonds.

Coconut (*see* note above)
(1) Add 110 g (4 oz) of medium desiccated coconut.
(2) Brush over with a dilute egg wash and dredge with fine desiccated coconut.
(3) Bake at 199°C (390°F).

Ginger (*see* note above)
(1) Add and mix in 55 g (2 oz) ginger crush or finely chopped ginger.
(2) Wash with egg whites and dredge with granulated sugar.

Almond Paste
(1) Use equal quantities of basic biscuit paste and a good quality almond paste, *see* page 256.
(2) Roll out the biscuit paste and the marzipan to equal thickness of 6–10 mm (¼–⅜ in).

(3) Egg wash the biscuit paste and lay on the almond paste.
(4) Lightly pass the rolling pin over to ensure the two pastes are joined securely and cut into cubes.
(5) Bake at 199°C (390°F).

LARGER BISCUITS

Derby Biscuits

(1) Roll out the wine biscuit dough to 3 mm ($\frac{1}{8}$ in) in thickness and cut out using a larger 6$\frac{1}{2}$ cm (2$\frac{1}{2}$in) fluted cutter.
(2) Egg wash and dust with castor sugar.
(3) Place onto papered baking sheets and bake at 199°C (390°F).

Jam or Jelly Biscuits

(1) Roll out the basic wine biscuit dough to approx. 2 mm ($\frac{1}{10}$ in) in thickness.
(2) Cut out with a 6$\frac{1}{2}$ cm (2$\frac{1}{2}$ in) fluted cutter.
(3) With half of these, cut out three holes in the form of a triangle using a 12 mm ($\frac{1}{2}$ in) plain tube.
(4) Place onto baking sheets and bake each half separately at 204°C (400°F) to achieve even baking.
(5) When cold, sandwich each half with boiling apricot purée with the half with the holes on top. Alternatively, a filling cream may be used for sandwiching.
(6) Fill the holes with three different coloured jams or jellies using a bag with a small plain tube.

VIENNESE

Method of mixing
Recipe 1 Well beat the ingredients together to form a smooth paste.
Recipes 2 and 4 Use method 2 of short and sweetpastry (*see* page 16).
Recipe 3 Use method 3 of short and sweetpastry (*see* page 16).

Tarts

(1) Using a star tube, pipe the mixing into paper cases using a spiral motion and leaving an impression in the centre.
(2) Bake at 204°C (400°F).
(3) When baked and cold, dust with icing sugar and pipe a spot of raspberry jam in the centre of each tart.

Piped Shapes

(1) Using a star tube, pipe various shapes out onto a baking sheet.
(2) Bake at 204°C (400°F).
(3) When baked and cold, sandwich in pairs using jam or a suitable cream.
Notes
(1) The piped shapes may be further decorated by dipping parts into chocolate.
(2) It is recommended *not* to use Recipe No. 1 for piped shapes since it produces a very short and crumbly article which is more suitable for tarts.

Nougat Viennese

Recipe 5
(1) Cream the butter, sugar and nougat.

(2) Fold in the flour and ground hazelnuts.

(3) Pipe into fancy shapes onto a baking sheet and bake at 182°C (360°F).

(4) When cold, sandwich with a suitable filling cream and dip parts or spin over with chocolate.

Frangipane Viennese

(1) Using a savoy bag with approx. 1 cm ($\frac{1}{2}$ in) star tube, pipe out rings onto a greased baking tray or silicone paper using the Viennese mixing.

(2) Fill the centre with frangipane mixture using a savoy bag with a plain tube.

(3) Bake at 182°C (360°F).

(4) When cool brush over the centres with apricot purée.

(5) Coat with a thin water icing and return to the oven for approx. $\frac{1}{2}$ minute.

Macaroon Viennese

Proceed as for frangipane Viennese, but instead of the frangipane mixing, fill the centre with macaroon mixing (*see* page 213).

African Tarts

Yield – 44

	kg	g	lb	oz
Sweet pastry (*see* page 16)	1	000	2	4
Viennese mixing (*see* page 94)	—	780	1	12
Jam or curd	—	170	—	6
Totals	1	950	4	6

(1) Roll out the sweetpastry to 3 mm ($\frac{1}{8}$ in) in thickness.

(2) Cut out rounds using a 6$\frac{1}{2}$ cm (2$\frac{1}{2}$ in) cutter (fluted or plain), and place upon clean baking sheets.

(3) Transfer the Viennese mixing to a savoy bag fitted with a 1 cm ($\frac{3}{8}$ in) star tube.

(4) Pipe a circle around the edge of the pastry round and across the centre to leave two half-moon shaped cavities.

(5) Bake in the oven at 204°C (400°F).

(6) When cold fill the cavities with two contrastingly coloured and flavoured jams or curds.

Alternative Variety   Instead of making two cavities, pipe a circle only, and afterwards fill the centre with one jam or curd. In this case the rounds can be smaller, i.e. cut out with a 5 cm (2 in) cutter.

Note   Other filling such as custard or fudge can be used.

Yields Allowing 45 g (1$\frac{1}{2}$ oz) approx. each

     Recipe 1 = 72

     Recipe 2 = 61

     Recipe 3 = 48

Flapjacks

(1) Melt the butter or fat in a bowl, and add the other ingredients. Mix thoroughly.

(2) Spread the mixing 6 mm ($\frac{1}{4}$ in) in thickness, on a baking sheet, putting a stick across to prevent the mixture flowing off the sheet during baking.

Viennese

	1				2				3				4				Nougat			
	kg	g	lb	oz	kg	g	lb	oz	kg	g	lb	oz	kg	g	lb	oz	kg	g	lb	oz
Soft flour	1	000	2	4	1	000	2	4	1	000	2	4	1	000	2	4	1	000	2	4
Baking powder	—	—	—	—	—	—	—	—	—	—	—	—	—	7	—	¼	—	—	—	—
Butter	1	000	2	4	1	000	2	4	—	375	—	13½	—	—	—	8	1	110	2	8
Cake margarine	—	—	—	—	—	—	—	—	—	—	—	—	—	665	1	8	—	—	—	—
Shortening	—	—	—	—	—	—	—	—	—	375	—	13½	—	—	—	—	—	—	—	—
Icing sugar	—	250	—	9	—	—	—	—	—	—	—	—	—	—	—	—	—	—	—	—
Castor sugar	—	—	—	—	—	305	—	11	—	305	—	11	—	345	—	12½	—	335	—	12
Eggs	—	—	—	—	—	125	—	4½	—	195	—	7	—	280	—	10	—	—	—	—
Milk	—	—	—	—	—	—	—	—	—	—	—	—	—	—	—	—	—	445	1	0
Nougat	—	—	—	—	—	—	—	—	—	—	—	—	—	—	—	—	—	—	—	—
Ground hazelnuts (slightly roasted)	—	—	—	—	—	—	—	—	—	—	—	—	—	—	—	—	—	220	—	8
Totals	2	250	5	1	2	430	5	7½	2	250	5	1	2	297	5	2¾	3	110	7	0

Flapjacks

	1				2				3			
	kg	*g*	*lb*	*oz*	*kg*	*g*	*lb*	*oz*	*kg*	*g*	*lb*	*oz*
Rolled oats	1	000	2	4	1	000	2	4	1	000	2	4
Butter	1	000	2	4	—	500	1	2	—	665	1	8
Shortening	—	—	—	—	—	250	—	9	—	—	—	—
Treacle	—	—	—	—	—	195	—	7	—	—	—	—
Castor sugar	1	000	2	4	—	—	—	—	—	335	—	12
Brown sugar	—	—	—	—	—	500	1	2	—	—	—	—
Ground hazelnuts	—	—	—	—	—	125	—	4½	—	—	—	—
Totals	3	000	6	12	2	570	5	12½	2	000	4	8

(3) Bake at 177°C (350°F) until a golden brown colour (approx. 25 minutes).
(4) When cool and set, cut into fingers or squares of the required size.

Shrewsbury Biscuits

	1st Quality				2nd Quality			
	kg	*g*	*lb*	*oz*	*kg*	*g*	*lb*	*oz*
Soft flour	1	000	2	4	1	000	2	4
Baking powder	—	—	—	—	—	10	—	⅓
Butter or cake margarine	—	625	1	6½	—	500	1	2
Soft castor or pulverized sugar	—	500	1	2	—	335	—	12
Whole egg	—	195	—	7	—	—	—	—
Milk	—	—	—	—	—	110	—	4
Ground cinnamon	—	5	—	⅙	—	5	—	⅙
Currants (optional)	—	165	—	6	—	165	—	6
Totals	2	490	5	9⅔	2	125	4	12½

(1) Make the paste by any of the methods detailed for short or sweetpaste (page 17). (If required, currants should be added after paste is made.)
(2) Roll out to 3 mm (⅛ in) in thickness, and cut out rounds using a 10 cm (4 in) finely fluted cutter.
(3) Lay out onto papered baking sheets and bake at 199°C (390°F) to a light golden brown colour.
(4) Dredge heavily with sugar as soon as the biscuits emerge from the hot oven.

WHOLEMEAL BISCUITS

(1) Mix the biscuit paste by the rubbing-in method of making short pastry (Method 1, page 17).
(2) Roll out the paste to 3 mm (⅛ in) in thickness.
(3) Dock well and cut out rounds using a 6½ cm (2½ in) cutter.
(4) Bake at 199°C (390°F) on biscuit wires or baking sheets.

Wholemeal Biscuits

	kg	g	lb	oz
Stone-ground coarse wholemeal flour	1	000	2	0
Soft white flour	—	110	—	4
Baking powder	—	7	—	$\frac{1}{4}$
Butter	—	445	1	0
Soft grained castor sugar	—	305	—	11
Milk	—	220	—	8
Salt	—	15	—	$\frac{1}{2}$
Totals	2	102	4	$7\frac{3}{4}$

(5) When cold, the base of these biscuits may be dipped in chocolate.

Method for Mixing Gingernuts and Parkin Biscuits

(1) Cream the fat, sugar, syrup, egg and/or milk.
(2) Thoroughly sieve the rest of the other dry materials and add to the cream.
(3) Work to a stiff clear paste.
Note In cold weather syrup or treacle is very viscous, and it will be necessary to warm it slightly so it will pour easily from the container and mix in more readily.

Gingernuts

	1				2				3			
	kg	g	lb	oz	kg	g	lb	oz	kg	g	lb	oz
Soft flour	1	000	2	4	1	000	2	4	1	000	2	4
Baking powder	—	15	—	$\frac{1}{2}$	—	15	—	$\frac{1}{2}$	—	—	—	—
Bicarbonate of soda	—	—	—	—	—	—	—	—	—	7	—	$\frac{1}{4}$
Tartaric acid	—	—	—	—	—	—	—	—	—	7	—	$\frac{1}{4}$
Ground ginger	—	15	—	$\frac{1}{2}$	—	15	—	$\frac{1}{2}$	—	15	—	$\frac{1}{2}$
Mixed spice	—	—	—	—	—	15	—	$\frac{1}{2}$	—	—	—	—
Butter/margarine	—	—	—	—	—	—	—	—	—	250	—	9
Shortening	—	195	—	7	—	220	—	8	—	—	—	—
Castor sugar	—	500	1	2	—	500	1	2	—	500	1	2
Golden syrup	—	500	1	2	—	500	1	2	—	500	1	2
Eggs	—	—	—	—	—	—	—	—	—	125	—	$4\frac{1}{2}$
Milk	—	60	—	$2\frac{1}{4}$	—	35	—	$1\frac{1}{4}$	—	—	—	—
Totals	2	285	5	$2\frac{1}{4}$	2	300	5	$2\frac{3}{4}$	2	404	5	$6\frac{1}{2}$

Gingernuts

(1) Roll the paste to 3 mm ($\frac{1}{8}$ in) in thickness, and cut into rounds using a 4 cm ($1\frac{1}{2}$ in) plain cutter. This is a sticky paste and the use of rice cones is recommended for dusting purposes.
(2) Place the biscuits on a lightly greased baking tray, evenly spaced.
(3) Splash with water immediately prior to placing them into the oven.
(4) Bake at 171°C (340°F) until a golden brown colour.

Parkin Biscuits

(1) Make the paste and scale in 35–45 g ($1\frac{1}{4}$–$1\frac{1}{2}$ oz) pieces.
(2) Mould round and place well apart on a greased baking sheet to allow for flowing during baking.

(3) Flatten with the palm of the hand, egg wash and place a split almond on each biscuit.

(4) Bake at 171°C (340°F).

Note Do not attempt to remove the biscuits from the baking sheet until they are cool.

Parkin Slabs or Cakes

(1) Proceed as for parkin biscuits. The mixture will be much softer, of a cake batter consistency.

(2) Deposit into paper-lined slab frames or pans. The height should be approx. 5 cm (2 in) when spread level.

(3) Bake at 171°C (340°F).

(4) If baked as a slab, cut into appropriately sized pieces.

Note A few flaked almonds may be sprinkled on top prior to baking.

Gingerbread

(1) Proceed as for parkin slabs, but the mixture should be only half as thick. Papered or well greased baking sheets may be used with a greased bar across the end to prevent the mixture flowing.

(2) After baking at 177°C (350°F) cut into squares of an appropriate size.

Grasmere Gingerbread Biscuits

(1) Make a crumble by rubbing the butter into the sieved dry ingredients. Do *not* apply pressure to form a paste.

(2) Spread the crumble onto a well greased tray to approx. 6 mm ($\frac{1}{4}$ in) in thickness.

(3) Lightly press level and bake at 204°C (400°F).

(4) After approx. 15 min remove from the oven, cut into rectangular shapes with the point of a sharp knife and return to the oven to finish baking.

(5) Remove after baking, separating into the individual biscuits.

Ashbourne Gingerbread Biscuits

(1) Proceed as for Grasmere gingerbread but make into a firm paste.

(2) Roll out into ropes approx. $2\frac{1}{2}$ cm (1 in) diameter and flatten to give a strip approx. 5 cm (2 in) wide.

(3) Cut into fingers approx. $2\frac{1}{2}$ cm (1 in) wide and place these on a lightly greased baking sheet.

(4) Bake at 204°C (400°F).

Brandy Snaps

(1) Mix ingredients to a smooth paste.

(2) Liberally grease a baking tray with fat.

(3) Roll out the paste into a long rope and with a knife, cut off pieces of equal size approx. 15 g ($\frac{1}{2}$ oz).

(4) Place these on the greased tray approx. 13 cm (5 in) apart and flatten with the hand or a fork.

Figure 37. Pressing out the brandy snap paste prior to baking

	Parkin Biscuits												**Parkin Slab**											
	1				**2**				**3**				**1**				**2**				**3**			
	kg	*g*	*lb*	*oz*	*kg*	*g*	*lb*	*oz*	*kg*	*g*	*lb*	*oz*	*kg*	*g*	*lb*	*oz*	*kg*	*g*	*lb*	*oz*	*kg*	*g*	*lb*	*oz*
Soft flour	—	500	1	2	—	500	1	2	—	500	1	2	—	500	1	2	—	500	1	2	—	500	1	2
Medium oatmeal	—	500	1	2	—	500	1	2	—	500	1	2	—	—	—	—	—	500	1	2	—	500	1	2
Wholemeal	—	—	—	—	—	—	—	—	—	—	—	—	—	500	1	2	—	—	—	—	—	—	—	—
Bicarbonate of soda	—	15	—	½	—	35	—	1¼	—	15	—	½	—	—	—	—	—	—	—	—	—	—	—	—
Baking powder	—	—	—	—	—	—	—	—	—	—	—	—	—	35	—	1¼	—	15	—	½	—	7	—	¼
Ground mixed spice	—	15	—	½	—	—	—	—	—	10	—	⅓	—	—	—	—	—	—	—	—	—	7	—	¼
Ground ginger	—	25	—	¾	—	—	—	—	—	15	—	½	—	25	—	¾	—	15	—	½	—	7	—	¼
Cake margarine/butter	—	—	—	—	—	155	—	5½	—	250	—	9	—	—	—	—	—	350	—	12½	—	—	—	—
Shortening	—	220	—	8	—	—	—	—	—	—	—	—	—	500	1	2	—	—	—	—	—	295	—	10½
Golden syrup	—	625	1	6½	—	440	—	15¾	—	430	—	15½	—	375	—	13½	—	560	1	4¼	—	260	—	9¼
Brown sugar	—	125	—	4½	—	—	—	—	—	310	—	11¼	—	375	—	13½	—	570	1	4½	—	220	—	8
Castor sugar	—	—	—	—	—	125	—	4½	—	—	—	—	—	—	—	—	—	—	—	—	—	—	—	—
Eggs	—	85	—	3	—	—	—	—	—	—	—	—	—	—	—	—	—	—	—	—	—	—	—	—
Milk	—	—	—	—	—	125	—	4½	—	—	—	—	—	210	—	7½	—	625	1	6½	—	80	—	2¾
Malt flour	—	—	—	—	—	—	—	—	—	—	—	—	—	25	—	¾	—	—	—	—	—	—	—	—
Totals	2	110	4	11¾	1	880	4	3½	2	030	4	$9\frac{1}{12}$	2	545	5	11¼	3	135	7	0¾	1	876	4	3¼

Brandy Snaps

	1				2				3				4			
	kg	g	lb	oz	kg	g	lb	oz	kg	g	lb	oz	kg	g	lb	oz
Soft flour	1	000	2	4	1	000	2	4	1	000	2	4	1	000	2	4
Butter	1	110	2	8	—	—	—	—	—	—	—	—	—	—	—	—
Cake margarine	—	—	—	—	—	—	—	—	—	500	1	2	—	290	—	10¼
Shortening	—	—	—	—	—	750	1	11	—	—	—	—	—	290	—	10¼
Golden syrup/treacle	1	000	2	4	1	250	2	13	1	000	2	4	1	000	2	4
Castor sugar	2	000	4	8	1	000	2	4	2	000	4	8	1	500	3	6
Ground ginger	—	35	—	1¼	—	35	—	1¼	—	35	—	1¼	—	25	—	¾
Ground mixed spice	—	7	—	¼	—	—	—	—	—	7	—	¼	—	—	—	—
Tartaric acid	—	—	—	—	—	—	—	—	—	15	—	½	—	45	—	1½
Totals	5	152	11	9½	4	035	9	1¼	4	557	10	4	4	150	9	4¾

(5) Bake at 171°C (340°F) until golden brown in colour. During baking, the mixture will flow out flat with a holey surface.

(6) Allow to cool slightly and then remove with a palette knife.

(7) Mould into the required shape whilst still warm. Once cold, they are very brittle and can easily snap.

(8) The brandy snap may be moulded into a cone shape using cream horn tins, or made into hollow cylinders by wrapping around wooden rods.

(9) These biscuits are usually filled with fresh whipped cream.

Note

(1) Smaller brandy snaps may be used for decoration of fancies and gâteau or torten.

(2) If these goods become too brittle to mould, they may be re-heated when they again become pliable.

(3) These goods are very hygroscopic, attracting moisture from the air to make them soft and sticky. They are best when consumed fresh, but if storage is necessary, an air tight container should be used.

Langue du Chat

	1				2				3			
	kg	g	lb	oz	kg	g	lb	oz	kg	g	lb	oz
Soft flour	1	000	2	4	1	000	2	4	1	000	2	4
Butter	1	000	2	4	—	695	1	9	—	—	—	—
Castor sugar	1	000	2	4	—	—	—	—	—	—	—	—
Icing sugar	—	—	—	—	—	695	1	9	1	000	2	4
Egg whites	—	625	1	6½	—	610	1	6	—	875	1	15½
Whipping cream	—	—	—	—	—	445	1	0	1	000	2	4
Totals	3	625	8	2½	3	445	7	12	3	875	8	11½

Methods

Recipe 1.

(1) Thoroughly grease a baking tray.

Gingerbread

	1				2				3				4				5 Grasmere				6 Ashbourne			
	kg	g	lb	oz	kg	g	lb	oz	kg	g	lb	oz	kg	g	lb	oz	kg	g	lb	oz	kg	g	lb	oz
Soft flour	—	500	1	2	—	500	1	2	1	000	2	4	1	000	2	4	1	000	2	4	1	000	2	4
Wholemeal	—	500	1	2	—	500	1	2	—	—	—	—	—	—	—	—	—	—	—	—	—	—	—	—
Bicarbonate of soda	—	15	—	1/2	—	—	—	—	—	—	—	—	—	—	—	—	—	—	—	—	—	—	—	—
Baking powder	—	—	—	—	—	25	—	3/4	—	—	—	—	—	40	—	1 1/2	—	—	—	—	—	—	—	—
Ground mixed spice	—	7	—	1/4	—	10	—	1/3	—	7	—	1/4	—	—	—	—	—	7	—	1/4	—	15	—	1/2
Ground ginger	—	15	—	1/2	—	—	—	—	—	15	—	1/2	—	15	—	1/2	—	15	—	1/2	—	805	1	13
Butter/cake margarine	—	190	—	6 3/4	—	335	—	12	—	195	—	7	—	250	—	9	—	780	1	12	—	—	—	—
Golden syrup/treacle	—	375	—	13 1/2	—	335	—	12	—	555	1	4	—	500	1	2	—	—	—	—	—	—	—	—
Soft brown sugar	—	250	—	9	—	—	—	—	—	555	1	4	—	—	—	—	—	415	—	15	—	—	—	—
Castor sugar	—	—	—	—	—	—	—	—	—	—	—	—	—	190	—	6 3/4	—	—	—	—	—	500	1	2
Milk	—	470	1	1	—	250	—	9	—	195	—	7	—	155	—	5 1/2	—	—	—	—	—	—	—	—
Eggs	—	250	—	9	—	—	—	—	—	—	—	—	—	—	—	—	—	—	—	—	—	—	—	—
Cake crumbs	—	—	—	—	—	85	—	3	—	—	—	—	—	—	—	—	—	—	—	—	—	—	—	—
Honey	—	—	—	—	—	85	—	3	—	250	—	9	—	60	—	2 1/4	—	—	—	—	—	—	—	—
Chopped ginger	—	—	—	—	—	—	—	—	—	—	—	—	—	—	—	—	—	—	—	—	—	—	—	—
Finely mixed peel	—	—	—	—	—	—	—	—	—	250	—	9	—	—	—	—	—	—	—	—	—	155	—	5 1/2
Sultanas	—	—	—	—	—	—	—	—	—	335	—	12	—	—	—	—	—	—	—	—	—	—	—	—
Split almonds	—	—	—	—	—	—	—	—	—	—	—	—	—	—	—	—	—	—	—	—	—	—	—	—
Totals	2	572	5	12 1/2	2	125	4	12 1/12	3	357	7	8 3/4	2	210	4	15 1/2	2	217	4	15 3/4	2	475	5	9

(2) Prepare the mixture using the sugar-batter method (*see* page 128).
(3) Transfer mixing to a savoy tube fitted with a 6 mm ($\frac{1}{4}$ in) plain tube.
(4) Pipe out the shapes required. Allow plenty of space for these to flow during baking.
(5) Bake at 204°C (400°F) until the edges are tinged a light golden brown colour.
(6) Remove from the tray whilst still warm.

Recipe 2.
(1) Cream the butter with 500 g (1 lb 2 oz) of the icing sugar.
(2) Gradually beat in the cream.
(3) Add the remaining sugar with the egg whites and whisk to a meringue.
(4) Blend both mixtures and then fold in the flour.
Proceed as with Recipe 1.

Recipe 3.
(1) Whip the egg white and sugar to a stiff meringue.
(2) Slightly whip the cream to thicken.
(3) Carefully fold the flour into the meringue.
(4) Lastly blend in the thickened cream.
Proceed as with Recipe 1.

Uses
(1) As a decoration for gâteaux and torten (*see* page 192).
(2) Sandwiched with an appropriate cream or filling, they make an attractive article, and if small enough can be served as petits fours. These biscuits may be either left plain or partly dipped in chocolate.
(3) If removed immediately they are baked, these biscuits can be curled or twisted, and in this form make an attractive accompaniment to ice cream dishes.

Marquis

These are langue du chat biscuits which are sandwiched with the following filling:
3 parts ganache (*see* page 171).
1 part crushed nougat (*see* page 281).
These biscuits may either be dipped into chocolate or left plain with the word *marquis* piped on each.

Bury Simnels

Yield 11 at 250 g (9 oz)
This must not be confused with the traditional simnel cake which is explained on page 144. It is included in this chapter because it is more of a biscuit than a cake.

	kg	g	lb	oz
Soft flour	1	000	2	4
Baking powder	—	25	—	$\frac{7}{8}$
Butter	—	400	—	$14\frac{1}{2}$
Demerara sugar	—	400	—	$14\frac{1}{2}$
Whole egg	—	250	—	9
Ground nutmeg	—	7	—	$\frac{1}{4}$
Sultanas	—	290	—	$10\frac{1}{2}$
Currants	—	290	—	$10\frac{1}{2}$
Cut peel	—	95	—	$3\frac{1}{2}$
Milk	—	125	—	$4\frac{1}{2}$
Totals	2	882	6	$8\frac{1}{8}$

(1) Make into a dough by *method 1* for short pastry on page 17.
(2) Weigh pieces at approx. 250 g (9 oz) and mould round.
(3) Flatten with a rolling pin to approx. 10 cm (4 in) in diameter and place onto greased baking sheets.
(4) Egg wash and decorate with split almonds in the form of a cross.
(5) Place into an oven at 204°C (400°F) for approx. 25 minutes to bake.
Almonds for decoration – Allow approx. 15 g ($\frac{1}{2}$ oz) split almonds for the decoration of each Bury simnel.

Marshmallow Biscuits

For these a sweetpastry is recommended (*see* page 16).
(1) Roll out the paste to 3 mm ($\frac{1}{8}$ in) in thickness, and cut out the following:

Rounds	–	approx. 5 cm (2 in) cutter.
Rings	–	outside cutter 6$\frac{1}{2}$ cm (2$\frac{1}{2}$ in).
		inside cutter 3 cm (1$\frac{1}{4}$ in).
Ovals	–	approx. 5$\frac{1}{2}$ × 4 cm (2$\frac{1}{4}$ × 1$\frac{1}{2}$ in) cutter.

(2) Bake these shapes on silicone paper or a clean baking sheet in an oven at 193°C (380°F) until they are baked to a golden brown.
(3) Beat up marshmallow (*see* page 169) and when it begins to stiffen, fill a savoy bag fitted with a 1$\frac{1}{4}$ cm ($\frac{1}{2}$ in) tube for the round and oval shapes, and a 1 cm ($\frac{3}{8}$ in) tube for the rings.
(4) Pipe a bulb of marshmallow on the rounds and ovals, and a ring on the others.
(5) Cover immediately with desiccated coconut either plain or toasted *or* leave plain for dipping into chocolate. For added decoration the coconut varieties may have liquid chocolate spun across (*see* page 237).

Note These biscuits, if left undressed, can be completely enrobed with chocolate couverture. However, if this is required, it is good practice to allow the dry biscuit a day or two to absorb moisture from the air before enrobing. If the biscuit is too dry when it is enrobed, the biscuit base will expand as it absorbs moisture, and this can lead to the chocolate flaking away.

Figure 38. Marshmallow biscuits showing the various finishes, using chocolate and coconut

Biscuit Base (Using Cake Crumbs)

	kg	g	lb	oz
Soft flour	1	000	2	4
Cake crumbs	1	000	2	4
Baking powder	—	50	—	1¾
Margarine	—	500	1	2
Castor sugar	—	250	—	9
Whole egg	—	250	—	9
Totals	3	050	6	13¾

(1) Sieve the baking powder with the flour.
(2) Cream the margarine with the sugar, and gradually beat in the egg to form a batter.
(3) Blend in the flour.
(4) Add and blend in the cake crumbs to form a paste.
(5) Roll out this paste and from it cut any size or shape of biscuit base desired.
Note This biscuit can be turned into any number of varieties by the addition of other materials such as nuts, fruit, cocoa, etc. (*see* page 91). It can be used as a base for marshmallow fancies (*see* opposite), or sandwiched with a suitable filling and decorated as a fancy.

8. Meringue Goods

A meringue is any mixture of beaten egg whites and sugar in almost any proportions. The recipes given below will make meringue of average lightness. If a lighter meringue is required less sugar will be needed and conversely a heavier meringue will require more sugar than that quoted.

However, whilst less sugar will make a lighter meringue it will not be so stable and the shape into which it is piped may be difficult to retain.

CHOICE OF MERINGUE

Cold

Used for basic shells, other plain shapes and for built up cases (*vacherins*).

Hot

Used for decorative shapes, particularly where star tubes are used. Containing more sugar it is a heavier meringue but will retain the shape into which it is piped. It is usually sold without the addition of filling.

Boiled

As this is partially cooked, it is used to decorate such goods as meringue pies in which the meringue is *flashed* off, i.e. put into a hot oven for a few minutes to colour only. It may also be used to make buttercream where it is blended into butter. It is a very stable meringue and can be left for some time before using without it losing its stability.

Equipment

Meringues are best made by machine because of the excessive amount of whisking required and because any trace of grease will prevent the egg whites from forming a stable foam when whipped, it is essential to sterilize both the bowl and the whisk with boiling water before use.

	Cold				Hot				Boiled			
	kg	g	lb	oz	kg	g	lb	oz	kg	g	lb	oz
Egg whites	1	000	2	4	1	000	2	4	1	000	2	4
Castor sugar	2	000	4	8	2	805	6	5	—	—	—	—
Lump sugar	—	—	—	—	—	—	—	—	2	000	4	8
Water	—	—	—	—	—	—	—	—	—	610	1	6
Cream of tartar	—	4	—	$\frac{1}{8}$	—	4	—	$\frac{1}{8}$	—	7	—	$\frac{1}{4}$
Totals	3	004	6	$12\frac{1}{8}$	3	809	8	$9\frac{1}{8}$	3	617	8	$2\frac{1}{4}$

CHOICE OF INGREDIENTS

The best meringues are made from fresh or frozen egg white and a hard grained castor sugar, but it may be made from reconstituted albumen or from meringue powders.

When egg whites are used the meringue has to be baked to coagulate the protein, but with the use of meringue powders, the meringue only requires drying out and a warm cupboard or prover is quite sufficient for this purpose.

Because they are not baked, such meringues do not have the delicate fawn colour associated with those made with egg whites and properly baked. They are also powdery and easily crumble; the flavour is also inferior lacking that slight caramel taste found in a good meringue.

One of these egg white substitutes is ethyl methyl cellulose, which is marketed under the name of *Edifas*. This has no nutritional properties whatsoever, but because it makes such a stable foam it is often added to an egg white mixture as a stabilizer (*see* page 2 for details).

Various other materials may be mixed into a meringue mixture as, for example, ground almonds or hazelnuts, coconut to make such goods as Japanese Biscuits and Coconut Macaroons (*see* pages 113–15).

Colours and flavours can also be added to enhance the appearance and flavour of what tends to be a rather sweet but otherwise bland-flavoured article. The addition of these materials must be done with care however, otherwise the stability of the meringue will break down and the mixture will flow.

This can be partially prevented by the use of a stabilizer which will also enable the mixture to be left for a time before use.

Stabilizers

Besides ethyl methyl cellulose another agent which can be employed is tapioca starch. This is used at the rate of 6% of the egg whites in the recipe, i.e. 60 g ($2\frac{1}{4}$ oz) per 100 g ($2\frac{1}{4}$ lb). It can only be used for cold meringues where it is incorporated by first thoroughly mixing with the sugar. Its use will help to prevent the meringue flowing towards the end of the piping operation, especially when additions are made, e.g. ground almonds.

Cold Meringue

(1) Add the cream of tartar to the egg whites and beat to a stable foam on high speed.
(2) Gradually add two-thirds of the sugar in a steady stream whilst the machine is whisking.
(3) Continue whisking until the meringue is very stiff and the mixture clumps around the whisk. This may take ten minutes or more. An indication of when the meringue is ready may be made when the note of the motor of the machine changes to show it is labouring. If in doubt continue whisking. The author has never known a meringue to break down due to over-whisking.
(4) Remove from the machine and lightly stir in the remaining sugar with a spatula.
The finished meringue is now ready to be piped into the required varieties and baked. This should be done immediately, as the meringue will lose its stability and aeration if left standing for a while before use.

Baking of Meringues

This should be between 110–132°C (230–270°F) with a good average temperature being 121°C (250°F). Too high a temperature must be avoided otherwise the meringues will crack and form a crust which will flake away when the meringue is handled after

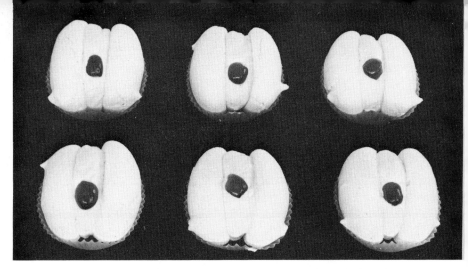

Figure 39. Meringue shells, sandwiched with fresh cream and decorated with a cherry

baking, and a hole will form in the centre. The aim should be to get an even light fawn colour throughout the meringue, but this can only be achieved by the use of egg white (not meringue powders) baked at the correct temperature.

Shells

(1) Fill a savoy bag fitted with a $1\frac{1}{2}$ cm ($\frac{5}{8}$ in) plain tube with the meringue.
(2) Pipe out bold oval shapes onto greaseproof, silicone or a good quality cap paper with the glazed side uppermost. The shells may be dredged with castor sugar prior to baking.
(3) Bake in an oven at 121°C (250°F) until set and a faint fawn colour.
(4) Carefully remove from the paper and gently press in the base with the thumb to form a hollow into which the cream is piped when the shells are sandwiched together.
(5) Stack the shells on their sides in a tray and place in a warm place to thoroughly dry out, away from dust and moisture for a few hours or overnight. On removal from the oven the centre of the shell is still soft but after drying it will be brittle throughout.
(6) The shells may be stored in an airtight tin in a warm place until required to be finished for sale. Because meringues contain such a high percentage of sugar they are very hygroscopic and if stored in a damp atmosphere, they will soon soften and become unattractive to eat. Also if cream is used for sandwiching, this should be done at the latest time before selling to prevent the meringue from becoming soft, due to the absorption of moisture from the cream.
(7) Shells may be finished off in two ways:
    (a) Sandwich with fresh cream and place in pairs on edge in a paper case.
    (b) Lay in a paper case with the base uppermost. Pipe cream in a decorative pattern on this base and embellish with tinned fruit, i.e. pineapple, orange segments, apricots, peach slices, etc., or fresh strawberries when in season.

Fingers may also be treated in the same way as shells. As an added attraction the ends may be dipped into chocolate before sandwiching.

Shapes

Various shapes such as flowers, birds, animals, snowmen, etc., may be piped in meringue and when baked, suitably finished with chocolate, etc., and sold as novelty goods.

Figure 40. Meringue mush-
rooms

Small shapes may also be made as decorative pieces for gâteaux or torten. Such a shape is a mushroom which is made as follows:

Mushrooms

(1) Pipe out small bulbs onto greased and floured baking sheets or silicone paper, avoiding getting any points. (These can be removed by dabbing with a damp brush.)
(2) After piping, dust lightly with cocoa powder, which will simulate the speckles seen on mushrooms.
(3) Pipe out elongated bulbs on another tray and finish them off with a point.
(4) Bake off both sheets at 132°C (270°F).
(5) When baked and cold, make an indentation in the base of the round bulb.
(6) Coat the flat base of the round bulb in chocolate and as each is spread, press the pointed end of the elongated bulb into the indentation to form the *stalk*. As the chocolate sets, the *stalk* will be securely fixed to the *head* of the mushroom.

MERINGUE CASES (VACHERINS)

Individual

(1) Prepare a sheet of paper (cap or greaseproof) with drawn rings of the size required, usually 7 cm (2¾ in) is sufficiently large enough.
(2) Place onto a baking sheet and on this lay a piece of greaseproof paper so that the drawn rings are visible.
(3) Using a savoy bag fitted with a 1 cm (⅜ in) plain tube, pipe out three rings for each case but fill in one ring for the base. Alternatively the bases may be stencilled out as in Japs (*see* page 110).
(4) Bake at 132°C (270°F).
(5) When baked and cold, remove from the paper and make up cases by cementing two rings to a base with meringue.
(6) Place in a cool oven at 110°C (230°F) to set the cementing meringue and thoroughly dry out the case, or, alternatively, place in a warm environment for a few hours or overnight.
(7) These cases may be filled with fruit and fresh cream and either finished off with a piece of fruit on top or a lid made of meringue. Meringue lids can be made to look very attractive and one favourite is a piped dahlia which once baked and perfectly dried out, may be sprayed with edible colour. Alternatively, the meringue itself may be coloured prior to being piped. Commercially these meringue cases can be piped in one operation with a base and two rings.

If the cases have to be filled with fruit and cream and left for a considerable time before being consumed, it is a good idea to mask the inside with chocolate prior to

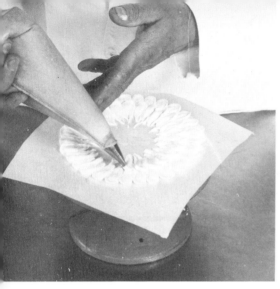

Figure 41. Piping the dahlia top for a vacherin

filling. This not only prevents the migration of moisture from the cream to the meringue which will cause it to soften, but as a bonus enhances its flavour.

Large Vacherins

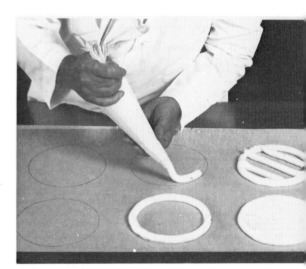

Figure 42. Piping the base and rings for a large round vacherin

Figure 43. A large round vacherin with a piped dahlia top

These can be made in several shapes, square and round being the most popular. They may be made in the same manner as the individual ones but for added strength the large rings may have a lattice piped in but leaving plenty of space between each row of piping.

Figure 44. A square vacherin with a top decoration of confiture pineapple wedges, glacé cherries and spun chocolate. The sides are masked with cream using a comb scraper and with a base of browned nibbed almonds

The base may be either piped or stencilled, or as an alternative a piece of thin sponge may be used.

Browned flaked or nibbed almonds, desiccated coconut or other coralettes may be used to mask the sides or sprinkled on top. Chocolate as well as glacé fruit may also be used to decorate these goods.

All meringue goods containing fresh cream should be stored at a temperature of approx. 4°C (40°F) until ready for sale.

Hot Meringue

(1) Place the sugar on a sheet of clean paper on a tray. Spread it evenly and place into an oven to warm thoroughly. Ensure that the edges do not crystallize.
(2) Whisk the egg whites and cream of tartar to a snow.
(3) Pour the warmed sugar into the beaten egg whites in a steady stream and continue whisking until a very firm meringue has been made.
(4) Add any colour or flavour required.
(5) Pipe out fancy shapes onto greased and floured baking sheets, silicone or greaseproof paper using a savoy bag fitted with a star tube.
(6) Decorate using coralettes, glacé fruit, nuts, etc., and bake at 132°C (270°F).

Figure 45. Fancy meringue shapes piped from a hot meringue and decorated with chocolate and coralettes

(7) When baked, remove and dry out thoroughly in a warm place.

(8) They may be finished off by dipping parts in chocolate.

Fancy meringues may either be piped large and sold individually, or made very small and sold in bags by weight (meringue biscuits).

Boiled Meringue (Italian)

(1) Place the lump sugar and water into a saucepan (preferably copper) and heat to boiling point. Remove any scum which may appear.

(2) Moisten 4 g ($\frac{1}{8}$ oz) cream of tartar* with about 30 g (1 oz) water and add to the boiling sugar syrup.

(3) Continue boiling to 118°C (245°F) observing the rules of sugar boiling (*see* page 13).

(4) Whilst the sugar syrup is boiling, whisk the egg whites with the remaining cream of tartar until a stable foam has been made. This should coincide with the sugar syrup reaching the required temperature.

(5) The whites should be whisked at slow speed whilst the hot sugar syrup is poured in a steady stream.

(6) When all the syrup has been incorporated, whisk at medium speed until the meringue is quite firm. This will take about 5 minutes.

Note   * As an alternative to cream of tartar 195 g (7 oz) of confectioner's glucose may be added at 107°C (225°F).

JAPANESE BISCUITS AND FANCIES

These are made by adding ground almonds or other ground nuts to a meringue, piping or stencilling into different shapes and baking into biscuits. When cold they are converted into fancies by the addition of various creams and other decorating media (*see* page 236). A wide variety of recipes exists and a selection is given here.

Recipe No. 1

(1) Beat the egg whites and stabilizer to a snow.

(2) Add $\frac{3}{4}$ of the castor sugar and beat into a firm meringue.

(3) Carefully blend in the scone flour.

(4) Fold a quarter of the meringue into the macaroon paste and when clear fold in another quarter.

(5) Finally fold in the remaining meringue, sugar and ground nuts.

(6) The mixture may now be treated in two ways.

Stencilling

Special rubber mats are available for this purpose. The mat is placed onto a well greased lightly floured baking sheet or a sheet of silicone paper and the jap mixture spread over with a palette knife. After removing the surplus, the mat is removed by lifting up from one corner carefully so that the shape of the biscuits is not distorted.

Figure 46. Spreading japanese mixing over a stencil mat to make japanese biscuits

Obviously the stencil can only be used for producing flat biscuits. Special shapes for torten and display pieces may also be stencilled out using specially cut stencils.

Piping

For flat biscuits, transfer the mixture to a savoy bag fitted with a 6 mm (¼ in) tube.

Figure 47. Alternative method of making japanese biscuits by piping the mixture onto silicone paper in the form of a spiral to fill the circle which has been pencilled onto the greaseproof paper underneath.

Mark the floured surface of the baking sheet with a cutter of the size of the biscuit required. With a spiral motion fill in the centre of the marked circle. Alternatively silicone paper may be used instead of greased and floured trays. Rings and bulbs can be piped out using larger tubes.
(7) Bake the biscuits at 182°C (360°F) until light fawn in colour.
(8) When baked, store in an airtight tin for future use. These biscuits are hygroscopic and will soon soften if exposed to the air.

Recipe No. 2
(1) Soften the raw marzipan with heat, and blend in half the sugar and cornflour.
(2) Gradually beat in half the egg whites to form a smooth paste.
(3) Whip the remaining egg whites and sugar to a firm meringue.
(4) Add half of the meringue to the paste and amalgamate thoroughly, but gently.
(5) Fold in the remaining meringue.
(6) Proceed as described in Recipe No. 1.

Recipes 2–6
(1) Beat the egg whites, cream of tartar and half the sugar to a meringue.
(2) Sieve and mix the dry ingredients and the remaining sugar thoroughly together.
(3) Add half the meringue to the dry ingredients and thoroughly amalgamate carefully.
(4) Add this to the rest of the meringue and carefully blend to a clear mixture.
(5) Proceed as described in Recipe No. 1.
Notes
(1) If a stabilizer is not used, great care must be exercised in the mixing of the dry ingredients into the meringue to ensure that it does not break down and become runny.
(2) Gâteaux and torten. Besides small fancies, jap mixtures may be either stencilled or

Japanese

	1				2				3				4				5				6			
	kg	g	lb	oz	kg	g	lb	oz	kg	g	lb	oz	kg	g	lb	oz	kg	g	lb	oz	kg	g	lb	oz
Macaroon paste	1	000	2	4	1	000	2	4	—	—	—	—	—	—	—	—	—	—	—	—	—	—	—	—
Raw marzipan	—	—	—	—	—	—	—	—	—	—	—	—	—	—	—	—	—	—	—	—	—	—	—	—
Ground almonds/hazelnuts	—	250	—	9	—	—	—	—	1	000	2	4	1	000	2	4		see below			—	500	1	2
Jap crumbs	—	—	—	—	—	—	—	—	—	—	—	—		see below			—	—	—	—	1	500	3	6
Desicated coconut	—	—	—	—	—	—	—	—	—	—	—	—	—	—	—	—	—	500	1	2	—	—	—	—
Coconut flour	—	500	1	2	—	610	1	6	—	—	—	—	2	000	4	8	—	500	1	2	—	—	—	—
Castor sugar	—	375	—	13½	—	665	1	8	1	305	2	15	1	250	2	13	2	000	4	8	1	000	2	4
Egg whites/albumen	—	15	—	½	—	—	—	—	1	000	2	4	—	—	—	—	1	250	2	13	1	250	2	13
†Scone flour	—	—	—	—	—	110	—	4	—	195	—	7	—	—	—	—	—	—	—	—	—	—	—	—
Cornflour	—	—	—	—	—	—	—	—	—	—	—	—	—	—	—	—	—	—	—	—	—	—	—	—
Cream of tartar	—	—	—	—	—	—	—	—	—	—	—	—	—	3	—	⅛	—	3	—	⅛	—	3	—	⅛
*Stabilising solution	—	125	—	4½	—	—	—	—	—	—	—	—	—	305	—	11	—	305	—	11	—	—	—	—
Totals	2	265	5	1½	2	385	5	6	3	500	7	14	4	558	10	4⅛	4	558	10	4⅛	4	253	9	9⅛
														up to the following may be added					up to the following may be added				
													—	250	—	9	—	250	—	9				

*5% solution of ethyl methyl cellulose (*see* page 125)
If this is not available the recipe can still be made but more care must be exercised at the mixing stage.

† *Scone flour*

Baking powder 65 g (2¼ oz)   } Sieve together at least 3 times
Medium flour 1 kg (2 lb 4 oz) }

piped out in large rounds either for use as gâteaux tops or as bases for torten (*see* page 181).

(3) Slices may be made from jap mixture spread onto a greaseproof paper or silicone paper lined baking sheet. Allow approx. 1110 g (2½ lb) per full-sized baking sheet (*see* continental slices which follow).

(4) Broken jap biscuits may be used either in further recipes as in numbers 4 and 6, or passed through a sieve and used to make jap fancies. Fine and coarse granules can be made by using sieves of two different size meshes.

Yields from 1 kilo (2¼ lb) of japanese mixture
Slices – 1 full-sized baking sheet (30 × 18 in).
Torten bases – 4 × 20 cm (8 in) or 3 × 25 cm (10 in).
Biscuits – (2 in diameter) – 100 approx. (piped) or 150 approx. (stencilled).

Continental Slices

Yield – 3 full-sized baking sheets (30 × 18 in).

These are made from a japanese mixture to which melted butter and a little flour is added.

	Recipe 1				Recipe 2			
	kg	g	lb	oz	kg	g	lb	oz
Ground almonds/hazelnuts	1	000	2	4	1	695	1	9
Jap crumbs	—		—	—	—	305	—	11
Castor sugar	1	195	2	11	—	805	1	13
Egg whites or albumen solution	1	000	2	4	1	000	2	4
Cream of tartar	—	7	—	¼	—	7	—	¼
Flour	—	195	—	7	—	95	—	3½
Melted butter	—	150	—	5½	—	125	—	4½
Totals	3	547	7	15¾	4	032	6	13¼

(1) Beat the egg whites, cream of tartar and castor sugar to a stiff meringue.
(2) Mix the dry ingredients together and carefully blend into the meringue.
(3) Blend in the melted butter with the minimum amount of handling.
(4) Spread the mixture onto baking sheets lined either with silicone paper or greased greaseproof paper.
(5) Bake at 193°C (380°F) until a light fawn colour. When cold, these sheets are left for 24 hours or more to soften, then cut into strips, sandwiched with a suitable cream and finished off as fancies.

Note The blending of the melted butter into the jap mixture must be done very lightly to prevent the mixture becoming runny and losing its aeration. The finishing of these slices is explained on page 240.

Coconut Macaroon Goods

There are many different types of coconut macaroons made by many different methods.

Recipe No. 1
(1) Beat the egg whites and sugar to produce a firm meringue.
(2) Stir in the coconut.
(3) Deposit onto wafer or silicone paper or greased and floured baking sheets in rocky heaps.

Coconut Macaroon Goods

	Macs (1)				Macs (2)				Macs (3)				Macs (4)				Pyramids				Slices			
	kg	g	lb	oz	kg	g	lb	oz	kg	g	lb	oz	kg	g	lb	oz	kg	g	lb	oz	kg	g	lb	oz
Desiccated coconut	1	000	2	4	—	835	1	14	1	000	2	4	1	000	2	4	1	000	2	4	1	000	2	4
Coconut flour	—	—	—	—	—	165	—	6	—	—	—	—	—	—	—	—	—	—	—	—	—	—	—	—
Castor sugar	1	000	2	4	1	390	3	2	—	140	—	5	2	335	5	4	—	335	—	12	2	000	4	8
Coarse gran. or lump sugar	—	—	—	—	—	—	—	—	—	860	1	15	—	—	—	—	—	280	—	10	—	—	—	—
Water	—	—	—	—	—	—	—	—	—	360	—	13	—	205	—	$7\frac{1}{2}$	—	170	—	$6\frac{1}{4}$	—	—	—	—
Cream of tartar	—	—	—	—	—	—	—	—	—	2	—	$\frac{1}{16}$	—	—	—	—	—	2	—	$\frac{1}{16}$	—	4	—	$\frac{1}{8}$
Egg white	—	415	—	15	—	585	1	5	—	360	—	13	—	835	1	14	—	170	—	$6\frac{1}{4}$	—	835	1	14
Rice cones	—	—	—	—	—	—	—	—	—	—	—	—	—	335	—	12	—	—	—	—	—	250	—	9
Totals	2	415	5	7	2	975	6	11	2	722	6	$2\frac{1}{16}$	4	710	10	$9\frac{1}{2}$	1	957	4	$6\frac{9}{16}$	4	089	9	$3\frac{1}{8}$

(4) Decorate with a cherry and bake at 177°C (350°F).

Recipe No. 2
(1) Place the egg whites, sugar and coconut flour in a bain-marie and whilst stirring heat to 49°C (120°F).
(2) Stir in the desiccated coconut.
(3) Proceed as 3 and 4 above.
  Alternatively, this mixture may be moulded into pyramids and baked.

Recipe No. 3
(1) Place the granulated sugar or lump sugar in a pan with the water and cream of tartar, and bring to the boil.
(2) Observing the rules of sugar boiling (*see* page 13) boil to 115°C (240°F).
(3) Meanwhile beat the egg whites and sugar to a firm snow.
(4) Continue to whip at slow speed while the boiling syrup is poured in a steady stream into the whites. Once all the syrup has been added, whip at medium speed for approx. 4–5 minutes.
(5) Transfer the Italian meringue just made to a bowl and stir in the coconut with a spatula.
(6) Proceed as 3 and 4 of Recipe 1.

Recipe No. 4
(1) Sieve the coconut and rice cones together.
(2) Mix the egg whites, water and castor sugar in a bain-marie and whilst stirring, heat to 52°C (125°F).
(3) Add the dry ingredients to the heated mixture and beat well with a spatula.
(4) Transfer to a savoy bag with 12 mm ($\frac{1}{2}$ in) tube and pipe out biscuits onto wafer, or silicone paper.
(5) Bake at 188°C (370°F).
Note These macaroons should resemble almond macaroon biscuits.

Recipe No. 5–Pyramids
(1) Mix the granulated or lump sugar with the water and heat to boiling point.
(2) Whip the egg whites, castor sugar and cream of tartar to a firm meringue.
(3) Pour the hot syrup into the meringue while continuing to whip at slow speed.
(4) Once all the syrup has been incorporated, whip for a further 4–5 minutes at medium speed.
(5) Finally add the coconut, and mix thoroughly.
(6) Mould into a pyramid shape, and place onto greased and floured baking sheets.
(7) Leave for one or two hours to dry and then bake at 188°C (370°F).

Notes on Recipes 1–5
(1) Further decoration can be made to these macaroons by dipping parts in chocolate when cold.
(2) For recipes 3, 4 and 5, the use of a mixing machine is essential for good results.

Recipe No. 6–Slices
(1) Whip the egg whites and cream of tartar to a firm snow.
(2) Add the remaining ingredients and blend lightly together.
(3) Transfer the mixing to a bain-marie and heat to approx. 43°C (110°F).
(4) Prepare strips of sweet pastry as for almond slices (*see* page 215).
(5) Spread the warm mixture evenly into the centre of the slice.
(6) Bake at 188°C (370°F).
(7) Whilst still warm, cut into fingers approx. $2\frac{1}{2}$ cm (1 in) in width.

9. Sponge Goods

The aeration of best quality sponge goods is achieved by beating the egg into a foam which is constituted by trapping air in the form of small cells. This property of egg is due mainly to the albumen of the egg white which when agitated partially coagulates thus forming a semi-rigid membrane around each air cell. Hence, besides becoming aerated, the egg also becomes stiffer. The sugar of the recipe added to the egg when being beaten helps to stabilize the foam.

In making sponges, the sugar is whisked with the egg to a thick light foam and the flour is carefully blended in to prevent the light structure from breaking down. Special stabilizers are now available which can help in preserving this structure, and their use is invaluable in the industry especially where machinery such as depositors are employed. In some cheap recipes, baking powder is used to assist aeration but in first quality sponge goods, aeration is caused solely by the air trapped by the egg in the beating process.

CHOICE OF INGREDIENTS

Flour

The use of a very soft flour is essential for first quality sponges. If strong flour has to be used it should be diluted with cornflour.

Sugar

A hard-grained castor sugar is recommended for the best aeration.

Egg

Fresh shell egg is reputed to give the best results. For exhibition work it is recommended that the eggs should be cracked open and sieved prior to use. Some people advocate leaving the cracked eggs overnight before use as this helps to strengthen the resulting batter. If not covered with a damp cloth, eggs, and particularly egg yolks, will form a skin.

Cake Colour (Yellow)

Although not essential, a little colour enhances the appearance but it must however be used with discretion.

Glycerine

The use of this is recommended to extend the shelf life of sponge goods.

Stabilizer

This is widely used in the industry to prevent the aerated batter from breaking down when the flour is added, *see* page 2.

Detailed Method of Making Good Quality Sponges

(e.g. Swiss roll recipes 1, 2, 3 and 4. Sandwich recipes 1, 2 and 3)

(1) Sterilize the mixing bowl and whisk in boiling water to remove any trace of fat or oil. The presence of fat will interfere with the whisking of the egg and will prevent a perfect sponge from being made.

(2) Weigh the ingredients.

(3) Mix the egg and sugar and warm to approx. 32°C (90°F) stirring over warm water. (*Not very hot water* as this might cook the egg.) An alternative way to warm the sponge is to place the sugar on a tray and heat it in the oven prior to adding it to the egg.

(4) Whisk the egg and sugar mixture until it reaches the consistency of thick cream. This stage can only be accurately judged by experience. It should be thick enough to leave the marks of the whisk for a few seconds after it is withdrawn. Care should be exercised however to ensure it is not overwhisked if a machine is used.

(5) While the egg and sugar are being whisked, prepare the baking pan or sheet, either with paper (as for Swiss rolls) or with grease and flour (and sugar for some varieties).

(6) Whisk in any colour, flavour, glycerine or water on slow speed.

(7) Blend in the sieved flour by hand. This must be done carefully so as not to break down the very light structure which has been built up by the whisking process. It is best to use the hand with fingers out-stretched, gently lifting the flour through the sponge and turning the bowl.

(8) Deposit the sponge into the prepared baking pan and bake at the correct time according to the variety made.

Method for Making Lower Quality Sponges

Methods for Swiss Roll Recipe 5 and 6.

Methods for Sandwich Recipe 4, 5 and 6.

(1) Make a sponge by beating an equal quantity of sugar with the egg.

(2) Make a batter from the milk beaten with an equal quantity of flour from the recipe together with the rest of the sugar and glycerine.

(3) Sieve the baking powder with the remaining flour.

(4) Add (1) to (2) and blend together by hand.

(5) Add (3) and blend by hand until smooth.

(6) Deposit as previously described.

Plain Sponge Sandwich

Yield 21 at 170 g (6 oz) each in a 15 cm (6 in) tin

On page 118 there are six recipes in order of quality. In the first two recipes up to 280 g (10 oz) of the whole egg may be replaced with egg yolks, and this is recommended especially for sponge drops and fingers.

Figure 48. Sponge sandwich: *Left* top iced with fondant   *Right* top dusted with icing sugar and cut into 6 segments

Sponge Sandwiches

	1				2				3				4				5				6			
	kg	g	lb	oz	kg	g	lb	oz	kg	g	lb	oz	kg	g	lb	oz	kg	g	lb	oz	kg	g	lb	oz
Soft flour	1	000	2	4	1	000	2	4	1	000	2	4	1	000	2	4	1	000	2	4	1	000	2	4
Castor sugar	1	000	2	4	1	000	2	4	1	000	2	4	1	000	2	4	1	000	2	4	1	000	2	4
*Whole eggs	1	460	3	4½	1	250	2	13	1	045	2	5½	—	835	1	14	—	500	1	2	—	400		14½
Milk	—	—	—	—	—	25	—	¾	—	205	—	7½	—	310	—	11¼	—	625	1	6½	—	700	1	9¼
Baking powder	—	—	—	—	—	—	—	—	—	10	—	⅓	—	15	—	½	—	30	—	1⅛	—	50	—	1¾
Glycerine	—	55	—	2	—	70	—	2½	—	70	—	2½	—	70	—	2½	—	85	—	3	—	85	—	3
Totals	3	515	7	14½	3	345	7	8¼	3	330	7	7⁵⁄₆	3	230	7	4¼	3	240	7	4⅝	3	235	7	4½

*Up to 280 g (10 oz)
of whole egg in Recipes 1 & 2
may be replaced with
egg yolks to improve quality.

For a 15 cm (6 in) jam and cream filled sandwich use the following:—

Jam   50 g (1¾ oz)
Fresh cream 140 g (1½ decilitres approx)   5 oz (¼ pint approx)

Varieties

Chocolate : Substitute 200 g (7 oz) flour with cocoa powder.

Almond : Substitute 200 g (7 oz) flour with ground almonds.
  Sieve well into the flour.

Lemon, Orange, Raspberry or Strawberry – Add colour and flavour to taste.

(1) Prepare sponge mixture as previously described.

(2) Give the sandwich pans a coating of fat and dust with flour. Alternatively a cream of fat and flour may be used.

(3) Deposit mixture weighed at 170 g (6 oz) into the sandwich pans and bake in an oven at approx. 204°C (400°F) for 25–30 minutes. (The sponge is done when no marks remain after drawing fingers lightly across the top.)

(4) When baked, turn the sponges out of the pans onto a cooling wire.

(5) When cold, sandwich with jam and, if required, cream.

(6) The top may be either dusted with icing sugar or iced with fondant, water icing or chocolate. Also it may be cut into segments and placed separately onto the cream filling.

Sponge Cakes (Frames or Bricks)

Yield – Allow 30 g (1 oz) of batter for each brick.
  These are suitable for individual cakes or trifles.

Recipe – Same as for Sponge Sandwich.

(1) Coat the sponge frames first with fat, then a dusting of castor sugar followed by a dusting of flour.

(2) Make the sponge mixing as previously described.

(3) Place the sponge mixing in a savoy bag and pipe the mixture to within 1¾ cm (½ in) of the top of each cavity in the sponge frame.

(4) Liberally dust the top with castor sugar.

(5) Bake on the oven sole at 210°C (410°F) for approx. 12 minutes until baked.

(6) Remove from oven and cool on a wire.

Sponge Goods Using Dried Egg

Dried egg is used on a fairly extensive scale for mass-produced sponge goods which are deposited by machine.

Since the aeration is achieved by the use of baking powder, such goods do not suffer from the effect of the machinery involved so that a uniform and consistent product can be produced.

The *all-in* method is used to make the sponge, the dry ingredients being first mixed and then made into the batter by the addition of the water and glycerine.

Sponge Goods Using Dried Egg

	Swiss Roll				Sandwich			
	kg	g	lb	oz	kg	g	lb	oz
Soft flour	1	000	2	4	1	000	2	4
Dried egg	—	450	1	0¼	—	310	—	11¼
Castor sugar	1	095	2	7½	1	000	2	4
Cream powder/Cream of tartar	—	60	—	2	—	30	—	1
Bicarbonate of soda	—	30	—	1	—	15	—	½
Cold water	1	305	2	15	—	750	1	11
Glycerine	—	—	—	—	—	35	—	1¼
Totals	3	940	8	13¾	3	140	7	1

Swiss Rolls

	1				2				3				4				5				6			
	kg	g	lb	oz	kg	g	lb	oz	kg	g	lb	oz	kg	g	lb	oz	kg	g	lb	oz	kg	g	lb	oz
Soft flour	1	000	2	4	1	000	2	4	1	000	2	4	1	000	2	4	1	000	2	4	1	000	2	4
Castor sugar	1	110	2	8½	1	000	2	4	1	000	2	4	1	000	2	4	1	000	2	4	—	860	1	15
Whole eggs	2	250	5	1	2	100	4	11½	1	950	4	6¼	1	595	3	9½	—	835	1	14	—	665	1	8
Milk	—	—	—	—	—	—	—	—	—	—	—	—	—	—	—	—	—	415	—	15	—	665	1	8
Baking powder	—	—	—	—	—	—	—	—	—	—	—	—	—	—	—	—	—	30	—	1⅛	—	55	—	2
Glycerine	—	—	—	—	—	50	—	1¾	—	70	—	2½	—	85	—	3	—	85	—	3	—	85	—	3
Hot water	—	30	—	1	—	—	—	—	—	—	—	—	—	—	—	—	—	—	—	—	—	—	—	—
Totals	4	390	9	14½	4	150	9	5¼	4	020	19	0¾	3	680	8	4½	3	365	7	9⅛	3	330	7	8

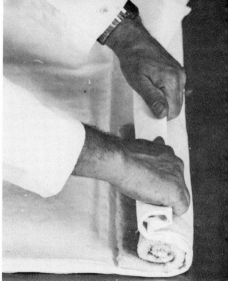

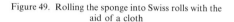
Figure 49. Rolling the sponge into Swiss rolls with the aid of a cloth

Swiss Rolls

Yield – A full sized baking sheet (30 × 18 in) should take approx. 1110 g (2½ lb) of sponge batter for a roll of normal size. For miniature rolls and sheets for cutting up into fancies (*see* chapter 17) only 890 g (2lb) or even less, 780 g (1¾ lb), will be required.

Varieties

Chocolate and almond	Same as for sponge sandwiches.
Lemon, Orange Raspberry or Strawberry	} Add colour and flavour to taste.
Sultana	Sprinkle clean and washed sultanas just prior to baking.
Cherry	Sprinkle chopped glacé cherries prior to baking.

(1) Line the baking sheets with greaseproof paper.
(2) Make the sponge as previously described.
(3) Deposit approx. 1110 g (2½ lb) of the sponge onto each baking sheet and spread level. This can be done with a special spreader or using a trowel palette knife shaped so that the handle can project over the edge of the tin.
(4) Bake in a hot oven at 238°C (460°F) for approx. 4 minutes.
(5) When baked remove from the oven and turn upside down onto a clean cloth. It is best placed onto several layers of cloth or absorbent paper if possible. If the roll is properly made and baked it should not stick to the cloth. However, the cloth can first be dusted with castor sugar if desired.
(6) Leave with the baking tin on top. The steam should now be trapped in the layers of cloth or paper and eventually moisten the roll.
(7) When absolutely cold, remove the tray and the greaseproof paper.
(8) Spread on a layer of jam, curd or cream and roll up with the aid of the cloth.
(9) Cut either into slices or in lengths of approx. 15 cm (6 in).

INDIVIDUAL SWISS ROLLS

Yield – 180
(1) Proceed as for ordinary Swiss rolls but with less sponge deposited on the tray (*see* above).
(2) After baking, and when cold, spread with jam, curd or cream.
(3) Cut into approx. 75 cm (3 in) squares.
(4) Roll up each square into a small Swiss roll.
(5) These can be dusted with icing sugar or covered in chocolate.

Varieties

Besides the addition to the recipe of flavouring substances and sprinkling sultanas or glacé cherries on top of the roll prior to baking, the fillings can also be varied using:
Jams – apricot, raspberry, pineapple.
Curds – lemon, orange, pineapple.

Creams – raspberry, strawberry, lemon, orange, pineapple, vanilla, chocolate, coffee, almond, hazelnut, praline.

With the cream could also be used the following:

Pineapple crush, ginger crush, chopped glacé cherries, chopped tinned oranges.

The actual roll may also be decorated as follows:

(1) Cover the roll first in a layer of boiling purée and then ice with a covering of warmed, appropriately flavoured and coloured fondant. Decorate using cherries, angelica, etc.

(2) Cover the roll first with boiling apricot purée. Roll out a sheet of either almond, coconut or sugar paste, trim to size and cover the roll. The paste may be textured with a roller prior to covering. Decorate if desired.

(3) Cover the roll in buttercream and mask with desiccated coconut or nibbed almonds either plain or roasted.

(4) *Chocolate Log*   Make a chocolate roll, using a buttercream filling (*see* recipe 174). After cutting into the required length, the roll may be finished in three ways.

Method A

(1) Mask each end with a white buttercream or filling cream, and into this pipe a spiral or circles of chocolate cream to simulate the end grain.

(2) Using a savoy bag fitted with a star tube, pipe lines of the chocolate cream lengthwise, completely covering the surface.

Method B

(1) Cover the roll with boiling apricot jam and chocolate coloured paste. Mark with a fork.

(2) For the ends, roll out a piece of paste into a long strip. Cover with chocolate, and when set, roll up like a Swiss roll. Cut thin slices off this and roll out to cover the ends to which they are attached, using purée.

Method C

(1) Cover with chocolate or butter/filling cream, and mark with a comb scraper.

(2) Mask each end with either the cream (Method A) or paste (Method B).

A side branch is often simulated by attaching a piece of roll cut on the cross before finishing with the cream or chocolate.

Usually a paper inscribed with the words *Season's Greetings* is attached, the whole roll being mounted on special log boards for ease of handling. Both buttercream and chocolate has been used for decorating the logs illustrated in Figure 50. The ends are finished with the paste as described under method B(2).

Note   Varieties 1, 2 and 3 together with a suitable centre, may be cut up into slices and used as fancies.

The Swiss roll mixture is also used for cream-filled fancies and these are described on page 249.

Figure 50. Christmas logs finished in two different ways

Sponge Curls

(1) Using a savoy bag with a plain tube, pipe a Swiss roll mixture onto greaseproof or silicone paper in the form of a spiral so that a flat disc approx. 10 cm (4 in) in diameter is formed.
(2) Bake at 238°C (460°F) for approx. 3 minutes and remove from the paper when cold.
(3) Fold the sponge over and fill with fresh or a suitable filling cream, and fruit if desired.
(4) Dust with icing sugar.

Butter Sponge (Light Genoese)

This is a good quality sponge into which melted butter up to $\frac{1}{2}$ the weight of the flour may be added and carefully incorporated. Any of the first three sandwich recipes on page 118 may be adapted for this but on page 139 will be found some special recipes.

The general method for mixing is as follows:
(1) Make the sponge as previously described.
(2) Blend the flour carefully into the batter. When almost mixed add the melted butter and finish mixing. [The temperature of the butter should not be below 49°C (120°F)].
(3) Deposit into greased and floured pans and bake as for sandwiches.

Note These are difficult to make successfully because the butter tends to break down the structure of the sponge. For success, keep the sponge warm so that the butter does not set before the mixture is deposited into the tin. Butter sponge or light genoese is used for high quality confectionery and can only be made successfully if the flour and butter are incorporated by hand. It is not suitable therefore for large scale production involving the use of mechanical machinery. Successful imitations however can be made by substituting the butter with nut oil for large scale production.

Sponge Drops and Fingers

Yield – This will depend upon the size but using a 12 mm ($\frac{1}{2}$ in) tube 320–340 single drops or fingers can be produced.

For these a good quality sponge sandwich recipe should be used (recipes 1 and 2 on page 118).

The use of egg yolk makes a considerable improvement and it is recommended that 280 g (10 oz) of the whole egg in these two recipes is replaced by egg yolks. This will give stability which is a great asset for this type of goods.

(1) Prepare a baking tray with a sheet of greaseproof paper.
(2) Make the sponge mixing and place some in a clean savoy bag fitted with a 12 mm ($\frac{1}{2}$ in) plain tube.
(3) Pipe either fingers or drops of uniform size onto greaseproof paper on a clean table top. Use separate sheets for the drops and fingers.

Figure 51. Piping sponge fingers onto silicone paper. Notice that the paper on which they are piped is marked with parallel lines to assist in achieving a uniform size.

(4) After the whole tray has been piped, cover liberally with castor sugar.
(5) Remove excess sugar by picking up the greaseproof sheet on which they have just been piped, holding it vertically, then placing it onto a baking tray.
(6) Bake immediately in an oven at 232°C (450°F) for approx. 4 minutes. The colour should be a light brown all over.

The addition of a stabilizer is also a great asset for this type of goods, since it prevents the sponge from breaking down as it stands before being piped out.

VARIETIES MADE FROM SPONGE DROPS AND FINGERS

(1) Sandwich with cream (butter-filling or fresh), or cream and jam, and place in paper cases.
(2) Dip each end of the fingers and half of the drop into chocolate before sandwiching.
(3) After sandwiching with jam, dip into boiling purée, brush off surplus and roll into desiccated coconut either roasted or plain. Apricot or raspberry may be used but the latter should have an addition of red colour.
(4) Place upside down in paper cases. Pipe on a whirl of fresh cream and decorate with fruit, i.e. segment of pineapple or oranges, etc.
(5) Small sponge fingers may be used also to mask the outside of a gâteau or torte.
(6) An attractive method of presenting sponge fingers for sale is to tie 4 or 6 together with silk ribbon. In high-class establishments customers are usually quite prepared to pay for this extra embellishment.

Madeleines

For these, special dariole moulds are required.
(1) Liberally grease the dariole moulds.
(2) Make up a sandwich sponge mixing and $\frac{2}{3}$ fill the mould using a savoy bag.
(3) Bake at 210°C (410°F) for approx. 12 minutes.
(4) When cold turn out of the moulds.
(5) Finish off by dipping into boiling jam or purée, brushing off surplus and rolling the sides in desiccated coconut either plain or toasted. The top may be decorated with a cherry.

Sponge Flans

These are made from any of the sponge sandwich recipes on page 118, the batter being deposited in special greased and floured sponge moulds which have a raised outside edge.

When baked these flans may be filled with various fruits and cream in the same way as for the short pastry flans.

Victoria Sponge

Yield – 16 at 220 g (8 oz) approx.

	kg	g	lb	oz
Soft flour	1	000	2	4
Baking powder	—	30	—	1
Butter	—	835	1	14
Castor sugar	—	835	1	14
Whole egg	—	835	1	14
Glycerine	—	45	—	$1\frac{1}{2}$
Totals	3	580	8	$0\frac{1}{2}$

(1) Make on the sugar batter method of cake making – (*see* page 128).
(2) Deposit approx. 220 g (8 oz) into well greased sandwich tins or small pans.
(3) Bake at 182°C (360°F) for approx. 25 minutes.
(4) Remove from the tins immediately they are baked and finish off as desired.

Note Any Madeira cake recipe (*see* page 134) deposited and baked in sandwich pans may be called a Victoria sandwich.

The above recipe may be flavoured in the same way as for sponges using the same quantity of agents mentioned on page 119.

Ginger Sandwich

Add to the above recipe – 20 g (¾ oz) ground ginger and 7 g (¼ oz) ground spice, sandwich with ginger marmalade.

Othellos

Continental in origin, these light sponge goods are decorated as fancies after being sandwiched with an appropriate cream and iced in fondant. On the Continent they are usually made by whisking the egg whites and yolks separately with the sugar. Without the aid of a stabilizer, they are difficult to make because, being so light, there is a risk of the mixture breaking down when the flour is incorporated, unless extreme care is exercised. The use of a stabilizer not only helps to overcome this difficulty but also eliminates the necessity of whisking the whites and yolks separately with the sugar.

The following recipe will give consistently good results. A stabilizer will also enable a strong flour to be used without adverse results.

	kg	g	lb	oz
Egg whites	1	000	2	4
*Stabilizing solution	—	125	—	4½
Castor sugar	—	535	1	3¼
Egg yolks	—	475	1	1
Soft white flour	—	665	1	8
Totals	2	800	6	4¾

Yield – 240 halves – 120 fancies.

* *Stabilizing solution.* Use a proprietary brand or a 5% solution of ethyl methyl cellulose (edifas).

5% solution = 1 oz stabilizer to 1 pint water.

This is brought into solution by first adding half the water boiling or very hot and adding the remainder cold. It should be allowed to stand until a gel forms before being used.

Method
(1) Place the egg whites, stabilizer and sugar into a clean bowl and whisk by machine to a stiff meringue.
(2) Using the whisk, stir in the yolks lightly until they are completely amalgamated.
(3) Carefully fold in the sieved flour, taking care not to overmix.
(4) Transfer the mixing to a savoy bag fitted with a 12 mm (½ in) tube.
(5) Pipe the mixing into bulbs approx. 5 cm (2 in) diameter onto a silicone papered or a greased and floured baking sheet.
(6) Bake in an oven at 204°C (400°F) for 7–8 minutes.

Figure 52. Desdemonas

(7) When cold, remove from the baking sheet, turn over and using a knife, scoop and remove some of the sponge from the centre.
(8) Sandwich with the appropriate cream (see below) and remove the peak so that they will stand correctly.
(9) Brush over or dip into boiling apricot purée and coat with the appropriately flavoured and coloured fondant.
(10) Place into paper cases and finish by piping a spiral of fondant, adding a piece of crystallized flower petal, cherry or nut for decoration. For Othellos a silver dragee could be added.

Traditionally Othellos are reserved for the chocolate coated variety which are sandwiched with a chocolate custard cream. Other varieties with their classical names are as follows:

Desdemonas

Othello bases sandwiched with vanilla-flavoured whipping dairy cream and finished with white fondant with kirsch.

Jagos

Same as Othellos except that coffee flavour is used.

Rosalinds

Same as Desdemonas except that a rose flavoured cream and fondant are used.

Note   On the Continent special Othello trays are available which are made with raised bumps over which the mixing is piped before being baked. Thus the hollows are baked into the bulbs which eliminates the necessity of removing the centres with a knife afterwards.

The Othello base is really a shell to enclose the filling and to form a surface which is coated with a sweet icing. It is therefore low in sugar to balance the overall sweetness.

FAULTS IN SPONGE CAKES

FAULTS \ CAUSES	Presence of grease or silicone in mixing bowl.	Breaking down batter when mixing in flour/fat, etc.	Use of too strong a flour.	Oven too cool.	Oven too hot.	Overbeating.	Underbeating.	Not spreading level.	Left too long in oven.	Too much egg/water.	Too much flour.	Too much sugar.	Underbaking.	Tin insufficiently greased.	Left too long before baking.
Poor volume.	✓	✓	✓	✓	✓	✓	✓			✓	✓				
Uneven shape.	✓	✓	✓		✓			✓			✓				
Pale crust colour.			✓										✓		
High crust colour.					✓				✓			✓			
Brown spots on surface.					✓				✓			✓			
Close texture.	✓	✓	✓				✓			✓	✓				
Open texture.				✓		✓						✓			
Tough texture.	✓	✓	✓				✓			✓	✓				
Thick crust.	✓	✓	✓	✓			✓		✓		✓				
Sticking to tin.														✓	
Dry texture.	✓	✓	✓	✓			✓		✓		✓				
Seams in texture.	✓	✓	✓							✓	✓	✓	✓		
Sunken top.						✓				✓		✓	✓		
Cracks on sponge drops.	✓	✓	✓			✓				✓	✓				✓
Peaked top.	✓	✓	✓		✓		✓	✓			✓				
Swiss rolls cracking.				✓					✓		✓				✓

10. Plain Cakes

Introduction

If the section of chapter 1 (page 5) is read, it must become patently obvious that thousands of different recipes are possible by altering the balance of the basic cake ingredients and varying the optional additions of fruit, nuts, etc. Further varieties are possible by altering the shape and dressings that may be put on before baking.

In selecting the recipes for this chapter, every attempt has been made to present ones which not only vary in quality but also differ in other respects such as the use of different materials.

It must always be remembered that balance does not only depend upon the ratio of the individual ingredients in the recipe, but their function also. The choice of flour, for example, is vital in this respect. A recipe which will make a perfect cake with one type of flour can give poor results with another.

For good consistent results the reader is advised to read the section which precedes the recipes before commencing to make any particular cake.

CAKE-MAKING METHODS

A batter temperature of approx. 21°C (70°F) is recommended for cakes, and therefore materials should be brought to this temperature prior to mixing.

Sugar Batter

(1) Beat the fat, margarine and/or butter to a light foam with the sugar. The time of beating will depend upon the creaming properties of the fat chosen. For a high-grade shortening this will be approx. 4 minutes, but for butter it will be at least three times as long. Colour and flavours should be added at this stage.
(2) Add the egg and beat well into the fat and sugar cream. If a machine is used this can be added in a steady stream over a period of about 2 minutes. If mixing by hand, it should be added in approx. four portions beating each well in.
(3) The flour (see note) is now added and carefully mixed into the batter. The aim should be to get a clear smooth batter without any lumps and yet not toughened.
(4) Lastly, add the liquid, e.g. milk, and any fruit or nuts and carefully blend into the batter to ensure even distribution.
Note Sometimes the batter curdles during the last stages of mixing in the egg. This may be due to a number of reasons. (a) Batter temperature is too high or too low – aim for 21°C (70°F). (b) Fat has poor emulsification properties. (c) Egg is added too quickly and not thoroughly beaten in. This trouble can be eliminated by beating in a small proportion of the flour from the recipe.

Flour Batter

(1) Whisk the sugar and the egg to a half sponge.
(2) Cream the fat, margarine and/or butter with an equal quantity of flour.
(3) Add (1) to (2) in approx. 4 portions, beating each portion of the sponge well into the fat/flour cream.
(4) Blend the rest of the flour (sieved with any remaining dry material, e.g. baking powder) into the batter and mix until smooth and free from lumps.
(5) Lastly add the liquid, e.g. milk, and any fruit or nuts and carefully blend into the batter to ensure even distribution.

Note It is very important that the sponge is at the same temperature as the fat and flour cream in order to achieve perfect amalgamation.

Blending

This method is used for the production of high-ratio cakes (high sugar and liquid) which are made using a special cake flour and fat.
(1) Sieve the flour with the rest of the dry ingredients, e.g. baking powder.
(2) Add to the fat and mix to a crumbly consistency (similar to ground almonds). Care must be exercised not to turn it into a paste.
(3) The liquid (eggs, milk or water) is now carefully blended in and mixed to a smooth batter. If there is water in the recipe, add this to bring the mixture to a batter before blending in the egg. The finished batter must be smooth and free from lumps.
Note Dry ingredients such as baking powder, ground almonds, cocoa powder, etc., are always first sieved with the flour.

Machine Mixing

(1) For all beating operations, use medium speed.
(2) For all blending operations, use bottom speed.
(3) Ensure that between each operation the bowl is scraped free of any adhering batter.
(4) To ensure that no toughening action is given, the flour may be blended in by hand. If the flour is mixed into the batter by machine, it should still have a final stir with the hands to ensure freedom from lumps and even distribution of fruit, etc.

CHOICE OF MATERIALS

(Refer also to the notes on Materials, pages 7–9)

Flour

Soft flour is required for cakes rich in fat, sugar and egg in which aeration is achieved by beating.

For cheap cakes which rely on baking powder for their aeration, a medium flour should be used. This flour may also be used in rich fruit cakes where its strength is available to help keep the heavy fruit from sinking.

Blends of flour can be made to suit any recipe. Strong flour may be brought to a blend soft enough to be used for rich cakes by adding cornflour. A medium blend can be made by mixing a soft with a strong breadmaking flour.

Specially milled cake flours are also available for use with high sugar and liquid (high-ratio) cakes (*see* page 6).

Fats

For best quality cakes a good cake margarine or butter should be used. However, although butter gives a superior flavour it has poor creaming properties, and if used on its own, aeration and hence the volume of the cake could suffer. To minimize this defect it is recommended that up to 50% of the butter should be replaced with a good shortening.

Normal lard need never be used because of its lack of creaming power, however specially prepared lards are now available which do not have this defect.

The use of shortening is usually reserved for cheaper cakes where it may be blended with margarine.

For high-ratio cakes we use a special 100% shortening which has been manufactured exclusively for this type of cake.

It is important that fats for cakemaking should be brought to the correct plastic condition before beating into a batter. Solid fats may first need to be warmed to bring them to this condition.

If margarine or butter is being substituted for shortening, or vice versa, the water content of the former must be taken into consideration in the balance of the recipe in which it is used.

Sugar

For rich cakes in which the sugar is beaten with fat, castor sugar should be employed.

The cheaper granulated sugar may be used for cheap cakes if it can be dissolved adequately in the liquid of the recipe.

The brown raw sugars are used in some rich cakes where they contribute flavour as well as colour. This type of sugar sometimes forms hard lumps which if added to a batter is difficult to disperse. The only way to eliminate such trouble is to pass the sugar through a sieve of an appropriate mesh.

Honey and Invert Sugar

Some cakes may have honey or invert sugar in the recipe. Since this caramelizes at a lower temperature than cane sugar, a slightly lower baking temperature is recommended. Because these agents are hygroscopic their use helps to keep the crumb moist.

Syrup

This too helps to keep the crumb of cake moist by its hygroscopic nature. Its use is more confined to ginger cakes.

Egg

Fresh or frozen egg will give the best results for the production of rich cakes.

Since there is some loss of aeration the use of liquid egg and dried egg is usually reserved for cheaper quality cakes where the aeration is assisted with the use of baking powder.

If eggs and particularly egg yolks are left a while before use, they should be covered either by putting them in a sealed container or covered with a damp cloth to prevent skinning.

For exhibition cakes, the eggs should be strained through muslin to eliminate any skin, etc., that might be present and so mar the texture.

Milk

Except for special occasions it is usual to use reconstituted milk from skimmed milk powder and this is quite satisfactory.

Fruit

The type of fruit used will be dictated by the recipe, but it should receive preliminary treatment prior to its use in a cake batter *see Bakery: Bread & Fermented Goods.*

Large fruit such as cherries or glacé pineapple may have to be cut into small dice before they can be successfully held up in a batter. Failure to do this could result in the fruit sinking.

Colour

Any colour should be added to the initial stage of cakemaking to ensure that it becomes adequately dispersed. The standard strength colour should always be used and accurately measured. For small quantities a dropping tube or pipette is a useful aid.

Caramel

For rich celebration cakes caramel (blackjack) is usually added to impart a rich dark colour to the crumb. If this is thick it must firstly be warmed and then added to the fat and flour or fat and sugar cream.

Flavour

This too may be added in the initial stages of mixing. In rich fruit cakes it may also be added with the fruit into which the flavour is thoroughly mixed.

If spirits are used, i.e. rum, brandy, etc., as in rich bridal cakes, it is added to the cake *after* it is baked, *see* page 155.

Glycerine

The use of glycerine in cakes is recommended to help keep the crumb soft and prolong their shelf life. The glycerine achieves this by attracting moisture from the atmosphere.

Raw Marzipan

Besides flavour, raw marzipan is often incorporated into a cake batter to help keep the crumb of the cake moist.

Choice of Method

The sugar batter method is recommended for fruit cakes which can usually benefit from the little toughening to which the batter is subjected in the final stages of mixing. This helps to strengthen the cake structure and so assist in supporting the fruit.

The flour batter method is recommended for plain rich cakes. It gives a superior crumb and texture and also greater volume than any other method. Because most of the flour is incorporated into the fat before the liquid is added, it can be more thoroughly mixed without the problem of toughening.

The blending method is usually reserved for high-ratio cakes (high sugar and liquid).

Special methods have been designed for use with continuous cake-making processes using materials tailored to suit this process, e.g. pumpable shortenings, details of which are not covered in this book.

Preparation of Cake Hoops

Cakes baked in hoops need the added protection of paper against the heat of the oven. A baking sheet is first covered in several thicknesses of paper. Then there are three methods of preparation:

(1) Cover the paper with a sheet of greaseproof paper and onto this place the cake hoops. Line the inside of the hoops with a strip of protective paper followed by a band of greaseproof or specially prepared paper liners. When the cake has been baked, a skewer or sharp pointed rod is run round the hoop to score the greaseproof paper before removing the hoops. In this way the cakes are removed with that portion of the greaseproof paper in contact with the cake. The main disadvantages of this method is that there is a danger of the batter escaping from under the hoop, particularly if the batter is soft and the baking sheet buckled. Unless trimmed with a pair of scissors, the cake also suffers from a poor appearance.

(2) Proceed as for (1) but without the greaseproof paper base. After banding, insert a disc of greaseproof or specially prepared paper. This may be cut as shown in figure 53 so that it fits snugly in the hoop and prevents any batter from seeping out.

(3) After preparing the baking sheet with paper, the hoops are placed on top, and special paper cases inserted. This eliminates the use of bands. This method is therefore widely used where a large volume of cakes is being made.

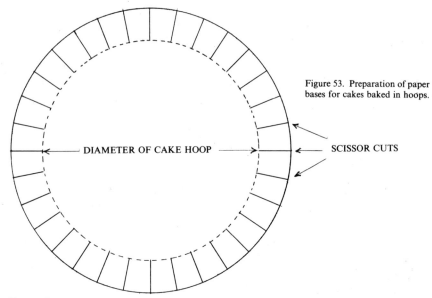

Figure 53. Preparation of paper bases for cakes baked in hoops.

DIAMETER OF CAKE HOOP

SCISSOR CUTS

Drumming

When large rich cakes containing a high proportion of fruit are baked, the outside bottom edge is often burnt. This can be prevented by the technique known as *drumming*. This is done by using a piece of greaseproof paper considerably larger than the cake hoops. The hoop is placed in the centre and the excess paper is twisted up to the rolled edge of the hoop in such a way that it forms a protective roll of paper against the lower edge where it is held so that no batter can possibly leak out, i.e. a drum has been made.

This technique is also useful for torten bases made from a sponge to prevent the mixture seeping out from the space between the torten ring and the baking sheet.

Protection of Slab Cakes

Cakes baked in large frames or tins also require the protection from heat given by paper. These are treated in the same way as the hoops except that the final lining paper has to be cut in the way shown in Figure 54.

When this is inserted into the frame, the ends of the long sides are wrapped round the ends of the short sides to effect a seal and so prevent the mixture leaking out.

Figure 54. Cutting a liner for a slab frame

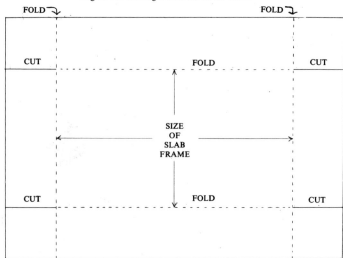

FOLD   FOLD

CUT   FOLD   CUT

SIZE
OF
SLAB
FRAME

CUT   FOLD   CUT

Size and Weight

The following calculations apply to Madeira and lightly fruited cakes. For heavily fruited cakes either the weights need to be increased or the hoop size reduced to achieve a cake of the same height. These calculations do not apply to wedding cakes which will be dealt with in Chapter 12.

Unlike wedding cakes which are made to a size, these cakes are made to a weight, and the size of hoops given are only a guide and can be altered to suit individual preferences, e.g. a thinner cake in a larger hoop may be preferred.

Approx. weight of cake	Approx. weight of batter	Size of Hoops	Approx. Baking Temperature
400 g (14 oz)	450 g (1 lb)	11½ cm (4½ in)	193–190°C (380–375°F)
450 g (1 lb)	510 g (1 lb 2 oz)	13 cm (5 in)	190–188°C (375–370°F)
680 g (1 lb 8 oz)	765 g (1 lb 11 oz)	15 cm (6 in)	188–185°C (370–365°F)
910 g (2 lb)	1020 g (2 lb 4 oz)	18 cm (7 in)	185–182°C (365–360°F)
1360 g (3 lb)	1530 g (3 lb 6 oz)	20 cm (8 in)	182–180°C (360–355°F)
1815 g (4 lb)	2040 g (4 lb 8 oz)	23 cm (9 in)	180–177°C (355–350°F)

Notes
(1) The above weights allow for a maximum baking loss of $12\frac{1}{2}\%$. This may be higher than required, particularly if the cakes are baked in a good humid atmosphere.
(2) The baking temperatures given are for rich Madeira cakes. This should be higher for leaner recipes.

Baking of Cakes

See notes on page 10.

MADEIRA

(*See* choice of materials, page 129).

Recipes 1,2 and 3 These may be made by either the sugar batter or the flour batter method of cake-making, the use of the latter giving a marginally better texture (*see* page 128).

Recipes 4 and 5 These are commercial recipes with a higher liquid ratio employing special high-ratio cake flour and require to be made by the blending method (*see* page 129).

(1) Make by one of the methods previously recommended.
(2) Scale at the appropriate weight in relation to the size required.
(3) Bake at the appropriate temperature in a humid atmosphere.

Note Madeira cakes may be decorated with a slice of citron peel prior to being placed into the oven.

PLAIN HIGH SUGAR AND LIQUID CAKES AND SLABS

It is recommended that the reader should peruse the notes on cake-making and recipe balance on pages 5–7 and choice of materials, page 129.

Because these cakes are aerated by baking powder it is not necessary to make the batter by the conventional manner. High sugar and liquid cakes (High Ratio) are made as on the *blending method—see* page 129.

Once the batter is made, deposit into hoops or slabs and bake as follows:

Angel Cake	171°C (340°F)
Other Recipes	
Cakes	182°C (360°F)
Slabs	177°C (350°F)

Madeira Cakes

	1				2				3				4				5			
	1st Quality				2nd Quality				3rd Quality				1st Quality				2nd Quality			
	kg	g	lb	oz	kg	g	lb	oz	kg	g	lb	oz	kg	g	lb	oz	kg	g	lb	oz
Soft flour	1	000	2	4	1	000	2	4	1	000	2	4	1	000	2	4	1	000	2	4
Special HR cake flour	—	—	—	—	—	—	—	—	—	—	—	—	—	20	—	$\frac{3}{4}$	—	30	—	1
Baking powder	—	5	—	$\frac{1}{5}$	—	7	—	$\frac{1}{4}$	—	25	—	$\frac{7}{8}$	—	—	—	—	—	—	—	—
Butter	—	610	1	6	—	470	1	1	—	—	—	—	—	390	—	14	—	530	1	3
Cake margarine	—	—	—	—	—	—	—	—	—	305	—	11	—	280	—	10	—	—	—	—
Shortening	—	195	—	7	—	235	—	$8\frac{1}{2}$	—	195	—	7	—	—	—	—	—	—	—	—
Castor sugar	—	805	1	13	—	710	1	$9\frac{1}{2}$	—	585	1	5	—	750	1	11	—	835	1	14
Eggs	1	000	2	4	—	890	2	0	—	500	1	2	—	680	1	$8\frac{1}{2}$	—	530	1	3
Milk	—	—	—	—	—	—	—	—	—	280	—	10	—	165	—	6	—	470	1	1
Salt	—	45	—	$1\frac{1}{2}$	—	55	—	2	—	—	—	—	—	3	—	$\frac{1}{8}$	—	7	—	$\frac{1}{4}$
Glycerine	—	—	—	—	—	—	—	—	—	—	—	—	—	—	—	—	—	—	—	—
Totals	3	660	8	$3\frac{7}{10}$	3	367	7	$9\frac{1}{4}$	2	890	6	$7\frac{7}{8}$	3	288	7	$6\frac{3}{8}$	3	402	7	$10\frac{1}{4}$

Yields   The best way of calculating the weight of this type of slab batter to any given size of tin or frame, is to use the following formula:
1 kg (2¼ lb) batter should be deposited in every 300 sq cm (48 sq in) of slab 3 in deep.
For example:
   If we require a slab of angel cake 25 cm × 20 cm × 8 cm (10 in × 8 in × 3 in) what weight of batter will be required?

$$Answer: \quad 25 \times 20 \text{ cm} = 500 \text{ sq cm (80 sq in)}$$

300 sq cm (48 sq in) require 1 kg (2¼ lb) batter.
500 sq cm (80 sq in) require –

Metric	*Imperial*
$\dfrac{1000}{300} \times \dfrac{500}{1}$	$\dfrac{36 \text{ (oz)}}{48} \times \dfrac{80}{1}$
= 1666.6 gm	= 60 oz (3 lb 12 oz)

Angel Cake

   Because this cake is not coloured by the traditional materials of margarine and egg, it is a very suitable base to receive colour, and may be so used for making Battenburg and Neapolitan layer cakes.
Suggested colour and flavour additions to the recipe as shown.

White	Vanilla flavour.
Yellow	Vanilla or lemon flavour and approx. 20 g (⅔ oz) yellow colour.
Pink	15 g (½ oz) raspberry colour/flavour and approx. 7 g (¾ oz) pink colour.
Orange	55 g (2 oz) orange combienne
Chocolate	40 g (1½ oz) chocolate combienne

Madeira Slab Cake – Standard Recipe

	1st Quality				2nd Quality			
	kg	*g*	*lb*	*oz*	*kg*	*g*	*lb*	*oz*
Soft flour	1	000	2	4	1	000	2	4
Baking powder	—	10	—	⅓	—	15	—	½
Butter	—	500	1	2	—	—	—	—
Cake margarine	—	—	—	—	—	305	—	11
Shortening	—	165	—	6	—	195	—	7
Castor sugar	—	665	1	8	—	595	1	5½
Eggs	—	835	1	14	—	500	1	2
Glycerine	—	40	—	1½	—	40	—	1½
Milk	—	—	—	—	—	250	—	9
Totals	3	215	7	3⅚	2	900	6	8½

(1) These may be made by either the sugar batter or the flour batter method, but the latter will give a better texture, *see* page 128.
(2) Deposit into tins or frames and bake at 182°C (360°F) in a humid oven for approx. 2¾–3 hours depending upon thickness.

High Sugar/Liquid Cakes and Slabs

	Madeira (1)				Madeira (2)				Madeira (3)				Madeira (4)				Angel				Chocolate			
	kg	*g*	*lb*	*oz*	*kg*	*g*	*lb*	*oz*	*kg*	*g*	*lb*	*oz*	*kg*	*g*	*lb*	*oz*	*kg*	*g*	*lb*	*oz*	*kg*	*g*	*lb*	*oz*
*Special cake flour	1	000	2	4	1	000	2	4	1	000	2	4	1	000	2	4	1	000	2	4	—	765	1	11½
Baking powder	—	20	—	⅔	—	15	—	½	—	25	—	¾	—	40	—	1⅓	—	30	—	1	—	30	—	1
Cream of tartar	—	—	—	—	—	—	—	—	—	—	—	—	—	—	—	—	—	15	—	½	—	—	—	—
Bicarbonate of soda	—	—	—	—	—	—	—	—	—	—	—	—	—	—	—	—	—	—	—	—	—	7	—	¼
Butter/margarine	—	375	—	13½	—	195	—	7	—	675	1	8½	—	—	—	—	—	—	—	—	—	—	—	—
Shortening	—	375	—	13½	—	195	—	7	—	—	—	—	—	—	—	—	—	—	—	—	—	—	—	—
*Special HR shortening	—	—	—	—	—	—	—	—	—	—	—	—	—	650	1	7½	—	640	1	7	—	570	1	4½
Castor sugar	1	000	2	4	1	000	2	4	—	750	1	11	1	250	2	13	1	225	2	12	1	235	2	12½
Milk powder	—	30	—	1	—	30	—	1	—	—	—	—	—	—	—	—	—	90	—	3½	—	140	—	5
Egg	—	750	1	11	—	500	1	2	—	695	1	9	—	595	1	5½	—	—	—	—	—	765	1	11½
†Egg whites	—	—	—	—	—	—	—	—	—	—	—	—	—	—	—	—	—	720	1	10	—	—	—	—
Milk	—	280	—	10	—	500	1	2	—	150	—	5½	—	150	—	5½	—	—	—	—	—	—	—	—
Cocoa powder	—	—	—	—	—	—	—	—	—	—	—	—	—	—	—	—	—	—	—	—	—	235	—	8½
Salt	—	15	—	½	—	15	—	½	—	7	—	¼	—	20	—	¾	—	15	—	½	—	15	—	½
Water	—	—	—	—	—	—	—	—	—	—	—	—	—	720	1	10	—	485	1	1½	—	945	2	2
Colour & flavour		as req.				as req.				as req.				as req.				as req.			—	—	—	—
Totals	3	845	8	10⅙	3	450	7	12	3	302	7	7	4	425	9	15 7/12	4	220	9	8	4	707	10	9¼

*See page 6
†or reconstituted albumen

Size and Yield The size of the tin or frame required for a given weight of batter may be calculated as follows:

Allow 30 g of batter for every 6 sq cm

Allow 1 oz of batter for every 1 sq in

In the above recipe (1st quality) we would need two frames 16 × 20 cm (7 in × 9 in).

Macaroon (or Almond) Cake

Yield – 18 at 230 g approx. (18 at 8 oz approx.)
       12 at 345 g approx. (12 at 12 oz approx.)

	kg	g	lb	oz
Soft flour	1	000	2	4
Butter or margarine	—	665	1	8
Shortening	—	140	—	5
Castor sugar	—	665	1	8
Eggs	—	930	2	$1\frac{1}{2}$
Macaroon paste	—	805	1	13
Totals	4	205	9	$7\frac{1}{2}$

(1) Cream the butter or margarine, shortening, castor sugar and macaroon paste until light.
(2) Add the eggs in about 4 portions beating in each addition well.
(3) Finally add the flour and blend in, taking care not to toughen the mixing.
(4) Scale the mixture into paper-lined tins of an appropriate size.
(5) Flatten the top and sprinkle on a few flaked almonds.
(6) Bake at 177°C (350°F) approx.

Note If macaroon paste is not available, a similar type of cake may be made by making the following adjustments to the recipe.

Add: Ground almonds 235 g ($8\frac{1}{2}$ oz)
                    by 470 g (17 oz)
Increase: Egg   by 100 g ($3\frac{1}{2}$ oz).

GENOESE

Sheet Genoese is used for a very wide variety of fancies as well as for gâteaux, layer cakes and Battenburgs.

The batter is spread level on a papered baking sheet (either 4 sided or with a stick at the end to restrain flow) using a trowel palette knife or a special spreader and baked. The normal spreading thickness for most purposes is 2 cm ($\frac{3}{4}$ in) but for petits fours 12 mm ($\frac{1}{2}$ in) might be more suitable.

Four types of Genoese can be made and notes about each are now given.

Light

This is made from butter sponge, *see* page 123 in which melted butter is incorporated into an egg sponge.

Because of the lightness of the crumb, this type of Genoese is unsuitable for cutting up into small fancies or for Battenburg etc.

Heavy

These were originally formulated from a recipe containing equal quantities of fat, sugar, egg and flour, and usually made on a sugar batter method.

This Genoese is suitable for cutting into fancies and Battenburg etc.

Genoese

	Boiled												Light											
	(1)				(2)				(3)				(1)				(2)				(3)			
	kg	g	lb	oz	kg	g	lb	oz	kg	g	lb	oz	kg	g	lb	oz	kg	g	lb	oz	kg	g	lb	oz
Soft flour	1	000	2	4	1	000	2	4	1	000	2	4	—	500	1	2	—	700	1	9	1	000	2	4
Baking powder	—	7	—	¼	—	—	—	—	—	7	—	¼	—	—	—	—	—	—	—	—	—	—	—	—
Butter/margarine	—	485	1	1½	1	000	2	4	—	805	1	13	—	250	—	9	—	500	1	2	—	500	1	2
Shortening	—	445	1	0	—	—	—	—	—	—	—	—	—	—	—	—	—	—	—	—	—	—	—	—
Castor sugar	1	055	2	6	1	125	2	8½	—	905	2	½	1	000	2	4	1	000	2	4	1	000	2	4
Whole egg	1	195	2	11	1	250	2	13	1	000	2	4	—	—	—	—	1	595	3	9½	1	250	2	13
Egg whites	—	—	—	—	—	—	—	—	—	—	—	—	—	890	2	0	—	—	—	—	—	—	—	—
Egg yolks	—	—	—	—	—	—	—	—	—	—	—	—	—	335	—	12	—	595	1	5½	—	—	—	—
Cornflour	—	—	—	—	—	—	—	—	—	—	—	—	—	500	1	2	—	305	—	11	—	—	—	—
Glycerine	—	95	—	3½	—	125	—	4½	—	—	—	—	—	—	—	—	—	—	—	—	—	—	—	—
Totals	4	282	9	10¼	4	500	10	2	3	717	8	5¾	3	475	7	13	4	695	10	9	3	750	8	7

Boiled

The special method used for the making of this type strengthens the crumb and enables the Genoese to be cut more cleanly without crumbs. It is especially recommended for petits fours which are cut a smaller size.

A bonus with this type of Genoese is that it has better keeping properties.

High ratio

Commercially the use of this type of Genoese is widespread. As with all high-ratio cakes, using the special H.R. flour and fat, it contains more liquid and sugar than the normal Genoese recipe, and this prolongs its shelf life.

However, when used in conjunction with sweet decorating ingredients like fondant, the resulting product tends to be too sweet for some palates.

The use of the high-ratio angel cake recipe has the advantage that it produces better coloured Genoese as well as white.

High-ratio Genoese

	1				2				3				4			
	kg	g	lb	oz	kg	g	lb	oz	kg	g	lb	oz	kg	g	lb	oz
High-ratio flour (cake)	1	000	2	4	1	000	2	4	1	000	2	4	1	000	2	4
Baking powder	—	45	—	1½	—	30	—	1	—	50	—	1⅓	—	55	—	2
High-ratio shortening	—	500	1	2	—	—	—	—	—	600	1	5½	—	720	1	10
Castor sugar	1	305	2	15	—	540	1	3½	1	140	2	9	1	622	3	10¼
Whole eggs	—	750	1	11	—	780	1	8½	—	845	1	14½	—	570	2	0½
Milk powder (skimmed)	—	110	—	4	—	70	—	2½	—	110	—	4	—	110	—	4
Cold water	—	500	1	2	—	280	—	10	—	585	1	5	—	765	1	11½
Salt	—	—	—	—	—	15	—	½	—	—	—	—	—	15	—	½
Cake margarine	—	—	—	—	—	540	1	3½	—	—	—	—	—	—	—	—
Glucose	—	—	—	—	—	180	—	6½	—	—	—	—	—	—	—	—
Glycerine	—	—	—	—	—	55	—	2	—	—	—	—	—	—	—	—
Cocoa powder	—	—	—	—	—	—	—	—	—	—	—	—	—	235	—	8½
Totals	4	210	9	7½	3	490	7	10	4	330	9	11⅓	5	092	12	3¼

Methods for Making Batters

Light – Normal method for butter sponges. *See* page 123.
    Baking Temperature 185°C (365°F).
Heavy – Normal sugar batter method for cakes. *See* page 128.
    Baking Temperature 199°C (390°F).
High ratio – Normal method for H.R. cakes. *See* page 129.
    Baking Temperature 193°C (380°F).

Boiled

(1) Heat the egg and sugar to approx. blood heat 38°C (100°F) and whisk to a thick sponge.
(2) Place the butter in a mixing bowl and heat until the water in the butter is boiling.
(3) Remove from the heat, stir in the flour and glycerine and beat to a smooth paste.
(4) Add the sponge to the paste in approx. three portions, beating the batter well after each addition to ensure freedom from lumps.
(5) Pour into a papered baking sheet and spread level to approx. 2 cm (¾ in) in thickness.

Heavy Genoese

	1				2				3				4				5			
	kg	g	lb	oz	kg	g	lb	oz	kg	g	lb	oz	kg	g	lb	oz	kg	g	lb	oz
Soft flour	1	000	2	4	1	000	2	4	1	000	2	4	1	000	2	4	1	000	2	4
Baking powder	—	15	—	$\frac{1}{2}$	—	15	—	$\frac{1}{2}$	—	20	—	$\frac{2}{3}$	—	15	—	$\frac{1}{2}$	—	15	—	$\frac{1}{2}$
Butter/margarine	—	585	1	5	—	500	1	2	—	500	1	2	—	805	1	13	—	890	1	14
Shortening	—	85	—	3	—	165	—	6	—	165	—	6	—	—	—	—	—	—	—	—
Castor sugar	—	705	1	$9\frac{1}{2}$	—	835	1	14	—	835	1	14	—	805	1	13	—	835	1	14
Eggs	—	835	1	14	—	725	1	$10\frac{1}{4}$	—	415	—	15	—	000	2	4	—	785	1	$12\frac{1}{2}$
Milk	—	—	—	—	—	205	—	$7\frac{1}{2}$	—	335	—	12	—	—	—	—	—	—	—	—
Glycerine	—	40	—	$1\frac{1}{2}$	—	40	—	$1\frac{1}{2}$	—	60	—	2	—	—	—	—	—	—	—	—
Raw marzipan	—	—	—	—	—	—	—	—	—	—	—	—	—	150	—	$5\frac{1}{2}$	—	—	—	—
Totals	3	265	7	$5\frac{1}{2}$	3	485	7	$13\frac{3}{4}$	3	330	7	$7\frac{2}{3}$	3	775	8	8	3	525	7	13

(6) Bake at 191°C (375°F) for approx. 40 minutes.

(7) When baked, store in a sealed tin until required. This cake will keep in a moist condition for a month if kept wrapped.

Varieties

Chocolate – Substitute 165 g (6 oz) of flour per kg with cocoa powder, add 2 oz water, and chocolate colour.

Almond – (a) Add 8 oz ground almonds.

(b) Add 12 oz raw marzipan and reduce sugar by 85 g (3 oz).

Walnut – Add 8 oz crushed walnuts.

Yields   The following batter weights are recommended for a sheet 46 × 70 cm (18 × 28 in).

Light	2225 g (5 lb)
Heavy and boiled	4000–4450 g (9–10 lb)
High ratio	3560–4000 g (8–9 lb)

Storage of Genoese

Sheet Genoese will keep for at least a week provided it is properly stored.

Once baked and cold it should be inverted onto boards or trays of a similar size and stored in a cupboard or prover. The paper should be left on the Genoese and not removed until it is required to be cut up into fancies, etc.

Preparation for Cutting

Before a sheet of Genoese can be cut into the required pieces and shapes, it must be free from any crust or loose skin. After peeling away the paper this can be carefully removed with a knife, but a useful utensil to use is a tool called a harp. This consists of a bow-shaped piece of metal from the sides of which a serrated wire cutter is stretched taut. This is placed over the Genoese sheet and by manipulating it to and fro it effectively trims it free of crust or skin. The serrated wire cutter is adjustable so that the sheet can be cut to a predetermined thickness without effort.

The particular use of this tool is to ensure the precision cutting of Genoese for such goods as Battenburg or layer cakes.

The crust and skin can be used in several products, and so should be carefully kept for future use.

Cutting of Genoese should be done with a sharp knife, so as to avoid the production of crumbs which can contaminate the decorating materials which are to be used and so spoil the ultimate appearance of the product.

To achieve uniformity of size and shape it is useful to have available a number of specially marked slats or strips of wood. These can be of different thicknesses for use when a strip has to be cut through. This technique is explained as follows:

(1) Place a slat of the required thickness on each side of the Genoese strip.

(2) Keeping the Genoese pressed down firmly between the two slats, rest a long-bladed knife on the slats and work it through the Genoese strip with a sawing motion. Alternatively, the harp previously described can be used for this purpose.

Apart from the function described above, these wooden cutting strips serve two other functions: (a) If marked in suitable width divisions they can be used as a ruler to divide the sheet, (b) Secondly, they are used as a straight edge with which to accurately cut the Genoese sheet.

Uses of Genoese are further explained in chapter 17.

Note   Cake Faults appear on page 152.

11. Fruit Cakes

Lightly-Fruited

The high price which dried fruit commands now makes it difficult to produce a cheap cake by use of a plain batter, and therefore one good quality basic recipe is given with variations for the production of the different varieties.

The introduction of high-protein cake flour has made possible a wide range of medium-quality fruit cakes, and these are also given, see page 147.

Best quality Lightly-Fruited Cakes (Standard Recipes)   (*see* choice of materials, page 129).

	kg	g	lb	oz
Soft flour	1	000	2	4
Baking powder	—	7	—	$\frac{1}{4}$
Butter or cake margarine	—	530	1	3
Shortening	—	165	—	6
Castor sugar	—	750	1	9
Eggs	—	860	1	15
Glycerine	—	45	—	$1\frac{1}{2}$
Colour & vanilla flavour		as required		
Fruit – *see* below	—	835	1	14
Totals	4	192	9	$4\frac{3}{4}$

Fruit

	Mixed Fruit	Sultana	Currant	Genoa
Sultanas	250 g (9 oz)	—	780 g (1.8 oz)	720 g (1.10 oz)
Currants	335 g (12 oz)	780 g (1.8 oz)	—	720 g (1.10 oz)
Diced cherries	85 g (3 oz)	—	—	110 g (4 oz)
Cut peel	165 g (6 oz)	165 g (6 oz)	165 g (6 oz)	165 g (6 oz)

(For preparation of fruit, *see* page 9 and *Bakery: Bread & Fermented Goods*.)

The above quantities are for lightly-fruited cakes. For medium-fruited, increase these quantities by 50% and for heavily fruited by 100%. For the heavier fruited cakes replace the flour with one of a medium strength and bake in a cooler oven.

(1) Make the cake on the sugar batter method.
(2) Proceed as for Madeira cakes.
(3) Prior to baking, the tops may be sprinkled with flaked almonds.

DUNDEE CAKES

These traditional Scottish cakes are a medium-heavy rich fruit cake with a golden brown moist crumb. To achieve the right degree of crumb colour it is usually necessary to add caramel (blackjack) and cake colour (yellow), but the amount will depend upon the degree of colour imparted by the brown sugar employed.

Figure 55. Dundee cake

Before baking, the tops of these cakes are evenly covered in split almonds usually with the rounded surface showing. They are glazed with stock syrup after baking.

Prepare and bake as for fruit cakes.

Note Sometimes this cake is defined as a rich sultana cake. In the recipe given the currants can be omitted if desired.

Rich Fruit Cakes

	Dundee				Paradise				Cherry				Simnel			
	kg	*g*	*lb*	*oz*	*kg*	*g*	*lb*	*oz*	*kg*	*g*	*lb*	*oz*	*kg*	*g*	*lb*	*oz*
Soft flour	1	000	2	4	1	000	2	4	1	000	2	4	1	000	2	4
Baking powder	—	10	—	⅓	—	10	—	⅓	—	10	—	⅓	—	—	—	—
Butter/margarine	—	500	1	2	—	665	1	8	—	500	1	2	—	805	1	13
Shortening	—	165	—	6	—	165	—	6	—	165	—	6	—	—	—	—
Castor sugar	—	—	—	—	—	—	—	—	—	665	1	8	—	805	1	13
Brown sugar	—	835	1	14	—	835	1	14	—	—	—	—	—	—	—	—
Egg	—	835	1	14	—	835	1	14	—	835	1	14	1	000	2	4
Milk (delete if rum is used)	—	85	—	3	—	—	—	—	—	—	—	—	—	—	—	—
Ground almonds	—	85	—	3	—	—	—	—	—	—	—	—	—	195	—	7
Currants	—	335	—	12	—	—	—	—	—	—	—	—	—	—	—	—
Sultanas	—	835	1	14	2	670	6	0	—	—	—	—	—	805	1	13
Cherries	—	165	—	6	—	890	2	0	1	500	3	6	1	195	2	11
Cut mixed peel	—	250	—	9	—	165	—	6	—	—	—	—	—	585	1	5
Cut citron peel	—	—	—	—	—	165	—	6	—	—	—	—	—	—	—	—
Roasted split almonds	—	—	—	—	—	165	—	6	—	—	—	—	—	—	—	—
Walnuts	—	—	—	—	—	335	—	12	—	—	—	—	—	—	—	—
Glacé apricots & pineapple	—	—	—	—	—	665	1	8	—	—	—	—	—	—	—	—
Rum (optional)	—	110	—	4	—	110	—	4	—	—	—	—	—	55	—	2
Glycerine	—	40	—	1½	—	30	—	1	—	—	—	—	—	—	—	—
Blackjack	—	15	—	½	—	15	—	½	—	—	—	—	—	—	—	—
Flavours	as required				—	—	—	—	as required				as required			
Spice	—	—	—	—	—	—	—	—	—	—	—	—	—	30	—	1
Totals	5	265	11	13⅓	8	720	19	9⅚	4	675	10	8⅓	6	475	14	9

PARADISE CAKE

These cakes are truly in the luxury class and because of the high cost of the nuts and glacé fruits used in their manufacture, may only have a very limited market. However expensive, if properly made they are a delicious item of confectionery.

Prepare as for fruit cakes but bake at a lower temperature.

CHERRY CAKE

These should be made with whole glacé cherries, but because of their weight, such cakes are very difficult to make successfully, unless great care is taken with the way the batter is made and the fruit prepared. The main fault with these cakes is the sinking of the cherries, which in extreme cases forms a layer along the base of the cake. We can help to support the whole cherries as follows:

Preparation of the Cherries

Fresh glacé cherries must be washed free of their preserving syrup, and thoroughly dried before being incorporated into the batter.

They may also be rolled in rice cones which not only absorb any surface moisture, but also prevent them slipping through the batter when it liquifies through the heat of the oven.

Strength of Flour

It is recommended that at least a percentage of strong flour is used in the batter to strengthen and help it support the cherries.

Mixing the Batter

Another way of causing the batter to support the cherries is to slightly toughen it by mixing. However, too much toughening in this way must be avoided since although it may keep up the cherries, the crumb will not be very palatable, and the cakes will be bound with a small volume, holes in the texture and a peaked top.

Use of Acid

The use of an acid strengthens the batter sufficiently to help keep the fruit from sinking. Therefore the addition of cream of tartar or tartaric acid can sometimes help.

Baking

The quicker the cake batter is set by heat, the more able it is to prevent the heavy cherries from sinking. The author has known a difference of 10°C (18°F) to make the difference between cherries keeping up in a batter and sinking. With this type of cake it is always advisable to place it into a hot oven initially, lowering the temperature for the final baking.

Size of Cherries

Where cherries are to be baked whole in a cake, it is advisable to obtain them as small as possible using alpine cherries if available.

SIMNEL CAKES

(Simnel Sunday – Mid-Lent or Mothering Sunday)

This traditional Easter cake is made from a fairly rich fruit cake mix, with a layer of marzipan baked in the centre. It is finished with a suitable decoration of marzipan on the top, which is flashed in a hot oven. Fondant icing may also be used in the final decoration.

Figure 56. Simnel cake

Almond Paste for Simnel Cakes

	Filling 1				Filling 2				Decoration 1				Decoration 2			
	kg	g	lb	oz	kg	g	lb	oz	kg	g	lb	oz	kg	g	lb	oz
Ground almonds	1	000	2	4	—	—	—	—	1	000	2	4	—	—	—	—
Raw marzipan	—	—	—	—	1	000	2	4	—	—	—	—	1	000	2	4
Castor sugar	1	000	2	4	—	—	—	—	—	600	1	5½	—	415	—	15
Icing sugar	—	—	—	—	—	750	1	11	—	400	—	14½	—	—	—	—
Whole egg	—	—	—	—	—	—	—	—	—	190	—	6¾	—	55	—	2
Egg yolks	—	290	—	10½	—	30	—	1	—	—	—	—	—	—	—	—
Ground rice	—	290	—	10½	—	—	—	—	—	—	—	—	—	—	—	—
Totals	2	580	5	13	1	780	4	0	2	190	4	14¾	1	470	3	5

Because of the high cost of the ingredients used in this cake – especially the almonds, the best quality of fruit cake is recommended.

For making cakes at 890 g (2 lb) in weight:

(1) Prepare 15 cm (6 in) cake hoops with paper and place on a well papered baking tray.
(2) Make the cake using the sugar batter method.
(3) Scale 220 g (8 oz) of the batter into the cake hoop and spread level.
(4) Weigh 220 g (8 oz) of the filling almond paste, mould into a ball and then roll out to approx. 14 cm (5½ in) diameter. Place this on top of the batter in the hoop.
(5) Weigh a further 220 g (8 oz) of the batter and place into the hoop on top of the almond paste.
(6) Spread level and bake in an oven at 182°C (360°F).
(7) When cool, the bands are removed and the tops of the cakes brushed with apricot purée.
(8) The top is now decorated with 195 g (7 oz) of the special almond paste in a variety of patterns as follows:

  (a) Mould the marzipan piece into a ball and roll out to the same size as the cake. Texture it by the use of marzipan rollers or a knife, before laying the piece on top of the cake.
  (b) Divide the paste into a number of evenly sized pieces, e.g. 12. Mould these into either round or pear shapes and place them around the edge of the cake.
  (c) Roll out the almond paste to approx. 12 mm (½ in) and cut out discs, hearts or other suitable shapes and place these around the edge of the cake.

(*d*) Roll the piece of almond paste into a rope and place on to encircle the top edge of the cake. Either with the fingers or using marzipan nippers, raise a pattern.

(9) Wash with egg yolk.

(10) Cut and attach greaseproof paper bands sufficiently wide so that they stand 12 mm (½ in) higher than the almond paste.

(11) Place the cakes into a hot oven approx. 232°C (450°F) to flash the almond paste to an attractive colour. Double tray the cakes to ensure that the bottoms of the cakes do not get burned.

(12) On removal from the oven, wash with a gum arabic solution, *see* page 220.

(13) With the exception of the cakes treated as 8 (*a*) the centre is now filled in with white or pale yellow fondant (suitably conditioned, *see* page 165).

(14) Finally decorate with preserved fruits, or Easter motifs, e.g. cut out flowers, chicks, rabbits, etc. An inscription incorporating the word Easter is also appropriate.

Note

(1) Any good quality mixed fruit cake recipe will be satisfactory for the cake but the one given is highly recommended.

(2) Two quite different recipes are given for each of the almond pastes required for filling and decorating. If ground almonds are required to replace the raw marzipan in Recipe No. 2 the 1000 g (2 lb 4 oz) of raw marzipan must be substituted as follows:

	kg	g	lb	oz
Ground almonds	—	580	1	5
Icing sugar	—	280	—	10
Whole egg/egg yolk	—	140	—	5
Totals	1	000	2	4

Instead of making individual simnel cakes, slabs may be made and cut up into slices afterwards. The recipe given will be sufficient for a slab of cake 50 cm × 46 cm (20 in × 18 in). For a slab sufficiently large to cover a full-sized baking tray of 18 in × 30 in we would require approx. 8 kg 900 g (20 lb) of cake batter with approx. ¾ of this weight of almond paste.

Baby Simnels

Very small simnel cakes can be baked in paper-lined hoops of approx. 5 cm (2 in). These would require approx. a total of 85 g (3 oz) of batter and 40 g (1½ oz) of almond paste for the centre. A rout mixing (*see* page 218) can be used for piping the top decoration and this is finished in the same way as the larger varieties.

Fruit High Sugar and Liquid Cakes and Slabs

To make a high sugar and liquid cake batter sufficiently stable to support fruit we need to use the special high-protein cake flour – *see* page 6.

The amount of fruit which such batters can carry will depend upon a number of factors:

(*a*) The formulation of the recipe.

(*b*) Size of the fruit used. In mixed fruit cakes the cherries, if used, should be chopped or quartered. The cherry cake recipe given contains added rice flour to help support whole cherries. However, these should be as small as possible (alpine cherries).

High Sugar/Liquid Fruit Cakes

	Fruit 1				Fruit 2				Fruit 3				Cherry			
	kg	g	lb	oz	kg	g	lb	oz	kg	g	lb	oz	kg	g	lb	oz
Special high-protein cake flour	1	000	2	4	1	000	2	4	1	000	2	4	1	000	2	4
Baking powder	—	20	—	$\frac{2}{3}$	—	25	—	$\frac{3}{4}$	—	10	—	$\frac{1}{3}$	—	25	—	$\frac{3}{4}$
Cream of tartar	—	—	—	—	—	—	—	—	—	—	—	—	—	7	—	$\frac{1}{4}$
Butter/margarine	—	250	—	9	—	555	1	4	—	—	—	—	—	555	1	4
Shortening	—	250	—	9	—	—	—	—	—	—	—	—	—	—	—	—
Special HR shortening	—	—	—	—	—	—	—	—	—	720	1	10	—	—	—	—
Castor sugar	1	000	2	4	—	720	1	10	1	030	2	5	—	720	1	10
Milk powder	—	—	—	—	—	40	—	1½	—	85	—	3	—	40	—	1½
Egg	—	500	1	2	—	680	1	8½	—	890	2	0	—	680	1	8½
Milk	—	595	1	5½	—	—	—	—	—	445	1	0	—	—	—	—
Rice flour	—	—	—	—	—	40	—	1½	—	—	—	—	—	85	—	3
Water	—	—	—	—	—	360	—	13	—	—	—	—	—	—	—	—
Salt	—	15	—	½	—	15	—	½	—	20	—	$\frac{2}{3}$	—	15	—	½
Mixed fruit	2	000	4	8	1	110	2	8	1	555	3	8	—	—	—	—
Cherries (whole)	—	—	—	—	—	—	—	—	—	—	—	—	1	000	2	4
Totals	5	630	12	10$\frac{2}{3}$	4	545	10	3$\frac{3}{4}$	5	755	12	15	4	127	9	3½

High Sugar/Liquid Fruit Slab Cakes

	Fruit 1				Fruit 2				Cherry 1				Cherry 2			
	kg	g	lb	oz	kg	g	lb	oz	kg	g	lb	oz	kg	g	lb	oz
Special high protein cake flour	1	000	2	4	1	000	2	4	1	000	2	4	1	000	2	4
Baking powder	—	—	—	—	—	7	—	$\frac{1}{4}$	—	20	—	$\frac{2}{3}$	—	20	—	$\frac{2}{3}$
Cream of tartar	—	—	—	—	—	7	—	$\frac{1}{4}$	—	10	—	$\frac{1}{3}$	—	10	—	$\frac{1}{3}$
Butter/margarine	—	375	—	13½	—	250	—	9	—	—	—	—	—	—	—	—
Shortening	—	375	—	13½	—	250	—	9	—	—	—	—	—	—	—	—
Special H.R. Shortening	—	—	—	—	—	—	—	—	—	720	1	10	—	805	1	13
Castor sugar	1	000	2	4	1	195	2	11	1	095	2	7½	1	095	2	7½
Milk powder	—	—	—	—	—	—	—	—	—	25	—	$\frac{3}{4}$	—	110	—	4
Egg	—	695	1	9	—	400	—	14½	—	805	1	13	—	890	2	0
Milk	—	345	—	12½	—	695	1	9	—	595	1	5½	—	—	—	—
Cornflour	—	—	—	—	—	40	—	1½	—	40	—	1½	—	40	—	1½
Rice flour	—	—	—	—	—	95	—	3½	—	160	—	5$\frac{3}{4}$	—	95	—	3½
Salt	—	20	—	$\frac{2}{3}$	—	15	—	½	—	20	—	$\frac{2}{3}$	—	20	—	$\frac{2}{3}$
Glycerine	—	—	—	—	—	40	—	1½	—	—	—	—	—	—	—	—
Mixed fruit (*see* below)	2	000	4	8	—	890	2	0	—	—	—	—	—	—	—	—
Cherries	—	—	—	—	—	—	—	—	1	780	4	0	1	555	3	8
Water	—	—	—	—	—	—	—	—	—	—	—	—	—	345	—	12½
Totals	5	810	13	1$\frac{1}{6}$	4	884	11	0	6	270	14	1$\frac{1}{3}$	5	985	13	7$\frac{2}{3}$

Fruit Content

The fruit quantity and mix can be varied to suit individual taste. The following is a suggestion for varying the fruit in recipe 1, page 147.

Fruit Variations

	Cherry Sultana				Sultana				Genoa				Cherry			
	kg	*g*	*lb*	*oz*	*kg*	*g*	*lb*	*oz*	*kg*	*g*	*lb*	*oz*	*kg*	*g*	*lb*	*oz*
Currants	—	—	—	—	—	—	—	—	—	665	1	8	—	—	—	—
Sultanas	1	220	2	12	1	665	3	12	—	665	1	8	—	—	—	—
Cut mixed peel	—	—	—	—	—	335	—	12	—	335	—	12	—	—	—	—
Cut citron peel	—	—	—	—	—	—	—	—	—	—	—	—	—	220	—	8
Cherries	—	780	1	12	—	—	—	—	—	335	—	12	1	780	4	0
Totals	2	000	4	8	2	000	4	8	2	000	4	8	2	000	4	8

Date and Walnut Cake

Add 280 g (10 oz) diced dates ⎫
Add 280 g (10 oz) broken walnuts ⎭ To each kg (2 lb 4 oz) of batter.

The dates should be diced using a little flour to prevent them sticking.

Recipe No. 3 on page 134 is also suitable for fruit slab provided the following adjustments are made.

Baking powder – reduce to 7 g ($\frac{1}{4}$ oz).

(1) Make the batter in the same manner as already described for the plain cakes on page 128.
(2) Once the batter is free of lumps, gently stir and distribute the fruit in the batter.
(3) Scale and deposit in lined hoops or tins.
(4) Bake at 182°C (360°F).

Yield Refer to hoop sizes and batter weights for Madeira or lightly fruited cakes on page 133.

First Quality Fruit Slabs – Standard Recipe

	Ginger (and Cherry)				Genoa			
	kg	*g*	*lb*	*oz*	*kg*	*g*	*lb*	*oz*
Soft flour	1	000	2	4	1	000	2	4
Baking powder	—	—	—	—	—	7	—	$\frac{1}{4}$
Butter	—	485	1	$1\frac{1}{2}$	—	530	1	3
Shortening	—	250	—	9	—	280	—	10
Castor sugar	—	695	1	9	—	695	1	9
Invert sugar	—	—	—	—	—	55	—	2
Egg	—	695	2	3	—	695	1	9
Ground almonds	—	—	—	—	—	95	—	$3\frac{1}{2}$
Lemon paste or zest	—	—	—	—	—	40	—	$1\frac{1}{2}$
Chopped stem ginger	2	445	5	8	—	—	—	—
Sultanas	—	—	—	—	—	805	1	13
Currants	—	—	—	—	—	610	1	6
Mixed cut peel	—	—	—	—	—	305	—	11
Totals	5	570	13	$2\frac{1}{2}$	5	117	11	$8\frac{1}{4}$

(1) Make on the sugar batter method, page 128.
(2) Before the Genoa slab goes into the oven, dress the top with flaked almonds (approx. 55 g (2 oz)) per slab.
(3) Deposit into well protected slab tins or frames and bake in a humid oven at 171°C (340°F) for approx. 3–3½ hours depending upon thickness.

Size and Yield The size of the tin or frame required for a given weight of batter may be calculated as follows:
Allow 35 g of batter for every 6 sq cm.
Allow 1¼ oz of batter for every 1 sq in.
For example: In the ginger cake recipe two slab tins or frames of the following approx. size 20 cm × 24 cm (8 in × 10 in) would be required.

Ginger Slab

When the ginger slab has been baked and allowed to cool the following decoration may be applied:
(1) Cut root ginger into slices.
(2) Water ice the top of the slab.
(3) Dip the slices of ginger into fine castor sugar and place these onto the iced top in neat rows to facilitate cutting of the slab.

Cherry Slab

The ginger slab recipe may be made into a cherry slab as follows:
(1) Replace the ginger with small alpine cherries. Remove the adhering syrup by rubbing them on a damp cloth.
(2) Add 85 g (3 oz) of milk to the batter just prior to adding the flour.
(3) Add the cherries and mix well.

Fig Cake

	kg	g	lb	oz		
Soft flour	1	000	2	4		Sieve well
Baking powder	—	30	—	1	A.	together.
Milk powder	—	65	—	2¼		
Mixed spice	—	30	—	1		
Margarine or butter	—	500	1	2		Thoroughly beat
Soft brown sugar	—	375	—	13½	B.	into a cream.
Golden syrup	—	500	1	2		
Whole egg	—	470	1	1	C.	
Figs	1	000	2	4	D.	Mash together
Boiling water	—	625	1	6½		and allow to cool.
Totals	4	595	10	5¼		

Yield – 10 cakes scaled at 450 g (1 lb).
(1) Add the egg C to B a little at a time, beating in each addition to form a batter.
(2) Carefully blend in A.
(3) Lastly blend in D.
(4) Scale into papered hoops or tins and bake at 193°C (380°F) on doubled trays for approx. 50 minutes.

Note It is a useful idea to pass the figs through a mincer before adding the boiling water.

Ginger Cakes

	1				2				3				4				5				6			
	kg	g	lb	oz	kg	g	lb	oz	kg	g	lb	oz	kg	g	lb	oz	kg	g	lb	oz	kg	g	lb	oz
Soft flour	1	000	2	4	1	000	2	4	1	000	2	4	1	000	2	4	1	000	2	4	1	000	2	4
Strong flour	—	—	—	—	—	—	—	—	—	—	—	—	—	—	—	—	—	—	—	—	—	—	—	—
Baking powder	—	25	—	3/4	—	—	—	—	—	20	—	2/3	—	20	—	2/3	—	50	—	1 3/4	—	30	—	1 1/8
Bicarbonate of soda	—	—	—	—	—	—	—	—	—	—	—	—	—	25	—	2/3	—	—	—	—	—	—	—	—
Ground ginger	—	25	—	3/4	—	15	—	1/2	—	15	—	1/2	—	20	—	2/3	—	45	—	1 1/2	—	15	—	1/2
Mixed spice	—	30	—	1	—	15	—	1/2	—	15	—	1/2	—	—	—	—	—	15	—	1/2	—	15	—	1/2
Butter/margarine	—	500	1	2	—	500	1	2	—	500	1	2	—	—	—	—	—	—	—	—	—	—	—	—
Shortening	—	—	—	—	—	375	—	13 1/2	—	—	—	—	—	220	—	8	—	345	—	12 1/2	—	250	—	9
Castor sugar	—	—	—	—	—	—	—	—	—	500	1	2	—	400	—	14 1/2	—	—	—	—	—	—	—	—
Soft brown sugar	—	500	1	2	—	500	1	2	—	500	1	2	—	—	—	—	—	300	—	10 3/4	—	250	—	9
Golden syrup/treacle	—	585	1	5	—	570	1	4 1/2	—	500	1	2	—	460	1	1/2	—	710	1	9 1/2	—	500	1	2
Whole egg	—	665	1	8	—	—	—	—	—	—	—	—	—	110	—	4	—	190	—	6 3/4	—	—	—	—
Milk	—	—	—	—	—	—	—	—	—	—	—	—	—	460	1	1/2	1	000	2	4	—	—	—	—
Cake crumbs	—	—	—	—	—	—	—	—	—	—	—	—	—	280	—	10	1	000	2	4	—	—	—	—
Salt	—	—	—	—	—	—	—	—	—	—	—	—	—	7	—	1/4	—	7	—	1/4	—	—	—	—
Cut preserved ginger	—	250	—	9	—	125	—	4 1/2	—	—	—	—	—	—	—	—	—	—	—	—	—	—	—	—
Cut mixed peel	—	250	—	9	—	—	—	—	—	—	—	—	—	—	—	—	—	100	—	3 1/2	—	125	—	4 1/2
Sultanas	—	335	—	12	—	—	—	—	—	—	—	—	—	—	—	—	—	305	—	11	—	—	—	—
Currants	—	335	—	12	—	—	—	—	—	—	—	—	—	—	—	—	—	—	—	—	—	—	—	—
Totals	4	500	10	1 1/2	3	100	6	15 1/2	3	050	6	13 1/3	3	002	6	11 5/6	5	067	11	6	2	192	4	14 7/8

Date and Fig Cake

	kg	g	lb	oz		
Soft flour	1	000	2	4		
Baking powder	—	40	—	$1\frac{1}{3}$	A.	Sieve together.
Bicarbonate of soda	—	15	—	$\frac{1}{2}$		
Castor sugar	1	000	2	4		Cream fat and sugar,
Shortening	—	145	—	$5\frac{1}{4}$	B.	beat in egg to form
Whole egg	—	295	—	$10\frac{1}{2}$		a batter.
Dates	—	595	1	5		Add boiling water
Water	—	735	1	$10\frac{1}{2}$	C.	to the dates, smash to a paste and allow to cool.
*Vanilla slice cuttings	—	890	2	0		Reduce cuttings
Water	—	345	—	$12\frac{1}{2}$	D.	to a paste and thoroughly mix with the water.
Figs	—	345	—	$12\frac{1}{2}$	E.	Chop or dice.
Totals	5	405	12	$2\frac{1}{12}$		

Yield – 12 at 450 g (1 lb) or 16 at 335 g (12 oz).
(1) Add C to B and mix thoroughly.
(2) Add D and mix thoroughly.
(3) Add A and mix to a batter.
(4) Lastly add the figs E and distribute evenly.
(5) Scale into papered square bread tins of an appropriate size.
(6) Bake at 188°C (370°F) until well cooked.
*See page 14.

Farmhouse Cake

	kg	g	lb	oz		
*Cake crumbs	1	000	2	4		
Milk	—	835	1	14	A.	Soak together.
Sugar	—	585	1	5		
Shortening	—	415	—	15	B.	Cream until light.
Coconut flour	—	165	—	6		
Eggs	—	415	—	15		
Glycerine	—	40	—	$1\frac{1}{2}$	C.	Mix.
Soft flour	—	890	2	0		
Baking powder	—	45	—	$1\frac{1}{2}$	D.	Sieve together.
Fruit – mixed	—	750	1	11	E.	Add.
Totals	5	140	11	9		

CAKE FAULTS

FAULTS \ CAUSES	Underbaking (TIME).	Overbaking (TIME).	Temperature of oven too low.	Temperature of oven too high.	Excessive sugar.	Excessive fat.	Excessive moistening agent.	Excessive baking powder.	Excessive flour.	Insufficient baking powder.	Insufficient moistening agent.	Disturbing before being baked.	Use of too weak a flour.	Use of too strong a flour.	Toughened batter.	Underbeating.	Overbeating.	Insufficient sugar.	Fruit too moist.	Insufficient steam in oven.
Sinking in centre.	✓				✓	✓	✓	✓				✓					✓			
Wet seam under top crust.	✓											✓								
Wet seam at base.							✓												✓	
Peaked tops.				✓					✓		✓			✓	✓					✓
Cauliflower tops.				✓				✓												
Poor volume.	✓		✓	✓	✓	✓	✓	✓	✓	✓	✓		✓	✓	✓	✓		✓		✓
Shrinkage/Loose bands.							✓													
Spots on crust.					✓															
Close-bound crumb.			✓	✓				✓	✓	✓	✓			✓	✓	✓	✓			✓
Loose woolly texture.									✓	✓					✓	✓				
Coarse dry texture.		✓		✓					✓	✓	✓		✓	✓	✓	✓	✓			
Uneven texture.	✓		✓	✓					✓		✓			✓	✓	✓				✓
Poor keeping properties.		✓	✓	✓	✓	✓	✓											✓		✓
Poor oven colour.	✓		✓															✓		
Excessive oven colour.		✓		✓	✓															✓

Yield – 11 at 440 g (1 lb approx.).
        22 at 220 g ($\frac{1}{2}$ lb approx.).

(1) Add C to B a little at a time, beating in each addition to form a batter.
(2) Add A and cream well together.
(3) Add D and carefully mix in.
(4) Add the fruit E and distribute evenly.
(5) Scale and deposit into paper cases in small bread tins.
(6) Sprinkle brown sugar on top and bake at 193°C (380°F).

Ginger Cakes

A very wide range of recipes exists for the production of ginger cakes. They range from a good quality cake batter containing cut preserved ginger to cheap recipes with a considerable quantity of cake crumbs and milk and flavoured with ground ginger. The selection of recipes given may all be made on the sugar batter method treating the syrup as sugar.

The batter may be scaled into hoops or tins and treated in the same way as Madeira cakes. The tops may be decorated with a slice of preserved ginger.

Readers are advised to read *Bakery: Bread & Fermented Goods* which gives further information on the materials used in this chapter.

12. Celebration Cakes

Almost any cake may receive special decorative treatment to turn it into a celebration cake.

However, wedding and other anniversary cakes are by tradition made from a heavily fruited cake, coated in almond and sugar icing and appropriately decorated.

We can turn any good plain cake recipe into such celebration cakes by substituting castor sugar with dark brown soft sugar and adding fruit, almonds, spices, caramel colour and sometimes spirits (e.g. rum).

Basically two types of plain batter are suitable for this treatment based upon the ratios of the main ingredients as follows:

	1	2
Flour	1 part	$1\frac{1}{4}$ parts
Egg	1 part	$1\frac{1}{4}$ parts
Sugar	1 part	1 part
Fats	1 part	1 part

In some recipes a small proportion of the flour is replaced by ground almonds, whilst in others it is an extra addition but the egg is increased to counteract its water absorption property. Before experimenting, however, it is advisable to read the notes on recipe balance on page 5 and the notes on choice of materials on page 129. The use of a soft flour tends to give a softer and more crumbly texture than the use of a strong flour which is recommended if a heavily fruited cake is required to be cut.

A small quantity of baking powder is used if the texture is required to be slightly more open, particularly in the case of Birthday or Christmas Cakes.

Since the price of dried fruit is so high, there is no advantage to be gained by trying to cheapen these rich cakes by reducing the main batter ingredients such as egg and fat and replacing them with milk and baking powder. Thus, in this chapter, only first class recipes based upon the ratios previously stated are given.

If we permute the wide range of ingredients in these cakes, particularly with regard to fruit, we would be able to produce a very wide range of acceptable recipes. Instead, it is felt prudent to supply only three giving sufficient information on how these may be varied to suit individual tastes.

WEDDING OR BRIDAL CAKES

Recipe 1. This is made using the sugar batter method (*see* page 128).

To increase the natural dark colour of this recipe and enhance the flavour, the flour and the nibbed almonds can be toasted in the oven prior to being mixed. (Ensure that they are first cooled.) Lemon paste may be replaced by the zest of 3 lemons.

Eggs in shell

The quantity of eggs given here is the actual weight of the egg in its shell. These should be first placed into warm water before breaking open. This not only warms the egg but aids the release of the contents, so that more egg is in fact extracted. Since fresh egg contains approx. 12% of shell the quantities of broken fresh egg or frozen egg required in these mixtures are shown in the brackets in the recipe.

Depositing the batter into the hoops or frames must be done with care.

	Recipe 1				Recipe 2			
	kg	*g*	*lb*	*oz*	*kg*	*g*	*lb*	*oz*
Soft flour	1	000	2	4	—	—	—	—
Strong flour	—	—	—	—	1	000	2	4
Butter	1	000	2	4	—	640	1	7
Shortening	—	—	—	—	—	180	—	6½
Eggs in shell	1	420	3	3	1	225	2	12
	(1	250)	(2	13)	(1	055)	(2	6)
Castor sugar	—	—	—	—	—	820	1	13½
Soft brown sugar	1	000	2	4	—	—	—	—
Ground almonds	—	250	—	9	—	180	—	6½
Nib almonds	—	165	—	6	—	—	—	—
Glycerine	—	70	—	2½	—	70	—	2½
Blackjack	—	40	—	1½	—	70	—	2½
Mixed spice	—	—	—	—	—	20	—	¾
Praline paste	—	—	—	—	—	40	—	1½
Orange paste	—	—	—	—	—	40	—	1½
Lemon paste	—	40	—	1½	—	40	—	1½
Egg colour	—	—	—	—	—	7	—	¼
Red colour	—	—	—	—	—	7	—	¼
Salt	—	15	—	½	—	15	—	½
Currants	3	005	6	12	2	890	6	8
Sultanas	1	000	2	4	1	445	3	4
Cut mixed peel	—	750	1	11	—	780	1	12
Rum	—	210	—	7½	—	110	—	4
Totals	9	795	22	0½	9	409	21	2¾

The batter should be placed into the hoops or frame in one solid mass from the scale plate.

Placing the batter in piecemeal encourages the formation of holes due to trapped pockets of air. The batter is fairly stiff and therefore the mixture needs to be distributed with the hands to fill every corner of the hoop or frame to eliminate cavities in the baked cake. It is a good idea to grease the inside lining slightly so that the batter will spread easily and fill the corners of the hoops or tin. Square corners are essential if the job of coating is to be made easy. The top is spread level usually with the back of the hand which has been moistened so that the batter does not stick. Some people make a slight concave on the top of the batter, to ensure that the cake bakes out perfectly flat. However, if a very rich cake like Recipe 1 is baked properly in a humid atmosphere, such precautions are unnecessary.

Maturing of Wedding Cakes

Traditionally these cakes are made at least one month before they are required to be decorated. They should be wrapped in greaseproof paper or foil and stored in an air-tight box. During this time, rum or brandy may be poured on at intervals and the cake left to absorb this spirit. Thin needles may be used to puncture the cake at several points to help the spirits to reach the centre. Alternatively the cake may be cut in half and the spirits added to the cut internal surface. When decorated, the two halves may be sandwiched with a layer of almond paste. This particular recipe may be made up to 3 months prior to finishing and during this time it is possible to get it to absorb up to one whole ¾ litre bottle of rum. With such treatment this recipe will keep in good condition for a long time. The author has had experience of eating this cake after ten years when the top tier had been saved for a christening cake. Its condition was still perfect.

This particularly rich cake produces a slightly more crumbly texture than Recipe No. 2 and therefore it should be baked into the same size and shaped units in which it is to be decorated.

Baking

The temperature of baking such a very rich fruited cake depends mostly upon the size and more especially its thickness (*see* page 10). As a general guide for cakes baked from Recipe No. 1 the temperature should never be higher than 177°C (350°F) for a large one. Ideally the oven should drop by 11°C (20°F) between the initial and final baking temperature. Steam in the oven and/or covering of the cakes with paper is essential for large cakes which require a long baking time.

Since small units require to be baked at a higher temperature than large ones, baking a 3 or 4 tier cake in the same oven can present difficulties if the baking is to be uniform for each size. This may be partially overcome by ensuring that the large cakes have more protection than the small ones and the cakes are baked in an oven in which the temperature is falling. In this way the small cakes will be baked at a higher average temperature than the larger ones. This problem is solved by baking a slab and cutting this into the differently sized units afterwards, *see* figure 57.

Baking Times

Size of Hoop or Frame	Approx. Baking Time	Size of Hoop or Frame	Approx. Baking Time
13 and 15 cm (5 and 6 in)	2 –2½ hours	23 cm (9 in)	3 –3½ hours
18 and 20 cm (7 and 8 in)	2½–3 hours	25, 28 and 30 cm (10, 11 and 12 in)	3½–4 hours

Recipe 2. This is made using the flour batter method, *see* page 128.

Although this is a first class recipe, it is more suited to be baked into cakes or slabs which have to be cut (*see later*). The author* of this particular recipe assures us that it reaches perfect maturity after one month and does not recommend a longer storage. He also recommends the production of square cakes cut from a slab and has produced a novel technique for this which is now explained.

Producing Square Cakes from a Baked Slab

(1) A frame is made to fit a normal sized baking sheet of 75 cm × 45 cm (30 in × 18 in).
(2) This is placed onto the necessary paper for heat protection, and lined with protective paper and greaseproof or silicone paper. The latter is recommended since it does not stick to the finished cake and can be easily removed afterwards.
(3) The required amount of mixture is now weighed in and spread level. The originator of this idea recommends that 33 lb of batter should be weighed for this size but at some slight sacrifice of thickness, 1½ times the recipe given will suffice.
(4) This cake is now baked at 182°C (360°F) dropping to 177°C (350°F) for 3¼ to 3½ hours.
(5) When required for finishing into decorated cakes it is cut as shown in Figure 57. This produces two large, four medium and four small square cakes which may be used for one size of a 3 tier cake, two sizes of a 2 tier and three sizes of a one tier.

Commercially these cakes may also be used for other celebration cakes, for birthdays and anniversaries, etc.

* Mr. Andrew Davidson.

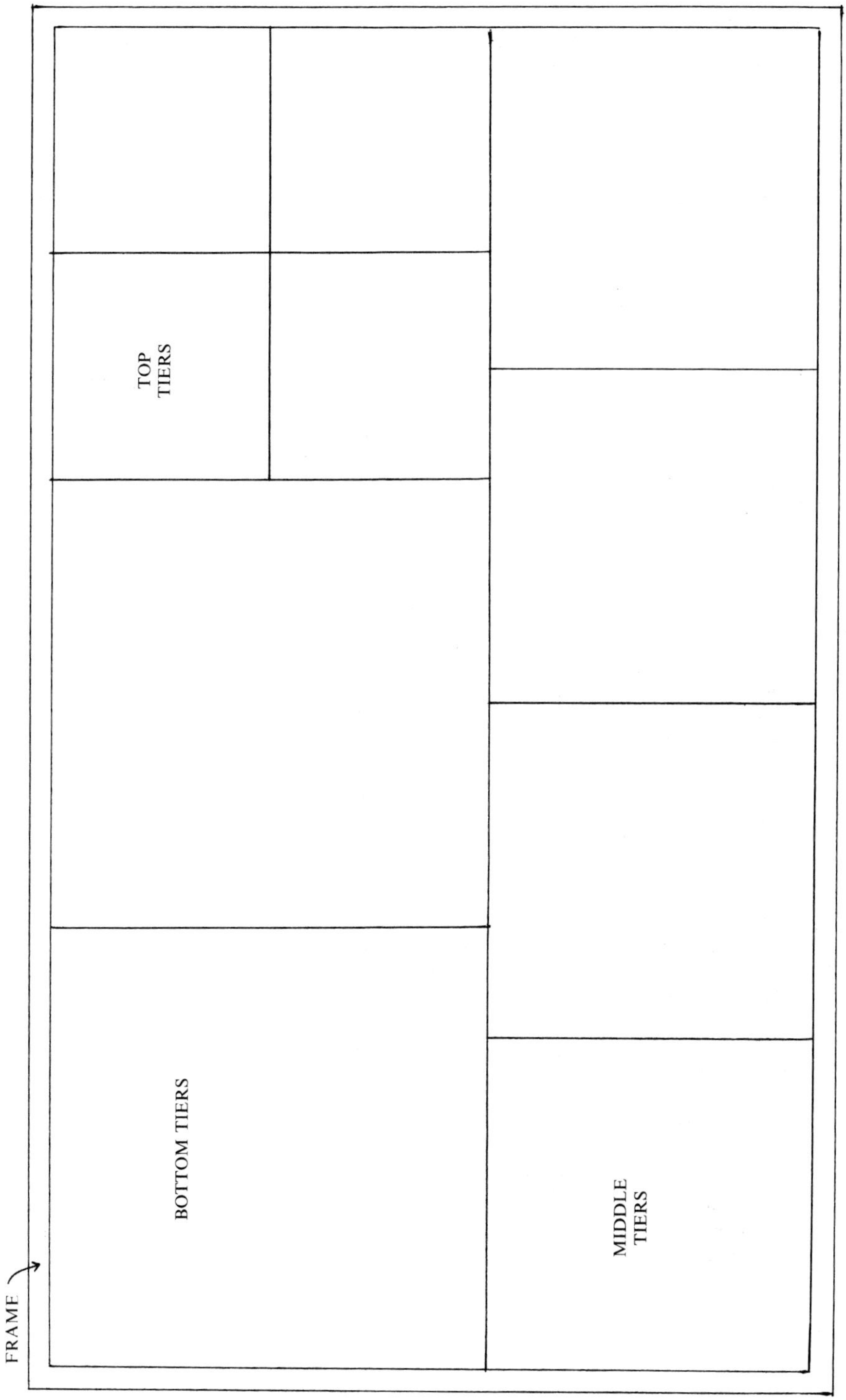

Figure 57. Cutting a slab of wedding cake into 3 different sizes

There is much to commend this technique. Baking is uniform, there is no waste, and used in the way described above, sizes and yields can be standardized.

The one disadvantage is that all the cakes, irrespective of size, are of the same thickness and therefore the proportion of a three tier cake is slightly out of balance. The top tier should always be slightly thinner than the base, although this can be compensated to a certain extent by the thickness of almond paste applied when decorating.

SIZES AND WEIGHTS

ROUND CAKES

When we peruse the available literature regarding the weight of batter recommended for a particular size of hoop, we can get very confused. Each advocate has arrived at the weight recommended by trial and error and there are great discrepancies.

Fortunately, with the aid of the electronic calculator we can easily determine the weight of batter required for any size of hoop as the following examples will show.

Let us assume that we are satisfied with the proportions of a cake baked in a 5 in hoop weighed in at 1 lb 8 oz. Provided we use the same recipe so that the specific gravity of the batter remains fairly constant, we can, by calculation, determine at what weight we need to scale the batter for any given size of cake.

Obviously the specific gravity of a cake batter will dictate the weight of batter required for any given size. For cake batters which are lighter and carry less fruit than Recipe No. 2, the weight required for the 5 in hoop will obviously be less and therefore the weights of all the other sizes will be decreased.

Let us assume that we want all our cakes at a standard thickness irrespective of size and we have chosen a thickness of batter of 2.3 in. (Because metric size hoops are not yet generally used this exercise will be done in imperial measures.) The cubic volume of our cake batter is now determined as follows:

$$\text{Area of the circle} \times \text{height}$$
$$\pi r^2 \times 2.3 \text{ in}$$
$$3.143 \times (2.5)^2 \times 2.3 \text{ in}$$
$$= 45.18 \text{ cubic in.}$$

Therefore 24 oz of batter occupies 45.18 cubic in.

We now calculate the cubic capacity required for the size of hoop we have decided to use.

Let us assume that this is 6 in in diameter. Using our calculator we find that the cubic volume of batter we now require is 65.06 cubic in. We now have a straightforward calculation to make in order to find the weight of batter required for this new size of hoop, i.e.

$$45.18 \text{ cubic in required} \quad 24 \text{ oz batter}$$

$$1 \text{ cubic in requires } \frac{24}{45.18} \text{ oz batter}$$

$$65.06 \text{ cubic in requires } \frac{24}{45.18} \times \frac{65.06}{1} \text{ oz batter}$$

$$= \quad 34\tfrac{1}{2} \text{ oz} = 2 \text{ lb } 2\tfrac{1}{2} \text{ oz batter}$$

The following table shows the weights of batter required for hoop sizes from 5 in to 12 in using this formula.

Table 1

Hoop Size	Cubic Volume of Batter Required	Weight of Batter Required Metric (to nearest 5 g)	Imperial
5 in	45.18	680	24 oz = 1 lb 8 oz
6 in	65.06	980	$34\frac{1}{2}$ oz = 2 lb $2\frac{1}{2}$ oz
7 in	88.55	1330	47 oz = 2 lb 15 oz
8 in	115.66	1745	$61\frac{1}{2}$ oz = 3 lb $13\frac{1}{2}$ oz
9 in	146.38	2210	78 oz = 4 lb 14 oz
10 in	180.72	2720	96 oz = 6 lb 0 oz
11 in	218.67	3290	116 oz = 7 lb 4 oz
12 in	260.24	3910	138 oz = 8 lb 10 oz

We have already stated that in order to achieve a correct proportion, as the cake gets progressively larger it should also get progressively thicker and the next two tables show how the weight of batter required is affected by these considerations.

In the first of these tables we are increasing the thickness by $\frac{1}{20}$ of an inch and in the second by $\frac{1}{10}$ of an inch.

Table 2

Thickness	Hoop Size	Cubic Volume of Batter Required	Weight of Batter Required Metric (to nearest 5 g)	Imperial
2.3 in	5 in	45.18 cubic in	680	24 oz = 1 lb 8 oz
2.35 in	6 in	66.47 cubic in	990	35 oz = 2 lb 3 oz
2.4 in	7 in	92.40 cubic in	1390	49 oz = 3 lb 1 oz
2.45 in	8 in	123.20 cubic in	1855	$65\frac{1}{2}$ oz = 4 lb $1\frac{1}{2}$ oz
2.5 in	9 in	159.11 cubic in	2395	$84\frac{1}{2}$ oz = 5 lb $4\frac{1}{2}$ oz
2.55 in	10 in	200.36 cubic in	3020	$106\frac{1}{2}$ oz = 6 lb $10\frac{1}{2}$ oz
2.6 in	11 in	247.19 cubic in	3715	131 oz = 8 lb 3 oz
2.65 in	12 in	299.84 cubic in	4520	159 oz = 9 lb 15 oz

Table 3

Thickness	Hoop Size	Cubic Volume of Batter Required	Weight of Batter Required Metric (to nearest 5 g)	Imperial
2.3 in	5 in	45.18 cubic in	680	24 oz = 1 lb 8 oz
2.4 in	6 in	67.89 cubic in	1020	36 oz = 2 lb 4 oz
2.5 in	7 in	96.25 cubic in	1445	51 oz = 3 lb 3 oz
2.6 in	8 in	130.75 cubic in	1970	$69\frac{1}{2}$ oz = 4 lb $5\frac{1}{2}$ oz
2.7 in	9 in	171.84 cubic in	2580	91 oz = 5 lb 11 oz
2.8 in	10 in	220.00 cubic in	3315	117 oz = 7 lb 5 oz
2.9 in	11 in	275.71 cubic in	4140	146 oz = 9 lb 2 oz
3.0 in	12 in	339.44 cubic in	5100	180 oz = 11 lb 4 oz

When metric size hoops become available this exercise can be done just as easily substituting metric figures for imperial. In the above table for example the thickness could be progressively increased in steps of 2 mm.

SQUARE CAKES

The same principle that we used for determining the weight of batter required for any size of cake hoop can also be used for square cakes.

Here the cubic volume of batter required is:

Area of frame or tin × height or thickness, i.e. width × length × height.

The thicknesses used in the previous two tables are now applied to square frames or tins of the same size to formulate the following tables for square cakes.

Table 4

Thickness	Hoop Size	Cubic Volume of Batter Required	Weight of Batter Required Metric (to nearest 5 g)	Imperial
2.3 in	5 in	57.5 cubic in	880	31 oz = 1 lb 15 oz
2.35 in	6 in	84.6 cubic in	1290	45½ oz = 2 lb 13½ oz
2.4 in	7 in	117.6 cubic in	1800	63½ oz = 3 lb 15½ oz
2.45 in	8 in	156.8 cubic in	2395	84½ oz = 5 lb 4½ oz
2.5 in	9 in	202.5 cubic in	3090	109 oz = 6 lb 13 oz
2.55 in	10 in	255.0 cubic in	3900	137½ oz = 8 lb 9½ oz
2.6 in	11 in	314.6 cubic in	4805	169½ oz = 10 lb 9½ oz
2.65 in	12 in	381.6 cubic in	5825	205½ oz = 12 lb 13½ oz

Table 5

Thickness	Hoop Size	Cubic Volume of Batter Required	Weight of Batter Required Metric (to nearest 5 g)	Imperial
2.3 in	5 in	57.5 cubic in	880	31 oz = 1 lb 15 oz
2.4 in	6 in	86.4 cubic in	1320	46½ oz = 2 lb 14½ oz
2.5 in	7 in	122.5 cubic in	1870	66 oz = 3 lb 2 oz
2.6 in	8 in	166.4 cubic in	2540	89½ oz = 5 lb 9½ oz
2.7 in	9 in	218.7 cubic in	3345	118 oz = 7 lb 6 oz
2.8 in	10 in	280 cubic in	4280	151 oz = 9 lb 7 oz
2.9 in	11 in	350.9 cubic in	5360	189 oz = 11 lb 13 oz
3.0 in	12 in	432 cubic in	6605	233 oz = 14 lb 9 oz

Coating in Almond Paste (For Recipes *see* pages 256 and 257)

After maturing, the cake is ready for finishing, the first stage of which is to coat it with almond paste. If we have started with a good quality cake we must also use a first class almond paste. (For special high quality cakes this almond paste may be flavoured with orange flower water.) For cakes which may be required to be stored for a long time, the almond paste should be of the boiled type and should not contain too much moisture. Such almond paste may be applied to the cake whilst still hot. Sometimes a bridal cake is required in several tiers each being supported by cake, almond paste and royal icing. Thus the bottom tiers have to support a considerable weight and this is only possible if the almond paste is very stiff.

Ratio of Cake to Almond Paste

The quantity of almond paste used and the way it is distributed between the various tiers, is a matter of personal preference and only guide lines can be laid. It is generally accepted that the weight of almond paste employed should be half that of the cake used.

However, the way this weight of almond paste is distributed is not so straightforward. Usually we only cover the top and sides but sometimes we need to sandwich the cake as well, particularly if the cake has already been cut in half to aid the absorption of spirit. If some of the paste is used in this way it must come from the total weight allocated and therefore the top coating, and possibly the sides as well, will have to be thinner as a result.

Since smaller tiers have a larger surface area in relation to their weight, the quantity of almond paste has to be disproportionately distributed, the large cakes probably having 40% of their weight in almond paste whilst the smaller tiers have 60%.

This disproportion is also carried through to the ratio of weight of paste required between the top coating and that of the side.

The following example of a 3 tier cake is given as a guide only.

	Weight of Baked Cake	*Size*	*Weight of Almond Paste*		
			Total Weight	*Top*	*Sides*
Bottom Tier	7 lb	11 in	3 lb 0 oz	2 lb 0 oz	1 lb 0 oz
Middle Tier	3 lb 15 oz	8 in	2 lb 7 oz	1 lb 10 oz	13 oz
Top Tier	1 lb 5 oz	5 in	14 oz	8 oz	6 oz
Totals	12 lb 10 oz		6 lb 5 oz	4 lb 2 oz	2 lb 3 oz

*Weights given in Table 2 less 10% baking loss.

Purpose of Almond Paste Coating

The purpose of the almond paste coating is threefold:
(1) It enhances the overall flavour of the cake.
(2) Properly coated, the cake is formed into a symmetrical shape which facilitates being easily coated in icing.
(3) The fat content of the cake is prevented from migrating into the icing and so spoiling the colour with stains.

Note The oil content of almond paste can also migrate into the royal icing to make it discoloured. This can be prevented by first coating the paste with boiling fondant.

Apricot Purée

This is used to make the almond paste adhere to the cake. It should be of good quality and well boiled prior to use in order to ensure against the possibility of fermentation after use.

It should be thinned with added sugar and water so that only a minimum quantity is used. For very high quality cakes, rum may be added instead of water. Fermentation will cause carbon dioxide gas to be produced which gets trapped between the cake and the almond paste and causes the latter to flake away. This can result in the collapse of the cake in extreme cases.

After covering the top and sides of the cake with marzipan, the traditional English Wedding Cake is coated and decorated with royal icing and artificial motifs.

Multi-tiered cakes are mounted on pillars which can be made from gum paste, plaster or plastic and an ornament or vase of flowers is usually placed on top.

RICH FRUITED BIRTHDAY OR CHRISTMAS CAKE

Optional Additions
Fruit Some of the fruit may be replaced with chopped glacé cherries.
Almonds Up to 165 g (6 oz) of ground almonds may be added.
Spirit Up to 110 g (4 oz) of rum may be added with the fruit.
(1) Follow the recipe using the sugar batter method (*see* page 128).
(2) Prepare in the same way as for wedding cakes (*see* page 154).
(3) The size and weights are the same as for wedding cakes (*see* page 158).
(4) The cakes are iced with almond paste and may either be coated and/or iced with royal icing or fondant.

	kg	g	lb	oz
Soft flour	1	000	2	4
Baking powder	—	10	—	$\frac{1}{3}$
Butter	—	610	1	6
Shortening	—	195	—	7
Dark brown soft sugar	—	805	1	13
Egg	1	000	2	4
Mixed spice	—	30	—	1
Glycerine	—	55	—	2
Blackjack	—	40	—	$1\frac{1}{2}$
Sultanas	1	390	3	2
Currants	1	390	3	2
Cut mixed peel	—	390	—	14
Vanilla flavour	—	as required		
Almond flavour	—	as required		
Orange paste	—	40	—	$1\frac{1}{2}$
Lemon paste	—	40	—	$1\frac{1}{2}$
Totals	6	995	15	$11\frac{1}{2}$

The orange and lemon paste may be replaced by
the zest and juice of 2 lemons and 2 oranges.

(5) The cakes are then appropriately decorated using royal icing fondant or other decorating mediums.

The techniques involved in the decoration of celebration cakes are fully explained in so many other books* that the author felt it to be inappropriate to include a further explanation in this publication.

Figure 58. A well-proportioned 3-tier wedding cake

Cake Design and Decoration by L. J. Hanneman and G. Marshall.
Modern Cake Decoration by L. J. Hanneman.
Both published by: Applied Science Publishers Ltd., Ripple Road, Barking, Essex.

WEDDING CAKE FAULTS

(For faults in the actual cake *see* page 152)

FAULTS	Insufficiently beaten.	Insufficient glycerine added.	Too much acid added.	Too much glycerine added.	Stored in damp conditions.	Cake/almond paste/icing too soft.	Apricot purée or almond paste fermented.	Use of oiled almond paste.	Paste not sealed with boiling fondant.	Insufficient or no blue added.	Poor storage.	Insufficient maturing.	Insufficient moisture in recipe.
Icing too hard.	√	√	√										
Icing too soft.				√	√								
Collapsed tiers.						√	√						
Icing flaking away from cake.							√						
Icing discoloured.								√	√				
Greyish coloured icing.										√			
Dry cake crumb.	√										√	√	√

CAUSES

13. Icings and Creams

The basic ingredients in an icing are sugar and water, but additions such as egg whites, gelatine and other gums, fats and milk may be made to produce a variety of different icings each enhanced by the flavour of the added ingredient which also sometimes contributes some physical characteristics.

Some icings like fondant are required to be used warm so that they set to a firm coating when cool.

Other icings are required for spreading or piping as in the case of royal icing which needs to be beaten to form a stiff paste before use.

1. Water

	kg	g	lb	oz
Icing sugar	1	000	2	4
Water	—	150	—	$5\frac{1}{2}$
Totals	1	150	2	$9\frac{1}{2}$

(1) Heat the water to boiling point.
(2) Remove from the heat and whisk in the sieved icing sugar to form a smooth icing.
Note Stock syrup (*see below*) may be used instead of water. More syrup will be required than that quoted for water resulting in a greater yield.

2. Stock Syrup

	kg	g	lb	oz
Lump or granulated sugar	1	000	2	4
Water	—	835	1	14
Totals	1	835	4	2

(1) Place the sugar and water in a saucepan (preferably copper) and heat gently.
(2) Once the sugar has dissolved bring to the boil.
(3) Cool and store in jars for future use.

3. Fondant

	kg	g	lb	oz
Lump or granulated sugar	1	000	2	4
Water	—	310	—	$11\frac{1}{4}$
* Glucose	—	165	—	6
Totals	1	475	3	$5\frac{1}{4}$

* This may be replaced by 7 g ($\frac{1}{4}$ oz) cream of tartar and 30 g (1 oz) water.

(1) Mix the sugar and water and bring to a temperature of 225°F observing the rules of sugar boiling (*see* page 13).

(2) Add the glucose and boil the mixture rapidly to 115°C (240°F) without agitation.

(3) Pour out onto a slab which has been splashed with water, between four steel bars to stop it flowing.

(4) Splash with cold water and allow to cool to approx. 37.7°C (100°F).

Manufacture of Fondant

Once the boiled sugar has cooled, remove the steel bars and with a wooden spatula, agitate the syrup by moving it backwards and forwards. Gradually the mass will thicken and turn white until it crystallizes into a hard white lump. Cover with a damp cloth and leave for ½–1 hour. Then rub down the mass to a thick creamy consistency. Store for future use in an air-tight container.

Hand-made fondant is never as perfectly made as the type which is purchased in bulk from a supplier.

Uses

(1) As an icing for fancies, torten, etc. (*see* chapters 14 and 17).

(2) Added to a boiled sugar solution to make fudge, coconut ice, etc. (*see* page 284).

(3) As an improver in fermented goods.

(4) An ingredient in such goods as fudge, coconut ice, buttercream, sugar paste and almond paste.

(5) As a centre for chocolates (*see* page 286).

(6) Used hot for covering the almond paste of wedding cakes (*see* page 161).

Preparation of fondant for icing

To bring fondant to the correct condition for coating purposes we need to apply gentle heat and dilute it with water or stock syrup.

Ideally, the latter should be used, since this will not only help preserve gloss but also increase the yield of the fondant. Since sugar is cheaper than fondant to purchase, this use of syrup is a sound economic reason.

Rules to be observed in preparing fondant for use as an icing

The whiteness and gloss of fondant is due to the light reflecting property of millions of minute crystals of sugar. The smaller these are the more light and hence more gloss is imparted. Therefore anything which will increase the size of these crystals will result in loss of gloss, and must be avoided. For the best results the following points should be observed:

(1) Always use freshly manufactured fondant.

(2) Break up into small lumps in a bain-marie.

(3) Apply gentle heat, but on no account should the temperature of the fondant be more than 38°C (100°F), otherwise loss of gloss results.

(4) Add stock syrup (*see* opposite) to reduce the fondant to the required consistency. The correct consistency is a matter of judgement, depending upon its temperature and the area of the goods to be covered. The warmer the icing the thinner will be its consistency. Large areas usually require fondant of a thicker consistency than small areas.

(5) The base which is to be covered must be prepared either by covering with a paste such as almond paste or with boiled purée. Unless the surface on which the fondant is placed is thus suitably prepared its moisture will migrate to the base causing the fondant to lose its gloss.

One technique employed by continental confectioners is to use the fondant much hotter for goods like petits fours glacés, and then place them in a hot oven for a minute after they have been coated and the fondant set. This causes the fondant to crystallize into small crystals on the surface which improves its gloss.

ADDITIONS

To improve the flavour

Chocolate

Melted chocolate up to 165 g per kg (6 oz per 2¼ lb) may be added to flavour fondant and although this will also impart colour, it is necessary to add chocolate colour as well. Block cocoa or unsweetened chocolate is recommended in preference to the ordinary sweetened type to reduce the excessively sweet flavour of this particular product.

Fruit

Extracts, combienne or juices may be added for flavouring purposes, the amount depending upon their strength, along with the appropriate colour. If juice is used, this may replace the syrup for reducing in the initial stages of preparation.

Evaporated Milk

This will impart a creamy consistency and taste to fondant and this is well recommended for chocolate centres. Like the fruit juice it may be used to reduce the fondant initially.

To improve the gloss

Gelatine – use up to 70 g per kg (2½ oz per 2¼ lb).
Piping jelly – use up to 140 g per kg (5 oz per 2¼ lb).
Egg whites – use up to 70 g per kg (2½ oz per 2¼ lb).
(The above three additions will affect the consistency and must be taken into account when the syrup is added.)
Marshmallow – use up to 140 g per kg (2½ oz per 2¼ lb).

Soft icings

Blends of marshmallow, Italian meringue and royal icing may be made, the latter imparting quick-setting properties to the icing. These ingredients are usually blended in the proportion of one part to two parts of fondant for the making of these soft-eating icings.

Dry Fondant (Drifon)

This is fondant in a powdered form which is reconstituted by merely adding water or syrup in the following proportions:
1 part water to 9 parts dry fondant,
or 1 part stock syrup to 2·8 parts dry fondant.
Two methods of reconstitution are given:
(1) Using a machine, place the water in the bowl, add the dry fondant and mix on low speed for approx. 15 minutes.
(2) Place the water and dry fondant in the bowl and mix until the powder is thoroughly

wetted. Cover and leave to reconstitute for at least 1 hour or preferably overnight. This method is recommended if the mixing is done by hand.

Warm to approx. 43°C (110°F) and reduce to the correct consistency before using in the same way as ordinary fondant.

One great advantage of this product is that fruit juice may be used as the reconstituting agent producing a fondant with a very superior flavour.

4. American

	kg	g	lb	oz
Lump or granulated sugar	—	890	2	0
Invert sugar	—	110	—	4
Water	—	280	—	10
Cream of tartar	—	3	—	$\frac{1}{8}$
Egg whites	—	205	—	$7\frac{1}{2}$
Totals	1	488	3	$5\frac{5}{8}$

This is an Italian meringue which is allowed to grain to form a frosted icing.
(1) Boil the sugars, water and cream of tartar to 115°C (240°F) observing the rules of sugar boiling (*see* page 13).
(2) Whisk the egg whites and pour on the boiling syrup.
(3) Continue whisking until it just begins to grain (crystallize).
(4) Use immediately whilst still warm. This icing will set with a thin dry crust.

5. Chocolate

	kg	g	lb	oz
Chocolate couverture	1	000	2	4
Stock syrup	—	375	—	$13\frac{1}{2}$
Totals	1	375	3	$1\frac{1}{2}$

(1) Melt the chocolate in a bain-marie.
(2) Warm the stock syrup to approx. 49°C (120°F).
(3) Add the syrup to the melted couverture a little at a time, beating in each addition thoroughly. The mixture will first thicken to a toffee-like consistency but as more syrup is used it will approach that of fondant.
(4) If necessary, adjust the consistency with syrup.

This icing is used warm like fondant for covering purposes, when it sets to form a skin, the icing remaining soft to eat.

6. Caramel

Use like the fudge filling (Recipe 1 on page 178).
(1) Boil the demerara sugar with the first quantity of water shown to 115°C (240°F).
(2) Mix the rest of the ingredients except the remaining water and slowly mix into the boiling syrup.
(3) Add the remaining water and mix until smooth.

	kg	g	lb	oz
Demerara sugar	1	000	2	4
Water	—	310	—	11¼
Butter or margarine	—	190	—	6¾
Hydrogenated shortening	1	000	2	4
Icing sugar	1	500	3	6
Fondant	2	000	4	8
Milk powder (skimmed)	—	375	—	13½
Cold water	—	105	—	3¾
Caramel colour		as desired		
Totals	6	480	14	9¼

7. Fruit

	kg	g	lb	oz
Granulated sugar	1	000	2	4
Water	—	750	1	11
Butter or margarine	—	250	—	9
Water	—	250	—	9
Cornflour	—	190	—	6¾
Fruit mixture	1	000	2	4
Egg or lemon colour		as desired		
Totals	3	440	7	11¾

(1) Bring the first quantity of water shown, the granulated sugar and the fat to the boil.
(2) Mix the cornflour with the remaining water, add to the syrup and boil until it is clear.
(3) Add the fruit mixture. This is made by mixing together equal proportions of the following: apricot jam – lemon curd – pineapple crush.

Royal

	kg	g	lb	oz
Icing sugar	1	000	2	4
Egg whites or albumen solution	—	145	—	5
Acid (Acetic, Citric or Tartaric) } optional		two drops		
Glycerine	—	10	—	⅓
Totals	1	155	2	9⅓

Method by Hand
(1) Scald all the utensils used with hot water.
(2) Using a spatula beat ⅔ of the sugar with the egg whites or albumen solution until it thickens.
(3) Add the remaining ⅓ and beat in well.

(4) Cover with a damp cloth or polythene sheet.
Method by Machine
(1) Thoroughly scald bowl and beater used.
(2) Place the icing sugar and egg whites or albumen solution in the machine bowl and mix on *bottom* speed until the required stiffness is reached. This is indicated when the icing can be drawn to a point after a spatula is inserted and then removed.

8. Stock Marshmallow (1)

	kg	g	lb	oz
Lump or granulated sugar	1	000	2	4
Water	—	530	1	3
Agar-agar	—	15	—	$\frac{1}{2}$
Glucose	—	500	1	2
Egg whites	—	85	—	3
Totals	2	130	4	$12\frac{1}{2}$

Method for Recipe 1
(1) Soak the agar in the 915 g (2 lb 1 oz) of water for 12 hours (or overnight). Boil to completely dissolve and pass through muslin or a nylon sieve.
(2) Add the sugar, heat to boiling point and then strongly to 107°C (225°F).
(3) Add the glucose and continue to boil rapidly to 121°C (250°F).
(4) After the glucose has been added, start to whisk the egg whites until a stiff snow has been reached.
(5) Pour the boiling syrup into the whites in a steady stream whilst continuing to whisk at low speed.
(6) Once all the syrup has been added, whisk at top speed for approx. 1 minute and then change the whisk for a beater.
(7) Continue to beat at medium speed for approx. 15 minutes after which the marshmallow is ready either to pipe out or to transfer to polythene bags or air-tight containers for future use.

Stock Marshmallow (2)

	kg	g	lb	oz
Lump or granulated sugar	1	000	2	4
Water	—	890	2	0
Glucose	—	960	2	$2\frac{1}{2}$
Gelatine	—	85	—	3
Water	—	165	—	6
Totals	3	100	6	$15\frac{1}{2}$

Method for Recipe 2
(1) Boil the sugar and first quantity of water to 107°C (225°F).
(2) Add the glucose and continue to boil rapidly to 121°C (250°F).
(3) Disperse the gelatine in the second quantity of water and blend into the syrup.

(4) Pack into polythene bags or air-tight containers for future use.

Preparation for use

(1) Add 250 g (9 oz) water to each kg (2 ¼ lb) of stock marshmallow, heat to approx. 71°C (160°F) and whip.

(2) Add 310 g (11¼ oz) egg whites to each kg (2¼ lb) of stock marshmallow and whip.

CREAMS

In Britain the use of the word cream is restricted by law to fresh dairy cream.

Hence we cannot describe cakes as *cream* cakes unless the cream used is in fact fresh dairy cream. We are also restricted to the number of substances which can be added and their amount.

Likewise the term *buttercream* can only be used for mixtures of fat and sugar provided they contain at least 22.5% butter and no other added fat. The name must also be presented as one word, e.g. butter cream or butter-cream is not allowed. Mixtures like buttercream which are made from other fats or margarines we must describe as fillings or icings.

Fresh Cream

This is one of the most delicious raw materials used in the bakery. It should be at least 12 hours old when delivered and stored at 4°C (40°F) until required for use. Provided the cream has not been contaminated and kept cool, it should keep for at least 5 days. Like milk, if the cream is not stored in a cool place it will soon turn sour and be unfit for use.

Great care should be taken in handling fresh cream since it can be a source of food poisoning (*see* first volume of *Bakery: Bread and Fermented Goods*).

The maintenance of a temperature of 4°C (40°F) for whipping cream gives the best volume and therefore should always be observed.

Goods containing fresh cream should always be kept cool, preferably in a refrigerated cabinet, before they are sold.

Freezing

Whipped cream as a filling in goods will freeze satisfactorily. However, if the unwhipped fresh cream is allowed to freeze, the emulsion will break and the cream is not able to be beaten to a stiff foam.

CHOICE OF CREAM FOR WHIPPING

Whipping Cream

Cream suitable for whipping into a firm foam must have a minimum butterfat content of 35%. Such creams are described as whipping cream and sold as such. These give the greatest volume when whipped. However, creams with higher butterfat contents can be whipped but although they form a firmer foam, they are not so light and have a lower volume.

Double Cream

This contains approx. 48% butterfat.

Sometimes we require to add juices or liqueurs with fresh cream which would have the effect of diluting the butterfat content and impair its whipping performance. In these cases the double cream should be used in preference to the whipping variety.

Whipping Fresh Cream

We require fresh cream to be whipped for two reasons:

(*a*) To increase its volume so that it becomes more economical to use.

(*b*) To produce a stable foam which can be piped or spread and retain its shape.

Whipping may be done by hand or machine. Cleanliness is essential. The bowls and whisk should be washed with scalding water, allowed to drain and cool beforehand. If a machine is used whipping may be done on medium speed until the correct consistency is reached. Overbeating will result in separation and the formation of globules of butter and this must be avoided. It is best to remove the cream from the machine and finish off by hand to reach the critical stage.

Certain types of machines have an air pump which forces air into the cream thus creating greater volume.

Additions

The additions which may be made to cream are strictly controlled by law, as follows: To 1 litre – 1000 g (2¼ lb) cream
add not more than:

Sugar $\qquad$ 13% = 130 g (4½ oz) for sweetening

Sodium alginate
Mixture of sodium bicarbonate,
    tetrasodium pyrophosphate, $\qquad$ 0.3% = 3 g ($\frac{1}{10}$ oz) total of
    and alginic acid $\qquad$ any or all for
Sodium carboxymethyl cellulose $\qquad$ stabilizing.
Carrageenan
Gelatine

Where large volumes of cream are being used, the use of the stabilizers shown above is very useful to prevent the cream *running back* and to maintain its firmness.

Providing goods are not sold as *cream* goods additions other than those mentioned above may be made. One such additive is Italian meringue which besides sweetening the cream also contributes to its final volume. The meringue is put into the initial stages so that it is beaten with the cream.

Marshmallow is another additive which may be used in the same way.

The use of these two additives prolong the shelf life of the cream due to the extra sugar and stabilizing agents used.

Ganache

	kg	g	lb	oz
Fresh cream	1	000	2	4
Chocolate couverture	1	670	3	12
Totals	2	670	6	0

(1) Melt the chocolate in a bain-marie.

(2) Place the cream in a clean saucepan and bring it to the boil.

(3) Remove from the heat and stir in the melted chocolate. Whisk until completely mixed and smooth.

Note Spirits and liqueurs may be used to flavour this mixture. The consistency can be altered by adjusting the ratio of chocolate to cream. For a thicker ganache, increase the chocolate and for a thinner one, increase the cream.

Ganache may be used in 4 ways:
(1) Used warm, it can be used for covering, like fondant, when it will set into a thin soft-eating coating.
(2) It may be refrigerated into a firm paste which can be moulded for chocolate centres and sweets.
(3) If whisked it may be used like buttercream.
(4) As a filling it may be used either on its own or mixed with other creamed fillings.

Imitation Ganache

Imitation cream and/or evaporated milk may be used either with couverture or chocolate-flavoured compounds (bakers' cake coatings) to give fillings which closely resemble ganache except for flavour.

Imitation Cream

This product looks and behaves like fresh cream, but has a longer life. It should be treated in every way identically with that of fresh dairy cream.

Because proprietary brands contain vegetable fat and not butter, the flavour of this product cannot compare with fresh cream. It is much cheaper and is therefore used to produce goods at a lower cost.

Good imitation creams should whip up to 3 times their volume.

ADDITION OF FLAVOURING MATERIALS

Because of the liquid nature of this type of cream, it is sometimes difficult to blend in certain flavouring materials without special consideration.

Nougat (Praline Paste)

(1) Warm the nougat and work it to a smooth paste.
(2) Mix in a quarter of its weight of cold water so that a smooth mixture is formed.
(3) Blend this into the whipped cream. Up to half its weight may be flavoured with this nougat mixture.

Caramel

Warm and thin down slightly with water before adding.

Juices and Liqueurs

Use fresh double cream if liquid additions are to be made.

Chocolate

This has to be blended in warm and fairly quickly to prevent the chocolate setting into pieces. The cream should be slightly warmer than usual to ensure a thorough amalgamation of the chocolate.

BUTTERCREAM

There is a great variety of recipes but all should be made free of lumps and easily spread or piped. Before dealing with these recipes, some general notes are made.
Notes
(1) Margarine may replace the butter to give a creamed filling which will fulfil all the functions of buttercream but is lacking in flavour.
(2) The unsalted variety of butter or margarine is recommended for the best flavoured cream. The flavour will be impaired by the presence of salt.

(3) The consistency is greatly influenced by temperature. If it is too soft it can be stiffened by cooling and conversely warmed if it is too stiff for piping.

(4) All buttercreams are emulsions and in certain cases the fat phase will separate from the liquid phase. If this happens, the mixture can usually be brought back to the right condition by beating with slight heat.

(5) All types of colours and flavours may be added (*see* below).

(6) Buttercream is prone to pick up off-flavours so it should always be stored away from strong odours, preferably in a cool place. It should not be kept in store for long periods because of the perishable nature of the butter used.

(7) It is very important that the raw materials used for making buttercreams are conditioned to ensure that they can be amalgamated easily to produce a cream free from lumps. This means that the butter must be free from lumps and very plastic. If cold it will have to be slightly warmed before beating. Fondant must also be plasticized and free from skin and hard lumps. Icing sugar may need sieving. It is a mistake to believe that lumps can be knocked out by the action of beating on the machine – invariably they remain to ruin the mixture completely.

Flavouring Buttercream and Creamed Fillings

Buttercream and creamed fillings will blend with a very large variety of flavouring materials, most of which are listed here:

(*1*) *Natural and Artificial Flavours, Essential Oils and Extracts* If these are of fruit extraction, e.g. lemon oil or flavour, tartaric or citric acid should be added to simulate the natural acidity of the fruit.

(*2*) *Fruit Extracts, Juices and Concentrates* These are very true flavouring materials and are excellent for use in creams.

(*3*) *Curds* made from lemons, oranges and pineapple will blend well and impart an excellent flavour to cream.

(*4*) *Chocolate* This has to be first melted and stirred in whilst still warm. The cream too must not be too cold otherwise the chocolate will solidify before it is dispersed. For very sweet creams the use of block cocoa or unsweetened chocolate is recommended. Chocolate may also be shredded and stirred in.

(*5*) *Nougat (Praline)* This is a paste made from roasted nuts and sugar. To blend it uniformly throughout the cream, it needs to be softened by first creaming it with a little buttercream before blending it into the rest.

(*6*) *Chestnut Purée* To make this, the chestnuts are boiled in water until soft. The husk and skin are first removed and the soft meat mashed to a purée. This may be sweetened and used as a filling cream on its own or added to the buttercream. (Chestnut purée may also be purchased in tins.)

(*7*) *Crushed Nuts* Any type of nut may be crushed and added.

(*8*) *Crushed Fruit* This makes a delicious addition to buttercream, but care must be taken to exclude as much juice as possible because this will separate out. Glacé fruits, e.g. cherries, angelica, pineapple, may also be added but are not as attractive in flavour as tinned or fresh fruit.

(*9*) *Spirits and Liqueurs* Any type may be added but the choice is usually limited to the liqueurs derived from fruits and would be used in combination with such fruits. Examples:

Kirsch, Maraschino and Cherry Brandy	– Pineapple and Cherries
Apricot Brandy	– Apricots
Peach Brandy	– Peaches
Grand Marnier, Curaçao	– Oranges
Tia Maria	– Coffee
Creme de Cacao	– Chocolate

Rum being derived from sugar, blends well with a variety of different flavours but it is especially good with chocolate and therefore, ganache.

Some fruits are so strong in flavour that the use of a liqueur in combination would be uneconomical, e.g. lemon.

(*10*) *Coffee*   Liquid or the powdered instant variety.

(*11*) *Milk*   Evaporated or condensed milk may be added to make a smoother buttercream and simulate the flavour of fresh cream.

(*12*) *Malt*   Malt extract or dried malt extract may be added.

(*13*) *Eggs*   The use of eggs, especially yolks, helps to enrich the buttercream. The use of egg whites is solely to make the cream lighter and smoother.

BUTTERCREAM RECIPES

1. German

	kg	g	lb	oz
Unsalted butter	1	000	2	4
Castor sugar	—	445	1	0
Fresh eggs	—	350	1	11
Totals	1	795	4	15

(1) Whisk the eggs and sugar to a firm sponge.
(2) Beat the butter to a light cream.
(3) Add the sponge to the butter in approx. 4 portions, beating well to form a smooth buttercream.

2. Icing Sugar

	kg	g	lb	oz
Unsalted butter	1	000	2	4
Icing sugar	1	000	2	4
Egg whites	—	85	—	3
Totals	2	085	4	11

(1) Cream the butter and sugar well together.
(2) Add the egg whites and continue beating until it is light.

3. Fondant

	kg	g	lb	oz
Unsalted butter	1	000	2	4
Fondant	1	110	2	8
Totals	2	110	4	12

(1) Work the fondant to a plastic mass free from lumps.
(2) Cream the butter and add the fondant a little at a time until it is all incorporated.

4. Pectin

	kg	g	lb	oz
Unsalted butter	1	000	2	4
Granulated sugar	—	665	1	8
Icing sugar	—	165	—	6
Egg whites	—	415	—	15
Water	—	85	—	3
* Pectin mixture	—	60	—	2
Totals	2	390	5	6

(1) Place the sugar, pectin mixture, water and egg whites in a bain-marie and slowly heat to approx. 38°C (100°F), stirring continuously. Allow to cool.
(2) Beat the butter and icing sugar until very light.
(3) Pour in the cooled pectin syrup and beat until light and smooth.

Pectin Mixture

	kg	g	lb	oz
Granulated sugar	1	000	2	4
Powdered pectin 40% strength	—	300	—	11
Totals	1	300	2	15

Mix the powdered pectin and sugar well together and store in an airtight tin for use as required.

5. Boiled

	kg	g	lb	oz
Unsalted butter	1	000	2	4
Icing sugar	—	250	—	9
Lump or granulated sugar	1	335	3	0
Castor sugar	—	250	—	9
Water	—	415	—	15
Eggs	—	250	—	9
Cream of tartar	—	4	—	$\frac{1}{8}$
Totals	3	504	7	$14\frac{1}{8}$

Method for 5 and 6
(1) Boil the lump or granulated sugar with the water to 118°C (245°F). The cream of

tartar moistened with water should be added when the syrup reaches 225°F. Observe the rules for sugar boiling (*see* page 13).

(2) Whisk the egg, sugar and egg whites to a stiff sponge foam, timing it so that it is ready when the syrup has reached the required temperature.

(3) Add the hot syrup in a steady stream to the sponge foam at slow speed. When incorporated, change to medium speed and beat for approx. 5 minutes.

(4) Beat the butter or butter and icing sugar to a light cream, add the sponge or meringue and beat until it is all incorporated.

6. Boiled

	kg	g	lb	oz
Unsalted butter	1	000	2	4
Lump or granulated sugar	1	000	2	4
Water	—	305	1	11
Egg whites	—	625	1	6$\frac{1}{2}$
Cream of tartar	—	4	—	$\frac{1}{8}$
Totals	2	934	7	9$\frac{5}{8}$

7. Custard

	kg	g	lb	oz
Unsalted butter	1	000	2	4
Icing sugar	—	500	1	2
Cold custard (*see* page 180)	1	000	2	4
Totals	2	500	5	10

(1) Beat the butter and icing sugar to a light and smooth cream.

(2) Blend in the custard and beat to a smooth buttercream.

8. Lemon

	kg	g	lb	oz
Unsalted butter	1	000	2	4
Fondant	2	000	4	8
Lemon curd	—	500	1	2
Totals	3	500	7	14

(1) Work the fondant to a plastic mass free from lumps.

(2) Beat the butter and gradually add the fondant beating until it is all incorporated.

(3) Lastly blend in the lemon curd. For a stiffer buttercream add 500 g (1 lb 2 oz) of icing sugar.

9. G.M.S.

	kg	g	lb	oz
Unsalted butter	1	000	2	4
Icing sugar	—	500	1	2
Castor sugar	—	625	1	6½
Eggs	—	500	1	2
* G.M.S. emulsion	—	125	—	4½
Totals	2	750	6	3

(1) Whip the eggs, castor sugar and G.M.S. emulsion to a firm sponge.
(2) Beat the butter and icing sugar to a light cream.
(3) Add the G.M.S. sponge in a steady stream whilst continuing to beat on slow speed. Once incorporated, beat on medium speed for approx. 5 minutes.

* G.M.S. Emulsion

	kg	g	lb	oz
Water	1	000	2	4
Glycerol monostearate	—	200		7
Totals	1	200	2	11

(1) Heat the water and stir in the GMS flakes. Whisk to form an emulsion.

10. Marshmallow

	kg	g	lb	oz
Unsalted butter	1	000	2	4
Icing sugar	—	165	—	6
Fondant	—	335	—	12
Marshmallow	1	000	2	4
Totals	2	500	5	10

(1) Beat the butter to a smooth light cream.
(2) Add the marshmallow and beat at medium speed for approx. 5 minutes.
(3) Add the icing sugar and beat in well.
(4) Plasticise the fondant and beat this in also.
(5) For recipe 11 add the evaporated milk.
(6) When all the ingredients are blended together beat on medium speed for another 5 minutes.

11. Marshmallow

	kg	g	lb	oz
Unsalted butter	1	000	2	4
Icing sugar	—	500	1	2
Marshmallow	—	665	1	8
Evaporated milk	—	220	—	8
Totals	2	385	5	6

CREAMED FILLINGS

1. Fudge

	kg	g	lb	oz
High grade shortening	1	000	2	4
Fondant	1	780	4	0
Icing sugar	1	780	4	0
Evaporated milk	—	335	—	12
Totals	4	895	11	0

Recipe 1
(1) Beat the shortening with the icing sugar.
(2) Plasticize the fondant, add and beat in well.
(3) Add the milk in a steady stream and beat for a further 2 minutes.

2. Fudge

	kg	g	lb	oz
Unsalted butter or margarine	1	000	2	4
Fondant	1	780	4	0
Evaporated milk	—	165	—	6
Totals	2	945	6	10

Recipe 2
(1) Warm the fondant and blend in the butter.
(2) Add the milk and beat to a smooth icing.
    These fillings may be used as an icing by heating in a bain-marie to a temperature of approx. 38°C (100°F) when it can be poured onto cakes in the same manner as fondant. When set, this icing forms a crust which facilitates wrapping.
Note This icing is also known as parfait icing.
    Other creamed fillings are made by substituting butter for unsalted margarine and/or shortening in the previous buttercream recipes.

3. Fruit

	kg	g	lb	oz
*Cider	1	000	2	4
Fruit pulp	—	500	1	2
Granulated sugar	—	500	1	2
Cornflour	—	165	—	6
Lemon juice	—	85	—	3
Totals	2	250	5	1

*This may be replaced in part or all by wine, fruit juice, milk or water.
(1) Place the ingredients in a clean saucepan.
(2) Gently heat, constantly stirring until the mixture thickens.
(3) Transfer to an earthenware basin and allow to cool.
(4) Cover with a damp cloth to prevent formation of skin.

4. Wine

	kg	g	lb	oz
Dry white wine	1	000	2	4
Granulated sugar	—	220	—	8
Lemon juice	—	220	—	8
Egg yolk	—	55	—	2
Gelatine	—	70	—	$2\frac{1}{2}$
Whipped, sweetened double cream	1	170	2	8
Totals	2	735	6	$0\frac{1}{2}$

(1) Place the wine, sugar, lemon juice and egg yolk in a clean saucepan and carefully cook the mixture, using a whisk to prevent the formation of lumps.
(2) Add the gelatine and stir until it dissolves.
(3) Add the sweetened, whipped cream and blend into a smooth cream.
Notes
(1) The wine may be replaced with cider.
(2) The consistency may be adjusted by altering the quantity of wine used, adjusting the gelatine content or using single cream instead of double.
(3) This filling may be used instead of fresh cream in cream goods.

CUSTARDS

These may be used in a number of different types of goods, i.e.
Vanilla slices – (*see* page 49).
Danish pastries (*see* first volume of *Bakery: Bread and Fermented Goods*).
Buttercream and creamed fillings – (*see* page 176).

Custards

	1				2				3				4			
	kg	g	lb	oz	kg	g	lb	oz	kg	g	lb	oz	kg	g	lb	oz
Milk	1	000	2	4	1	000	2	4	1	000	2	4	1	000	2	4
Cornflour	—	100	—	3½	—	155	—	5½	—	80	—	2¾	—	100	—	3½
Sugar	—	155	—	5½	—	600	1	5½	—	195	—	7	—	195	—	7
Eggs	—	195	—	7	—	—	—	—	—	250	—	9	—	—	—	—
Egg yolks	—	—	—	—	—	305	—	11	—	—	—	—	—	—	—	—
Egg whites	—	—	—	—	—	610	1	6	—	—	—	—	—	—	—	—
Butter	—	—	—	—	—	—	—	—	—	100	—	3½	—	80	—	2¾
Powdered gelatine	—	—	—	—	—	—	—	—	—	—	—	—	—	15	—	½
Vanilla flavour	as required				as required				as required				as required			
Totals	1	450	3	4	2	670	6	0	1	625	3	10¼	1	390	3	1¾

Recipes 1, 2 and 3
(1) Use a little of the milk to make a paste with the cornflour.
(2) Mix the sugar with the rest of the milk and bring to the boil.
(3) Pour this onto the cornflour paste stirring vigorously to prevent the formation of lumps.
(4) Return the mixture to the heat and bring to boiling point, stirring continuously.
(5) Whisk the egg and/or yolk and white and whilst stirring slowly pour on the hot gelatinized liquid.
(6) Put the mixture into a bain-marie and gently heat until it thickens.
(7) Lastly, if there is any butter in the recipe, this should be stirred into the hot custard.
(8) Cover and leave to get cold before serving.

Recipe 4
(1) Mix the gelatine and cornflour with a little of the milk and make a paste.
(2) Add the sugar to the milk and bring to the boil.
(3) Pour the hot liquid onto the paste whilst stirring.
(4) Return to the heat and bring to the boil, stirring continuously.
(5) Proceed as for 7 and 8 in the previous recipe.

14. Torten

Introduction

Before introducing the reader to these special examples of the confectioner's art, some notes of explanation are appropriate.

Torte is the German term for a large flat tart or gâteau. The plural is *Torten*.

The true description is therefore of German origin, but even in this country these goods differ in the materials used and the way they are made up into this type of cake.

There are many interpretations. In some cases a large decorated gâteau is called a torte, but the generally accepted definition is that of a large flat gâteau, already divided into a number of segments, each similarly decorated. The torte may either be sold as a whole unit or the individual segments sold separately as slices. In this event it is important that the slice is placed in a protective carton if it is to be taken from the shop. However, in Germany, a slice of torte is a very popular accompaniment to an afternoon cup of coffee or tea and is very prominent in all the coffee houses.

If the reader peruses this chapter it will be seen that there are so many different types of bases, fillings and decorative materials one can use, that it is difficult for torten to be classified. One point should be made however.

Because torten is sold by the slice, it is very important to ensure that the interior should look as attractive as the exterior and to this end special layering techniques aimed at providing good contrast between the base and the filling should be used, to create interest when the torte is cut. If fruit is used, for example, it should be incorporated in such a way that it is clearly visible when the torte is cut.

Many torten are made from a sponge which besides being layered with cream and other fillings, is also soaked with a liqueur-flavoured syrup, or even sweetened fruit juice. Such a sponge is made low in sugar so that excessive sweetness is avoided. A high egg quantity is also used to improve cutting qualities.

The base often comprises a disc of japanese, sweetpaste or a similar biscuit-like article.

A typical section of a torte would appear as shown in Figure 59.

Figure 59. Section of a typical torte incorporating a layer of fruit

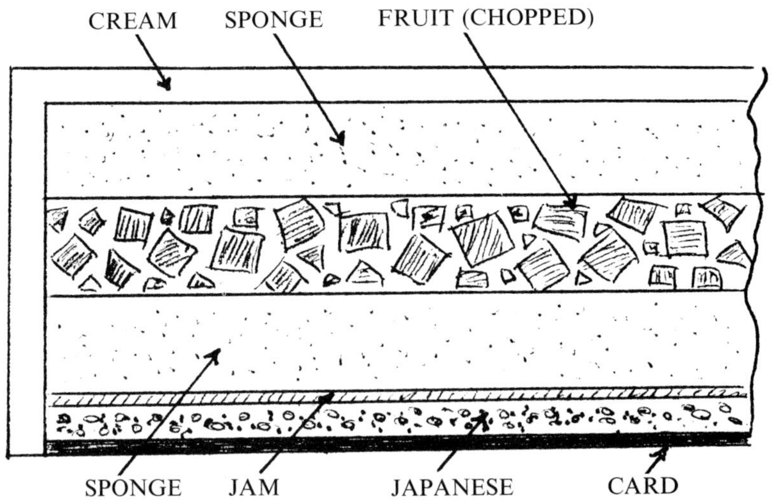

CREAM   SPONGE   FRUIT (CHOPPED)

SPONGE   JAM   JAPANESE   CARD

If fruit such as cherries is to be incorporated they would replace the centre layer of sponge.

As an alternative to layering horizontally, we can bake the sponge in a thin sheet, like Swiss roll and cut it into strips. After spreading with an appropriate cream, these strips are rolled up and placed vertically onto the base. The section would then appear as shown in Figure 60.

Figure 60. Section of a torte made from a roll so that vertical layers are formed

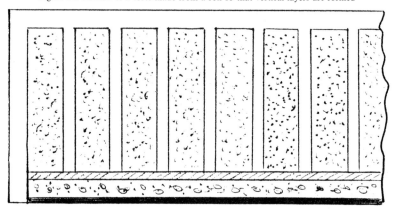

Yet another alternative is to bake sheets of differently coloured sponge and cut these into rings using a number of graduated sized cutters. This is known as a harlequin. For a 25 cm (10 in) torte these should be approx. as follows:

5, 10, 15 and 20 cm (2, 4, 6 and 8 in).

By interchanging alternately sized rings we can then make a checkerboard pattern when the segment is cut as shown in Figure 61.

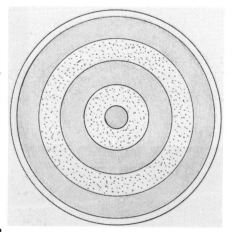

Figure 61 A. Plan of a torte showing how the rings of coloured sponge should be arranged to produce the checkerboard effect shown in the section. The two coloured rings are interchanged between each layer.

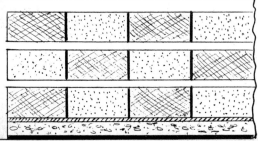

B. Section of the checkerboard torte.

Size   It is recommended that these should not be more than 6 cm ($2\frac{3}{8}$ in) in height. The diameter may vary between 20–30 cm (8–12 in) in diameter.

Method of Assembly (see Figures 62-70)   The following method has been adopted by the author for the assembly and coating of a basic torte.

(1) A disc of either japanese or sweetpaste is placed onto a circular torten card and given a coating of raspberry or another jam of good quality.

The torten card is made in waxed cardboard and should have a size about 12 mm ($\frac{1}{2}$ in) larger in diameter than the jap (or sweetpaste) base. Cake strawboards may also be used for this purpose, although they may prove more expensive.

(2) The sponge is now assembled on the base in at least three layers (unless fruit is used) with a liberal layer of flavoured cream between. This sponge may either be baked in one piece and cut into three afterwards or it might be more convenient to bake three very thin sponges.

The discs of sponge should be the same size as the base of either japanese or sweetpaste and if necessary should be trimmed to this size. Before each sponge disc is layered with cream it should be liberally sprinkled with a suitably flavoured syrup. For high class torten this should be flavoured with liqueur (*see* page 187 and Figures 62 and 63).

Stages in the making of a cherry torte: Figure 62. Applying the syrup to the first layer of sponge which has been sandwiched to a jap base with jam.

Figure 63. Applying the cherries to form a layer in the centre of the torte.

(3) After assembly, a cakeboard is placed on top and pressure applied to ensure a perfectly flat top surface.

(4) The top and sides are now completely masked in a suitably flavoured (and coloured) buttercream, employing a suitable turntable.

(5) Using a celluloid scraper, plain or serrated, the side is coated by holding the scraper against the edge of the torten card or strawboard, so that an even layer of cream is perfectly applied when the turntable is revolved. The card or strawboard acts like a template in this application (*see* Figure 64).

Figure 64. Applying the side coating of cream, using a serrated plastic scraper to form a ribbed pattern.

(6) Using a long wide-bladed knife, the top is levelled by sweeping the knife from the outside edge to the centre from about four positions of the turntable (*see* Figure 65). After practice, a smooth and level top with a clear unbroken edge can be accomplished. Alternatively the top may be coated by sweeping a knife or straight edge over and cutting off with a palette knife as the sides are coated.

Figure 65. Use of a long wide-bladed knife to apply the smooth top coating.

(7) Because of the card under the torte, the latter may be handled more easily to facilitate the application of edge or side decoration. The card is intended to stay with the torte and therefore unless it is sold by the slice, is sold with the cake to the customer. In this event special card containers are often supplied to ensure that the customer gets the torte home undamaged.

Figure 66. Applying toasted desiccated coconut to the bottom edge for decoration

(8) Special dividers can now be used which when placed upon the buttercream top will leave marks which will indicate where the cut needs to be made to divide the torte.

Figure 67. Marking the top into 12 divisions with the torte divider

(9) The use of a shield made out of a disc of a stiff paper into which has been set a round cutter will ensure that a sprinkling of corallettes can be placed into the centre without any being scattered over the top and so spoil the surface.

Figure 68. Sprinkling decoration to for centrepiece.

(10) Each segment is suitably decorated and the torte is now ready for sale.

69 Piping lines of cream over the marks left by the torte divider

Figure 70. The finished torte

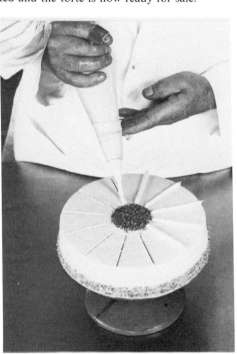

Other Types of Torten

Many varieties of torten are made from a suitable base with wine cream or fresh cream with fruit. Obviously such torten require refrigeration to keep them in perfect condition.

There are also many torten which are traditional and therefore should be made only in a certain way and from specified materials. Examples of such torten are Sacher, Kirsch, Dobos, etc.

Special anniversaries and traditional holidays may be celebrated with specially made and decorated torten (or gâteaux). Some of these celebrated in Britain are as follows:

New Year's Day – January 1st.

St. Valentine's Day – February 14th.

Mother's Day – Mid-lent Sunday.
St. Patrick's Day – March 17th.
Easter
Halloween – October 31st.
Guy Fawkes' Day – November 5th.
Christmas – December 25th.
In addition to these there are birthdays, children's parties, etc., when such special
cakes might be appropriate.

Flavours

Most continental torten are flavoured with liqueurs in combination with fruit or
nuts. The following shows some useful combinations:

Fruit, etc.	*Liqueurs*
Apricot	Apricot Brandy
Cherry	Kirsch, Cherry Brandy, Maraschino
Chocolate	Rum
Coffee	Tia Maria, Rum, Brandy
Ganache	Rum, Brandy
Orange	Grand Marnier, Curaçao, Cointreau
Pineapple	Kirsch
Peach	Peach Brandy
Praline	Rum

Lemon is so strongly flavoured that it is usually unnecessary to add any liqueur. The
syrup used to flavour such torten should be strongly flavoured with the juice of the fruit
itself. If tinned fruit is used the juice should be employed for the syrup with which to
soak the sponge. If spirits such as rum, for example, are added, the sweetness might
have to be adjusted by the addition of extra sugar (icing) or golden syrup.

Buttercream

A good quality buttercream should be used for torten (*see* pages 174–178). It should
be made from unsalted butter so that the true flavour of the liqueur, for example, is not
impaired.

Torten Bases

There are a bewildering number of individual recipes published in the various recipe
books of continental origin, but basically, although variations can easily be made, there
are three basic types. These are:
Butter sponge (Vienna)
Roll – (Roulade)
Sponge biscuit (Dobos)
Variations can be made to these as follows:

Butter

Plain sponges are usually used but some melted butter can be incorporated to form a
butter sponge if desired. The sponge should be kept warm to facilitate the blending of
the butter.

Chocolate

It is usual to replace up to 110 g (4 oz) per kg ($2\frac{1}{4}$ lb) of flour (including cornflour)
with cocoa powder and add 55 g (2 oz) sugar. In some chocolate roulade mixtures
chocolate couverture is added.

Torten Bases

	Sponge						Dobos				Roulade			
	Vienna 1		Vienna 2		Almond		1		2		Almond		Plain	
	kg g	lb oz	kg g	lb oz	kg g	lb oz	kg g	lb oz	kg g	lb oz	kg g	lb oz	kg g	lb oz
Medium strong flour	— 470	1 1	— —	— —	— —	— —	— —	— —	— —	— —	— 570	1 4½	— —	— —
Soft flour	— —	— —	— 765	1 11½	1 000	2 4	1 000	2 4	1 000	2 4	— —	— —	1 000	2 4
Cornflour	— 530	1 3	— 235	— 8½	— —	— —	— —	— —	— —	— —	— 430	— 15½	1 670	3 12
Whole egg	1 170	2 10	1 305	2 15	2 000	4 8	— —	— —	— —	— —	— 185	— 6¾	1 670	3 12
Egg yolk	— —	— —	— 220	— 8	— 305	— 11	— 665	1 8	1 000	2 4	— 430	— 15½	— —	— —
Castor sugar	— 820	1 13½	1 085	2 7	1 195	2 11	— 915	2 1	1 335	3 0	1 430	3 3½	— 30	— 1
Baking powder	— 15	— ½	— —	— —	— —	— —	— —	— —	— —	— —	— —	— —	— —	— —
Water	— 110	— 4	— 75	— 2¾	— —	— —	— —	— —	— —	— —	— —	— —	— —	— —
Glycerine	— —	— —	— 75	— 2¾	— —	— —	— —	— —	— —	— —	— —	— —	— —	— —
Raw marzipan	— —	— —	— —	— —	— —	— —	— —	— —	— —	— —	— 860	1 15	— —	— —
Ground almonds	— —	— —	— —	— —	— 750	1 11	— —	— —	— —	— —	— —	— —	— —	— —
Egg whites	— —	— —	— —	— —	— —	— —	1 335	3 0	1 670	3 12	— —	— —	— —	— —
Melted butter	— 85	— 3	— —	— —	— 415	— 15	— 415	— 15	1 335	3 0	— —	— —	— 835	1 14
Totals	3 200	7 3	3 760	8 7½	5 665	12 12	4 330	9 12	6 340	14 4	3 905	8 12¾	5 205	11 11

Almond

Ground almonds can be used to replace up to $\frac{1}{3}$ of the flour content, or alternatively raw marzipan can be used if first mixed with additional egg yolks to form a smooth paste.

METHODS FOR MAKING BASES

Vienna Butter Sponge

Yields – Recipe 1 – 8 bases of 23 or $25\frac{1}{2}$ cm diameter (9 or 10 in).
Yields – Recipe 2 – 10 bases of 23 or $25\frac{1}{2}$ cm diameter (9 or 10 in).
 Prepare the torten hoops as follows:
(1) Cut greaseproof or silicone paper squares sufficiently large enough to cover the ring. Drum these hoops as described on page 132.
(2) Grease the sides of the torten rings, secure a band of brown paper to the outside and place on a good protection of paper or cardboard.

Method for Sponge

(1) Sieve and blend the flours together (and baking powder for Recipe No. 1).
(2) Mix the eggs, sugar, water (and glycerine for Recipe 2). Warm and whisk to a full sponge (*see* page 116).
(3) Carefully blend in the sieved flours.
(4) For Recipe 1 add the melted butter and carefully blend into the sponge.
(5) Deposit approx. 400 g (14 oz) into torten rings.
(6) Bake at 188°C (370°F) for approx. 40–45 minutes.

Dobos – Method for Recipe 1

(1) Whisk half the sugar with the egg yolks to form a sponge.
(2) Whisk the remaining half of the sugar with the egg whites to form a meringue.
(3) Melt the butter, blend into the egg yolk and sugar mixture and then carefully incorporate the meringue.
(4) Lastly add the flour and mix to a smooth batter.
(5) Grease and flour a baking sheet and spread this mixture to a thickness of approx. 3 mm ($\frac{1}{8}$ in) thick either in a sheet for slices, etc., or in discs for torten.
    The latter is best done using a stencil, but if this is not possible, it should be spread with a scraper inside a torte ring.
(6) Bake at 215°C (420°F) until crisp and brown.
(7) Trim the discs of baked sponge prior to assembly.

Dobos – Method for Recipe 2

(1) Cream the butter and half the sugar quantity to a light batter.
(2) Gradually add the yolks a little at a time, beating in each addition.
(3) Whisk the egg whites and the remaining sugar into a stiff meringue.
(4) Blend the meringue into the batter.
(5) Carefully fold in the flour and mix to a smooth batter.
(6) Proceed as with 5–7 in previous method.

VARIETIES FROM VIENNA SPONGE BASES

Fruit Torten

A wide variety of fruit torten may be made using fruit in many different forms and incorporating it in many different ways. The sponge is invariably soaked with the fruit juice to which the appropriate liqueur has been added. Some ideas on the make-up of these torten are as follows:

Lemon

Interior filling   Lemon-curd or lemon buttercream in which either lemon curd or lemon paste has been blended.
Coating   Lemon-flavoured buttercream.
Decoration   Lemon jelly slices with lines of piped buttercream.

Orange

Interior filling   Orange curd or buttercream which is flavoured with orange paste or liqueur with segments of tinned mandarin oranges either layered or chopped and mixed in.
Coating   Orange or liqueur-flavoured buttercream.
Decoration   Segments of tinned mandarin orange or orange jelly slices with lines of piped buttercream. The segments of orange can first be glazed with apricot purée, but must first be *dry*.

Pineapple

Interior filling
   (*a*) Layer of paste made from sweetened tinned pineapple juice and good quality cake crumbs which can be flavoured with kirsch liqueur if required.
   (*b*) Kirsch-flavoured buttercream with either fresh or tinned pineapple pieces either layered or chopped and mixed in. (Drained pineapple crush can be used for this.)
Coating   Kirsch-flavoured buttercream.
Decoration   Wedges of glacé or confiture pineapple (*see* page 231) arranged on a piped line. An attractive flower form can be made by inserting the pineapple wedge into a V cut in a cherry.
   This is set onto each segment with a diamond of angelica to simulate a leaf.

Apricot/Peach

Interior filling   Buttercream flavoured with the appropriate fruit brandy with either tinned or reconstituted cooked fruit, halves in the case of apricot, and slices for the peach. Alternatively, the fruit may be cut into small pieces and incorporated into the buttercream.
Coating   Buttercream flavoured with the appropriate fruit brandy.
Decoration   Apricot – Firm well drained halves, glazed with apricot purée and set onto piped buttercream lines.
Peach – Selected well drained slices set onto piped buttercream lines.

Cherry

Interior filling   Buttercream flavoured with kirsch, maraschino or cherry brandy with a layer of stoned cherries (tinned or fresh). See page 183. Alternatively, the cherries may be cut up and incorporated with the buttercream.
Coating   Buttercream flavoured with the appropriate liqueur.
Decoration   Two glacé cherries arranged in their natural growing position with a line of piped chocolate coloured buttercream on each segment, or a whole cherry placed on each segment with diamonds of angelica. Maraschino-flavoured cherries are available for this purpose. Other decorations can be made especially with the use of chocolate.

Strawberry/Raspberry

Interior filling

(*a*) Buttercream into which sieved strawberry or raspberry has been mixed. This can be obtained from the tinned or frozen fruit.

(*b*) Use the flavoured buttercream with a layer of strawberries. The fresh fruit is the best, but frozen can also be used.

Coating Appropriately flavoured buttercream.

Decoration Fresh strawberries or raspberries set onto a rosette of buttercream on each segment. Select the fruit so that the size is uniform. It might be necessary to cut large strawberries in half. If fresh fruit is unobtainable, jelly fruit can be used or the torte left plain. Both the tinned and frozen forms of these fruits are unsuitable to use as decoration, because they lack firmness.

Other Fruit Torten

The fruit torten previously described are basically made up from sponge and buttercream with a filling of fruit, only pieces of which are used for decoration.

Other torten may be made from suitably flavoured and layered sponge, but the whole of the top covered with fruit arranged in various patterns as for fruit flans (*see* page 26).

Several different fruits may be placed on in segments to make what might be regarded as a Tutti Frutti Torte.

Glazing of the fruit is important not only for appearance, but to help prevent the fruit from drying out.

The best type of glaze to use is pectin and there are proprietary ones available which consist of a thick syrup to which a measured amount of citric acid is added. This rapidly sets the syrup to a jelly but gives enough time for it to be poured onto the fruit before it sets.

A novel way to cover the top and sides of such a torte is as follows:

(1) Make the glaze by pouring the recommended quantity of acid into the syrup as directed.

(2) Pour this onto a sheet of greaseproof paper and spread to a thin layer.

(3) When set, reverse the greaseproof paper with the jelly over the torte and wash the back with water.

(4) After a short while the layer of jelly will be released from the wet greaseproof paper and it will be transferred to the top of the torte.

(5) The greaseproof paper is now peeled away to leave a layer of pectin glaze completely covering the torte.

(6) A knife is now used to trim off the excess at the base.

Nut Torten

The nuts used for these varieties are mainly almond, hazelnut and walnut. They are usually incorporated in the sponge base either by replacing some of the flour with the ground nut or by adding crushed or nibbed nuts to the sponge batter.

Interior filling

(*a*) Buttercream containing crushed roasted nuts and praline.

(*b*) Softened nut paste made by adding syrup to the ground nut.

Coating Buttercream either left plain or flavoured with praline.

Decoration Whole or split nuts which may be roasted, placed upon piped lines in buttercream. The nuts may be used unblanched.

Praline (or Nougat)

Praline (or nougat) paste is an ideal flavouring agent with which to flavour buttercream for nut torten, but it can also be used on its own without the addition of nuts. Used in this way, a higher quantity of the paste may be incorporated to give it a more pronounced flavour.

To blend the praline paste into the buttercream so that it is free from lumps, the paste may first have to be warmed and worked to a pliable and smooth consistency. To ensure a smooth amalgamation of the paste and buttercream, the latter should be added a little at a time to the paste and each addition well mixed until all the buttercream is incorporated.

To soften the sponge bases of these nut and praline torten, a rum syrup may be used.

Chocolate

Figure 71. Two chocolate torten coated in chocolate buttercream.
Left This is decorated using chocolate "cut-outs" arranged as a flower for the centre, and chocolate-piped filigree shapes on the segments (*see* page 279)
Right Small round langue du chat biscuits are used in the decoration of this torte (*see* page 99)

Interior filling   Chocolate buttercream made by blending liquid couverture into the buttercream.

Coating   Either chocolate buttercream, a thin coating of chocolate couverture or chocolate icing (*see* page 167).

Decoration   Shapes cut out or piped from chocolate couverture and placed upon lines piped in chocolate buttercream. Other shapes such as langue du chat biscuits may also be used (*see* page 99).

The sponge bases may be made from chocolate sponge in which some of the flour is replaced by cocoa powder. A rum syrup is a very suitable medium with which to soak the sponge. Rum can also be added to the chocolate buttercream if desired.

Ganache

This is made similarly to the chocolate torte, except that ganache (*see* page 171) is used instead of chocolate buttercream. Rum may also be used to flavour in the same way.

Figure 72. A ganache coated torte. Chocolate coralettes are used to decorate the centre and bottom. On each segment a line of white cream is piped and on this is placed a diamond of angelica and a chocolate filigree flower (*see* page 279)

Coffee

Interior filling   Buttercream flavoured with coffee extract. Rum or Tia Maria may also be added.
Coating   The same flavoured buttercream.
Decoration   Small marzipan modelled coffee beans set on lines piped in buttercream.

The sponge may be coffee flavoured by the addition of instant coffee or coffee extract to the sponge batter. The bases may be soaked with syrup containing either rum or Tia Maria.

Black Forest (Schwarzwalder) (Also *see* page 199)

This is a traditional torte from Germany. There the sponge bases are specially prepared, but a good quality chocolate sponge is perfectly satisfactory. Kirsch-flavoured syrup may be used for soaking the sponge. Use three thin rounds of chocolate sponge.
Interior filling   Cooked cherries (suitably sweetened) or tinned cherries with kirsch-flavoured whipped dairy cream.
Decoration   Chocolate shavings around the edge and in the centre. Place a glacé cherry or a rosette of cream piped onto each segment. Dust with icing sugar and refrigerate.

Kirsch

This is another traditional torte from Switzerland. It simply consists of two layers of sponge soaked with a kirsch-flavoured syrup and sandwiched with a pale pink coloured buttercream between two large discs of japanese. The torte is finished by masking with buttercream and roasted nib or flaked almonds or sieved jap crumbs. The top is dusted with icing sugar and marked with the back of a knife in a lozenge design. Glacé cherries or crystallized flower petals can be used in the centre as an added decoration.

To ensure that the sponge is saturated with the syrup, it is usual to allow it to lie in a shallow pan into which a measured amount of the syrup is first placed. The sponge is left until all the syrup has been absorbed.

Marzipan

Use the almond butter sponge recipe for the bases.

Figure 73. Kirsch torte. The centre motif of marzipan is made from two halves of glacé cherries with stalks piped in chocolate and some thin strips of citron peel to imitate leaves

Interior filling   Strawberry jam and vanilla-flavoured buttercream.
Coating
Sides – buttercream masked with roasted nib almonds.
Top – disc of pink marzipan.
Decoration   Rout biscuit filled with strawberry jam placed in each segment.

Almond

Use the almond butter-sponge recipe for the bases.
Interior filling   Vanilla-flavoured buttercream.
Coating
Sides – buttercream masked with roasted nib almonds.
Top – buttercream.
Decoration   Segments of rout biscuit embellished with a piece of cherry and angelica.

Dobos

The making of the Dobos bases is explained on the following pages:
Recipe 188.
Method 189.
The detailed method for the making of a Dobos Torte is now explained.
Method of assembly
(1) For this torte we need five thin discs of the Dobos sponge. Select the best for the top and sandwich the others liberally with the caramel cream (*see* opposite).
(2) Ice the selected top disc with the hot caramel (*see* opposite) and when cold, cut into the desired number of segments.
 This is best done by inverting the caramel iced surface onto a cutting board and with a sharp knife cutting first through the sponge and then the caramel.
(3) Coat the top and sides with the caramel cream.
(4) Mask the sides with roasted nib or flaked almonds.
(5) Arrange the caramel coated segments on top.
To make and use the Caramel
(1) Place some sugar in a copper pan with the lemon juice and heat to melt the sugar first and then bring it to the caramel degree (but not too dark) (*see* page 13).
(2) When the sugar is sufficiently coloured, stir in the butter or margarine.

(3) Pour the hot caramel onto the baked torte top and spread with a palette knife.
(4) Allow the caramel to set and then, using a knife with a saw-like action, cut into the
desired number of segments.
Yield – 10 torten
Caramel

	kg	g	lb	oz
Granulated sugar	1	000	2	4
Lemon juice	—	55	—	2
Butter	—	85	—	3
Totals	2	40	2	9

Caramel Cream

	kg	g	lb	oz
Fresh dairy cream	1	000	2	4
Granulated sugar	—	305		11
Lemon juice	—	—		$\frac{1}{2}$
Totals	1	305	2	$15\frac{1}{2}$

To make the caramel cream
(1) Weigh the sugar into a copper pan, add a drop of lemon juice and place on the heat
to melt the sugar and then bring it to the caramel degree – a light amber at approx.
160°C (320°F).
(2) Remove from the heat and add a little water (beware of steam) to bring the caramel
to a syrup which when cold has the consistency of golden syrup.
(3) Start whisking the fresh double dairy cream, add the cold caramel syrup to flavour
and sweeten and continue whisking until it is thick.
Note Dobos may also be made into slices by baking the mixture in strips and
sandwiching together after first cutting the caramel-coated layer into the appropriately
sized slices.

Sacher (This is the original recipe of this Austrian speciality)
Yield – 7 Torten

	kg	g	lb	oz
Soft flour	1	000	2	4
Butter	1	000	2	4
Castor sugar	1	095	2	$7\frac{1}{2}$
Egg yolks	1	095	2	$7\frac{1}{2}$
Egg whites	1	595	3	$9\frac{1}{2}$
Chocolate	1	250	2	13
Vanilla extract		as required		
Totals	7	035	15	$13\frac{1}{2}$

(1) Add half the sugar to the butter and beat into a cream.
(2) Melt the chocolate and blend into the cream.
(3) Add the yolks a little at a time and beat into the cream.
(4) Whisk the whites to a stiff snow and stir in the rest of the sugar to form a meringue.
(5) Carefully fold the flour into the meringue and then the butter and egg yolk cream.
(6) Deposit the batter into a well greased torte ring and bake at 176°C (350°F).
(7) When cold, sandwich the sponge with apricot jam and mask the top and sides with apricot purée.
(8) Coat the top and sides with the special chocolate coating and with chocolate write the word *Sacher* on top.

Chocolate Icing

	Soft				Fudge			
	kg	g	lb	oz	kg	g	lb	oz
Plain chocolate couverture (shredded)	1	000	2	4	1	000	2	4
Granulated sugar	1	000	2	4	1	195	2	11
Water	—	835	1	14	—	610	1	6
Totals	2	835	6	6	2	805	6	5

Soft Icing
(1) Shred the chocolate into small pieces and gently heat [not above 43°C (110°F)] to melt.
(2) Place the sugar and water in a saucepan and warm to form a syrup.
(3) Add the syrup to the chocolate and stir well to form a smooth glossy icing.

Fudge Icing
(1) Boil the sugar, shredded chocolate couverture and water to 107°C (225°F) (thread degree) stirring the mixture constantly.
(2) Once this condition is reached, pass the mixture through a conical strainer into a cool container.
(3) Pour a little of the icing onto a cold slab and rub down with a palette knife until it commences to grain or crystallize.
(4) Return the grained icing to the mass and stir this to cause the rest of the icing to grain.
(5) Pour immediately over the prepared bases and allow to set.

Linzer (Austrian)
(1) Make up into a paste by the creaming method 2 (*see* page 16).
(2) Use half the pastry allocated to each torte for the base, roll this out to fill a torten ring and place onto a clean baking tin surrounded by the ring.
(3) With the remaining pastry, make a rope which will encircle the base and cut the rest into strips.
(4) Brush the edge of the base with a little water and attach the rope of pastry.
(5) Spread red currant jam on the base and cover with a lattice of pastry from the strips already cut.
(6) Egg wash these strips and bake the torte at 180°C (360°F).

Figure 74. Linzer torte

Yield – 8 torten for Recipe 1, 14 for Recipe 2.

	Recipe 1				Recipe 2			
	kg	*g*	*lb*	*oz*	*kg*	*g*	*lb*	*oz*
Soft flour	1	000	2	4	1	000	2	4
Butter	1	000	2	4	2	350	5	4½
Icing sugar	1	555	3	8	2	350	5	4½
Egg	—	335	—	12	1	405	3	2½
Egg yolks	—	335	—	12	—	—	—	—
Ground almonds	—	780	1	12	2	350	5	4½
Sponge crumbs	—	—	—	—	2	350	5	4½
Baking powder	—	—	—	—	—	50	—	1¾
Ground cinnamon	—	—	—	—	—	30	—	1
Zest of lemon or lemon paste	—	30	—	1	—	50	—	1¾
Totals	5	035	11	5	11	935	26	13

Strawberry Dairy Cream

Yield – 4 Torten

	kg	*g*	*lb*	*oz*
Sweet paste	1	000	2	4
Viennese sponge base	1	000	2	4
Strawberries	3	115	7	0
Strawberry pulp	—	390	—	14
Dairy cream (whipping)	2	225	5	0
Red currant jelly	—	220	—	8
Lemon juice	—	30	—	1
Leaf gelatine	—	55	—	2
Totals	8	035	18	1

(1) Roll out the sweetpaste to approx. 2 mm ($\frac{1}{10}$ in) in thickness and cut out a disc using a 25 cm (10 in) torten ring.
(2) Transfer to a baking tray and bake in an oven at approx. 193°C (380°F) to a light golden brown colour.
(3) Spread the sweetpaste base with the red currant jelly or jam and place a disc of Viennese sponge on top.
(4) Cover this with the strawberries which have been previously washed and dried.
(5) Soak the leaf gelatine in water for at least 1 hour, then drain and add it to the strawberry pulp and lemon juice. Warm to dissolve the gelatine.
(6) Whip the fresh cream and into this blend the gelatine solution.
(7) Spread the gelatined cream on top of the strawberries and shape with a flat top and straight sides which may be spread with a comb scraper if desired.
(8) Place some curled chocolate in the centre and decorate the segments with a rosette of the cream and whole fresh strawberries.
(9) The lower bottom edge can be dressed in roasted nuts if desired.

TECHNIQUES FOR TORTEN FINISHES

A quick commercial method for applying the fresh cream to dairy-cream torten is as follows:
(1) Surround the sweetpaste and Viennese sponge base with the torte ring.
(2) Cover with the fruit.
(3) Fill to the top of the hoop with cream using a straight edge to level it off against the sides of the hoop, and chill in a refrigerator.
(4) Lift the hoop away from the torte and mark the sides with a comb scraper.

If these torten are to be deep-frozen the following technique should be followed:
(1) Prepare the torte in the usual way with the bases covered with the fruit.
(2) Fill with the cream as described in (3) above making sure that it is pressed down the sides so that no air pockets are formed.
(3) After levelling the top, lay on a disc of waxed paper.
(4) Several torten may be stacked one upon the other and stored in the deep freeze until required.
(5) To finish, take from the deep freeze and leave with the wax paper removed until the

hoop can be removed easily by hand. If the torte is required immediately, it can be held over heat for a second or so when the hoop can be easily lifted off to give a smooth perfectly coated side. No further coatings to either the top or the sides are necessary.

Figure 75. Method of stacking partially finished torten for storing in a deep freeze.

Black Forest (Schwarzwälder) Torte

This torte may also be made by this method in the following way:
(1) Lay a disc of chocolate sponge inside the torten ring and cover with a compote of black cherries.
(2) Fill to within 12 mm ($\frac{1}{2}$ in) of the top with whipped cream flavoured with kirsch liqueur.
(3) Lay in another thin disc of chocolate sponge and press down to leave approx. 6 mm ($\frac{1}{4}$ in) to the top of the torte ring.
(4) Sprinkle this chocolate sponge liberally with kirsch liqueur syrup.
(5) Fill to the top with chocolate or kirsch flavoured cream and level off.
   These may now be refrigerated and released from its ring by warming.
(6) Decorate with a rosette of cream and a cherry on each segment and chocolate showing in the centre.
   Other types of fruit-filled dairy cream torten can be made using an alternative fruit filling. One such torte is as follows:

Swedish Apple

Proceed as for the Strawberry Dairy Cream Torte but with the following variations:
(1) Spread the sponge with a layer of softened marzipan.
(2) Use finely chopped apples for the fruit filling. Sultanas soaked in rum may also be added.
(3) To decorate the torte, pipe a rosette of cream and sprinkle on some roasted flaked nuts.

Note The fresh cream need not be stabilized with gelatine except in hot weather or if fruit pulp juices or liqueurs are added. If such additions to the cream are made, use the double cream, otherwise whipping cream is perfectly satisfactory.

Wine Cream

(1) Proceed as for the previous torten for 1, 2 and 3.
(2) Cover the Viennese sponge with a compote of various fruits (without the juice or syrup) to within 12 mm ($\frac{1}{2}$ in) from the edge.
(3) Place a torte hoop over the base.
(4) Make the wine cream (*see* recipe on page 179) and pour it into the torte hoop. This recipe will be sufficient for 4 torten.
(5) When cold remove the hoop, divide into 16 segments and decorate each segment using a rosette of fresh cream and cherries and/or small grapes.

Notes
(1) The compote may be made from one fruit if desired and the appropriate liqueur may be added to the wine cream, e.g. if cherries are used, Kirsch or Maraschino can be added. Obviously the fruit used in the decoration would have to be similarly appropriate.
(2) The Viennese sponge can also be varied. Almond for example would blend very well with cherry, peach or apricot.

Lemon Cream Cheese

Yield – 4 Torten

	kg	g	lb[*]	oz
Cream cheese filling (*see* opposite)	3	905	8	12½
Rum	—	110	—	4
Syrup (*see* page 164)	—	220	—	8
Icing sugar (for decoration)	—	110	—	4
Whipped cream (for decoration)	—	110	—	4
Roasted nib almonds (for decoration)	—	110	—	4
4 sponge rounds 23 cm (9 in) diameter × 2 cm (¾ in) thick	—	890	2	0
Totals	5	455	12	4½

Lemon Cream Cheese Filling

	kg	g	lb	oz
Cream cheese	1	000	2	4
Sugar	—	335	—	12
Lemon curd	—	890	2	0
Leaf gelatine	—	95	—	3½
Sultanas (soaked in rum)	—	335	—	12
Whipped cream	1	250	2	13
Totals	3	905	8	12½

(1) Soak the gelatine in water until it is pliable and then melt over heat.
(2) Mix the cream cheese, sugar and lemon curd and then blend in the gelatine solution (keep this mixture warm to prevent premature setting).
(3) Whip the cream and carefully stir it in with the sultanas which have been previously soaked by leaving overnight in rum.

Method for Torte Assembly

(1) Split the sponge rounds into two discs approx. 6 mm (¼ in) and 12 mm (½ in) thick.
(2) Place the thicker sponge in a 9 in torten ring on a card or board.
(3) Mix the rum with the syrup and liberally sprinkle over the sponge (first soak the sultanas in the rum, drain and then mix the remainder into the syrup).
(4) Spread on top the lemon cream cheese filling, level off and refrigerate.
(5) Cut the thin sponge layer into 12 or 16 segments, dust liberally with icing sugar and lay on top of the set filling.
(6) Carefully remove the torten ring and decorate using whipped cream and a sprinkling of roasted flaked almonds.

Variations

(1) A thin round of puff pastry may be used as a base before the sponge layer is placed into the ring.
(2) The disc of sponge may be omitted from the top of the torte.

Other Varieties

Many other varieties of cold-set cream cheese torten may be made using fruits other than sultanas. For example, blackcurrant, red currant, strawberry, raspberry, cherry, pineapple, apricot, orange, apple may all be used usually being incorporated in a layer on top of a sponge round with the filling on top. Some fruit may be incorporated with the filling, e.g. pineapple crush. The following filling is suitable for these varieties:

Cream Cheese Filling

Yield – 4 Torten

	kg	g	lb	oz
Cream cheese	1	000	2	4
Sugar	—	290		10½
Lemon juice	—	55		2
Leaf gelatine	—	110		4
Egg yolks	—	55		2
Whipped cream	1	110	2	8
Milk	—	970	2	3
Totals	3	590	8	1½

(1) Mix the curd, sugar and yolks until smooth.
(2) Gradually blend in the milk.
(3) Soak the gelatine and when pliable heat to melt.
(4) Add the gelatine solution to the mixture, but keep this warm to prevent premature setting.
(5) Whip the cream and blend it into the mixture.
(6) Deposit into the torte ring on top of the fruit, level off and refrigerate.

Notes A prepared mix is now available in various flavours and merely requires the addition of water for it to be reconstituted.

Slices may also be easily made with a base of puff pastry or sponge, a layer of fruit and topped with the cream cheese filling, using a suitably sized frame.

15. Gâteaux, Layer Cakes and Battenburgs

GÂTEAUX

The dividing line between torten and gâteaux is difficult to define. The Kirsch Sacher and Linzer torten described on pages 195 and 196 are not sold already divided into segments and therefore can be regarded as gâteaux, although they are termed torten in their country of origin.

Any large decorated sponge can be called a gâteau, although this term can also be applied to large cakes made from bases other than sponge, e.g. Gâteaux St. Honoré.

The term *large* is relative. On the continent it is usual to see gâteaux and torten up to 30 cm (12 in) in diameter. In Britain the size is much smaller and 15 cm (6 in) is commonplace.

Shape is not important. The sponge base may either be baked in sandwich pans or in small cottage (bread) tins which are finished off in the inverted position to give gâteaux with sloping sides.

The same filling, coating and decorating mediums used for torten can also be used for gâteaux. The sponge can be similarly flavoured and contain nuts, chocolate pieces, fruit, etc., according to the variety required.

Many gâteaux are completely coated in fondant icing and the following is the general method by which this should be done:

(1) Split the base sponge into two or three layers and sandwich with an appropriately flavoured buttercream or similar filling.
(2) Mask the top and sides with boiled apricot purée.
(3) Lay the sandwiched bases on a wire placed over a tray. If the sponge has been baked in a cottage pan, lay in the inverted position.
(4) Warm the fondant in a bain-marie and reduce to a pouring consistency with stock syrup (*see* page 164).
(5) Pour the fondant over the gâteau base so that it is completely covered. Use a palette knife to spread it evenly over the top. The surplus fondant will collect in the tray underneath the draining wire and can be re-used.
(6) When the fondant has set, remove from the wire, trim the bottom edge and transfer to a strawboard or card.
(7) Decorate suitably and present for sale.

Note For a perfectly smooth fondant coating it is advisable first to mask the sponge base in a thin layer of almond or sugar paste. This is particularly recommended if the sponge base is of a crumbly nature.

Decoration of Gâteaux

The number of ways a gâteau can be decorated are endless, but with the cost of labour at a premium it is sound sense to restrict the decoration to the minimum required to produce an attractive product. This can usually be accomplished by a few well placed lines in conjunction with decorative materials, either natural or prefabricated. An example of this is shown in Figure 76.

Fudge Iced Gâteaux

Quick and very decorative finishes can be applied to gâteau bases baked in a paper case supported by cottage pans. Any genoese type mixture can be used for the bases

Figure 76. Fondant coated gâteau. Two thin ropes of almond paste are placed at the base of half a flower, the petals of which are wedges of confiture pineapple (*see* page 231) arranged round a cherry centre. Lines of chocolate-coloured fondant are piped and three diamonds of angelica complete the design

Figures 77 to 82. Fudge-coated gâteau (*see* text for explanation)

Figure 77.

Figure 78.

although it is important that they are not toughened or baked in too hot an oven so that flat tops are produced.

The fudge icing (*see* page 178) is liberally spread and smoothed over the top and then the following variations can be made:

(*a*) Using the end of a small palette knife, make impressions in the surface so that as the blade is pulled away, points are formed which fall over the hollows made. This finish may be decorated with a sprinkling of roasted nuts (*see* Figure 77 (left)).

(*b*) Use the small palette knife in a paddling motion over the surface to produce the design shown. A sprinkling of coloured almond decor or corallettes completes the design (*see* Figure 77 (right)).

In the next eight examples chocolate has been used and marbled into the textured surface as follows: (*see* Figure 78).

Liberally coat the top of the gâteau with fudge and with the edge of the small palette knife blade make a circular impression in the icing, starting at the centre and working towards the edge of the gâteau by the use of a turntable.

Into the hollow impression pipe liquid chocolate or chocolate coloured icing. Using a sharp pointed knife, pull through the icing from the outside edge to the centre at any desired number of intervals, sixteen being quite easily made as shown in Figure 79. In

Figure 79.

Figure 80 (left) the chocolate is only piped in three lines around the outside edge, whilst in Figure 80 (right) they are piped into the hollows from the centre to the edge before being marbled into the fudge icing.

In Figure 81 (left) we have reversed the direction of the marbling after stopping the chocolate piping short of the edge whilst in Figure 81 (right) we revert to the original direction of marbling, but pipe the chocolate lines at four intervals as shown. Half a walnut placed in the centre of each of these examples completes the design.

Figure 82. These two gâteaux show the effect of marbling chocolate lines into the fudge icing which has been textured by pulling the edge of the palette knife horizontally at intervals over the surface. In Figure 82 (right) the lines are pulled in alternate directions at right angles to the hollows, whilst in Figure 82 (left) they are pulled at an angle.

Although not shown here, variations can be made to these two examples by pulling the chocolate line in one direction only. These may also have a sprinkling of coloured almond decor or corallettes to complete the design.

Figure 80.

Figure 81 (*above*)   Figure 82 (*below*)

Marbling in Fondant

Attractive decorative finishes can also be applied using fondant of two contrasting colours. The top is first iced in a light colour, and lines of a darker coloured fondant are then piped on at intervals. A knife blade is then drawn across so that the dark line is marbled into the surface. By using a utensil consisting of several wires spaced at intervals the marbling can be done in one operation.

There are some gâteaux which are not made from a sponge base and these are now described:

Nougat

Yield – 3 Gâteaux

	kg	g	lb	oz
Puff pastry trimmings (*see* page 57)	1	000	2	4
Icing sugar	—	165	—	6
Whipped fresh cream	—	835	1	14
Nougat nibs (*see* page 282)	—	665	1	8
Totals	2	665	6	0

(1) Roll out the puff pastry trimmings very thinly and cut into 3 discs of 23 cm (9 in) diameter for each torte. These will shrink to about 20 cm (8 in) in the baking.
(2) Prick each piece with the docker and allow to rest for approx. 30 minutes.
(3) Dust each piece liberally with icing sugar.
(4) Bake in an oven at 232°C (350°F) until brown and crisp (some of the sugar will caramelize).
(5) Keep some of the fresh cream aside to coat the sides. Mix the remainder with the nougat nibs.
(6) Trim the puff pastry discs all to the same size and an even round shape and select the best for the top.
(7) Sandwich together using the nougat cream, placing the selected disc inverted on top.
(8) Mask the sides with the whipped cream reserved for this purpose and the rest of the nougat nibs.
(9) Liberally dust the top with icing sugar and mark on a diamond pattern with the back of the knife.

St Honoré

(1) Roll out the shortpastry or puff pastry trimmings to form a disc for each gâteau. In the case of shortpastry this should be 23 cm (9 in) but because puff pastry will shrink when baked, it should be rolled out to 25½ cm (10 in) diameter.
(2) Transfer the disc to a baking sheet, dock well and brush the outer edge with egg.
(3) Make the choux paste using the éclair recipe and transfer to a savoy bag using a 12 mm (½ in) plain tube.
(4) Pipe a rope of choux paste round the edge. For the puff pastry disc, pipe approx. 12 mm (½ in) from the edge to allow for shrinkage.
(5) Brush the choux paste ring with egg using a soft brush and making sure that the shape is not disturbed.
(6) Bake in an oven at 204°C (400°F) until the choux paste ring is thoroughly cooked.

Yield – 4 Gâteaux

	kg	g	lb	oz
Short pastry or puff pastry trimmings (*see* page 57)	1	000	2	4
Choux paste (use ⅓ of the éclair recipe on page 62)	1	610	3	12
Genoese cubes (*see* page 137)	1	000	2	4
Sweetened fresh cream	2	000	4	8
Crystallized violets, cherries and pineapple	—	665	1	8
Green nib almonds	—	220	—	8
Apricot purée	—	110	—	4
Roasted nib or flaked almonds	—	665	1	8
Granulated sugar	—	665	1	8
Totals	7	935	18	0

(7) Meanwhile pipe the rest of the choux pastry into petits choux buns, sufficient to provide 16 for each gâteau. They should be no larger than the size of a walnut and washed carefully with egg.

(8) Bake the petits choux buns at 221°C (430°F) until they are well browned and thoroughly baked.

(9) When cold, the centre of the gâteau is now filled, first with cubes of Genoese and the sweetened fresh cream. The Genoese cubes may be first soaked in a liqueur-flavoured syrup or fruit juice.

(10) The cold petit choux buns are now filled with sweetened fresh cream.

(11) Place the granulated sugar in a saucepan with 195 g (7 oz) of water, heat to dissolve and then rapidly boil to the crack degree 138°C (280°F) observing the sugar boiling precautions (*see* page 13).

(12) Once the boiling sugar is ready, immediately dip four of the petits choux buns into any four of the following for each gâteau:
  (*a*) Broken crystallized rose petals.
  (*b*) Broken crystallized violet petals.
  (*c*) Chopped glacé pineapple.
  (*d*) Chopped glacé cherries.
  (*e*) Green nibbed almond decor.
  (*f*) Red nibbed almond decor.
  (*g*) Yellow nibbed almond decor.
  (*h*) Browned nibbed almonds.

(13) Attach these to the choux paste ring with a spot of the hot boiled sugar. Arrange the buns in rotation around the edge so that there are four buns of each dressing on each gâteau, making 16 in all.

(14) Brush the outside edge with apricot purée and mask with roasted flake or nib almonds.

(15) Finish the decoration with piped lines of cream on top and decorate with glacé fruit.

(16) This gâteau is designed to be consumed at a dinner or banquet and it is usual just prior to service to cover with spun sugar.

Note There are many variations of this traditional dish. Instead of fresh cream, other fillings can be used as, for example, a mixture of fresh cream and custard or a special custard made lighter by the addition of beaten egg whites. In some recipes no Genoese is used. Tinned or fresh fruits may also be used, both with the filling and to decorate the top. The version given of this traditional gâteau is adapted from the original French recipe.

Japanese

Figure 83. Japanese gâteau

(1) Make a japanese mixture (*see* page 112), transfer it to a savoy bag with a 1 cm ($\frac{3}{8}$ in) plain tube and pipe out discs in a spiral fashion onto silicone paper. Three discs are required for each gâteau.
(2) Dust with castor sugar and bake at 177°C (350°F).
(3) When cold remove from the paper and trim to the size required.
(4) Sandwich the discs with nougat or chocolate flavoured buttercream.
(5) Mask the sides with buttercream and coarsely dressed jap crumbs.
(6) The top may be left with the spiral pattern showing, chocolate spun over the decoration or dusted with icing sugar.

Layer Cakes

These can be regarded as gâteaux made up from layers of sponge or Genoese and buttercream or a similar filling and rectangular in shape. Usually the size is dictated by the size of the baked sponge before being cut up and layered. If this is baked in the standard-sized baking sheet of 30 in × 18 in (75 cm × 45 cm) a useful size would be 3 in × 6 in (approx. $7\frac{1}{2}$ × 15 cm) which gives a yield of 30.

As with torten and gâteaux, the interior can contain layers of fruit, chocolate, nuts, etc., incorporated with the sponge and filling medium.

Layer cakes may be completely enrobed with icing or buttercream, etc., but often the sides and top only are coated. The disadvantage of this latter practice is that the ends tend to become dry. They may also be covered with almond paste or chocolate.

Decoration may be applied in the same way as for a gâteau, but often the top is

Figure 84. Layer cakes: The sides are masked with buttercream and toasted desiccated coconut. *Left* The top is coated in fondant and a flower spray is arranged on top using confiture pineapple (*see* page 231), glacé cherries, angelica diamond and chocolate lines. *Right* Chocolate and white chocolate buttercream is used for the coating and decoration of this layer cake

marked into slices and each suitably decorated with the intention of it being divided when it is consumed by the customer.

As with torten, the make-up of the layer cake can provide interest for the customer, particularly if the ends are not coated. Interesting patterns can be produced by sandwiching different coloured sponges.

Items other than sponge may also be used. For example, frangipane sandwiched between two sheets of japanese with buttercream and enrobed with chocolate makes a very attractive variety.

The three layer cakes illustrated (Figure 85) are of Swiss origin and are explained as follows:

Left A suitably layered sponge is sandwiched between two layers of japanese, the top layer made by piping lines with a savoy tube. After assembly, the sides are masked in chocolate couverture. The top inscription is executed in chocolate on a marzipan plaque.

Middle The shape is first built up with sponge suitably layered. Chocolate couverture is then used to completely cover the shape and three pieces of crystallized violet petals complete the decoration.

Right After layering the sponge, the top is covered first in a thin layer of buttercream and then with half slices of pineapple confiture and a cherry. Finally the sides are covered with chocolate couverture.

Figure 85. Swiss layer cakes

Figure 86. Battenburgs

Battenburgs (Fig. 86)

These are assembled from the following materials:
Genoese in two colours (e.g. pink and white) (*see page 137*).
Apricot purée
Almond paste (*see page 257*).

(1) Remove the crust and trim the two sheets of Genoese. *or victoria base*.
(2) Sandwich the two sheets with a liberal layer of boiled purée. The purée should be of good quality so that it makes a good contribution to the overall flavour as well as being the medium by which the various portions of Genoese are held together.
(3) The sandwiched strip is now cut into strips approx. $2\frac{1}{2}$ cm (1 in) wide and each strip laid on its side.

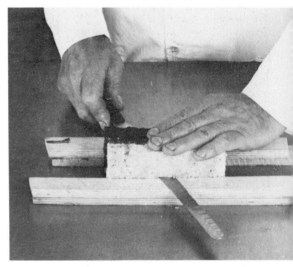

Figure 87. Method used to slice battenburg accurately, using slats of wood of the required thickness

(4) After the whole sheet has been so treated, again coat liberally with apricot purée.
(5) The strips are now alternately reversed and cemented together, white to pink to form the end checkerboard pattern.
(6) Roll out the almond paste to approx. 3 mm ($\frac{1}{8}$ in) trimmed to the same size as the length of the Genoese strip. Use icing sugar for dusting purposes.
(7) Liberally cover the almond paste with the purée.
(8) Lay the composite strip of Genoese onto the almond paste at one end and roll it over four times so that it picks up the paste and becomes completely enveloped.
(9) A knife is used to cut the strip free from the rest of the almond paste and a second

strip is covered in the same way. Several pieces may be so wrapped before the almond paste has been used up and another piece pinned out. Any remaining paste which is insufficient to cover at least one side of the strip may be worked into the next almond paste piece set aside for rolling out.

(10) The Battenburg strip may be left plain or receive some decoration before being cut up into individual cakes. It is usual to crimp the sides either with the fingers or with marzipan nippers.

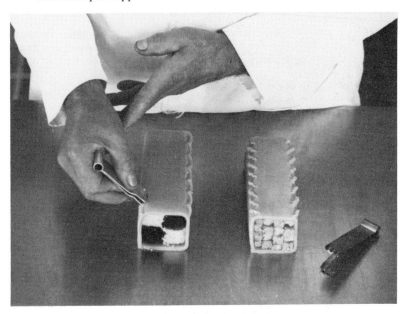

Figure 88. Showing the use of marzipan nippers (*extreme left*) to reproduce a design on the edge of the battenburg

(11) The top may also be marked with a knife or decorated using cherries and angelica, or prefabricated decoration, without or with linework done in fondant or chocolate. The almond paste may be first textured with a roller to give a more interesting finish.

The Battenburgs just described are commercially produced, but it is possible to produce 16 square and 9 square checkerboard patterns using 4 or 3 different colours. These are time consuming to make and therefore are usually only to be found in exhibitions.

Yet another variation can be made by cutting and cementing together two differently coloured pieces of Genoese in such a way that a triangle is formed. These and the square varieties can be made into very attractive fancies (*see* page 251).

Note Because the ends are exposed it is advisable for Battenburgs (and layer cakes) to be wrapped in film before being sold to the public. If this is done the decoration needs to be carefully considered, since it would have to be of a type which will not be spoiled by the film when wrapped.

16. Almond and Other Nut Goods

This chapter deals with goods in which almonds and other nuts are the main basic ingredient along with sugar.

Besides ground almonds there are three other proprietary made-up products available from which most almond goods may be made. These are raw marzipan, almond paste and macaroon paste. There are two broad classifications into which almond goods recipes can conveniently fall:

(1) Those where the ratio of ground almonds to sugar is 1:2.

(2) Those where the ratio of ground almonds to sugar is 1:1.

To the above we add egg whites or in some cases egg, to produce a wide range of different products.

Whichever of the three made-up products we use, we must retain the correct ratio of almonds/sugar demanded by the recipe. It is therefore important that we know the composition before the ground almonds and sugar are replaced by the use of these products:

Raw marzipan –	Contains 2 parts almonds and 1 part sugar.
Almond paste –	The ratio of almonds/sugar must first be known. A good quality almond paste may have up to 40% almond content but a ratio of 1 of almonds to 2 of sugar is more usual.
Macaroon paste –	This is a stiff macaroon mixture made from 1 part almond and 2 parts sugar with albumen solution.

Once we know the almond content, we can substitute the ground almonds using these products and making the necessary adjustments to the sugar content.

Example 1   To obtain an almond/sugar ratio of 1:2.

Using raw marzipan   3 parts raw marzipan = 2 parts almonds + 1 part sugar.

3 parts raw marzipan + 3 parts sugar = 2 parts almonds + 4 parts sugar.

Therefore, by adding an equal amount of sugar to raw marzipan we get the almond/sugar ratio of 1:2.

Using almond paste   If the paste already contains a ratio of almond/sugar of 1:2 it may be used without any further addition of sugar.

Example 2   To obtain an almond/sugar ratio of 1:1.

Using raw marzipan   3 parts raw marzipan + 1 part sugar = 2 parts almonds + 2 parts sugar.

Therefore, by adding sugar at the rate of $\frac{1}{3}$ of the raw marzipan we get the almond/sugar ratio, of 1:1.

Using almond paste   Here we need to use ground almonds as follows:

3 parts almond paste = 1 part almonds + 2 parts sugar.

3 parts almond paste + 1 part almonds = 2 parts almonds + 2 parts sugar.

Therefore by adding ground almonds at the rate of $\frac{1}{3}$ of the almond paste we get the almond/sugar ratio of 1:1.

Macaroon paste is not suitable for replacing ground almonds in all recipes because it is made from granulated sugar which is restricted to macaroon goods. For producing these, all that is necessary is to add additional whites of egg and in some cases water, and beat.

Methods.

Using ground almonds
(1) Mix dry ingredients together.
(2) Add egg whites or egg.
(3) Beat well. If a machine is used beat for 3 minutes at top speed.

Using raw marzipan
(1) Warm the marzipan and make it pliable.
(2) Add the sugar and mix.
(3) Gradually beat in ⅔ egg whites to produce a soft paste.
(4) Whisk the remaining ⅓ to a stiff foam and add in two portions as follows:
(5) Blend in the first portion and mix until clear.
(6) Fold the remainder in lightly.

Although a certain amount of beating is necessary to achieve aeration in almond goods, it should not be overdone otherwise a fault known as *blowing* results. This is the formation of a large hole at the base of such goods as congress tarts or the concave bottom in the case of macaroons. Rice flour is often included in macaroon biscuits to close the texture and make goods more *chewy*.

Baking Because of the high sugar content, all almond goods have to be baked at the low temperature of approx. 177°C (350°F) and there should be some humidity in the oven.

Sugar The type of *crack* which is required on the surface of the macaroon is largely dictated by the type of sugar used. The large crack associated with macaroon biscuits is mainly due to the use of granulated sugar, whilst the use of icing sugar will result in goods which bake out with a smooth glossy surface. The crack also depends upon the length of time before goods are baked and the humidity in the oven. Macaroons should be baked off as soon as possible after piping out on trays.

Egg whites Fresh, frozen or solutions of albumen made from the dried product, are all suitable for making almond goods. Substitute meringue powders which are not made from hen albumen are *not* satisfactory.

Consistency Because the moisture content varies between various batches of almonds and almond products, the amount of egg white required to be added might have to be varied slightly to achieve perfect results.

Macaroon Biscuits

Yields – Recipe 1 – 134 ⎫
       Recipe 2 – 90 ⎬ This gives a biscuit weighing approx. 28 g (1 oz).
       Recipe 3 – 38 ⎭

	Ground Almonds				Raw Marzipan				Macaroon Paste			
	kg	g	lb	oz	kg	g	lb	oz	kg	g	lb	oz
Ground almonds	1	000	2	4	—	—	—	—	—	—	—	—
Raw marzipan	—	—	—	—	1	000	2	4	—	—	—	—
Macaroon paste	—	—	—	—	—	—	—	—	1	000	2	4
Medium granulated sugar	2	000	4	8	1	000	2	4	—	—	—	—
Ground rice	—	125	—	4½	—	85	—	3	—	—	—	—
Egg white/albumen solution	—	610	1	6	—	415	—	15	—	60	—	2¼
Totals	3	735	8	6½	2	500	5	10	1	60	2	6¼

Figure 89. *Right* Macaroon Biscuits
Centre Congress tarts
Left Fancy macaroons

(1) Line a baking sheet with wafer paper after a light dusting in rice cones.
(2) Mix by one of the methods described on page 213.
(3) Transfer the mixture to a savoy bag fitted with a plain 16 mm (⅝ in) tube and pipe bulbs of the appropriate size onto the wafer paper giving adequate room to allow for flowing during baking.
(4) Place a split almond in the centre of each biscuit for decoration.
(5) Bake in an oven at 177°C (350°F) in a humid atmosphere for 30–40 minutes depending upon size.
(6) When baked, rub off the surplus paper from the base of each biscuit before presenting them for sale.
Note Silicone paper may be used instead of wafer.

CONGRESS TARTS

Yields [using a 5 cm (2 in) patty pan] for 150 tarts (machine blocked)

	kg	g	lb	oz
Shortpastry	1	000	2	4
Macaroon mixing	1	780	4	0
Totals	2	780	6	4

Use the macaroon biscuit recipe but increase the egg whites or albumen solution as follows:
Recipe No. 1 (ground almonds) 890 g (2 lb)
Recipe No. 2 (raw marzipan)   445 g (1 lb)
Recipe No. 3 (macaroon paste) 140 g (5 oz)

Notes
(1) Instead of egg whites 150 ml (5 oz) of water can be added to Recipe No. 3.
(2) To each kg of finished mixing 60 g ($2\frac{1}{4}$ oz) of scone flour (*see* page 112) and 30 g ($1\frac{1}{8}$ oz) of extra egg whites or albumen may be added if desired.

Method
(1) Roll out shortpastry (*see* page 16) 2 mm ($\frac{1}{10}$ in) in thickness, cut with a round cutter and line shallow patty pans. Alternatively, block out with the machine.
(2) Pipe in a spot of raspberry jam.
(3) Mix the congress tart macaroon mixture by one of the methods described on page 213.
(4) Transfer to a savoy bag with a 12 mm ($\frac{1}{2}$ in) plain tube and $\frac{2}{3}$ fill each tart.
(5) The top may be decorated by laying on two thin strips of paste in the form of a cross prior to baking or piping on softened shortpaste.
(6) Dust with castor sugar and then bake at 177°C (350°F) in a humid atmosphere for approx. 30 minutes.

Scotch Macaroons
(1) Roll out well rested puff pastry (*see* page 38) to 2 mm ($\frac{1}{10}$ in) in thickness.
(2) Using a $6\frac{1}{2}$ cm ($2\frac{1}{2}$ in) diameter cutter, cut out rounds and place onto baking sheets. Allow a further 2 hours resting period.
(3) Make the congress tart macaroon mixing and transfer to a savoy bag with a plain 12 mm ($\frac{1}{2}$ in) tube.
(4) Pipe a bulb of macaroon mixing into the centre of each puff paste disc and dust with castor sugar.
(5) Bake at 177°C (350°F) in a humid atmosphere for approx. 30 minutes.

Slices

Method 1
(1) Roll out shortpastry to form long ropes approx. $2\frac{1}{2}$ cm (1 in) in diameter.
(2) Lay a rolling pin in the centre of these ropes and by moving the pin backwards and forwards with pressure, extend the width to approx. 8 cm (3 in) with the sides thicker than the centre.
(3) Transfer to a clean baking sheet and then using the thumb and forefinger notch the sides as for shortbreads (page 85).
(4) Dock the centre of each strip and pipe in a little raspberry jam.
(5) Using the congress tart mixing in a savoy bag $\frac{2}{3}$ fill the cavity.
(6) Sprinkle on flaked almonds and bake at 177°C (350°F) for approx. 45 minutes.
(7) When cold they are cut into $2\frac{1}{2}$ cm (1 in) slices with a sharp knife. (The use of a damp cloth will prevent dragging the sides of the filling.)

Method 2
(1) Roll out shortpastry 2 cm ($\frac{1}{10}$ in) in thickness and line special tins specially made for slices. They are 8 cm (3 in) wide having sides turned up approx. $2\frac{1}{2}$ cm (1 in) and can be of any convenient length.
(2) Proceed with 4–7 of Method 1.

French Macaroon Mixing
    Instead of using egg whites, fresh or whole egg is employed using the method of mixing reserved for ground almonds (*see* page 213).
    The egg is used at the following quantities:
Recipe No 1 (ground almonds) 1110 g (2 lb 8 oz)
Recipe No 2 (raw marzipan)   555 g (1 lb 4 oz)
Recipe No 3 (macaroon paste) 165 g (6 oz)

French Macaroon Tarts and Slices

Tarts
(1) Proceed to line patty tins with shortpastry as for congress tarts.
(2) Pipe in some apricot jam and fill $\frac{2}{3}$ with the French macaroon mixture.
(3) Dust with icing sugar and sprinkle with small flaked almonds.
(4) Bake at approx. 193°C (380°F).
Slices
(1) Proceed as for almond slices using the French macaroon mixture.
(2) Dust well with castor sugar and sprinkle with flaked or nib almonds.
(3) Bake at approx. 193°C (380°F).
(4) Allow to cool and cut into $2\frac{1}{2}$ cm (1 in) slices.

Fruit Varieties

Proceed in the same way as for tarts and slices, but instead of jam place in a quantity of chopped fruit, e.g. apples, blackcurrants, cherries, pineapples or sultanas.

Fancy Macaroons

Soften the macaroon biscuit recipes (on page 213) by adding extra egg whites as follows:
Recipe No 1 (ground almonds) 155 g ($5\frac{1}{2}$ oz) approx.
Recipe No 2 (raw marzipan)   105 g ($3\frac{3}{4}$ oz) approx.
Recipe No 3 (macaroon paste) 15 g ($\frac{1}{2}$ oz) approx.

Frangipane Macaroon Ovals

(1) Make the macaroon mixture as described on page 213.
(2) Transfer into a savoy tube fitted with a 1 cm ($\frac{3}{8}$ in) plain tube.
(3) Pipe oval rings onto silicone paper.
(4) Fill the centre with frangipane mixture (*see* pages 27 and 28).
(5) Bake at 177°C (350°F).
(6) When cooled, coat the centre first with hot raspberry jam and then with water icing.
(7) Replace in the oven for $\frac{1}{2}$ minute to improve the glaze.

Other Piped Varieties

(1) Proceed as for (1) and (2) above.
(2) Pipe the mixture into fingers, buttons, ovals or rounds onto greaseproof paper.
(3) Sprinkle with nib or flaked almonds and dust with either castor sugar or icing sugar. By varying the dressing agents and the shapes, a wide variety can be made.
(4) Bake at 188°C (370°F) on a reversed baking sheet.
(5) After cooling, lift off the paper containing the macaroons, reverse onto a clean surface and wash the back carefully with water to remove them from the paper.
(6) Sandwich with any of the following:
    (*a*) Jam or other preserve.
    (*b*) Fresh cream.
    (*c*) Softened almond paste.
    (*d*) Nougat mixed with chocolate.
(7) After sandwiching, part may be dipped into chocolate or chocolate spun over (*see* page 237).

Sweetpastry Varieties

(1) Roll out sweet pastry to 2 mm ($\frac{1}{10}$ in) in thickness.

(2) Cut out various shapes with a knife or with cutters and transfer to a clean baking sheet.
(3) Half-bake in a temperature not exceeding 193°C (380°F) until the pastry has set without colour.
(4) When cold, coat each with the macaroon mixing and dip into nibbed almonds.
(5) Transfer to the baking sheet, replace in the oven and cook until coloured.

Moss Biscuits
(1) Colour raw marzipan green.
(2) Pass it through a coarse sieve and take off pieces with a palette knife.
(3) Place the pieces onto a silicone papered tray.
(4) Allow to rest for at least 6 hours and flash off by putting them into an oven at 218°C (425°F) until the edges are tinged with colour.

Italian Macaroon Biscuits
(1) Proceed as for shortpastry varieties (1), (2) and (3).
(2) When cold pipe a Parisian rout mixing (*see* recipe on page 218) in various patterns using a star tube and decorate with glacé fruit, e.g. cherries, angelica etc.
(3) Leave overnight or for at least 6 hours, and then flash off by putting them into a hot oven at 249°C (480°F) for a few minutes to obtain a brown tinge at the edges.
(4) Piping jelly or chocolate may be used for further decoration in some varieties.

Figure 90. Italian macaroon varieties

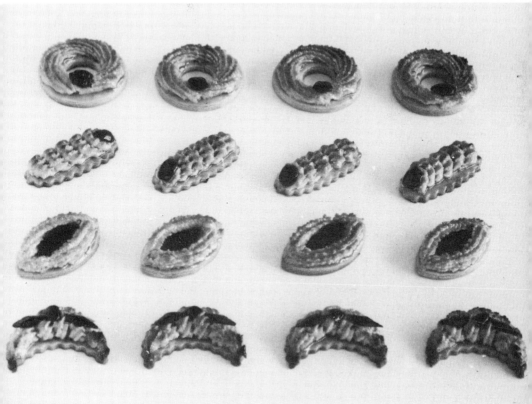

Almond Dessert Biscuits

Using Ground Almonds	Parisian Routs				English Routs				Parisian Biscuits				Fancy Macs				Dutch Macs				Bouleé			
	kg	*g*	*lb*	*oz*	*kg*	*g*	*lb*	*oz*	*kg*	*g*	*lb*	*oz*	*kg*	*g*	*lb*	*oz*	*kg*	*g*	*lb*	*oz*	*kg*	*g*	*lb*	*oz*
Ground almonds	1	000	2	4	1	000	2	4	1	000	2	4	1	000	2	4	1	000	2	4	1	000	2	4
Castor sugar	1	000	2	4	—	595	1	5½	1	250	2	13	1	000	2	4	—	180	—	6½	1	000	2	4
Icing sugar	—	—	—	—	—	250	—	9	—	—	—	—	—	—	—	—	2	250	5	0	—	250	—	9
Egg whites	—	320	—	11½	—	—	—	—	—	625	1	6½	—	610	1	6	—	805	1	13	—	250	—	9
Fine desiccated coconut	—	—	—	—	—	—	—	—	—	250	—	9	—	—	—	—	—	—	—	—	—	—	—	—
Egg yolks	—	—	—	—	—	250	—	9	—	—	—	—	—	—	—	—	—	—	—	—	—	—	—	—
Ground rice	—	—	—	—	—	—	—	—	—	—	—	—	—	180	—	6½	—	—	—	—	—	—	—	—
Totals	2	320	5	3½	2	095	4	11½	3	125	7	0½	2	790	6	4½	4	235	9	7½	2	500	5	10

Using Raw Marzipan

Raw marzipan	1	000	2	4	1	000	2	4	1	000	2	4	1	000	2	4	1	000	2	4	1	000	2	4
Castor sugar	—	500	1	2	—	340	—	12¼	—	710	1	9½	—	500	1	2	—	500	1	2	—	570	1	4½
Icing sugar	—	—	—	—	—	140	—	5	—	—	—	—	—	—	—	—	1	000	2	4	—	140	—	5
Egg whites	—	220	—	8	—	—	—	—	—	320	—	11½	—	305	—	11	—	500	1	2	—	125	—	4½
Fine desiccated coconut	—	—	—	—	—	—	—	—	—	140	—	5	—	—	—	—	—	—	—	—	—	—	—	—
Honey	—	35	—	1¼	—	—	—	—	—	—	—	—	—	—	—	—	—	—	—	—	—	—	—	—
Egg yolks	—	—	—	—	—	140	—	5	—	—	—	—	—	—	—	—	—	—	—	—	—	—	—	—
Ground rice	—	—	—	—	—	—	—	—	—	—	—	—	—	105	—	3¾	—	—	—	—	—	—	—	—
Totals	1	755	3	15¼	1	620	3	10¼	2	170	4	14	1	910	4	4¾	3	000	6	12	1	835	4	2

Ratafia Biscuits

Use the basic macaroon biscuit recipe on page 213, but with the following additions:

	Ground bitter almonds	Egg whites
Recipe No. 1	210 g (7½ oz)	105 g (3¾ oz)
Recipe No. 2	140 g (5 oz)	70 g (2½ oz)
Recipe No. 3	70 g (2½ oz)	35 g (1¼ oz)

(1) Mix and beat all the ingredients together. If using a machine beat on top speed for 3 minutes.
(2) Pipe small bulbs onto greaseproof or silicone paper.
(3) Bake at 188°C (370°F).
(4) If greaseproof paper has been used, remove the biscuits by damping the underside.
Note These are sold by weight either on their own or mixed with other dessert biscuits.

Almond Dessert Biscuits

These small biscuits are sold by weight. They are often served at buffets and banquets where they are also known as petits fours secs (a very small biscuit).

Almond dessert biscuits may be made either from ground almonds or raw marzipan and recipes for both are given. Macaroon paste is unsuitable because it contains granulated sugar which is too coarse for this type of biscuit.
Mixing Methods
Ground almond recipes
(1) Mix the dry ingredients together.
(2) Add the egg whites (or yolks) and beat to form a smooth paste.
Raw marzipan
(1) Warm the raw marzipan and make it plastic—ensure that it has no hard skin.
(2) Add the sugar and mix.
(3) Gradually add the egg whites (or yolks) mixing in each addition thoroughly to form a paste free from any lumps.

For small quantities made by hand, it is advisable to use a round bowl and a celluloid scraper which may be employed for mixing the ingredients and scraping them free from the bowl so that a thorough homogenous mixture is made.

Parisian Routs

This makes a very stiff paste and it is an advantage to warm the mixture before use to facilitate the piping of the various shapes.

Figure 91. Parisian rout varieties

(1) Transfer the mixture to a savoy bag fitted with an appropriate tube – a 15 or 16 star is used for most shapes. An adaptor to use this size tube may be used or it may be slipped inside a plain savoy tube.
(2) Pipe out into decorative shapes onto silicone paper, wafer paper or greased and lightly floured baking sheets.
(3) Decorate with pieces of cherry, angelica, glacé, pineapple and nuts.
(4) Leave for at least 6 hours or overnight.
(5) Flash by placing them in an oven at 249°C (480°F) for a few minutes to obtain a brown tinge at the edges.
(6) On removal from the oven, wash over with a solution of warm gum arabic (*see below*) to obtain a glaze.

Gum Arabic Solution

	kg	g	lb	oz
Hot water	1	000	2	4
Powdered gum arabic	—	200	—	7
Totals	1	200	2	11

Mix well and continue heating until all the gum arabic has dissolved. Use warm and reheat for subsequent use. The solution may be kept in a jar in the refrigerator.

English Routs

Figure 92. English routs – *see* text for explanation of varieties

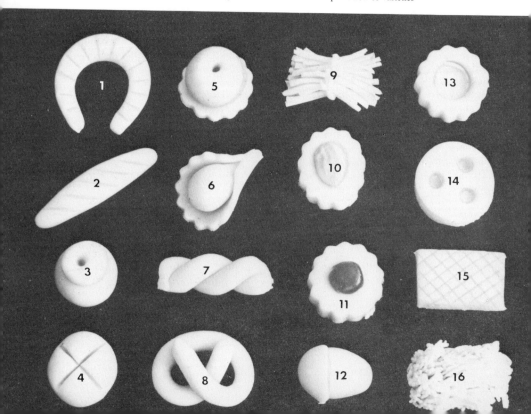

Yield – Allow 10 g ($\frac{1}{3}$ oz) for each variety.
(1) Mix to a firm paste – avoid excess mixing as this will cause oiling.
(2) Make into any of the varieties illustrated in Figure 92 and explained below.
(3) Place onto silicone paper or greased and floured baking sheets.
(4) Wash with egg.
(5) Leave for at least 6 hours or overnight.
(6) Flash by placing in an oven at 249°C (480°F) on double trays until the edges are golden brown in colour.
(7) Glaze by brushing over a solution of gum arabic (*see* opposite).

Varieties (*see* Figure 92)

1	5	9	13
2	6	10	14
3	7	11	15
4	8	12	16

The sixteen varieties are shown prior to baking and finishing.

(1) Roll the paste first into a ball and then into a long baton shape. Arrange this in the form of a crescent and simulate the folds by marking with a knife.
(2) Proceed as (1) above, but place it straight onto the tray. With a knife mark the cuts which are a feature on this type of shaped bread.
(3) Make a cottage loaf shape by dividing a ball of paste into two pieces, one twice as large as the other. Mould round, flatten slightly and place the smaller ball on top of the larger. Make an impression in the top with a pointed modelling tool.
(4) Make a coburg loaf shape by moulding the paste into a ball and marking a cross with a knife.
(5) Pin out the dough to 2 mm ($\frac{1}{16}$ in) and using a $2\frac{1}{2}$ cm (1 in) fluted cutter, cut out a disc. Mould a piece of the paste into a ball and arrange this on top of the disc. Mark the centre with a sharp pointed modelling tool so that the shape resembles an apple.
(6) Repeat the first part of (5) above but mould the ball of paste into a pear shape. Wrap the disc around the shape.
(7) Roll out the paste into a rope, divide into two and twist one round the other.
(8) Roll out the paste into a thin rope and arrange in a pretzel shape as shown.
(9) Pin out the paste to 2 mm ($\frac{1}{16}$ cm) in thickness. First cut into approx. 3 cm ($1\frac{1}{4}$ in) strips and then cut into 2 mm ($\frac{1}{16}$ in) strips. Assemble a number of these together and *tie* with another strip to resemble sticks of firewood.
(10) Pin out the paste to 12 mm ($\frac{1}{2}$ in) in thickness. From this cut an oval using 2–$2\frac{1}{2}$ cm ($\frac{3}{4}$–1 in) fluted cutter. Into the centre place a split almond.
(11) Proceed with (10) above but use a round cutter and decorate with half a cherry.
Note Other nuts, e.g. walnuts, or glacé fruits, e.g. pineapple, may also be used to decorate shapes in (10) and (11).
    Varieties (10) and (11) can be further decorated once they are baked by spinning over chocolate (*see* page 237).
(12) Pin out the paste to 2 mm ($\frac{1}{16}$ in) and using a 12 mm ($\frac{1}{2}$ in) plain savoy tube, cut out a disc. Shape some paste into the form of an acorn and wrap the disc over the fatter end. When finished, this disc which is now formed into a cap may be dipped into chocolate and corals if desired.
(13) Pin out the paste to 6 mm ($\frac{1}{4}$ in) in thickness and from this cut out two discs using 3 cm ($1\frac{1}{4}$ in) fluted cutter. Cut the centre from one of these discs using a 2 cm ($\frac{3}{4}$ in) cutter, and join the two discs. When baked, fill the centre cavity with jam, jelly or curd.
(14) Pin out the paste slightly thinner than described in (13) and use a slightly larger cutter to cut out two discs. use a 6 mm ($\frac{1}{4}$ in) savoy tube to make 3 holes in one of

these discs and join the two. When baked, fill the three cavities with three different coloured jams, jellies or curds.

(15) Pin out the paste to 12 mm ($\frac{1}{2}$ in) and cut into rectangles. Mark the top with a knife in a lattice pattern.

(16) Press some of the parts through a sieve and assemble in a bunch. If the paste is green it will look like moss.

Parisian Biscuits

(1) Mix to a soft paste.
(2) Pipe out biscuits $2\frac{1}{2}$ cm (1 in) diameter onto silicone, or wafer paper, using a 1 cm ($\frac{3}{8}$ in) plain tube.
(3) Dredge with fine desiccated coconut, removing the excess by lifting up the paper and shaking.
(4) With a clean index finger, make an impression in the centre of each biscuit.
(5) Bake at 177°C (350°F) until golden brown in colour.
(6) When cold, pipe a spot of coloured fondant in the impression.

Fancy Macs

(1) Mix to a soft paste.
(2) Pipe out $2\frac{1}{2}$ cm (1 in) diameter biscuits onto silicone or wafer paper, using a 1 cm ($\frac{3}{8}$ in) plain tube.
(3) Decorate using a wide variety of nuts as follows:

(a) Split almonds	(b) Strip almonds
(c) Nib almonds	(d) Coloured nib almonds
(e) Walnuts	(f) Hazelnuts
(g) Cashew nuts	

(4) Bake in an oven at 177°C (350°F) until golden brown in colour.

Dutch Macs

(1) Mix to a soft paste and warm.
(2) Transfer the mixture to a savoy bag fitted with a 6 mm ($\frac{1}{4}$ in) plain tube.
(3) Pipe out ovals onto greaseproof paper. The mixture should flow flat.
(4) Leave for at least 6 hours or overnight.

Figure 93. Dutch macaroons

(5) Cut the crusted surface through with a sharp-pointed knife (a razor blade can be used for this purpose).
(6) Bake at 171°C (340°F).
(7) When cool, remove from the paper by damping the back with water.
(8) Sandwich the biscuits with jam, jelly or any other similar ingredient.

Boulée

(1) Mix the ingredients to a smooth paste.
(2) Make into small balls.
(3) Dip the balls into softened royal icing (*see below*) drain and roll into the following:
    (*a*) Nib almonds   (*b*) Flaked almonds
    (*c*) Strip almonds   (*d*) Coloured nib almonds
    (*e*) Desiccated coconut
(4) Place onto either silicone paper or greased and floured trays.
(5) Allow the balls to rest at least 6 hours or overnight.
(6) Bake at 177°C (350°F) until golden brown in colour.
Note This mixture may be flavoured and appropriately coloured to give a wider variety.

Royal Icing for Dipping

Egg whites – 1 part   ⎱
Icing sugar – 4 parts   ⎰   beat together.

Figure 94. Boulee (1) Covered in nib almonds   (3) Covered in flaked almonds
                      (2) Covered in desiccated coconut   (4) Covered in strip almonds

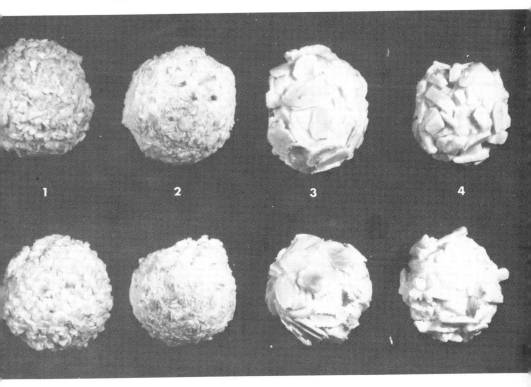

Figure 95. Florentines

Florentines

	Recipe 1				Recipe 2			
	kg	g	lb	oz	kg	g	lb	oz
Prepared nuts	1	000	2	4	1	000	2	4
Butter or margarine	—	665	1	8	—	720	1	10
Castor sugar	—	720	1	10	1	000	2	4
Chopped fruit	—	890	2	0	1	000	2	4
Soft flour	—	—	—	—	—	125	—	$4\frac{1}{2}$
Fresh or artificial cream	—	220	—	8	—	—	—	—
Milk	—	—	—	—	—	415	—	15
Totals	3	495	7	14	4	260	9	$9\frac{1}{2}$

Yields – Recipe 1 – 180–200
Yields – Recipe 2 – 220–240 depending upon size

Prepared nuts Although the almond is the main nut used in this classical recipe, other nuts such as hazel, walnuts, brazil, pecan, cashew, pine and peanuts may also be used. The nuts require to be blanched and chopped or in the case of almonds, nib, flake or strips may be used or a mixture of these. Small flaked almonds are well recommended.
Chopped fruit Any type of dried fruit may be used or a dry mixture. Normally the fruit would consist of diced cherries, sultanas and finely chopped peel, but a proportion of other diced glacé fruit may be used and/or ginger and pineapple crush.
Quality The best quality florentines are made with butter and fresh cream, but this may be made marginally cheaper by employing margarine and artificial cream, or even milk. It may be further cheapened by the use of baker's cake coating instead of couverture for finishing.
(1) Melt the butter or margarine in a saucepan.
(2) Add the sugar, bring to the boil and remove from the heat. Stir in the cream or milk.
(3) Add and stir in the nuts (and flour for Recipe 2).

(4) Lastly add the fruit and blend into the mixture.
(5) Deposit the mixture into small heaps on either:
   (*a*) A well greased and floured baking tray.
   (*b*) A siliconed papered tray.
   (*c*) Flat silicone papered cases.
   (*d*) Discs of wafer paper, on flour-dusted baking sheets.
   Allow plenty of room for these goods to flow during baking.
(6) Bake at the following temperatures: Recipe 1 – 182°C (360°F), Recipe 2 – 193°C (380°F), until they are baked to a light golden brown colour.
(7) A better circular shape may be made if, when the florentines are immediately removed from the oven, a larger round cutter is placed over and used to pull the edges into a perfect circle. To produce florentines commercially which have a uniform shape and size, they may be baked in special metal rings approx. 8 cm (3 in) diameter and $\frac{1}{2}$ cm ($\frac{3}{16}$ in) in thickness. These may be treated with a silicone resin to aid the release of the florentine when baked and cold.
(8) Leave until quite cold and crisp before removing.
(9) Coat the underside with chocolate.

Coating florentines with chocolate If couverture is used, temper as described on page 227.

There are several methods by which the backs of these goods may be coated with chocolate. The first method results in the best shaped florentine, but is less commercial in terms of the labour required.

Method 1
(1) Spread the liquid chocolate onto greaseproof or silicone paper on a slab.
(2) Before it sets, lay the florentines with the flat side down on the chocolate.
(3) When the chocolate has set, trim round by using an appropriately sized cutter.

Figure 96. Trimming florentines with a round cutter after laying them onto a sheet of liquid chocolate

(4) Remove from the paper.
(5) Spread some more chocolate on the already coated side and before it sets, mark
    wavy lines using a comb scraper.

Figure 97. Coating the backs of florentines with chocolate using a comb scraper

(6) Display showing both the nut and the chocolate coated sides.
Note   Besides obtaining a perfect shape this method prevents the liquid chocolate
from passing through the porous surface to spoil the top appearance.

The debris left may be warmed and passed through a fine sieve to recover the
chocolate. The pieces of florentine can be made into attractive decorative pieces and
used on torten, etc.

Method 2
(1) Coat the flat surface of the florentine and lay them chocolate side down onto
    greaseproof or silicone paper.
(2) When the chocolate has set, remove and finish in the same manner as (5) in Method
    1.

Method using Wafer Paper
(1) Since the wafer paper effects a seal, there is no danger of the chocolate running
    through and spoiling the top appearance. Therefore they can be coated and left
    nut-side down for the chocolate to set.

Square Florentines

Yields – 1335 g (3 lb) per 75 cm × 45 cm (30 in × 18 in) baking sheet.

$7\frac{1}{2}$ cm (3 in) square = 60

$6\frac{1}{2}$ cm ($2\frac{1}{2}$ in) approx. = 77

(1) Deposit the florentine mixture onto either a silicone paper or wafer paper lined baking sheet and spread level.

(2) Bake and afterwards cut into appropriately sized squares (or rectangles if preferred).

(3) Finish by coating the wafer side with chocolate as already described opposite.

Notes Any shape may be cut from these sheets, or alternatively large discs can be baked, divided into segments and used for the top of gâteaux and torten.

Very small florentines approx. 4 cm ($1\frac{1}{2}$ in) in diameter may be made into petits fours, but for these the fruit and the nuts need to be finely chopped.

Toscaner

Yields – 2560 g ($5\frac{3}{4}$ lb) per 75 cm × 45 cm (30 in × 18 in) baking sheet.

Recipe 1 = 180 approx.

Recipe 2 = 130 approx.

Recipe 3 = 116 approx.

	1				**2**				**3**			
	kg	g	lb	oz	kg	g	lb	oz	kg	g	lb	oz
Ground almonds	1	000	2	4	—	—	—	—	—	—	—	—
Macaroon paste	—	—	—	—	1	000	2	4	—	—	—	—
Raw marzipan	—	—	—	—	—	—	—	—	1	000	2	4
Butter or margarine	—	500	1	2	—	375	—	$13\frac{1}{2}$	—	335	—	12
Castor sugar	—	500	1	2	—	165	—	6	—	—	—	—
Egg	1	250	2	13	—	720	1	10	—	780	1	12
Flour	—	250	—	9	—	205	—	$7\frac{1}{2}$	—	165	—	6
Water	—	—	—	—	—	105	—	$3\frac{3}{4}$	—	—	—	—
Totals	3	500	7	14	2	570	5	$12\frac{3}{4}$	2	280	5	2

Recipe 1

(1) Beat butter or margarine, sugar and ground almonds.

(2) Add egg a little at a time and beat in well.

(3) Lastly add and blend in the flour.

(4) Spread the mixture level on a silicone papered tray and bake in an oven at 177°C (350°F) until the mixture is set.

Recipe 2

(1) Beat the butter or margarine, sugar and macaroon paste.

(2) Mix the egg and water. Gradually add and beat into the batter.

(3) Proceed as for Recipe 1.

Recipe 3

(1) Soften the raw marzipan with heat.

(2) Add the butter a little at a time and beat in.

(3) Proceed as (2) in Recipe 1.

Finishing

(1) When cold, the top of these are spread with the following topping whilst still hot.

Topping
   Heat the following ratio of ingredients in a saucepan:
   Butter – 3 parts
   Sugar – 3 parts
   Confectioner's glucose – 3 parts
   Small flaked almonds – 3 parts
   Water – 2 parts
Yield   The weight of topping required is approx. half the weight of the baked cake.
(1) Return the sheet now spread with the topping to an oven at approx. 193°C (380°F)
     and continue baking until the topping is a golden brown in colour.
(2) When cool, turn the sheet upside down onto a slab.
(3) Remove the paper and cut the sheet into appropriately sized and shaped pieces.
     These are usually rectangles and triangular shapes. It is necessary to cut these
     upside down to facilitate cutting through the crisp caramelized topping.
(4) Melt chocolate and temper (*see* page 277) and dip the base and sides to leave the
     topping to show.

Petits Fours

   These make ideal petits fours if made smaller. The temperature of the oven for
baking may be increased by 11°C (20°F) for baking the thinner slice involved. The yield
for such goods will be approx. double that of the afternoon tea fancy.

   Several concoctions similar to the florentine mixture can be made and used as a
filling for tarts or slices. The following is well recommended.

Nut Filling

Yield – 250 approx.

	kg	g	lb	oz
Strip almonds	1	000	2	4
Castor sugar	1	000	2	4
Butter	—	835	2	0
Honey	—	500	1	2
Sultanas	1	000	2	4
Evaporated milk	—	500	1	2
Rice Crispies	—	250	—	9
Totals	5	085	11	9

(1) Place the sugar, evaporated milk, honey and butter in a saucepan, melt and bring
     to the boil.
(2) Add and blend in the sultanas, nuts and rice crispies.
     The following can now be made:

Tarts

   Deposit the filling into sweetpaste lined patty tins and bake at 182°C (360°F).

Slices   Roll out sweetpaste to 3 mm ($\frac{1}{8}$ in) and $\frac{3}{4}$ bake. Spread with the filling and finish
the baking at 182°C (360°F) until golden brown in colour. When cool the slices may be
half dipped into chocolate.

Sicilians
Yields
Recipe 1 – 165
Recipe 2 – 110
Recipe 3 – 50
(* *see* page 112).

	1 Ground Almonds				2 Raw Marzipan				3 Macaroon Paste			
	kg	g	lb	oz	kg	g	lb	oz	kg	g	lb	oz
Ground almonds	1	000	2	4	—	—	—	—	—	—	—	—
Raw marzipan	—	—	—	—	1	000	2	4	—	—	—	—
Macaroon paste	—	—	—	—	—	—	—	—	1	000	2	4
Medium granulated sugar	2	000	4	8	1	000	2	4	—	—	—	—
Ground rice	—	125	—	4½	—	85	—	3	—	—	—	—
Egg white/albumen solution	—	305	—	11	—	210	—	7½	—	30	—	1
Honey	—	305	—	4	—	210	—	2¾	—	30	—	1
Zest of orange	—	45	—	1½	—	30	—	1	—	15	—	½
*Scone flour	—	305	—	4	—	210	—	2¾	—	30	—	1
Sultanas	—	890	2	0	—	610	1	6	—	280	—	10
Totals	4	975	10	5	3	355	6	15	1	385	3	1½

(1) Make the basic macaroon mixture with the honey and zest by one of the methods described on page 213.
(2) Slowly stir in the scone flour.
(3) Add and mix in the sultanas.
(4) Transfer to a savoy bag fitted with 2 cm (¾ in) tube and pipe out long strips onto silicone or greaseproof paper.
(5) Bake on double trays at 177°C (350°F).
(6) If greaseproof paper has been used, remove by damping the back.
(7) With a sharp knife cut into pieces approx. 6½ cm (2½ in) in length.
(8) They may be finished off by either dipping the ends into chocolate or alternatively spinning chocolate over the top (*see* page 237).

Marzipan Wafers

	kg	g	lb	oz
Raw marzipan	1	000	2	4
Icing sugar	0	500	1	2
Cornflour	0	250	0	9
Milk	0	250	0	9
† Egg	0	750	1	11
Totals	2	750	6	3

†The egg content is variable and it may be necessary to increase it to 890 g (2 lb) according to the shape and thickness required to be stencilled. Egg whites may also be used instead of egg in which case 60 g (2 oz) less will be required. It is advisable to use the latter, if the wafer mixture is required to be coloured.

(1) Work down the marzipan with half the egg or egg whites to a smooth paste.
(2) Add and blend in the icing sugar and cornflour.
(3) Finally blend in the remaining egg and milk. The mixture must be free from lumps and pliable.
(4) Leave covered overnight. This increases the pliability of the mixture which facilitates the manipulation of the hot shapes.
(5) Stencil the mixing in the required shape onto baking trays which have been well greased and lightly floured.
(6) Place into an oven at 216°C (420°F) and half-bake.
(7) Cool and return to the oven until coloured.
(8) Moulded shapes may be made by placing the hot stencilled wafer over a templet to set.
   Examples: Cornets using cream horn tins.
            Cylinders using wooden rollers.

Notes
(1) These can be partly dipped into chocolate and filled with cream to make attractive fancies (*see* Figure 116 page 254).
(2) Flaked nuts may be sprinkled on prior to baking.

Almond Paste
   This is dealt with on page 256.

17. Fancies

These may be described as any small cake which is decorated. The base may be made of sweetpastry with a suitable filling such as frangipane; Genoese; japanese sponge and many other types of mixings.

Decorating Materials

There is a fairly comprehensive list of decorating materials which are used extensively in the decoration of all types of cakes as described in the first volume of *Bakery: Bread and Fermented Goods*. Some decorative materials can be made by the confectioner, and a review of these is appropriate before describing how they may be used to decorate fancies, gâteaux, etc.

Roasted Nuts

Roasted nuts, whether they are nibbed or flaked almonds or desiccated coconut, are more attractive and palatable and most confectioners will produce these for decoration purposes. However, to achieve a uniform colour the following should be observed.
(1) The oven temperature should not exceed 177°C (350°F), the best temperature being 149°C (300°F).
(2) Spread the layer of nuts to be roasted very thinly over the tray.
(3) Mix the nuts at least twice during the roasting.

Coloured Nuts

Although coloured nib almonds are available for sale through sundriesmen it is also possible for the confectioner to colour his own nib almonds for decorative purposes. All that is necessary is to steep the almonds in a fairly strong solution of edible colour, drain, spread thinly on a tray and place in a cool oven to dry.

Crumbs

Some types of crumb, i.e. japanese and macaroons, etc., are very suitable for dressing fancies and gâteaux, etc. The crumbs must be very dry so that they easily crush when rolled with the rolling pin. They are then first passed through a fine sieve and then a coarse currant sieve to obtain two sizes of granule.

Marzipan and Sugar Paste

Cut-out shapes and flowers can easily be made from paste for decorative purposes. *See* Figure 271.

Chocolate

Cut-outs and piped shapes can easily be produced from this ingredient for the decoration of fancies and gâteaux, etc. The paste shapes can also be embellished with chocolate. *See* Figure 279.

Confiture and Glacé Fruit

Some glacé fruits such as cherries and angelica are readily available, but good quality glacé or confiture pineapple is not so easily obtained and the confectioner is well recommended to make his own from tinned pineapple as follows:

Tinned pineapple	A 10 tin size
Sugar	1360 g (3 lb)

| Citric acid | 7 g ($\frac{1}{4}$ oz) |
| Water (including juice of fruit) | 2270 g (5 lb) (4 pints) |

(1) Pour off the juice from the fruit into a measure and make up to 2270 g (4 pints).
(2) Add the sugar and acid and bring to a clear syrup with heat.
(3) Immerse the fruit and bring to the boil.
(4) Remove from the heat and leave for 24 hours.
(5) On the second day, replace over the heat and re-boil.
(6) Remove from the heat and leave for 24 hours.
(7) Repeat operations (5) and (6) for 5 more days making 7 days intermittent boiling in all.
(8) At the end of the process, remove the fruit and store for future use. The syrup may be used for stock syrup.

Apricot Purée

This can easily be made from sieved apricot jam to which additional sugar and a little water is added and re-boiled. When cold, it should set to a firm jelly.

Although used as a decorating material in its own right, the use of jam has other functions as follows:

(1) It seals the base against evaporation of moisture and so helps to prolong its shelf life.
(2) It acts as an adhesive for such materials as marzipan, etc.
(3) It adds flavour and moistness to a cake.
(4) Since it prevents migration of moisture, it helps to keep the gloss on fondants, therefore the base of fondant coated goods should always be covered first with apricot purée.

Therefore not only should a good quality apricot jam be used in the first instance, but it should be used liberally.

Buttercream Filling Ingredients

(*see* page 174)

Fancies from Sweetpaste Bases

The following fancies are made from unfilled sweetpaste bases which are baked blind (*see* page 22).

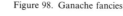

Figure 98. Ganache fancies

Ganache

	kg	g	lb	oz
Sweetpaste (*see* page 16)	1	000	2	4
Ganache (*see* page 171)	1	500	3	6
Sultanas	—	750	1	11
Stock syrup (*see* page 164)		as required		
Rum		as required		
Icing sugar		as required		
Totals	3	250	7	5

(1) Roll out the sweetpaste to $1\frac{1}{2}$ mm ($\frac{1}{16}$ in), line the appropriate patty tins and bake blind.
(2) Soak the sultanas for at least 24 hours in the syrup to which a good quantity of rum has been added.
(3) Drain the sultanas free of syrup and place a few in the base of the unfilled pastry case.
(4) Fill with the ganache and spread level.
(5) Dust with icing sugar using a mask to get the different patterns shown.
(6) Finish with a rosette of ganache or buttercream, and decorate with a silver dragee or similar decoration.

Other Varieties

Cherries   Instead of sultanas use cherries which have been soaked in syrup to which kirsch has been added.
Pineapple   Either pineapple crush or chopped tinned pineapple may be used as the filling.
Ginger   Use either ginger crush or chopped glacé ginger as the filling.
  As an alternative finish, the ganache may be coated with chocolate or chocolate flavoured fondant and either left plain or decorated.
  Wine cream or fresh dairy cream can be used instead of ganache in combination with a wide variety of fruits both fresh and tinned, to produce attractive fancies. Besides being used with the filling, the fruit may be used in the decoration (*see* Figure 2, page 22).

Frangipane

  Prepare the bases as described on page 27. These may be decorated in a great many different ways, but a useful selection is shown in Figures 99 and 100 and these are now explained.

Round Varieties (*see* Figure 99)

(1)   (i) Pipe a bulb or filling or buttercream into the centre of each tart.
   (ii) Roll out sugar or a suitable nut paste to approx. 2 mm ($\frac{1}{16}$ in) and cut out circles with either a plain or fluted cutter. The paste may be coloured in a contrasting colour to the cream or suitably textured.
   (iii) Cut the centre of the paste in the form of a cross and lay over the filling so that it shows through the incision.
(2) Spread the top with filling or buttercream and cover with any of the following dressings (*see* Figure 99).

Figure 99. Frangipane fancies – *see* text for explanation of varieties

    (*a*) Chocolate corallettes
    (*b*) Nonpareils
    (*c*) Desiccated coconut, plain or toasted
    (*d*) Nibbed nuts, plain, coloured, or toasted
    (*e*) Jap or macaroon crumbs
(3)   *Oysters* (*see* Figure 99)
      (i) Three-quarters cut through the top of the frangipane filling, lift up and pipe in filling or buttercream using a star piping tube for a decorative effect.
     (ii) Cover the top with a red jam or jelly and finish off with a sprinkling of green nib nuts.
  Baskets
    This is not illustrated but is made in a similar manner to the previous variety.
      (i) Cut through the top completely and divide into two.
     (ii) Using a star tube, pipe a scroll of filling or buttercream on each side of the tart.
    (iii) Replace the cut tops over the cream in such a way that they meet in the centre to form a basket shape showing the filling on each side.
    (iv) A thin strip of angelica can be used to simulate a handle.
(5)   (*see* Figure 99)
      (i) Coat the top with chocolate or suitable icing which can be appropriately flavoured and coloured.
     (ii) The edge can be masked in coconut, almond nibs etc., for a further decorative effect and a centre decor can be used. In the illustration, chocolate with a silver dragee is used.

(6) (*see* Figure 99)

    (i) Coat the top of the tart with boiling apricot purée.

    (ii) Using a small star tube, pipe a whirl of filling or buttercream around the edge.

    (iii) Fill the centre with chocolate or a suitable icing.

    (iv) Decorate the centre with a small piece of decor.

(7) *Mushrooms* (*see* Figure 99)

    (i) Using chocolate-coloured filling or buttercream in a small star tube, pipe lines from the outside edge of the tart to the centre.

    (ii) When the whole top has been thus covered, place into the centre a short stem of almond or sugar paste cut from a rope of approx. 12 mm ($\frac{1}{2}$ in) diameter.

(8) (*see* Figure 99)

    (i) Use a $2\frac{1}{2}$ cm (1 in) round cutter and cut a disc of the frangipane mixture from the centre.

    (ii) Dust the top with icing sugar.

    (ii) Fill the cavity with a rosette of filling or buttercream.

    (iv) Cover the top of the disc which was removed with red jam or jelly or chocolate, and replace.

Note Besides the varieties just described, the basic tart is also shown in Figure 99 (4). Notice the flat top which is essential for some of these varieties to be made.

Other varieties can be made by covering the top with a mixture of glacé fruits and boiling apricot purée.

Examples

    (*a*) Cherries

    (*b*) Pineapple

    (*c*) Mixed glacé fruits

(1) **Boat Shaped Varieties** (*see* Figure 100)

Figure 100. Frangipane fancies – *see* text for explanation of varieties

(i) With a filling or buttercream, cover the top using a palette knife to build it into two flat walls.

(ii) Spin over a liquid chocolate in two directions (*see* opposite).

(iii) Place a piece of decoration in the centre.

(2) (*see* Figure 100)

(i) Cover the top in a decorative pattern using filling or buttercream in a bag fitted with a small star tube.

(ii) Finish off in a manner similar to (1) above.

(3) (*see* Figure 100)

Cover the top in the same way as described under Variety No. 1 but dip one of the flats into a suitable dressing. In the illustration toasted coconut has been used, but any nibbed nuts and even chocolate can be used.

(4) (*see* Figure 100)

(i) Cover the top with boiled red jam.

(ii) Pipe on three rosettes in a filling or buttercream.

(iii) Place on three chocolate buttons or Smarties (sweets).

(5) (*see* Figure 100)

(i) Spread the top with boiling apricot jam.

(ii) Arrange half-glacé cherries to cover and again brush over boiling apricot purée to maintain the glaze.

(6) (*see* Figure 100)

(i) Spread the top with boiling apricot purée.

(ii) Coat with a suitable icing or chocolate. Fondant icing has been used in this example.

(iii) Decorate using cherries, angelica, etc.

Japanese

The making of these bases is described on page 110. The selection of decorative treatments illustrated is now described.

Figure 101. Japanese fancies

Varieties

(1) The japanese bases are made in the form of fingers, two of which are sandwiched together with a filling, buttercream or ganache, using a star tube. They may either be left plain or have liquid chocolate spun over for decorative effect (*see* Figure 102).

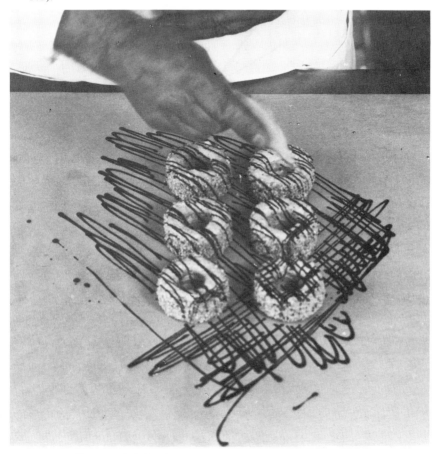

Figure 102. Spinning chocolate for a decorative effect on Japanese fancies

(2) A flat base and a circle are sandwiched with a rope of filling, buttercream or ganache, and the centre hole may be filled with a mixture of chopped glacé fruits and apricot purée. This may be left plain or decorated with spun chocolate.

(3) Two ovals are sandwiched in a similar way using a star tube to give a decorative pattern to the filling used, and again either left plain or decorated with spun chocolate.

Note Parts of these bases may be dipped into chocolate either before or after sandwiching.

The varieties shown in the next two figures are made from the stencilled bases described on page 110. They are sandwiched together with a suitable filling, buttercream or ganache, and then decorated. However, before describing the forms in which this decoration can be applied it is advisable to give some thought to obtaining uniform thickness. The following method produces jap fancies of uniform thickness, and is well recommended.

(1) Lay the bases on a clean baking tray which has the usual upturned edges. Pipe a bulb of the filling onto each base, sufficient that when the top base is pressed down to the correct depth, enough of the filling is squeezed out to mask the sides.

(2) Place another base on the top of each bulb of filling and cover the whole with a sheet of greaseproof paper.

(3) Place a larger baking tray on top and allow it to rest on the upturned edges of the first tray. This will effectively press down the bases to give a uniform thickness for each fancy.

(4) Chill to set the filling and then remove the tray.

(5) Using a small palette knife, mask the sides of the jap fancy with the surplus filling and roll the sides in a suitable dressing. This can be jap or macaroon crumbs, desiccated coconut, nibbed nuts, chocolate vermicelli etc. To speed this operation, two japs can be done simultaneously and split apart after dressing the sides.

Now this basic preparation is done, the jap fancy is ready to receive a number of finishes as follows:

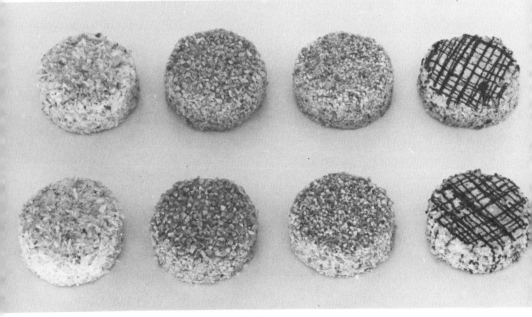

Figure 103. Japanese fancies. From *left* to *right* dressed as follows: coconut, nib almonds, Japanese crumbs, plain with spun chocolate

Coat the top with the filling cream and dip into any of the dressings described under (5) above. Obviously the same dressing should be used for the sides as well as the top. This variety can be made more attractive by spinning over liquid chocolate. This is the most commercial of the varieties shown being economic in terms of labour required for decoration.

Figure 104 (right) is finished by piping a circle of the filling cream around the outside edge and filling the centre with fondant. A piece of cherry completes the decoration.

Figure 104. Japanese fancies – *see* text for explanation of varieties

Figure 104 (centre) is simply finished by coating the top with fondant icing. This is done by piping a spiral of the conditioned fondant from the centre to the outside edge in such a way that it just flows sufficiently to cover the top. If the fondant is of the correct consistency and temperature, and the minimum amount piped on from a bag fitted with a small tube, it should not flow over the edge. In the illustration a little crushed rose petal has been sprinkled into the centre.

Figure 104 (left) is finished in a similar way using chocolate and violet petals for decoration.

Figure 105. Japanese fancies – *see* text for explanation of varieties

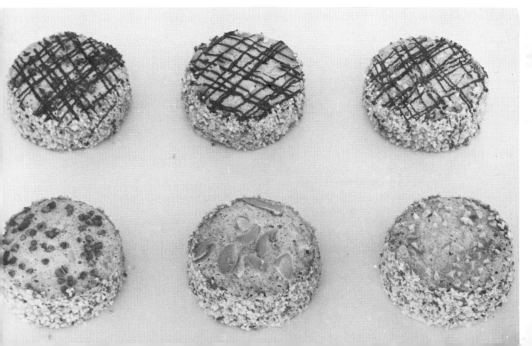

Instead of coating the top of the biscuit, we can sprinkle coloured almond decor, nibbed or flaked almonds over the jap shape before it is baked, using the biscuit with this side showing for decorative effect. Figure 105 shows the use of decor (left), flaked almonds (centre) and almond nibs (right) and the effect of spinning chocolate over these surfaces.

Continental Slices

These are produced from a sheet of butter enriched japanese mixing as explained on page 113.
(1) Allow the japanese sheet to soften by leaving it at least 24 hours after baking.
(2) Cut into strips approx. $7\frac{1}{2}$ cm (3 in) wide.
(3) Sandwich three strips using a good quality buttercream in which a liberal amount of nougat paste (praline paste) has been incorporated or just nougat paste on its own.
(4) Cover the sides with the filling and make sure they are smooth.
(5) Enrobe with either a chocolate-flavoured cake coating or tempered chocolate couverture, milk or plain.
(6) Using a comb scraper, spread the coating in a zig-zag fashion to produce a design.
(7) When the chocolate or coating has set, cut into slices.
(8) A sprinkling of coloured or crystallized flower petals can be applied in the centre before the chocolate sets, to improve the appearance.

Genoese Fancies (for recipes *see* page 137)

Before cutting up genoese into fancies some consideration ought to be given to their size and shape.

In these days of streamlined production resulting from the high cost of labour, a shape which can be easily cut without much waste of genoese is recommended.

These are the square, rectangle, diamond and triangle, since these can be cut with a straight edge and a sharp knife. Squares and rectangles can be cut with very little waste but with diamonds and triangles some waste is inevitable (*see* Figures 106 and 107).

The size chosen for a fancy is governed by several considerations.

PRODUCTION OF SQUARES CUT FROM SHEET OF GENOESE
46×76 cm (18×30 in)

Size	Number	Trimming Allowance
$2\frac{1}{2}$ cm (1 in)	$17 \times 29 = 493$	$2\frac{1}{2}$ cm (1 in approx.)
3 cm ($1\frac{1}{4}$ in approx.)	$14 \times 23 = 322$	$1\frac{1}{4}$ cm ($\frac{1}{2}$ in)
$3\frac{1}{2}$ cm ($1\frac{3}{8}$ in approx.)	$12 \times 21 = 252$	4 cm ($1\frac{1}{2}$ in)
4 cm ($1\frac{1}{2}$ in approx.)	$11 \times 19 = 209$	4 cm ($1\frac{1}{2}$ in)

Time of Production This will be approx. the same per 100 fancies whatever their size, so that the cost of producing a sheet of $2\frac{1}{2}$ cm (1 in) square fancies costs over twice that of producing a sheet cut for 4 cm ($1\frac{1}{2}$ in) square fancies.

Raw Material Cost Although small fancies are going to require more fondant, etc., for decoration, the more fancies which can be obtained from a sheet of genoese the lower the cost of the raw materials used.

Psychological factors Once the actual cost of production has been calculated, the selling price has to be determined. This decision is partly influenced by getting the right answers to two questions.
(1) Can the 4 cm ($1\frac{1}{2}$ in) size square fancy be sold at twice the $2\frac{1}{2}$ cm (1 in) size square fancy?
(2) Can twice as many large fancies be sold? Only by knowing the current market can

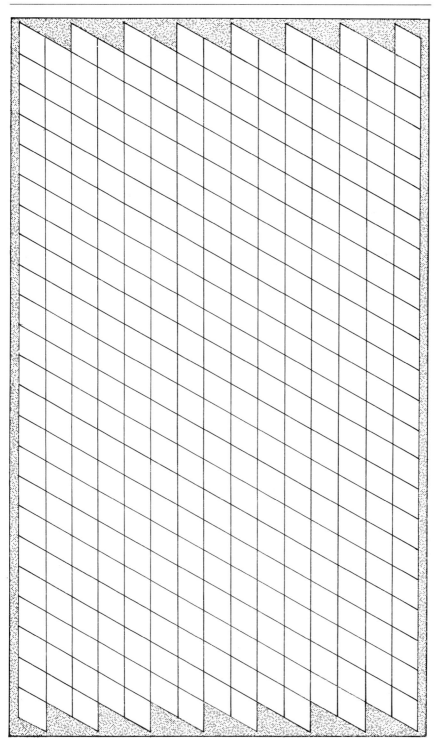

Figure 106. Showing sheet of genoese cut into diamonds. The shaded portion is the scrap left after cutting

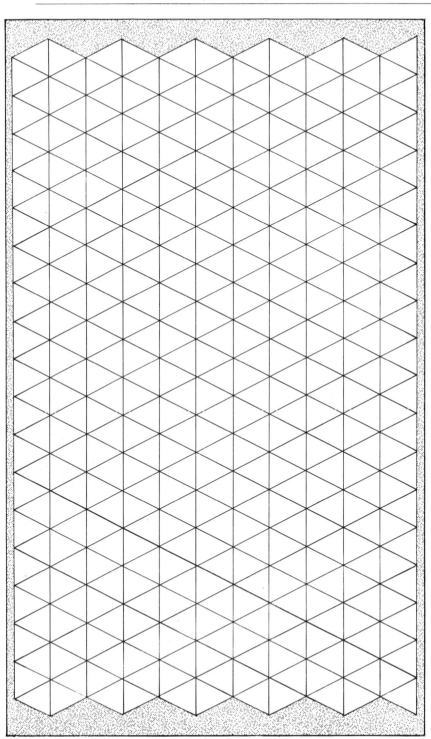

Figure 107. Showing sheet of genoese cut into triangles. The shaded portion is the scrap left after cutting

these questions be answered, but until they are the reader should keep an open mind about an acceptable size for sale to the public.

Genoese Slices

The genoese is first trimmed to an appropriate thickness and width. The use of the harp as shown in Figure 109 is recommended to achieve slabs of uniform thickness.

Figure 108 Genoese slices – *see* text for explanation of varieties

They are then sandwiched with a cream, jam, nougat or similar filling and can be decorated as follows:
(1) (i) Spread the top and sides of the genoese with boiled apricot purée. The sides may be covered in a filling or buttercream as an alternative.

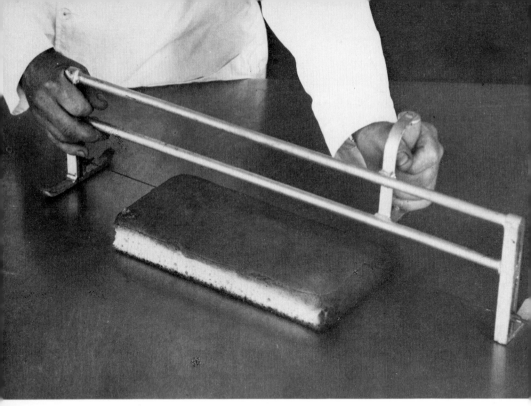

Figure 109. Use of the harp to trim genoese

    (ii) Cover the sides in a dressing of roasted nuts or coralettes or crumbs.
   (iii) Using a star tube, pipe two borders in buttercream, ganache or similar medium.
   (iv) Fill the centre between the borders with thinned fondant, icing, chocolate or jelly.
   (v) The centre can be left plain or decorated using glacé fruits, chocolate linework, or marbled.

Note To cut into thin slices, first mark with a tracy cutter, and then use a knife, dipping the knife into a jar of hot water and wiping off the moisture between each cut in order to sever the fondant coating cleanly.

(2) Use the same design as (1) but use ropes of marzipan (plain or decorated using nippers) instead of buttercream etc.

(3) Instead of using purée and fondant, etc., the whole slice may be completely covered with buttercream, or another suitable similar ingredient.

(4)   (i) Coat top and sides with buttercream, etc.
    (ii) Cover the sides with a suitable dressing of roasted nuts, coralettes or crumbs.
   (iii) After marking the strip into divisions of the required width, decorate using glacé fruit, cut-outs and other prefabricated decorations and then cut into slices.

(5)   (i) Spread the top of the genoese strip with boiling purée.
    (ii) Lay on three or more ropes of coloured marzipan or other paste in the centre.
   (iii) Place the strip on a draining wire with a drip underneath and enrobe with suitably coloured fondant, icing or chocolate.
   (iv) After marking, cut into slices as described in variety (1).

(6) Instead of marzipan (as in (ii) above) a suitable stiff cream or ganache can be used.

(7)   (i) Spread the top and sides with boiling purée.

(ii) Cover completely with a layer of marzipan or similar paste.

(iii) Mark and cut into slices.

(iv) Decorate with glacé fruit, cut-out or similar decoration.

The marzipan or paste may be textured with rollers in which case no added decoration should be necessary.

(8) Instead of flat rectangular slices, triangular slices may be made and coated with buttercream and other creams, or marzipan, etc.

   (i) Build up the genoese into at least 4 layers to form a square cross section.

   (ii) With a sharp knife cut from corner to corner to form a triangular strip.

   (iii) Finish off as already described under other varieties.

Dipped Fancies

Although the term *dipped* means that the genoese pieces are dipped into conditioned and coloured fondant usually by hand, today, enrobing gives a better finish. Where large numbers are involved, enrobing machines can be used. These arrange for pieces of genoese to pass on a moving wire under a curtain of liquid conditioned fondant or chocolate, etc. The production of crumbs is minimized by this method and a more even coating of icing or chocolate results.

Hand-enrobed fancies should be prepared as follows:

(1) Trim, and sandwich the genoese sheet with a suitably flavoured filling.

(2) Before the genoese is cut into the appropriate shape, a decision must be made as to whether the top is covered in purée or almond paste. If just purée is used, the genoese should be cut first and then coated with purée. If covered with paste, the genoese should be first coated with purée and then covered with paste. Cutting into the shapes is best done with the sheet inverted and the paste at the base.

(3) Once the pieces are cut, lay out onto a dipping wire with about 2 cm ($\frac{3}{4}$ in) between them. Place the wire on a dripping tray.

(4) Condition the fondant (*see* page 165) and transfer to a savoy bag with a 6 mm ($\frac{1}{4}$ in) tube.

(5) Cover each genoese piece on the wire with the fondant.

Figure 110. Fondant-dipped genoese fancies

(6) When the fondant has set, the coated pieces are lifted from the wire and placed into paper cases.

(7) Decorate with appropriate decorating materials and/or linework in fondant or chocolate.

Note Before the genoese pieces are covered in fondant, a number of materials may be first arranged on the pieces so that the fondant enrobes these also. Suitable materials for such treatment are as follows:

Buttercream and other creams, ganache, glacé fruits and jelly slices.

OTHER VARIETIES FROM GENOESE

Jam and Coconut

(1) Trim and cut the genoese into squares, etc.

(2) With the aid of a fork, dip each piece into boiling jam, either apricot or raspberry.

(3) Brush off surplus jam and dress the sides in roasted desiccated coconut.

(4) Place in paper cases and decorate with a rosette of buttercream and a cherry, nut, etc. [Figure 111 (5)]. Alternatively, cut ¾ through the top and pipe in a rosette of cream. [Figure 111 (1)].

Marzipan

(1) Trim and cut the genoese into suitable shapes.

(2) Roll out marzipan or another suitable paste, and purée the surface.

(3) Cut into strips and wrap it around the genoese shape. The paste may be textured and the top edge may be crimped.

(4) Fill the centre with fondant or chocolate and decorate with a piece of decoration. [Figure 111 (6) and (8)]. Alternatively the whole may be covered in marzipan [Figure 111 (3)].

The following two novelties may be made quite easily:

Cauliflower [*see* Figure 111 (2)]

(1) Roll out green almond or an alternative paste to 3 mm (⅛ in) in thickness and cut out circles using a 3 cm (1¼ in) cutter.

Figure 111. Genoese fancies—*see* text for explanation of varieties

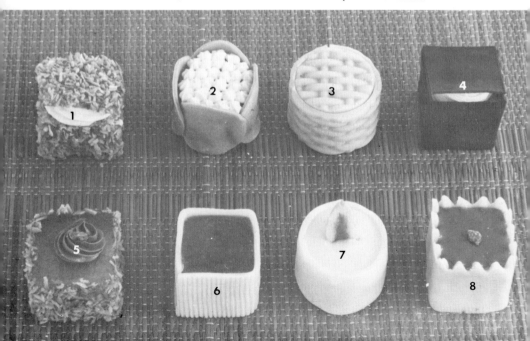

(2) Trim and cut the genoese into circles using a cutter of 4 cm ($1\frac{1}{2}$ in).
(3) Spread cream or jam on the sides and attach the green discs so that they overlap.
(4) Fill in the centre with small stars of white buttercream so that the fancy represents a cauliflower.

Nightlights [*see* Figure 111 (7)]
(1) Trim and cut the genoese into circles using a cutter of 4 cm ($1\frac{1}{2}$ in).
(2) Roll out uncoloured almond paste or white sugar paste and cover the surface with purée and cut into strips so that when wrapped around the genoese $\frac{1}{2}$ cm ($\frac{1}{4}$ in) overlaps. Wrap round each genoese piece.
(3) Fill the centre with white fondant.
(4) Tint a split almond yellow and place in the centre vertically to imitate the flame.

Chocolate boxes [*see* Figure 111 (4)]
(1) Spread some chocolate or cake coating onto greaseproof paper to a thickness of approx. 2 mm ($\frac{1}{10}$ in). When just set, cut into squares of approx. 4 cm ($1\frac{1}{2}$ in). Allow the chocolate to harden and remove from the greaseproof paper.
(2) Trim and cut the genoese into squares.
(3) Jam or buttercream the sides and attach a chocolate square to each side.
(4) Pipe a rosette of buttercream on top and lay on another square to completely enclose the genoese in chocolate.

VARIETIES FROM A SWEETPASTE BASE

For these varieties use either a chocolate, almond or plain good quality sweetpaste, *see* page 16.

Almond Fancies
Marzipan Mixture

	kg	g	lb	oz	
Raw marzipan	1	000	2	4	Mix to a
Apricot jam	—	750	1	9	smooth paste.
Totals	1	750	3	13	

Cushions

(1) Roll out the sweetpaste to approx. 3 mm ($\frac{1}{8}$ in) and cut out using a round cutter of 5–6 cm (2–$2\frac{1}{2}$ in) diameter.
(2) Bake at 204°C (400°F).
(3) When cool, pipe a ring of almond mixture around the edge of the bottom biscuit using a 1 cm ($\frac{3}{8}$ in) tube.
(4) Fill the centre with a good preserve or fruit crush such as pineapple crush.
(5) Sandwich with another biscuit.
(6) Spread the tops with chocolate cake coating or tempered chocolate, milk or plain, and mark with a comb scraper to give a pattern.
(7) Decorate with a sprinkling of coloured decoration.

Rings

(1) Roll out the sweetpaste (*see* page 16) to 3 mm ($\frac{1}{8}$ in) in thickness and cut out rings using a cutter of 5–6 cm (2–$2\frac{1}{2}$ in) and a cutter $2\frac{1}{2}$ cm (1 in) smaller for the centre.
(2) Bake at 204°C (400°F).

(3) When cool, pipe the marzipan mixture onto the sweetpaste ring using a 12 mm ($\frac{1}{2}$ in) plain tube.
(4) Sprinkle the marzipan mixture or dip it into roasted nib or chopped flaked almonds.
(5) Enrobe with chocolate cake coating or tempered chocolate couverture.
(6) Decoration can be applied by spinning milk chocolate over dark or vice versa.

Saris

(1) Pipe out macaroon biscuits approx. 5 cm (2 in) diameter and bake off, *see* page 213.
(2) When cold, mask the underside with a nougat-flavoured buttercream to form a shallow cone.
(3) Coat the buttercream with plain or milk couverture and present for sale with the chocolate side uppermost.

Bossanovas

(1) Pipe out and bake macaroon biscuits as described above.
(2) Coat the base of the macaroon biscuit with chocolate couverture.
(3) Pipe on a rosette of whipped cream and decorate with a sprinkling of roasted flaked almonds or, in season, fresh strawberries.

Ganache

(1) Roll out the paste to 3 mm ($\frac{1}{8}$ in) in thickness, cut out a variety of shapes, such as rounds, crescents, horseshoes, etc. and bake off.
(2) Soften and beat up the ganache (*see* page 233) to form a light cream.
(3) Pipe this onto the baked base in various decorative forms using a star tube.
(4) Either leave plain, or place on nuts either nibbed or whole and enrobe in chocolate. Further nuts may be used for decoration after enrobing.

Figure 112. Fancies from a roll – *see* text for explanation of varieties

FANCIES FROM A ROLL (*see* page 121)

Slices 1

These are slices cut from a long roll which consists of a sponge roll enclosing a suitable filling.

There are four basic varieties which are governed by the shape of the section as follows:

A

(1) Cut the roll into pieces approx. 46 × 19 cm (18 × 7½ in).
(2) Liberally spread some apricot purée on the long edge.
(3) Cover a 5 cm (2 in) diameter rolling pin with greaseproof paper and around this wrap the sponge, preferably whilst still warm, making sure that the ends are secured with the apricot purée or liquid chocolate.
(4) Using a savoy bag (without a tube) fill the centre with an appropriate filling (see later) when the rolling pin is removed.
(5) Transfer to a semi-circular template and place in a refrigerator to chill the filling and facilitate the cutting into slices.
(6) Finish as explained on page 250.

B

For this we need a template consisting of two flats of wood set in the form of a V.
(1) Cut 3 strips of roll for the sides and the base. A useful size is 6½ cm (2½ in) wide by 46 cm (18 in) long.
(2) Lay two strips, one on each side of the V template.
(3) Fill to the top with the filling cream.
(4) Lay on a similar strip and transfer to the refrigerator to chill.
(5) Finish as explained on page 250.

C

(1) Use a semi-circular 7½ cm (3 in) template for this variety. Plastic guttering purchased from a builder's merchant makes a very useful template for this purpose.
(2) Cut strips approx. 13 cm (5 in) wide and 46 cm (18 in) long, and lay these in the template.
(3) Fill to the top with the filling cream.
(4) Lay on a strip of sponge 8 cm (3 in) wide.
(5) Chill by placing in a refrigerator.
(6) Finish as explained on page 250.

D

This variety is not strictly completely enclosed in sponge. The tops and base only consist of sponge, the sides consisting of the filling which is masked in a suitable dressing such as roasted nuts, grated chocolate, coralettes, etc.

Fillings Usually these rolls are filled with (*a*) stabilized fresh cream, (*b*) wine cream or (*c*) a mixture of fresh cream and custard in which fresh fruit in season, tinned fruit or a fruit compote is incorporated.

If a fruit compote is used, the juice should be thickened by boiling with a little cornflour and the cream added when cool.

An example of such a filling is the apple one, as follows:

(1) Boil the apple juice and sugar.
(2) Make a paste of the cornflour and a little water.
(3) Add the boiling juice, return to the heat and boil to thicken and clear.
(4) Stir in the chopped apples.
(5) Allow to cool and then fold in the whipped cream.

Fillings for Roll Slices

Apple

	kg	g	lb	oz
Whipped cream	1	000	2	4
Chopped apples	—	805	1	13
Apple juice	—	280	—	10
Sugar	—	140	—	5
Cornflour	—	70	—	$2\frac{1}{2}$
Totals	2	295	5	$2\frac{1}{2}$

Slices 2

These are slices cut from a roll which may be finished as follows:
(1) Place a rope of coloured almond paste at the long edge of the sheet.
(2) Spread the sheet with a good quality buttercream into which has been mixed one of
    the following:
    (*a*) Chopped glacé cherries.
    (*b*) Chopped glacé pineapple.
    (*c*) Any other glacé fruit.
(3) Roll up the roll starting at the edge with the almond paste.
(4) Chill by placing it in the refrigerator.

Finishing Before cutting into slices these rolls may be finished as follows:
(1) Coat in buttercream or apricot purée and cover with roasted nuts. Dust with icing
    sugar.

Figure 113. Roll slices

(2) Dust with icing sugar and using a wire bent into a special shape, heat and burn a pattern into the icing.

(3) Cover with a thin coating of almond paste which can be textured by a roller prior to use.

(4) Coat in buttercream or fresh cream and cover with grated chocolate, chocolate curls or corallettes.

(5) Cut or mark the roll into slices and decorate each slice individually using any of the usual acceptable decorating ingredients.

Battenburg Slices

Figure 114. Battenburg fancies

(1) Make up battenburg as described on page 210.

(2) Cut the battenburg either in half horizontally and then into slices, or diagonally to make triangular slices.

(3) Melt tempered chocolate or cake coating.

(4) Dip the base of each slice into the melted chocolate, wipe off the surplus by scraping the slice against the lip of the container, and set the slice down onto greaseproof paper.

(5) When set, place into paper cases.

Petits Fours*

The term *petits fours* means small fancy biscuits and in this context the author's interpretation of *small* is a cake or biscuit which can be consumed in one or at most, two mouthfuls.

Any small confection can be a petit four whether it be made from genoese and iced with fondant, or made from ground almonds into a small dessert biscuit.

Petits fours which are covered in icing or sugar are called petits fours *glacé* whilst varieties which are not so iced such as almond dessert biscuits are called *sec*.

Therefore any of the fancies described in this chapter could be classified as petits fours provided they are made small enough to come into this category.

One category not so described is made by dipping various fruits or fruit segments into a boiling sugar solution.

Fruits suitable for this treatment are as follows:

(*a*) Grapes
(*b*) Orange segments
(*c*) Pineapple segments
(*d*) Cherries
(*e*) Strawberries (in season)

Sugar Solution

	kg	g	lb	oz
Cube or granulated sugar	1	000	2	4
Water	—	310	—	$11\frac{1}{4}$
Totals	1	310	2	$15\frac{1}{4}$

Boil ingredients to 154°C (310°F).

Dip the fruit into the boiling syrup and transfer onto an oiled slab to set.

Some fruits, i.e. dates, can be stuffed with marzipan before they are dipped. Also nuts, i.e. walnuts, almonds and brazil nuts can receive the same sort of treatment.

TRUFFLES

	kg	g	lb	oz
Cake crumbs	1	000	2	4
Nougat paste	—	750	1	11
Apricot jam	—	375	—	$13\frac{1}{2}$
Roasted nib almonds	—	95	—	$3\frac{1}{2}$
Roasted nib hazelnuts	—	195	—	7
Chopped sultanas	—	95	—	$3\frac{1}{2}$
Chopped cherries	—	305	—	11
Rum	—	50	—	$1\frac{3}{4}$
Totals	2	865	6	$7\frac{1}{4}$

*See *Patisserie* by the same author.

Many confectioners regard this type of fancy as an economic way to utilize their cake crumbs and the author has seen some very poor examples comprised merely of cake crumbs, bound together with an apricot purée flavoured with rum flavour and rolled in chocolate corallettes. The following example is of higher quality than this and worthy of the reader's consideration.

(1) Mix the nougat paste and jam.
(2) Add the cake crumbs and mix.
(3) Add the rum and mix.
(4) Finally add the chopped fruit and nuts and blend in.
(5) Mould into small balls and place into a refrigerator to chill.
(6) (*a*) Enrobe in either bakers cake coating or tempered chocolate couverture *or*
    (*b*) Cover with the above and roll into chocolate coralettes.
(7) Finish by sprinkling coloured almond nibs (decor) or crystallized flower petals onto each truffle.

Note The cake should be of good quality for use in this recipe.

Rum Truffle Slice

Rum truffles can also be made from good quality cake crumbs mixed with chocolate couverture or ganache (*see* page 171) in varying amounts. A suitable good quality recipe is as follows:

	kg	g	lb	oz
Cake or sponge crumbs	1	000	2	4
Cream	—	250	—	9
Chocolate couverture	—	250	—	9
Totals	1	500	3	6

(1) Melt the chocolate couverture.
(2) Boil the cream, stir in the melted chocolate and make a ganache.
(3) Stir in the crumbs.
(4) Spread onto a papered tray, to approx. $1\frac{1}{2}$ cm ($\frac{5}{8}$ in) and chill.
(5) Coat the top with chocolate couverture and mark with a comb scraper before it sets.
(6) Cut into rectangles of an appropriate size.

Note Cuttings from vanilla slices can also be used, but because the mixing is not cooked, the shelf life may have to be reduced.

EXAMPLES OF SWISS-DECORATED FANCIES

Figures 115 and 116 show examples of typical Swiss-decorated fancies which were demonstrated at the Richemont School in Lucerne. All are made up from the various bases already described, but some detailed explanation is now given.

Row 1. This is a very thin sponge sheet (called a Roulade), first coated with a buttercream and then wrapped around cubes of confiture pineapple (*see* page 231) so that a square slice is formed when the roll is cut. The outside is coated with chocolate before cutting.

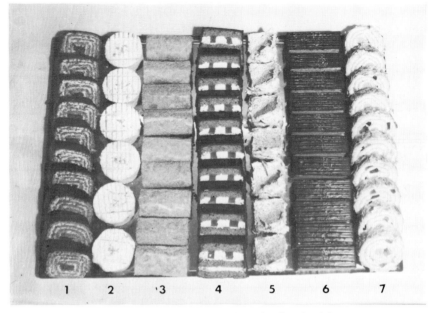

Figure 115. Swiss fancies – *see* text for explanation of varieties

Row 2. Japanese with the tops coated with buttercream marked with a knife and decorated with a sprinkling of crushed violet petals.

Row 3. Small rolls filled with a lemon cream.

Row 4. Chocolate sponge layered with vanilla buttercream with two rows of confiture pineapple placed in the top layer. The top and sides are coated with chocolate prior to cutting into slices.

Row 5. Squares of sponge the top of which is almost severed cornerwise and a rosette of buttercream piped in. The top is dusted with icing sugar.

Row 6. Continental slices (*see* page 240).

Row 7. Sponge roll (*see* page 250).

Figure 116. Swiss fancies – *see* text for explanation of varieties

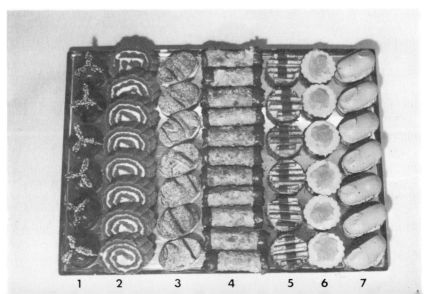

Row 1. A shortbread or almond biscuit base on which is piped a bulb of ganache (*see* page 171). This is then dipped into chocolate couverture and decorated with three strips of confiture fruit which has been rolled in granulated sugar.

Row 2. A chocolate sponge roll (Roulade) which has been piped out with a plain savoy tube in lines instead of the usual spreading. The sponge is layered with vanilla buttercream and after rolling, is cut into slices.

Row 3. Two oval chocolate shortbread or almond biscuits sandwiched with a vanilla buttercream. The tops are coated with a chocolate buttercream, dusted with icing sugar and marked with a knife.

Row 4. Made from marzipan wafer rolls (*see* page 229) over which small flaked almonds are sprinkled prior to baking. The hollow roll is filled with an almond buttercream and the ends dipped into chocolate.

Row 5. Japanese finished with three small chocolate curls (*see* page 280). Final decoration is made by laying a thin strip of paper in the centre and dusting with icing sugar.

Row 6. Chocolate biscuits dipped into chocolate, covered with a ring of textured marzipan, the centre of which is adorned with chopped pineapple confiture (*see* page 231).

Row 7. Piped japanese shells, half dipped in chocolate and sandwiched with buttercream to oval japanese biscuits.

18. Modelling Pastes

ALMOND PASTE

The latest legislation in Britain makes no distinction between almond paste, almond icing and marzipan.

Legally marzipan sold as such shall contain not less than 23.5% of dry almond substance and no other nut ingredient. Not less than 75% of the remainder shall be solid carbohydrate sweetening matter.

This code of practice, however, shall not apply to:

(1) Articles such as cake decorations, figures and petits fours.
(2) Single articles of sugar confectionery weighing less than 85 g (3 oz).
(3) Any articles weighing less than 30 g (1 oz) in a composite chocolate and/or sugar confectionery assortment.
(4) Bars or blocks coated with chocolate and/or sugar confectionery, which have a declared net weight not exceeding 110 g (4 oz).

If when sold, it is claimed that flour confectionery contains or is wholly or partly covered with marzipan, then the marzipan shall comply with the standard of composition already stated above. However, this legal definition of marzipan must not be confused with raw marzipan which is a specially prepared product (*see* page 212).

Recipe 1

	kg	g	lb	oz
Ground almonds	1	000	2	4
Icing sugar	1	000	2	4
Castor sugar	1	000	2	4
Whole egg	—	320	—	$11\frac{1}{2}$
Egg colour		as desired		
*Almond flavour		as desired		
Totals	3	320	7	$7\frac{1}{2}$

Recipe 2

	kg	g	lb	oz
Ground almonds	1	000	2	4
Lump or granulated sugar	1	555	3	8
Confectioner's glucose		220		8
Water		500	1	2
Egg yolks		150		$5\frac{1}{2}$
Egg colour		as desired		
* Almond flavour		as desired		
Totals	3	425	7	$11\frac{1}{2}$

Method for Recipe 1

(1) Sieve the icing sugar and ground almonds and mix well together.
(2) Mix the castor sugar and egg in a bain-marie and heat to approx. 49°C (120°F).
(3) Blend both mixtures together and mix to a smooth paste.

   This makes an almond icing which is slightly granular. If a smooth icing is required, replace the castor sugar with 750 g (1 lb 11 oz) icing sugar and 250 g (9 oz) fondant. In this case the mixture need not be heated.

Method for Recipe 2

(1) Place the sugar and water in a pan and boil to 107°C (225°F). Add the glucose and boil to 115°C (240°F). Observe sugar-boiling precautions (*see* page 13).
(2) Allow the syrup to cool slightly and blend in the almonds.
(3) Lastly stir in the egg yolks and mix to a smooth paste. The consistency may be altered by adjusting the egg quantity.

   * Alternatively 250 g (9 oz) of the sweet ground almonds in both these recipes may be replaced with bitter almonds.
Note   The above recipe No. 2 may be used hot to ice cakes by first preparing them with a greaseproof or silicone paper band and pouring the hot almond paste directly onto the cake where it will flow flat and set.

   In the following recipes ensure that before use, the raw marzipan is free from any crust, skin or lumps.

Recipe 3

	kg	g	lb	oz
Raw marzipan	1	000	2	4
Icing sugar	—	500	1	2
Fondant	—	500	1	2
Egg colour		as desired		
Totals	2	000	4	8

(1) Slightly warm the marzipan.
(2) Plasticise the fondant and blend into the marzipan.
(3) Mix in the sugar to form a smooth paste.

4. Modelling 1

	kg	g	lb	oz
Raw marzipan	1	000	2	4
Icing sugar	1	000	2	4
Glucose	—	125	—	4½
Totals	2	125	4	12½

(1) Warm the marzipan and glucose and blend together.
(2) Add the icing sugar and mix to a smooth paste.

   This recipe is more suitable for the modelling of animal shapes where the glucose prevents the marzipan from drying out and so preserves its attractive eating qualities.

5. Modelling 2

	kg	g	lb	oz
Raw marzipan	1	000	2	4
Icing sugar	1	170	2	10
Water	—	20	—	$\frac{3}{4}$
Gum tragacanth	—	3	—	$\frac{1}{10}$
Totals	1	193	4	15*

*Approx.

(1) Mix the water and gum.
(2) Add 165 g (6 oz) icing sugar and make into a paste.
(3) Warm to soften the marzipan, and blend in the gum paste.
(4) Add the sugar and mix to a firm paste.

This recipe is suitable for the modelling of flowers. The gum tragacanth increases the plasticity of this paste which greatly facilitates modelling technique, causing the paste to rapidly set and hold the shape of the petals, etc. Goods moulded from this paste will be dry and brittle to eat.

6. Modelling 3

	kg	g	lb	oz
Ground almonds, coconut or hazelnuts	1	000	2	4
Lump or granulated sugar	1	610	3	10
Confectioner's glucose	—	250	—	9
Water	—	500	1	2
Egg yolks or whites	—	250	—	9
Totals	2	610	8	2

(1) Boil the sugar and water to 107°C (225°F).
(2) Add the glucose and boil to 115°C (240°F).
(3) Stir in the ground almonds.
(4) Cool the mixture and blend in the egg.

Notes This paste is not as smooth as in the previous two recipes because the ground nuts have not been passed through granite rollers as the almonds in raw marzipan. However, it makes an acceptable alternative if raw marzipan is unobtainable or if an alternative variety of nuts is required to be used. Instead of egg, fondant may be employed. Obviously if the paste is to be coloured, either the latter or egg whites must be used.

Coconut will produce a rather friable paste which is difficult to model. The hazelnut paste is naturally brown in colour.

The consistency of the paste may be softened by the addition of either more fondant or egg.

MODELLING IN ALMOND PASTE

Almost any shape may be modelled in almond paste but the choice is governed by three considerations:

(*a*) The labour involved – this should not be such as to make the goods made prohibitive in price.

(*b*) The shape should be broken down into simple parts which can easily be shaped and assembled.

(*c*) The amount of almond paste involved should be small because of its high cost.

Particularly appropriate are animal and bird shapes, fruits, flowers and some human shapes like clowns' heads. Besides being able to produce modelled goods which can be sold individually, almond paste may also be used to produce decorative pieces for use on gáteaux and torten.

Modelling Almond Paste

Both the recipes 4 and 5 give pastes which are suitable for modelling. Once made, the paste should always be kept covered otherwise a crust will form which is difficult to eliminate. It is advisable to keep the made-up paste sealed in a polythene bag. Edible colour may be added in either the liquid, paste or powder form, but if very deep colours are required, e.g. carmine for roses, the latter types are recommended. Differently coloured pastes should never be kept together in the same bag, otherwise one colour might become contaminated by another.

When almond paste is overworked it becomes oiled, i.e. the natural almond oil is expressed and will ooze out of the paste. If this happens, it becomes almost impossible to model and the appearance is spoiled. Therefore the paste should never be worked down on a slab excessively.

Cleanliness is essential in the handling of the paste because it picks up the slightest trace of dirt with which it comes into contact.

Modelling Fruits

For fruits of a realistic size the weight of marzipan or almond paste required will vary between 125–200 g (4½–8 oz) according to the type of fruit it is intended to imitate.

Commercially the cost of almonds makes fruits of this size rather expensive and smaller sizes are finding more favour. Another way of reducing the cost of this expensive item is to form the shape around a centre of sponge. However, this is only

Figure 117. Marzipan fruits – *see* text for explanation of varieties

suitable for round fruits, the banana shape, for example, being unsuitable for this treatment. The modelling almond paste recipe No 1 is suitable for these and they are made as follows:

(1) Colour the paste as follows:
 Green – apples, pears and peaches.
 Yellow – apples, bananas, lemons, peaches, pears.
 Orange – oranges.

(2) Mould the paste into the required shape using modelling tools where necessary (*see* Figure 118). The rough surface on the orange and lemon is made by rolling the shape between two boards on which has been glued sago. This gives perfect indentations.

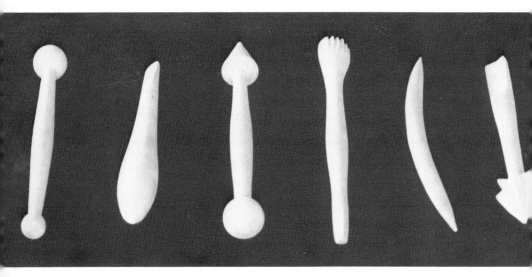

Figure 118. Selection of modelling tools

(3) Set the shapes into a bed of cornflour in order to retain the shape.

(4) Allow the shapes to lie overnight to set and then finish by adding colour, etc.

Finishing

Apples (see Figure 117)

 Use either green or yellow paste depending upon the type of apple it is intended to imitate. Apply either liquid colour by means of an aerograph spray (*see* Figure 119) or

Figure 119. Spraying colour onto marzipan fruits with an aerograph air brush

by dabbing on powder colour. Use a fine paint brush to add streaks of red colour. The waxy texture of the skin of an apple can be imitated by dressing the surface with a hard fat, i.e. cocoa butter. This is best applied by rolling the fruit shape in the hand which has been previously greased. Care must be exercised however to ensure that the colour which has been added, particularly powder colour, is not smudged spoiling the appearance. For the stems, use either brown marzipan, a stalk of maidenhair fern or a thin strip of angelica coloured brown. A clove can be used to imitate the calyx.

Pears (see Figure 117)

Use either green or yellow marzipan depending on the type of pear it is intended to imitate. Using a toothbrush and a piece of wire, scatter some chocolate colour over the shape after the right depth of shading has been achieved with other desired colours, i.e. red. The stalk and calyx are made in the same way as for apples.

Bananas (see Figure 117)

Spray a little green colour at each end of the shape modelled in yellow marzipan. Paint on chocolate brown marks using a fine paint brush. Rub on a little hard fat or cocoa butter, to imitate the waxy texture of the skin.

Lemons (see Figure 117)

Use yellow marzipan and tint the ends with green colour. Glaze with confectioner's varnish (*see* below).

Oranges (see Figure 117)

Fill the impression left at the top of the orange shape with a piece of chocolate-coloured marzipan to imitate the calyx. Glaze with confectioner's varnish (*see* below).

Peaches (see Figure 117)

Using yellow or green marzipan either spray orange or red colour on each side of the peach shape or use powdered colour. Dust with cornflour to imitate the bloom.

Small fruits may also be finished in the same way as those above and make either good petits fours or decorative pieces for gâteaux or torten.

Other fruits which can be easily modelled in marzipan are cherries, grapes and plums.

For exhibition purposes the fruit may be shown cut open, e.g. orange, or peeled, e.g. banana with the skin peeled back or a peach cut open to show the stone.

Varnish

Special confectioner's edible varnish is available from most flavour manufacturers, but if required for exhibition purposes the following may be used:

	kg	g	lb	oz
Isopropryl alcohol or rectified spirit of wine (ethyl alcohol)	1	000	2	4
Best white shellac	—	150	—	5½
Totals	1	150	2	9½

(1) Place the flakes of shellac in a bottle and pour on the alcohol.
(2) Stopper the bottle and shake.
(3) Stand it in a warm place and over a period of two to three days shake the bottle to dissolve the shellac.
(4) Strain through fine muslin and transfer to a well corked bottle.
(5) Use a soft paint brush (i.e. sable hair) to paint the varnish onto the marzipan. Wash the brushes in methylated spirit afterwards.

An edible varnish which may be used is made as follows:

	kg	g	lb	oz
Rectified spirit of wine				
(ethyl alcohol)	1	000	2	4
Gum benzoin	—	700	1	9¼
Totals	1	700	3	13¼

Dissolve the gum in the alcohol, strain through muslin and store in a well stoppered bottle until required for use.

Modelling Flowers

Almost any flower can be modelled in marzipan, but to achieve realistic results it is best to use a real flower as a model, dissecting it if necessary to see how the petals, etc., are assembled. The most popular flowers are the rose and carnation, but to show the techniques used for other types the narcissus and the fuchsia are also shown.

Rose

(1) Use the modelling almond paste Recipe 2 on page 258 of the required colour.
(2) Make a ball and from this fashion a pinnacle leaving sufficient paste to form a base.
(3) From another ball of paste, make a small petal by tapping the outside edge with the tips of the fingers until it is very thin, keeping the centre thicker for rigidity. Use a little cornflour to prevent the paste from sticking to the table or slab.
(4) Damp the centre with water and wrap the petal around the pinnacle leaving one side of the top edge furled back.
(5) Repeat, making the petals progressively larger and build up the rose by tucking one petal into another.
(6) As the last petals are applied, they should be first cupped in the palm of the hand

Figure 120. Marzipan flowers: Stages in the making of roses, petals and rosebuds. A fully-blown rose is also shown

and both sides furled back. These petals are put on haphazardly there being no regular pattern in nature. Five petals are sufficient to produce a good imitation of a rose – two for the centre bud and three surrounding. For a fully blown rose another four could be attached. Rose buds can be made from just the pinnacle surrounded by one or two petals.

(7) Cut the rose away from its base with a sharp knife.

(8) If the rose is to be finished off with a stem, the bulbous seed pod and green calyx must be attached.

For leaves, green marzipan either cut or made from a special mould can be attached to the stem. The veins can be imitated with the back of the knife.

Notes

(1) Two-tone effects can be made by inlaying differently coloured marzipan into the ball of paste before shaping the petal.

(2) Deep-coloured roses, e.g. carmine, are best coloured by holding the set shape in steam and brushing on powdered colour with a soft brush.

(3) Dried maidenhair or asparagus fern can be used to good effect with the rose when it is displayed on cake tops. Two rose buds and one fully blown rose are usually sufficient for this purpose.

Carnation

(1) Roll out a thin rope of marzipan of the required colour and press it onto the table top or slab.

(2) Using a greased palette knife slide it along to spread one edge of the paste very thinly so that it sticks to the work surface.

(3) Insert the knife between the marzipan and the work top and cut the strip of paste free. In doing this operation the thin edge will become ruffled in the same way as a carnation petal (*see* Figure 122).

(4) Gather the strip into the form of a carnation, keeping the ruffled or serrated edge uppermost.

(5) If the top edge of the petal is required to be tinted a different colour as in the variegated type, liquid colour can be applied with a paint brush to the thinned edge before removing the strip from the work top.

Figure 121. Marzipan flowers: carnation

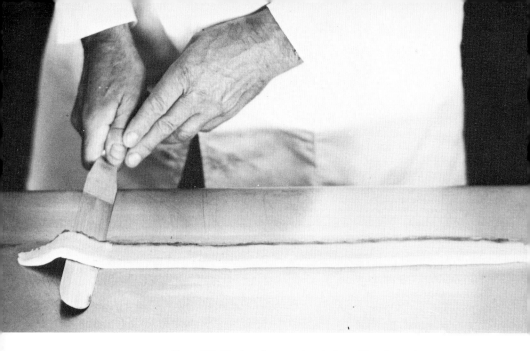

Figure 122. Marzipan flowers: – stage in the making of carnations

Narcissus

(1) Form a ball of white or pale-cream coloured marzipan from a saucer shape on a base.
(2) Using a pair of scissors cut into six and roughly cut out the shape of the petal.
(3) Fashion and thin the edges of these petals with the fingers and mark them with the modelling tool.
(4) Make a small ball from yellow marzipan, use the modelling tool to serrate the edge and tint it with red colour.
(5) Attach the centre to the petal.
(6) Place three spots of light green marzipan in the centre of the bell and give the petals a twist.
(7) Use a sharp knife to remove the flower from its base.

Figure 123. Marzipan flowers: stages in the making of narcissus

Fuchsia

(1) Roll out yellow marzipan very thinly and from this cut five pieces approx. 12 mm ($\frac{1}{2}$ in) in length for stamens.
(2) Make a pinnacle of pink marzipan and to this fix a narrow petal similar to that of a rose.
(3) Fix the stamens inside this petal and wrap round two more interlocking similar to a rose bud.
(4) Using deep red marzipan form a saucer shape on a base and cut out the shape of four petals using scissors.
(5) Fashion these with the fingers, to give petals which are long and pointed.
(6) Having allowed the centre petals and stamen to set, remove from its base with a knife and attach to the centre of the red petals.
(7) Cut the whole flower away from the base, thin the stem and curve the red petals backwards.

Other marzipan modelled flowers often seen in exhibitions are dahlias, freesias, chrysanthemums, lilies and orchids, but these are more difficult and time-consuming to make.

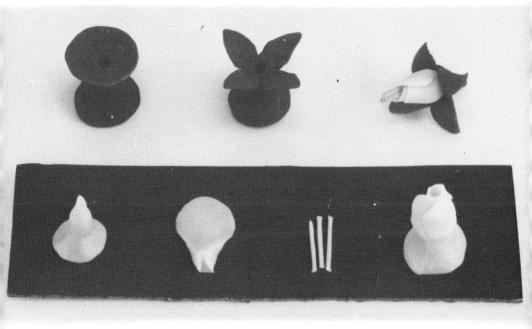

Figure 124. Marzipan flowers: stages in the making of fuchsia

Modelling Animal Shapes (*see* Figures 125–135)

Whilst it is possible to very closely imitate fruits and flowers, this is not so easy with animals, especially if they are required to be made quickly. However, all we need is to characterise the shape with features by which the animal may be recognized.

There are many basic shapes which may be used to imitate the body and this can be manipulated to show various positions such as standing, sitting, lying down or begging.

Likewise there are basic head shapes which can be attached to these body shapes.

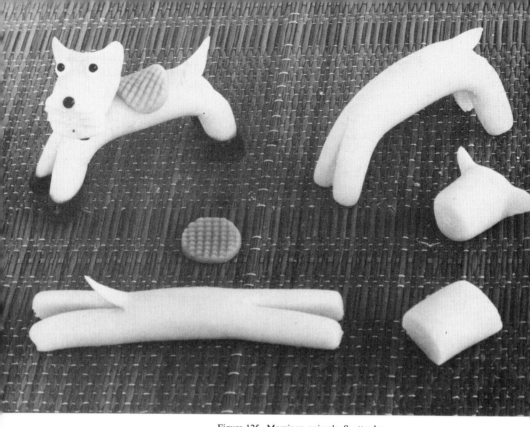

Figure 125. Marzipan animals: Scotty dog

Figure 126. Marzipan animals: Dachshund dog

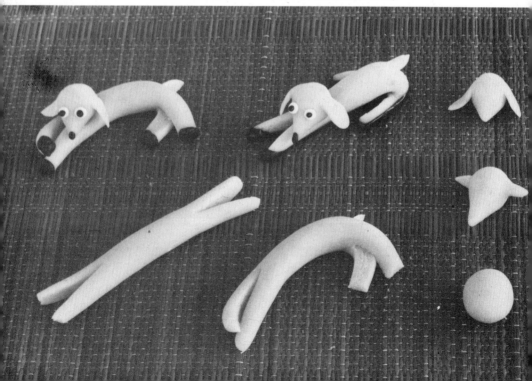

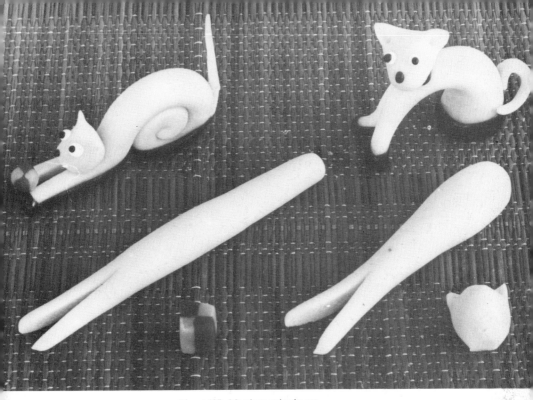

Figure 127. Marzipan animals: cat

Figure 128. Marzipan animals: rabbit

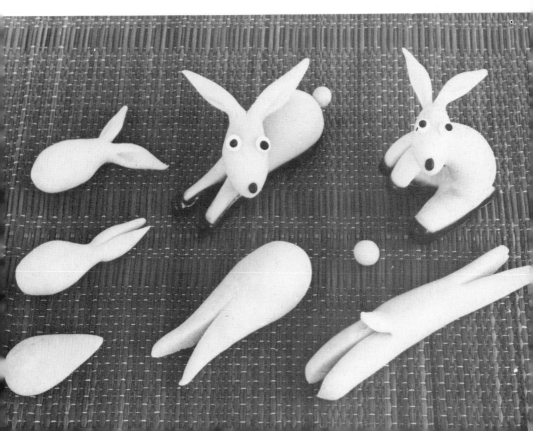

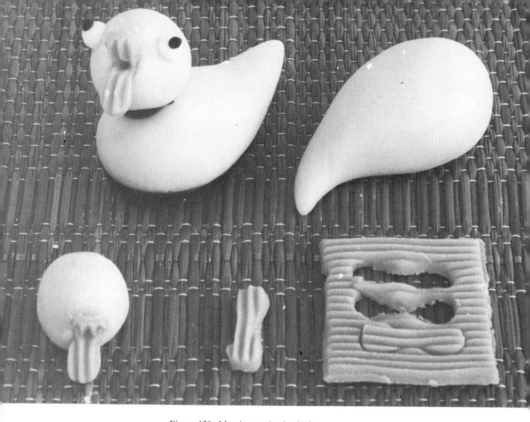

Figure 129. Marzipan animals: duck

Figure 130. Marzipan animals: chick

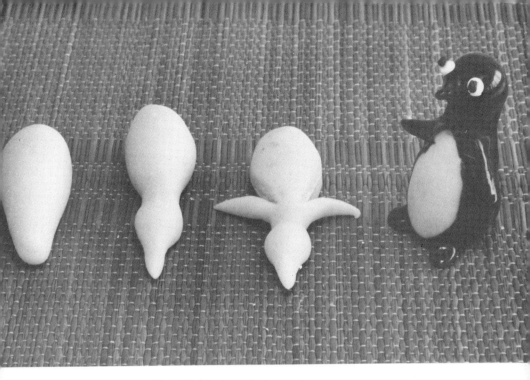

Figure 131. Marzipan animals: penguin

Figure 132. Marzipan animals: squirrel

Figure 133. Marzipan animals: sea lion

Figure 134. Marzipan animals: teddy bear

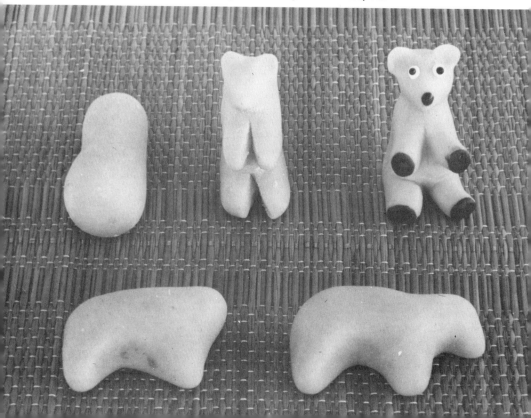

Figure 135. Television characters modelled in marzipan displayed in the Salon Culinaire at the International Catering Exhibition in London "Hotelympia"

Embellishments such as chocolate and royal icing are used to depict the various features such as eyes, mouth, paws, etc.

The modelling marzipan recipe No 1 is more suitable for this purpose.

The weight of the marzipan used for the individual animals will be dictated by the selling price, but is recommended to be between 45–55 g (1½–2 oz) each.

For some shapes it is necessary to employ the use of a template on which a given shape may be moulded and allowed to set before the other features are added, e.g. the head.

The proportion of marzipan used for the head is not critical and usually this is made larger than life. A proportion of ⅓ for the head and ⅔ for the body is quite satisfactory for most animals.

The animal shapes illustrated are shown in stages to minimise the explanation necessary for their make-up. The eyes are made by first piping a bulb of royal icing and then on top of this a bulb of chocolate.

SMALL CUT-OUT SHAPES
(Using Modelling paste No 1 on page 257)

Many attractive shapes may be cut out of marzipan and used for the decoration of all types of cakes and fancies. The marzipan may receive a decorative treatment prior to it being cut as follows:
(1) Textured with rollers to give an attractive surface, i.e. ribbed, basket, etc.
(2) Chocolate spun over in either a regular or irregular pattern. This can be done on the textured marzipan with good effect.
(3) Spread with either chocolate or royal icing and dress with:

(*a*) Castor sugar.

(*b*) Desiccated coconut.

(*c*) Small flake or nib almonds.

(*d*) Coloured coralettes.

Specially made cutters are available for cutting out the following shapes, besides the usual range of cutters for hearts, diamonds, etc.: Leaves, flowers, animals, birds, bells, candles, stars, Father Christmas, Snowmen, Christmas trees.

To obtain more realism these shapes often need further embellishment. The eyes, for example, need to be piped onto the animal shapes whilst flowers will require a yellow centre which can either be piped in with icing or jelly or a prefabricated sugar centre used. The use of the airgraph spray or a paint brush to apply colour is recommended in some cases.

Very small cut-out shapes are ideally suited for the decoration of individual fancies, since their use is economic in terms of labour.

Cutters can easily be made by a tinsmith, but the design is worthy of some consideration. It should be made so that it tapers away from the cutting end. Using this type several pieces can be cut out before being removed. This is easily effected by turning the cutter upside down when the pieces will fall out in a neat pile.

Figure 136A shows a number of such cutters and the shape of the cut-out pieces they produce. These can be further embellished by dipping various parts in chocolate.

Figure 136B shows four other simple shapes which may be used and these are now explained in detail.

Flowers

(1) Colour the marzipan to a deep colour.

(2) Roll out very thinly using fine castor sugar so that a crystallised effect is given to the surface.

(3) Cut out and place onto greaseproof paper in rows.

(4) Using a piece of dowel rod with the edges sanded off, press each cutout in the centre. This will cause the cut-out flower shape to form a cup and also fixes it onto the paper (*see* Figure 137 on page 274).

(5) When used, the centre is filled with a bright yellow jelly which should be first warmed so that it flows slightly.

Note These very attractive flowers may be used with diamonds of angelica for decorative purposes.

Figure 136A Examples of marzipan cutters and the shapes which result from their use.

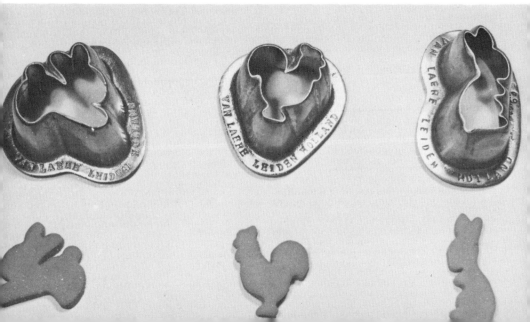

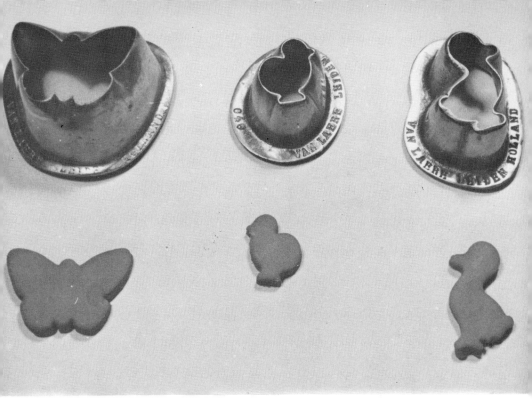

Figure 136A.

Figure 136B.

Holly-leaves

(1) Roll out green marzipan very thinly.
(2) Cut out the holly shapes and lay them in rows on greaseproof paper. It is a good idea to slightly dampen the paper so that the cut-outs are fixed in position and will not blow away when the airgraph spray is used.
(3) Spray on green colour.
(4) Pipe a bulb of bright red softened royal icing at the base.
(5) Place the sheet in a warm oven for a few minutes to help set the icing glossily to make the berry more realistic.
(6) If possible spray with an edible varnish.

Note These shapes will keep for a long time. The varnish not only helps to keep the paste free from damage but also discourages insects which like to feed on such foodstuffs.

Figure 137. Cupping marzipan flowers

Chicks

(1) Roll out yellow marzipan thinly using castor sugar.
(2) Cut out the shapes and place in rows onto greaseproof paper (slightly damp).
(3) Allow to harden before finishing off as follows:
    (a) Using the airgraph spray or a fine paint brush colour the beak a bright orange. Alternatively, pipe a beak with bright orange royal icing.
    (b) Either pipe in an eye using chocolate-coloured royal icing or add a spot of colour with a fine paintbrush or pen.

Robins

(1) Roll out white marzipan thinly using icing sugar for dusting purposes.
(2) Cut out the shapes and place in rows on greaseproof paper (slightly damp).
(3) Allow to harden and finish off as follows:
    (a) Using an airgraph spray colour the breast area an orange-red and the rest of the body a light chocolate brown.
(4) Either use chocolate-coloured royal icing to pipe in the eye or a fine paintbrush.
(5) When placing these onto cakes it adds to the realism by first piping a branch of a tree, mounting the robin thereon and piping in its legs.

OTHER MARZIPAN DECORATIONS

Yule-logs

(1) Make a rope of almond paste.
(2) Melt some chocolate and cover the marzipan, using a palette knife to spread the chocolate evenly.
(3) Use a comb scraper and mark the surface.

(4) When set, cut into suitably sized lengths. For small logs 4 cm (1½ in) is sufficient.
(5) Before placing onto a cake for decorative effect dust with icing sugar to imitate snow.

A more realistic effect can be made by first thinly rolling out the paste, spreading it with chocolate and rolling up like a Swiss roll to form a long rope. When cut, the ends will appear to resemble the ends of a log.

Snowballs

These can be made from either almond paste or sugar paste (*see* below). Whilst a solid ball of paste may be used for this, it is recommended that cherries be used.

(1) Roll out the paste to approx. 2 mm ($\frac{1}{10}$ in) and cut out circles sufficiently large to wrap up the cherry used.
(2) After the cherry has been completely covered with paste they may be finished off in two ways:
   (*a*) Roll them in white royal icing which has been previously spread onto the work top. This will give a rough-cast effect.
   (*b*) Place a few at a time in a small bowl with some icing sugar. Rotate the bowl so that the paste-covered ball picks up icing sugar on its surface.

Note   The size of these will depend upon the size of the cherries used and the thickness of paste into which they are wrapped. Small alpine cherries are recommended for snowballs with which to decorate fancies.

Sugar Paste

	Recipe 1				Recipe 2			
	kg	*g*	*lb*	*oz*	*kg*	*g*	*lb*	*oz*
Icing sugar	1	000	2	4	1	000	2	4
Marshmallow	—	665	1	8	—	—	—	—
Granulated sugar	—	—	—	—	—	200	—	7¼
Glucose	—	—	—	—	—	200	—	7¼
Water	—	—	—	—	—	60	—	2¼
Leaf gelatine	—	—	—	—	—	30	—	1
Royal icing	—	—	—	—	—	200	—	7¼
Totals	1	665	3	12	1	690	3	13

Recipe 1
(1) Add the icing sugar to the marshmallow and work into a smooth paste.

Recipe 2
(1) Add the water to the granulated sugar and glucose and bring to the boil.
(2) Soak the gelatine in some water and then add to the sugar syrup.
(3) Allow to cool slightly and stir in the royal icing.
(4) Add the icing sugar and make into a smooth paste.

Notes
(1) Both the above recipes give a paste which will set hard. For a softer eating paste the following should be added:
   Hard fat or cocoa butter – 85 g (3 oz).

(2) As this paste skins, always keep wrapped in a polythene bag or in an airtight container.

Uses

(1) Covering for all types of gâteaux and fancies.

It may be coloured and flavoured. It is useful to cover cakes which have to be coated with fondant or chocolate since it provides a flat smooth surface which greatly facilitates obtaining a perfect coating.

(2) The paste may be used for making cut-out or modelling shapes in a manner similar to marzipan.

(3) It may be used in the same way as gum paste for making models, caskets and table decorations etc.

Gum Paste

	kg	g	lb	oz
Icing sugar	1	000	2	4
Cornflour	—	125	—	4½
Gum tragacanth (powdered)	—	15	—	½
Cold water	—	125	—	4½
Totals	1	265	2	13½

(1) Mix the icing sugar, cornflour and gum tragacanth thoroughly together.

(2) Add the water and mix to a clear smooth paste.

Notes

(1) This paste should be left for at least an hour and mixed again prior to use to enable the gum tragacanth to become thoroughly dissolved in the paste.

(2) Always keep covered, either in a polythene bag or in an airtight container. Once exposed to the air, gum paste rapidly dries and hardens.

Use The main use of gum paste is to make decorations, display pieces, models or caskets, and some hints on its use are given here.

Moulded Decorations

(1) Dust surface with cornflour and press the paste into the mould.

(2) Cut off the surplus paste.

(3) To ease the moulded piece out of the mould it is sometimes a good tip to attach another piece of paste which has been moistened to pull it out.

(4) On very fine filigree-moulded shapes a piece of muslin can be attached to keep the shape intact.

Display pieces, models and caskets*

Before starting on these more elaborate goods we need working drawings and often templates.

---

* Further details on the use of a gum paste to make models and caskets are to be found in two other publications written by the same author:

Models   Cake Design and Decoration by L. J. Hanneman and G. Marshall, published by Applied Science Publishers, Essex.

Caskets   Patisserie by L. J. Hanneman, published by Wm. Heinemann Ltd., London.

19. Chocolate Goods

Although the uses of chocolate described in this chapter refer to chocolate couverture, many of the techniques described can be applied to the substitute cake coatings which were known as *baker's chocolate* or *cooking chocolate* before these descriptions were prohibited by law. (In Britain it is now illegal to apply the word *chocolate* to any product other than couverture).

However, the use of these substitute products will not produce such good results, as they lack the flavour, snap and gloss of couverture. The advantage is the ease with which such products can be used, since no tempering is necessary. All one has to do is to warm them to approx. 38–40°C (100–110°F) and use.

Tempering of Chocolate Couverture

Before chocolate can be successfully used it must be free from contamination by moisture and must be tempered. This process can be explained as follows:

Cocoa butter can be regarded as being a mixture of two fats – A with a low melting point and latent heat, and B with a high melting point and latent heat. Type A has crystals of fat which are soft and feel greasy, whilst the B type crystals of fat impart the gloss and snap required in well tempered chocolate.

To eliminate the A-type crystals, the couverture should be completely melted, then cooled to the setting point of the A crystals, when B crystals are produced as well. The mass is now heated to the temperature at which only the A crystals will melt, leaving some B crystals. On setting, the whole mass will crystallise out in the B crystal form. (This process is known as *seeding*).

There are several techniques used to temper chocolate:

(1) For this a double-jacketed pan known as a bain-marie or porringer is used. It consists of a small pan in which the chocolate is contained and a larger pan which is filled with warm water. The small pan is placed inside the larger one and the heat is transferred by the water. To melt the chocolate this water must not exceed 39°C (120°F).

When all the chocolate has melted, transfer the small pan into another large one containing very cold water (some *ice* may be used). Stir continually until some of the chocolate sets on the bottom. Transfer again to the pan of hot water where it remains until the solid chocolate just begins to melt. Remove and stir until all the solid chocolate has melted and has been dispersed. The temperature at this stage should be cool, approx. 29°C (84°F) for milk and 30°C (80°F) for plain.

(2) Melt the chocolate in a bain-marie. Remove from the heat and stir in flakes of solid chocolate, shredded from a block of well tempered chocolate. The proportion depends on the amount of liquid chocolate and its temperature which should be sufficient only *just* to melt the shreds of solid chocolate being stirred in.

(3) Once a quantity of liquid-tempered chocolate has been obtained, it can be used to *seed* fresh batches of un-tempered chocolate. The usual procedure is to have a large bowl of liquid chocolate available and as the tempered chocolate is used, it is replaced by the liquid un-tempered variety. This is how chocolate is tempered for large scale use in a factory.

Moulding

When tempered chocolate sets, it contracts and this action makes it easy for all types of figures to be moulded. Moulds may be either metal, usually tinned or plastic, the latter having the advantage of being flexible and so aiding release of the figure from the mould. The temperature of setting is important. Although it needs to be cool, it is a mistake to place the mould in a refrigerator. This will cause uneven contraction and result in a cracked figure.

DETAILED METHOD OF MOULDING EGGS AND FIGURES

(1) Make sure that the moulds are clean, dry and polished by rubbing cotton wool onto the surface.
(2) Temper the chocolate couverture as previously described.
(3) Fill the figure or mould to the brim with the liquid chocolate.
(4) Turn upside down and empty the mould of chocolate (*see* Figure 138).
(5) Wipe the brim free of surplus chocolate and place brim downwards onto greaseproof paper.
(6) Place in a cool room and allow the chocolate to set in the mould.
(7) Repeat the operation if the coating of chocolate is too thin. Except for the very small moulds, most require two thicknesses of chocolate for strength.
(8) Leave the moulds in a cool room until the chocolate has contracted sufficiently for the chocolate shape to be removed from the mould. This might take as long as two hours. The release of the chocolate from the mould is easier from plastic moulds than from tin.
(9) To finish off Easter eggs, the two halves have to be joined with chocolate. This is best done by heating a clean tray and placing the brim of one half of the chocolate

Figure 138. Chocolate moulding. The rabbit mould in this figure has just been filled and is being held so that the surplus chocolate can run back into the pan. Tapping the mould with a spatula helps to eliminate any air bubbles which might form. In the extreme *right* of the picture are some egg moulds just filled

Figure 139.
A variety of moulded chocolate figures

egg on the heated tray for a few seconds so that the chocolate melts. When this happens the two halves can be secured by placing the two edges together.

(10) The Easter eggs can be further decorated by piping stiffened chocolate in a shell pattern around the join. Also marzipan flowers and inscriptions may be piped on.

Dipping

Chocolate may be used for sweets by dipping various centres, e.g. fondants. It must be well-tempered and at such a temperature that the first one has started to set whilst the sixth is being dipped.

Several varieties of pastries, marzipan shapes and animals are enhanced by having a part dipped in chocolate. Whole enrobed cakes and biscuits will keep fresh and moist for very much longer periods.

Piping

When a liquid is added to chocolate, it thickens and in this state it can be piped. Piping chocolate loses its characteristic gloss and some of its snap and is not, therefore, recommended for piped off-pieces. Substances which may be added to thicken chocolate are as follows:

(1) Water or milk – not recommended.
(2) Glycerine – recommended – helps to maintain gloss.
(3) Piping jelly – recommended – helps to maintain gloss.
(4) Gelatine – recommended – helps to maintain gloss.
(5) Spirits and liqueurs – adds to flavour.

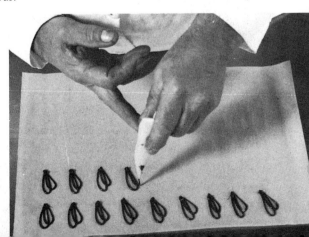

Figure 140. Piping chocolate filigree shapes

Note   Some chocolate is more suitable for piping than others, having a lower cocoa-butter content, and is therefore thicker when in the heated condition.

Thinning

To make chocolate thinner we must add cocoa butter. This is useful if a very thin covering is required.

Flavouring

Chocolate or block cocoa may be used to flavour icings and creams and the crumb of cakes. Block cocoa (lacking in sugar) is especially useful to flavour very sweet ingredients such as fondant. Although the chocolate is used mostly in the liquid state, solid flakes may be scattered or mixed in items like fresh cream.

Carving

The very nature of chocolate makes it an ideal foodstuff from which figures may be carved. All that is needed is a flair for this type of sculpture work and a sharp knife. In the first instance, a sufficiently large block of chocolate has to be provided and it might be necessary for the chocolate to be first melted, tempered and then poured into a suitably sized frame or mould.

Decoration

(1) Shapes may be piped out onto greaseproof paper from drawn designs. When set, these shapes may be used to decorate gâteaux, torten, fancies, etc.
(2) Chocolate may be spread out onto greaseproof paper and when nearly set, a cutter or knife can cut out shapes which, when set, can be removed from the sheet and used for decoration. *See* Figure 111(4) on page 246.
(3) Spread chocolate out onto marzipan or sugar paste, and as it is setting, spread with a serrated scraper to obtain a corrugated effect. Cut out shapes with a cutter or knife when chocolate has set and use shapes for decoration.
(4) Spread chocolate onto marzipan or sugar paste and before it sets, sprinkle on a variety of dressings, e.g. nibbed almonds, coloured decorations, coconut (white and browned), violet petals, rose petals, etc. Cut out shapes as in (3).
(5) Texture marzipan or sugar paste with rollers. Place melted chocolate in a greaseproof bag with a fine aperture. Pipe lines of chocolate at speed (*spinning*) over the textured paste, in different directions, (*see* page 237). Cut out shapes as in 3.
(6) *Curls* (Figure 141).   Pour some chocolate onto a marble, metal or melamine slab and spread backwards and forwards until it just sets. With a sharp knife, cut the chocolate off the slab using a shearing action. The chocolate will form long curls, the thickness depending upon the length of the shearing action. *Flakes* may be done in the same way but the chocolate has to be more firmly set.

Figure   141. Making
chocolate curls

Plastic Chocolate

If confectioner's glucose and couverture are blended homogeneously together, they will form a plastic paste which may be modelled into roses, etc. The proportions should be approx. 2 of chocolate to 1 of glucose, both warmed to about 32°C (90°F) before being blended together.

CHOCOLATE CENTRES

The following selected items are suitable for cutting up into small shapes before being dipped into chocolate.

Nougat

	Recipe 1				Recipe 2			
	kg	*g*	*lb*	*oz*	*kg*	*g*	*lb*	*oz*
Granulated sugar	1	000	2	4	1	000	2	4
Confectioner's glucose	—	335	—	12	—	—	—	—
Nibbed almonds	1	000	2	4	1	750	1	11
Lemon juice	—	—	—	—	—	30	—	1
Totals	2	335	5	4	2	780	4	0

Method for Recipe 1
(1) Stir the sugar and glucose over gentle heat until all the sugar has dissolved and melted.
(2) Raise the temperature and cook until pale amber in colour. (Observe sugar-boiling precautions, *see* page 13).
(3) Warm and then stir in the almonds and remove from the heat.
(4) Turn out onto a greased or oiled slab, and keep turning it over until cool enough to mould.

Method for Recipe 2
(1) Stir the sugar and lemon juice over gentle heat until all the sugar has dissolved and melted.
(2) Proceed as for Recipe 1.
Note For the best decorative effect, the sugar should be amber in colour before the almonds are added so there is a contrast between the brown colour of the sugar and the white of the almonds. However, if desired, roasted nib almonds may be stirred in, or the almonds added earlier and browned in the boiling sugar.

USES

Chocolate Centres

Whilst the nougat is still pliable and warm, roll out with a rolling pin or pass through greased pastry rollers to the required thickness. Using a caramel cutter, cut into appropriately sized squares or rectangles. Once cold, these individual pieces can be dipped into or enrobed in chocolate.

Moulding

Whilst still warm and pliable, nougat can be moulded into various shapes such as baskets. Once set it is very brittle but it can be readily softened again by heating, e.g.

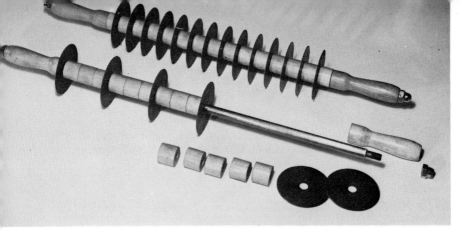

Figure 142. Caramel cutters (*see* page 281)

placing it into a warm oven. This is often required before the final shaping can be done. A strong pair of scissors is useful for cutting the nougat when it is pliable. Where nougat pieces have to be joined, e.g. handles or a basket, boiled sugar should be used as the cement.

Decoration

Various shapes cut from a sheet of nougat may be used for decorating gâteaux etc.

When set, nougat is easily crushed with a rolling pin and the pieces may then be sieved to give nibs for masking the sides of gâteaux. The crushed pieces should first be sieved through a coarse sieve to remove very large particles (which need re-crushing) and then through a medium sieve to give nibs of a uniform size.

Ingredient

The fine nibs and dust are suitable for mixing into fresh cream or buttercream for flavouring purposes (*see* nougat gâteau on page 206).

The nougat may also be ground to a paste by passing it through granite rollers. Such a paste is sometimes called praline and this, too, can be incorporated into creams for flavouring purposes.

Nougat Montelimart

	kg	g	lb	oz
Granulated sugar	1	000	2	4
Water	—	280	—	10
Honey	—	280	—	10
Confectioner's glucose	—	280	—	10
Egg white	—	110	—	4
Chopped glacé cherries	—	140	—	5
Green nib almonds	—	140	—	5
Nib almonds or hazelnuts	—	70	—	$2\frac{1}{2}$
Flaked almonds or hazelnuts	—	70	—	$2\frac{1}{2}$
Totals	2	370	5	5

(1) Boil the sugar and water rapidly to 107°C (225°F).

(2) Add the honey and glucose and continue to boil as rapidly as possible to 135°C (275°F) (Observe sugar-boiling precautions, *see* page 13).

Fudges

	1				2				3				Chocolate 1				Chocolate 2			
	kg	g	lb	oz	kg	g	lb	oz	kg	g	lb	oz	kg	g	lb	oz	kg	g	lb	oz
Light brown sugar	1	000	2	4	—	—	—	—	—	500	1	2	—	—	—	—	—	—	—	—
Granulated sugar	—	—	—	—	1	000	2	4	—	500	1	2	1	000	2	4	1	000	2	4
Confectioner's glucose	—	—	—	—	—	500	1	2	1	000	2	4	—	445	1	0	—	250	—	9
Water	—	—	—	—	—	155	—	5½	—	305	—	11	—	—	—	—	—	—	—	—
Fresh milk	—	180	—	6½	—	—	—	—	—	—	—	—	—	—	—	—	—	—	—	—
Condensed milk	—	180	—	6½	—	500	1	2	—	—	—	—	—	—	—	—	—	—	—	—
Evaporated milk	—	—	—	—	—	—	—	—	—	125	—	4½	—	—	—	—	—	305	—	11
Butter/margarine	—	250	—	9	—	375	—	13¼	—	125	—	4½	—	60	—	2¼	—	60	—	2¼
Fondant	—	—	—	—	—	500	1	2	—	500	1	2	—	—	—	—	—	125	—	4½
Marshmallow	—	—	—	—	—	500	1	2	—	—	—	—	—	—	—	—	—	—	—	—
Unsweetened chocolate	—	—	—	—	—	—	—	—	—	—	—	—	—	250	—	4½	—	85	—	3
Totals	1	610	3	10	3	530	7	15	3	055	6	14	1	755	3	10¾	1	825	4	1¾

(3) Whip the egg whites to a stiff snow and then beat them into the hot syrup. Continue beating until the mixture becomes firm in consistency. This operation is best executed on a machine.
(4) Warm the cherries and nuts and blend into the mixture.
(5) Pour onto wafer-lined trays or frame, spread level and also cover the surface with wafer paper.
(6) Press down the surface with a weighted flat board and leave until perfectly cold, preferably overnight.
(7) Cut into the appropriately sized pieces ready for dipping into chocolate.

Fudges

Method for Recipe 1
(1) Mix the milk and sugar and bring to the boil.
(2) Add the butter a little at a time and boil to 121°C (250°F). Keep the mixture well stirred so that it partially grains before pouring out.
(3) Once the temperature reaches 121°C (250°F) pour out into a greased tray of a size which will give a slab of the required thickness, to cut into centres.

Note
(1) This recipe will also make toffee if allowed to boil to 124°C (255°F) before pouring out. *In this case do not stir.*
(2) There is considerable frothing in these recipes which contain milk and fats, and it is therefore advisable to use a large saucepan in which the mixture only occupies ¼ of its capacity.

Method for Recipe 2
(1) Mix all except the fondant and marshmallow and cook to 118°C (245°F).
(2) Once this temperature has been reached remove from the heat and stir in the fondant and marshmallow.
(3) Proceed as for (3) in Recipe 1.

Method for Recipe 3
(1) Dissolve the sugar into the water on low heat.
(2) Add the glucose and boil to 130°C (265°F).
(3) Remove from the heat and stir in the remainder of the ingredients.
(4) Proceed as for (3) in Recipe 1.

Method for Chocolate 1
(1) Boil sugar and water to 115°C (240°F), stirring continuously.
(2) Once this temperature is reached, remove from the heat, add the butter and chocolate, and stir until creamy.
(3) Proceed as for (3) in Recipe 1.

Method for Chocolate 2
(1) Mix the sugar, glucose, milk and butter and boil to 113°C (236°F).
(2) Stir thoroughly and then add the chocolate and fondant.
(3) Proceed as for (3) in Recipe 1.

Toffee

Proceed as for fudge but without stirring. For a more brittle toffee, boil to 138°C (280°F).

Toffee

	kg	g	lb	oz
Granulated sugar	1	000	2	4
Confectioner's glucose	—	530	1	3
Condensed milk	—	220	—	8
Hard white fat	—	110	—	4
Water	—	95	—	3½
Totals	1	955	4	6½

Coconut Ice

	Recipe 1				Recipe 2			
	kg	g	lb	oz	kg	g	lb	oz
Granulated sugar	1	000	2	4	1	000	2	4
Confectioner's glucose	—	—	—	—	—	205	—	7½
Water	—	390	—	14	—	390	—	14
Cream of tartar		Trace			—	—	—	—
Desiccated coconut	—	110	—	4	—	110	—	4
Fondant	—	—	—	—	—	415	—	15
Totals	1	500	3	6	2	120	4	12½

Method for Recipe 1
(1) Dissolve the sugar in the water and bring to the boil.
(2) Continue boiling but add the cream of tartar (approx. 1½ g) at 104°C (220°F).
(3) Boil to 112°C (234°F).
(4) If the syrup hasn't already grained, stir slightly and then blend in the coconut.
(5) Proceed as for (3) in the Fudge recipe No 1 (*see* page 283).

Method for Recipe 2
(1) Dissolve the sugar, glucose and water and bring to the boil.
(2) Add the fondant and boil to 113°C (236°F).
(3) Blend in the coconut.
(4) Proceed as for (3) in the Fudge recipe No 1 (*see* page 283).

A quite acceptable coconut ice can be made from scraps of fondant, etc. These are boiled with a little water to approx. 113°C (236°F) and coconut stirred in. Because such scraps are usually tinted in various colours it is advisable to add chocolate and chocolate colour to mask the different colours and flavours of the scraps used.

Butterscotch

	kg	g	lb	oz
Brown sugar	1	000	2	4
Confectioner's glucose	—	250	—	9
Water	—	305	—	11
Salted butter	—	125	—	4½
Totals	1	680	3	12½

(1) Boil sugar, water and glucose to 143°C (290°F) observing sugar boiling precautions (*see* page 13).

(2) Remove from the heat and stir in the butter in small portions.

(3) Proceed as for (3) in the Fudge recipe No 1 (*see* page 283).

Fondants

	kg	*g*	*lb*	*oz*
Fondant	1	000	2	4
Condensed milk	—	150	—	$5\frac{1}{2}$
Yeast water	—	30	—	$1\frac{1}{4}$
Totals	1	180	2	$10\frac{3}{4}$

(1) Warm the whole mixture to 65°C (150°F) and transfer to a dropping funnel.

(2) Deposit into cornflour moulds.

(3) When set carefully remove and brush off surplus cornflour with a soft brush before dipping or enrobing with chocolate.

Cornflour Moulds

These are made by first filling a deep tray with cornflour compacting slightly and spreading level.

Impressions are now made into the cornflour with shapes usually glued onto a wooden slat so that several impressions can be made at once.

These are now filled with the hot fondant from the dropping funnel.

Yeast Water

Yeast : 1 part

Water : 3 parts.

Note Yeast is used to introduce enzymes which will partially liquify the fondant once it has been dipped and so make the centre more attractive to eat. However, ordinary water can be used if desired.

Rubber Moulds

Fondant centres may be made by depositing the liquid hot fondant into special flexible rubber moulds, *see* Figure 143.

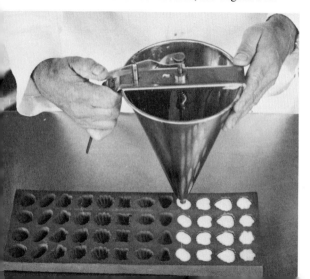

Figure 143. Depositing fondant into a rubber mould for chocolate centres

The fondant used for this purpose needs to be heated to at least 83°C (180°F) so that it readily forms a crust once it cools inside the rubber mould and makes it possible for easy release. Such centres are not so soft as the ones made in the cornflour moulds. *Note* The consistency and moisture content of fondant varies from manufacturer to manufacturer and being hygroscopic it is also influenced by the environment and storage conditions, e.g. age. Therefore it might be necessary either to increase or reduce the water content of the recipe to make a fondant centre which has a soft texture whilst being readily released from the mould.

CHOCOLATE GOODS

FAULTS	Room temperature too high.	Incorrect tempering.	Using the chocolate at too low a temperature.	Heated to too high a temperature.	Using the chocolate too warm.	Contaminated with water.
Failure to set properly.	√	√		√		√
White streaks.	√	√			√	
White bloom on surface.			√			
Lack of gloss.		√		√	√	

Appendix

TEMPERATURE CONVERSIONS

There are two methods by which the degrees in one scale can be converted into another. To change Celsius (Centigrade) into Fahrenheit:

Method 1
Multiply by $\frac{9}{5}$ and add 32.

Method 2
Add 40, multiply by $\frac{9}{5}$ and subtract 40.

To change Fahrenheit into Celsius:

Method 1
Subtract 32 and multiply by $\frac{5}{9}$.

Method 2
Add 40, multiply by $\frac{5}{9}$ and subtract 40.

Examples
(1) Change 25°C into Fahrenheit.

Method 1
$25 \times \frac{9}{5} = 45$.
$45 + 32 = 77°F$ (Answer)

Method 2
$25 + 40 = 65$
$65 \times \frac{9}{5} = 117$
$117 - 40 = 77°F$ (Answer)

(2) Change 41°F into Celsius

Method 1
$41 - 32 = 9$.
$9 \times \frac{5}{9} = 5°C$ (Answer)

Method 2
$41 + 40 = 81$
$81 \times \frac{5}{9} = 45$
$45 - 40 = 5°C$ (Answer)

A temperature conversion table appears on page 290.

Conversion Tables

These tables will be useful for recipe conversion.

The numbers in heavy type can be either °C or °F. If the heavy type number is °C, the equivalent in °F is on the right. If the heavy type number is °F, the equivalent in °C is on the left.

°C		°F	°C		°F	°C		°F	°C		°F
−40	**−40**	−40	0·5	**33**	91·4	21·0	**70**	158·0	71	**160**	320
−34	**−30**	−22	1·1	**34**	93·2	21·5	**71**	159·8	76	**170**	338
−29	**−20**	−4	1·6	**35**	95·0	22·2	**72**	161·6	83	**180**	356
−23	**−10**	+14	2.2	**36**	96·8	22·7	**73**	163·4	88	**190**	374
−17·7	**−0**	+32	2·7	**37**	98·6	23·3	**74**	165·2	93	**200**	392
−17·2	**1**	33·8	3·3	**38**	100·4	23·8	**75**	167·0	99	**210**	410
−16·6	**2**	35·6	3·8	**39**	102·2	24·4	**76**	168·8	100	**212**	413
−16·1	**3**	37·4	4·4	**40**	104·0	25·0	**77**	170·6	104	**220**	428
−15·5	**4**	39·2	4·9	**41**	105·8	25·5	**78**	172·4	110	**230**	446
−15	**5**	41·0	5·5	**42**	107·6	26·2	**79**	174·2	115	**240**	464
−14·4	**6**	42·8	6·0	**43**	109·4	26·8	**80**	176·0	121	**250**	482
−13·9	**7**	44·6	6·6	**44**	111·2	27·3	**81**	177·8	127	**260**	500
−13·3	**8**	46·4	7·1	**45**	113·0	27·7	**82**	179·6	132	**270**	518
−12·7	**9**	48·2	7·7	**46**	114·8	28·2	**83**	181·4	138	**280**	536
−12·2	**10**	50·0	8·2	**47**	116·6	28·8	**84**	183·2	143	**290**	554
−11·6	**11**	51·8	8·8	**48**	118·4	29·3	**85**	185·0	149	**300**	572
−11·1	**12**	53.6	9·3	**49**	120·2	29·9	**86**	186·8	154	**310**	590
−10·5	**13**	55·4	9·9	**50**	122·0	30·4	**87**	188·6	160	**320**	608
−10·0	**14**	57·2	10·4	**51**	123·8	31·0	**88**	190·4	165	**330**	626
−9·4	**15**	59·0	11·1	**52**	125·6	31·5	**89**	192·2	171	**340**	644
−8·8	**16**	60·8	11·5	**53**	127·4	32·1	**90**	194·0	177	**350**	662
−8·3	**17**	62·6	12·1	**54**	129·2	32·6	**91**	195·8	182	**360**	680
−7·7	**18**	64·4	12·6	**55**	131·0	33·3	**92**	197·6	188	**370**	698
−7·2	**19**	66·2	13·2	**56**	132·8	33·8	**93**	199·4	193	**380**	716
−6·6	**20**	68·0	13·7	**57**	134·6	34·4	**94**	201·2	199	**390**	734
−6·1	**21**	69·8	14·3	**58**	136·4	34·9	**95**	203·0	204	**400**	752
−5·5	**22**	71·6	14·8	**59**	138·2	35·5	**96**	204·8	210	**410**	770
−5·0	**23**	73·4	15·6	**60**	140·0	36·1	**97**	206·6	215	**420**	788
−4·4	**24**	75·2	16·1	**61**	141·8	36·6	**98**	208·4	221	**430**	806
−3·9	**25**	77·0	16·6	**62**	143·6	37·1	**99**	210·2	226	**440**	824
−3·3	**26**	78·8	17·1	**63**	145·4	37·7	**100**	212·0	232	**450**	842
−2·8	**27**	80·6	17·7	**64**	147·2	43	**110**	230	238	**460**	860
−2·2	**28**	82·4	18·2	**65**	149·0	49	**120**	248	243	**470**	878
−1·6	**29**	84.2	18·8	**66**	150·8	54	**130**	266	249	**480**	896
−1·1	**30**	86·0	19·3	**67**	152·6	60	**140**	284	254	**490**	914
−0·6	**31**	87·8	19·9	**68**	154·4	65	**150**	302	260	**500**	932
−0	**32**	89·6	20·4	**69**	156·2						

The numbers in heavy type can be either litres or pints. For example, if the heavy type number is 5, 5 litres are equivalent to 8·7990 pints and 5 pints are equivalent to 2·8412 litres.

Litres – Pints

(8 pints = 1 imperial gallon)

litres		pints	litres		pints	litres		pints
0·5682454	1	1·7598	19·8886	35	61·5930	38·6407	68	119·6664
1·1365	2	3·5196	20·4568	36	63·3528	39·2089	69	121·4262
1·7047	3	5·2794	21·0251	37	65·1126	39·7772	70	123·1860
2·2730	4	7·0392	21·5933	38	66·8724	40·3454	71	124·9458
2·8412	5	8·7990	22·1616	39	68·6322	40·9137	72	126·7056
3·4095	6	10·5588	22·7298	40	70·3920	41·4819	73	128·4654
3·9777	7	12·3186	23·2981	41	72·1518	42·0502	74	130·2252
4·5460	8	14·0784	23·8663	42	73·9116	42·6184	75	131·9850
5·1142	9	15·8382	24·4346	43	75·6714	43·1867	76	133·7448
5·6825	10	17·5980	25·0028	44	77·4312	43·7549	77	135·5046
6·2507	11	19·3578	25·5710	45	79·1910	44·3231	78	137·2644
6·8189	12	21·1176	26·1393	46	80·9508	44·8914	79	139·0242
7·3872	13	22·8774	26·7075	47	82·7106	45·4596	80	140·7840
7·9554	14	24·6372	27·2758	48	84·4704	46·0279	81	142·5438
8·5237	15	26·3970	27·8440	49	86·2302	46·5961	82	144·3036
9·0919	16	28·1568	28·4123	50	87·9900	47·1644	83	146·0634
9·6602	17	29·9166	28·9805	51	89·7498	47·7326	84	147·8232
10·2284	18	31·6764	29·5488	52	91·5096	48·3009	85	149·5830
10·7967	19	33·4362	30·1170	53	93·2694	48·8691	86	151·3428
11·3649	20	35·1960	30·6853	54	95·0292	49·4373	87	153·1026
11·9332	21	36·9558	31·2535	55	96·7890	50·0056	88	154·8624
12·5014	22	38·7156	31·8217	56	98·5488	50·5738	89	156·6222
13·0696	23	40·4754	32·3900	57	100·3086	51·1421	90	158·3820
13·6379	24	42·2352	32·9582	58	102·0684	51·7103	91	160·1418
14·2061	25	43·9950	33·5265	59	103·8282	52·2786	92	161·9016
14·7744	26	45·7548	34·0947	60	105·5880	52·8468	93	163·6614
15·3426	27	47·5146	34·6630	61	107·3478	53·4151	94	165·4212
15·9109	28	49·2744	35·2312	62	109·1076	53·9833	95	167·1810
16·4791	29	51·0342	35·7995	63	110·8674	54·5516	96	168·9408
17·0474	30	52·7940	36·3677	64	112·6272	55·1198	97	170·7006
17·6156	31	54·5538	36·9360	65	114·3870	55·6880	98	172·4604
18·1839	32	56·3136	37·5042	66	116·1468	56·2563	99	174·2202
18·7521	33	58·0734	38·0724	67	117·9066	56·8245	100	175·9800
19·3203	34	59·8332						

The numbers in heavy type can be either litres or imperial gallons. For example, if the heavy type number is 5, 5 litres are equivalent to 1·0999 imperial gallons and 5 imperial gallons are equivalent to 22·730 litres.

Litres-Imperial Gallons

litres		imp. gall.	litres		imp. gall.	litres		imp. gall.
4·5459631	1	0·21997	159·109	35	7·6991	309·125	68	14·9583
9·092	2	0·4400	163·655	36	7·9191	313·671	69	15·1783
13·638	3	0·6599	168·201	37	8·1391	318·217	70	15·3983
18·184	4	0·8799	172·747	38	8·3591	322·763	71	15·6182
22·730	5	1·0999	177·293	39	8·5790	327·309	72	15·8382
27·276	6	1·3199	181·839	40	8·7990	331·855	73	16·0582
31·822	7	1·5398	186·384	41	9·0190	336·401	74	16·2782
36·368	8	1·7598	190·930	42	9·2390	340·947	75	16·4981
40·914	9	1·9798	195·476	43	9·4589	345·493	76	16·7181
45·460	10	2·1998	200·022	44	9·6789	350·039	77	16·9381
50·006	11	2·4197	204·568	45	9·8989	354·585	78	17·1581
54·552	12	2·6397	208·114	46	10·1189	359·131	79	17·3780
59·098	13	2·8597	213·660	47	10·3388	363·677	80	17·5980
63·643	14	3·0797	218·206	48	10·5588	368·223	81	17·8180
68·189	15	3·2996	222·752	49	10·7788	372·769	82	18·0380
72·735	16	3·5196	227·298	50	10·9988	377·315	83	18·2579
77·281	17	3·7396	231·844	51	11·2187	381·861	84	18·4779
81·827	18	3·9596	236·390	52	11·4387	386·407	85	18·6979
86·373	19	4·1795	240·936	53	11·6587	390·953	86	18·9179
90·919	20	4·3995	245·482	54	11·8787	395·499	87	19·1379
95·465	21	4·6195	250·028	55	12·0986	400·045	88	19·3578
100·011	22	4·8395	254·574	56	12·3186	404·591	89	19·5778
104·557	23	5·0594	259·120	57	12·5386	409·137	90	19·7978
109·103	24	5·2794	263·666	58	12·7586	413·683	91	20·0178
113·649	25	5·4994	268·212	59	12·9785	418·229	92	20·2377
118·195	26	5·7194	272·758	60	13·1985	422·775	93	20·4577
122·741	27	5·9393	277·304	61	13·4185	427·321	94	20·6777
127·287	28	6·1593	281·850	62	13·6385	431·866	95	20·8977
131·833	29	6·3793	286·396	63	13·8584	436·412	96	21·1176
136·379	30	6·5993	290·942	64	14·0784	440·958	97	21·3376
140·925	31	6·8192	295·488	65	14·2984	445·504	98	21·5576
145·471	32	7·0392	300·034	66	14·5184	450·050	99	21·7776
150·017	33	7·2592	304·580	67	14·7383	454·596	100	21·9975
154·563	34	7·4792						

The numbers in heavy type can be either grams or ounces. For example, if the heavy type number is 5, 5 grams are equivalent to 0·17635 ounces and 5 ounces are equivalent to 141·7475 grams.

Grams – Ounces
(16 ounces = 1 lb (Avoirdupois))

gram		oz.	gram		oz.	gram		oz.
28·3495	1	0·03527	992·2325	35	1·23445	1927·7660	68	2·39836
56·6990	2	0·07054	1020·5820	36	1·26972	1956·1155	69	2·43363
85·0485	3	0·10581	1048·9315	37	1·30499	1984·4650	70	2·46890
113·3980	4	0·14108	1077·2810	38	1·34026	2012·8145	71	2·50417
141·7475	5	0·17635	1105·6305	39	1·37553	2041·1640	72	2·53944
170·0970	6	0·21162	1133·9800	40	1·41080	2069·5135	73	2·57471
198·4465	7	0·24689	1162·3295	41	1·44607	2097·8630	74	2·60998
226·7960	8	0·28216	1190·6790	42	1·48134	2126·2125	75	2·64525
255·1455	9	0·31743	1219·0285	43	1·51661	2154·5620	76	2·68052
283·4950	10	0·35270	1247·3780	44	1·55188	2182·9115	77	2·71579
311·8445	11	0·38797	1275·7275	45	1·58715	2211·2610	78	2·75106
340·1940	12	0·42324	1304·0770	46	1·62242	2239·6105	79	2·78633
368·5435	13	0·45851	1332·4265	47	1·65769	2267·9600	80	2·82160
396·8930	14	0·49378	1360·7760	48	1·69296	2296·3095	81	2·85687
425·2425	15	0·52905	1389·1255	49	1·72823	2324·6590	82	2·89214
453·5920	16	0·56432	1417·4750	50	1·76350	2353·0085	83	2·92741
481·9415	17	0·59959	1445·8245	51	1·79877	2381·3580	84	2·96268
510·2910	18	0·63486	1474·1740	52	1·83404	2409·7075	85	2·99795
538·6405	19	0·67013	1502·5235	53	1·86931	2438·0570	86	3·03322
566·9900	20	0·70540	1530·8730	54	1·90458	2466·4065	87	3·06849
595·3395	21	0·74067	1559·2225	55	1·93985	2494·7560	88	3·10376
623·6890	22	0·77594	1587·5720	56	1·97512	2523·1055	89	3·13903
652·0385	23	0·81121	1615·9215	57	2·01039	2551·4550	90	3·17430
680·3880	24	0·84648	1644·2710	58	2·04566	2579·8045	91	3·20957
708·7375	25	0·88175	1672·6205	59	2·08093	2608·1540	92	3·24484
737·0870	26	0·91702	1700·9700	60	2·11620	2636·5035	93	3·28011
765·4365	27	0·95229	1729·3195	61	2·15147	2664·8530	94	3·31538
793·7860	28	0·98756	1757·6690	62	2·18674	2693·2025	95	3·35065
822·1355	29	1·02283	1786·0185	63	2·22201	2721·5520	96	3·38592
850·4850	30	1·05810	1814·3680	64	2·25728	2749·9015	97	3·42119
878·8345	31	1·09337	1842·7175	65	2·29255	2778·2510	98	3·45646
907·1840	32	1·12864	1871·0670	66	2·32782	2806·6005	99	3·49173
935·5335	33	1·16391	1899·4165	67	2·36309	2834·9500	100	3·52700
963·8830	34	1·19918						

The numbers in heavy type can be either kilograms or pounds. For example, if the heavy type number is 5, 5 kilograms is equivalent to 11·023 pounds and 5 pounds are equivalent to 2·268 kilograms.

Kilograms – Pounds

kg.		lb.	kg.		lb.	kg.		lb.
0·453592	**1**	2·20462	15·876	**35**	77·162	30·844	**68**	149·914
0·907	**2**	4·409	16·329	**36**	79·366	31·298	**69**	152·119
1·361	**3**	6·614	16·783	**37**	81·571	31·751	**70**	154·324
1·814	**4**	8·818	17·237	**38**	83·776	32·205	**71**	156·528
2·268	**5**	11·023	17·690	**39**	85·980	32·659	**72**	158·733
2·722	**6**	13·228	18·144	**40**	88·185	33·112	**73**	160·937
3·175	**7**	15·432	18·597	**41**	90·390	33·566	**74**	163·142
3·629	**8**	17·637	19·051	**42**	92·594	34·019	**75**	165·347
4·082	**9**	19·842	19·504	**43**	94·799	34·473	**76**	167·551
4·536	**10**	22·046	19·958	**44**	97·003	34·927	**77**	169·756
4·990	**11**	24·251	20·412	**45**	99·208	35·380	**78**	171·961
5·443	**12**	26·455	20·865	**46**	101·413	35·834	**79**	174·165
5·897	**13**	28·660	21·139	**47**	103·617	36·287	**80**	176·370
6·350	**14**	30·865	21·772	**48**	105·822	36·741	**81**	178·574
6·804	**15**	33·069	22·226	**49**	108·026	37·195	**82**	180·779
7·257	**16**	35·274	22·680	**50**	110·231	37·648	**83**	182·984
7·711	**17**	37·479	23·133	**51**	112·436	38·102	**84**	185·188
8·165	**18**	39·683	23·587	**52**	114·640	38·555	**85**	187·393
8·618	**19**	41·888	24·040	**53**	116·845	39·009	**86**	189·598
9·072	**20**	44·092	24·494	**54**	119·050	39·463	**87**	191·802
9·525	**21**	46·297	24·948	**55**	121·254	39·916	**88**	194·007
9·979	**22**	48·502	25·401	**56**	123·459	40·370	**89**	196·211
10·433	**23**	50·706	25·855	**57**	125·663	40·823	**90**	198·416
10·886	**24**	52·911	26·308	**58**	127·868	41·277	**91**	200·621
11·340	**25**	55·116	26·762	**59**	130·073	41·731	**92**	202·825
11·793	**26**	57·320	27·216	**60**	132·277	42·184	**93**	205·030
12·247	**27**	59·525	27·669	**61**	134·482	42·638	**94**	207·235
12·701	**28**	61·729	28·123	**62**	136·687	43·091	**95**	209·439
13·154	**29**	63·934	28·576	**63**	138·891	43·545	**96**	211·644
13·608	**30**	66·139	29·030	**64**	141·096	43·999	**97**	213·848
14·061	**31**	68·343	29·484	**65**	143·300	44·452	**98**	216·053
14·515	**32**	70·548	29·937	**66**	145·505	44·906	**99**	218·258
14·969	**33**	72·753	30·391	**67**	147·710	45·359	**100**	220·462
15·422	**34**	74·957						

Index

Accordions, 58
Acid:
    for cherry cakes, 144; for puff pastry, 39
Aeration, 1:
    biological, 1; chemical, 1, 3–5; mechanical, 1
Adsorption, 6
A.F.D. egg, use of, 20
African tarts, 93
Almond:
    buns, 78; cake, 137; dessert biscuits, 218–223; fancies – cushions, 247, rings, 247–248, saris, 248, goods, 212–230; sponge, 119; Swiss roll, 121; torten, 189; turnovers, 52; wine biscuits, 91
Almond paste:
    for bridal cakes, 160; for macaroons, 212; for modelling, 257–259; for modelling animals, 265–270; for modelling flowers, 262–265; for modelling fruits, 259–261; for simnel cakes, 145; for wedding cakes, 160; legal requirements, 256; recipes, 256–258
Aluminium phosphates, 4
American cookies, 89
American icing, 167
Ammonia gas, 5
Ammonia flavour, 5
Ammonium bicarbonate, 5
Ammonium carbonate, 5
Angel cakes, 7, 135–136, 171
Animal shapes, 265–271
Apple:
    fresh, 32; meringue flan, 26; solid pack tinned, 32; strudel, 35, 55
Apricot:
    purée, 232; purée for wedding cakes, 161; puffs, 47; purses, 48; squares, 48; tarts, 22
Arabic, gum solution, 220
Arrowroot in fruit pies, 21
Ashbourne gingerbread biscuits, 97

Bakewell filling, 29
Baking, 10:
    biscuits, 84; cherry cakes, 144; egg

custard tarts, 20; jam tarts, 18; large pies, 24; large tarts, 24; meringues, 105; powder, 3; choice for chemically aerated goods, 72; choice for pastry, 18; quantity used, 7; temperatures, 10; Scotch shortbread, 85
Balance of recipe, 5
Banana tart, 22
Banbury, 53:
    filling, 53
Bases for torten, 187
Basic chemically aerated bun dough, 77
Base for biscuits, 103
Basic rules for a normal balanced recipe, 6
Basic scone recipes, 73
Batons glacés, 47
Battenburg, 210–211:
    slices, 251
Batter:
    flow, 7; temperature, 2
Beating:
    action, 2; speed, 2; temperature, 2; type of beater, 2; type of ingredients used, 2
Beaumé degrees, 13
Bicarbonate of soda, 3
Biological aeration, 1
Birthday cakes, 161–162
Biscuits:
    American cookies, 89; almond dessert, 218–223; Ashbourne gingerbread, 97; base, 103; boulée macaroons, 223; Derby, 92; Dutch, 88–89; Dutch macaroon, 222–223; Easter, 88; fancy macaroon, 222; Grasmere ginger-bread, 97; Italian macaroon, 217; jam, 92; Japanese, 110–113; jelly, 92; labelling, 83; langue du chat, 99; macaroon, 213–214; Marquis, 101; marshmallow, 102; meringue, 110; moss, 217; Parisian, routs, 219–220; parkins, 96–97; ratafia, 219; rice, 88; Shrewsbury, 95; wholemeal, 95–96; wine, 90–92
Blow degree, 12
Boiled buttercream, 175
Boiled paste, 66–67:
    uses of, 67
Boiling sugar, 12